The Trade in Lunacy

STUDIES IN SOCIAL HISTORY

edited by
HAROLD PERKIN
Professor of Social History, University of Lancaster

For a list of books in the series see back endpaper

THE TRADE IN LUNACY 1972.

A Study of Private Madhouses in England
in the Eighteenth and Nineteenth Centuries

William Ll. Parry-Jones

Lecturer in Psychiatry, University of Oxford
Fellow of Linacre College, Oxford

LONDON: Routledge & Kegan Paul
TORONTO: University of Toronto Press

First published 1972 in Great Britain by
Routledge & Kegan Paul Limited
and in Canada and the United States of America by
University of Toronto Press
Printed in Great Britain by
Richard Clay (The Chaucer Press), Ltd.
Bungay, Suffolk
RKP ISBN 0 7100 7051 9
UTP ISBN 0 8020 1830 0
UTP Microfiche ISBN 0 8020 0155 6

To my mother and father

Contents

CONTENTS

Illustrations

Figures   *page*

Tables

xi

Acknowledgments

THIS study has involved the co-operation of a great many archivists and librarians throughout England and Wales. I acknowledge, with gratitude, their help, without which the location of many of the sources used in this book would not have been possible. In particular, I am grateful to Miss Marjorie Jones, formerly Assistant County Archivist at the Oxfordshire County Record Office, for her ready assistance. My thanks are due also to those who made available, for my inspection, material preserved in various private collections. I am grateful to Dr A. Barr, of the Oxford Regional Hospital Board, for his advice on the statistical aspects of the study and for making arrangements for the processing of data in his department.

I should like to thank Dr R. A. Hunter and Dr Ida Macalpine who put their extensive knowledge and insight at my disposal and who read the MS. in its early stages. A general acknowledgment is made to those who kindly gave permission for the reproduction of material in their possession, the details being given in the appropriate places in the book, Finally, I am deeply indebted to my wife for her unfailing help, encouragement and forbearance.

Abbreviations

B.H.Q.N.C.N.	Brislington House Quarterly News Centenary Number, 1906
B.M.	British Museum, London
Bod. Lib.	Bodleian Library, Oxford
C.L.	Commissioners in Lunacy
C.R.O.	County Record Office
H.C.	House of Commons
H.L.	House of Lords
H.P.D.	Hansard's Parliamentary Debates
J.H.C.	Journals of the House of Commons
J.H.L.	Journals of the House of Lords
M.C.L.	Metropolitan Commissioners in Lunacy
MSS.	Manuscripts
O.C.R.O.	Oxfordshire County Record Office
P.R.	Parliamentary Return
P.R.O.	Public Record Office, London
Publ. Lib.	Public Library
Q.S.	Quarter Sessions
R.C.P.L.	Royal College of Physicians, London
R.O.	Record Office

S.C.	Select Committee
S.C.H.L.	Select Committee of the House of Lords
U.C.N.W.	University College of North Wales, Bangor
V.M.	Visiting Magistrates

1

Introduction

A PRIVATE madhouse can be defined as a privately owned establishment for the reception and care of insane persons, conducted as a business proposition for the personal profit of the proprietor or proprietors. The history of such establishments in England and Wales can be traced for a period of over three and a half centuries, from the early seventeenth century up to the present day. In the course of their lifespan these institutions were referred to by a variety of terms, ranging from 'houses for lunatics', 'madhouses', 'private madhouses', 'private licensed houses' to 'private asylums' and finally, the 'mental nursing homes' of the present century. Other types of institutions for the insane were referred to only rarely as 'madhouses'.

During the eighteenth century, an awareness of the need for public responsibility for the care of lunatics slowly emerged. A small number of hospitals and asylums were established with funds raised by voluntary subscription, but they afforded no relief to the large majority of patients and, with the increase in population, private madhouses flourished. The economic and social changes of the late eighteenth and early nineteenth centuries led to an increase in the numbers of the insane poor requiring some form of institutional care. The county asylum movement, as part of the overall humanitarian movement of the early nineteenth century, reflected the full assumption of public responsibility for pauper lunatics. However, the establishment of county asylums took place only slowly and very little provision was made in them for non-pauper patients, who continued to be catered for by the private madhouses and the public subscription asylums. The private madhouse made an important contribution until the middle of the nineteenth century, particularly with regard to pauper lunatics and retained considerable, although declining, influence until the close of the century. In view of this, it is surprising that the role of the private madhouse during the late eighteenth and the whole of the nineteenth century has been overlooked to such a degree by medical and psychiatric historians. Whilst a number of works on psychiatric history contain isolated references to private madhouses and a few short descriptions of individual houses have been published, there has been no consecutive study of the general role of these establishments. The constitution of the private madhouse, as an establishment run for profit, always exposed it to accusations of malpractice and its history was chequered by repeated disclosures of various infamous practices. The more disreputable aspects of the private madhouse system have received considerable attention and this has led, generally, to a biased conception of the private madhouse. The lack of a broad, objective appraisal of the functioning of these establishments motivated the researches upon which this volume is based.[1]

One of the features of psychiatric historiography is the meagre use that has been made of manuscript material. The importance of original records in the writing of a reliable history of any aspect of psychiatry has been stressed by R. A. Hunter (1959)[2] and, in this work, an attempt has been made to extract as much information as possible from manuscript sources. It was decided, for several reasons, to concentrate attention on the private madhouses in provincial England and Wales. This decision was aided by the fact that an administrative distinction between provincial houses and those in the London area had been drawn by legislation of 1774. Moreover, preliminary research revealed that the metropolitan houses had always received greater publicity and documentation in the reports of parliamentary enquiries and in other publications. This decision to focus attention on the provinces was influenced, also, by a personal interest in the history of the two private madhouses in Oxfordshire.

---

[1] The research presented in this book formed the basis of a thesis for the degree of M.D. of the University of Cambridge in 1968.

[2] Hunter, R. A. (1959), 'Some Notes on the Importance of Manuscript Records for Psychiatric History', *Archives IV*, pp. 9–11.

The scope of the research did not encompass either Irish or Scottish madhouses.

The research followed three main lines. Firstly, an exhaustive study was conducted into the total records extant relating to the private licensed houses in Oxfordshire, at Hook Norton and Witney. The records cover the period 1775–1857 and these dates have been used to delineate, broadly, the area for wider research, although the period considered in the greatest detail, because it is the best documented, has been the second quarter of the nineteenth century. The principal manuscript source relating to the houses at Hook Norton and Witney has been a large accumulation of documents comprising approximately 3,500 items, filed with the records of the Oxfordshire Court of Quarter Sessions. They are representative of the most comprehensive series which have survived in England and Wales.[1] No previous research has been carried out on these records, which include the reports of statutory visits by both the Visiting Magistrates and the Commissioners in Lunacy; plans of the two licensed houses; treasurer's accounts; miscellaneous correspondence and a series of documents concerning 745 consecutive admissions to the two licensed houses, during the period 1828 to 1856, and the corresponding discharges. By correlating and interpreting the data obtained from these records, an account is obtained of the life-history, the prevailing conditions and the therapeutic practice of these two establishments. Furthermore, these records are valuable for their illumination of aspects of the local application of national lunacy legislation.

Secondly, an attempt was made to ascertain the extent and distribution of surviving manuscript material relating to private licensed houses elsewhere in England and Wales. In order to locate private madhouse records, a survey of lunacy records amongst catalogued collections in record repositories in England and Wales was carried out, by means of a circular letter in the form of a questionnaire. It was attempted, in addition, to trace surviving madhouse records held in non-official custody. Subsequently, a selective study was undertaken of some of the records located by these means. In this way, it was possible to examine a representative sample of all the categories of record available and also to study the records of private madhouses of varying character situated in widely different parts of the country. Thirdly, parliamentary papers and printed works published in the eighteenth, nineteenth and twentieth centuries have been investigated,

---

[1] A catalogue of these documents is included in Appendix B.

with particular emphasis on those published in the first half of the nineteenth century. Material extracted from a number of lesser-known books, pamphlets and articles, located in record repositories and libraries in various parts of the country, has been incorporated.

From the outset, it was intended to assemble, as comprehensively as possible, facts relevant to an evaluation of the development, the character and the role of private madhouses. This volume embodies, therefore, both a systematic statement of facts collected in the course of research and a number of conclusions derived from their collation and interpretation. It is in no way claimed that this work covers the field exhaustively and, indeed, one of the delights of this kind of historical research remains the fact that new information can emerge at any time from the most unexpected sources.

The selection of the particular chapter grouping adopted was influenced by the need to overcome the difficulties inherent in integrating material of local and national significance. The historical development and background of the private madhouse system, from the early seventeenth century to the present day, is outlined in Chapter 2, with special reference to lunacy legislation and to the prevailing social conditions. The number of private licensed houses, their geographical distribution, their capacity, lifespan and the provisions available for the various categories of the insane are discussed in Chapter 3. In Chapter 4, the range and quality of private-madhouse proprietors is examined and reference is made to the published works of a number of the more notable individuals. Some contemporary descriptions of provincial private licensed houses are considered in Chapter 5, with particular reference to four houses which achieved prominence in the nineteenth century. A detailed account is given in Chapter 6 of the private licensed houses at Hook Norton and Witney, Oxfordshire, utilizing the entire scope of the surviving records. General statistics concerned with admissions and discharges to the two houses are presented. Aspects of the care and treatment of the insane in madhouses are discussed in Chapter 7, with particular reference to the use of mechanical restraint. The outcome of treatment is considered, together with some of the clinical data extracted from the Oxfordshire MSS. In Chapter 8, the principal abuses and defects of the private-madhouse system as a whole are reviewed, together with an evaluation of the various sources of information utilized. Finally, Chapter 9 attempts a summary of the main themes and findings of this work.

Particular attention is drawn to the contents of Appendix A. This contains a breakdown of the various categories of manuscript source relating to lunacy and to private madhouses in particular, from the late eighteenth century onwards. The changes in the format, content and volume of the documents relating to private madhouses are considered in conjunction with a detailed interpretation of the legislative developments of the period.

2

The 'Trade in Lunacy'[1] in its Historical and Legal Perspective

W<small>HILST</small> there is little information regarding the precise treatment of the insane in medieval times, there is evidence that the mentally afflicted were accommodated at times alongside the physically diseased in the infirmaries of the period.[2] In addition, monastic houses often gave shelter to lunatics in company with vagabonds and vagrants. The priory of St Mary of Bethlehem, London, founded in 1247, was one such establishment, and by the beginning of the fifteenth century it was functioning as a receptacle for lunatics. In 1547, it was given by Henry VIII to the city of London as a hospital for poor lunatics and, until the early eighteenth century, Bethlem Hospital was the only public institution for the insane, although the numbers admitted were small. From a legal viewpoint, a distinction was drawn, at an early period, between lunatics and idiots, and legislative provision for the protection of their estate was made in the Statute de Prerogativa Regis, of uncertain date, but usually printed as a statute of 17 Edward II, c. 9 & 10, 1324. Until the beginning of the nineteenth century, the emphasis was placed on the protection of the estate rather than on the treatment of the insane person concerned. The Poor Law Act of 1601, 43 Eliz., c. 2, served to focus attention on the poor and unemployed, but no separate provisions for the insane were made and harmless lunatics and idiots

---

[1] A phrase seen, not infrequently, in eighteenth- and nineteenth-century literature.
[2] Clay, R. M. (1909), *The Medieval Hospitals of England*, pp. 31–4.

6

continued to be left at liberty as long as they were not considered to be dangerous and caused no social disturbance. However, a change in social attitudes towards lunatics in the community was to take place in the seventeenth century.[1] This marked the beginning throughout Europe of the period of 'The Great Confinement'[2] of the insane in company with criminals, vagrants and the unemployed, a process that was reflected in England in the increasing use for this purpose of houses of correction and, later, the workhouses. The Act of 1714, 12 Anne, c. 23, distinguished, for the first time, between impoverished lunatics and 'Rogues, Vagabonds, Sturdy Beggars and Vagrants'. It was enacted that two or more justices of the peace could authorize the apprehension of lunatics who were 'furiously mad, and dangerous', by the town or parish officials, and order their confinement, 'safely locked up, in such secure place . . . as such justices shall . . . direct and appoint', where, if necessary, the lunatic could be chained. Apart from such restraint, which was to be applied only during the period of madness, no treatment was provided for, although the lunatic was exempted from whipping. The cost of detention, in the case of pauper lunatics, had to be paid out of the funds of the lunatic's parish of legal settlement. The charge for 'curing' such persons was added to these expenses by the Vagrant Act of 1744, 17 Geo. II, c. 5, which was essentially a re-statement of the Act of 1714. It is likely that the provisions of the latter reflected the prevailing practice during the late seventeenth century. One of the methods which had become adopted by the parishes for the disposal of lunatics placed in their charge was to board them out, at the expense of the parish, in private dwelling houses, which gradually acquired the description of 'mad' houses. For example, it is known that such an establishment existed in the parish of Horningsham, Wiltshire, in 1770, the lease of which was taken over by the parish officers in that year.[3] Boarding-out remained an important mode of management of lunatics and idiots until the mid-nineteenth century and, as has been observed by Fessler (1956), it constituted one of the roots of origin of the private-madhouse system.[4]

In the seventeenth century, it is known that lunatics from the more

---

[1] *Vide* Rosen, G. (1968), *Madness in Society*, pp. 151–71.
[2] Foucault, M. (1967), *Madness and Civilization*, pp. 38–64.
[3] Wilts. C.R.O., Horningsham parish records, 482/44.
[4] Fessler, A. (1956), 'The Management of Lunacy in Seventeenth-Century England. An Investigation of Quarter Sessions Records', *Proc. R. Soc. Med. 49*, p. 906.

affluent classes were cared for individually, often in the custody of medical men or clergymen. An example of this system is provided by the case of one Edmund Francklin of Bedford, who was found lunatic by inquisition in 1630 and later cared for, privately, by Dr Helkiah Crooke, physician to Bethlem Hospital.[1] Similarly, in 1679, it is recorded that Anne Grenville, the youngest daughter of the Bishop of Durham, was placed in the charge of, 'a person famous for the ordering of distempered persons', a physician who lived at Worcester.[2] There is evidence, in addition, that, during the seventeenth century, there were many establishments run specifically as madhouses, which provided accommodation for a number of lunatics. The following references have been singled out as representative of the range of this evidence.[3] In 1815, it was claimed that there had been an asylum at Box, Wiltshire, for 200 years.[4] There was a madhouse at Glastonbury, in 1656, where the Reverend George Trosse was confined.[5] It is recorded that, in 1661, the Reverend John Ashbourne, who kept a small madhouse in Suffolk, was murdered by one of his own patients.[6] Thomas Willis (1683) referred to a madman 'being placed in a house convenient for the business'[7] and, in 1673, John Archer, self-styled 'one of His Majesties Physicians in Ordinary', advertised his house for lunatics, placed 'in an excellent air nere the City'.[8] An advertisement for the house kept by James Newton 'on Clarkenwell Green', London, dated c. 1674, has survived.[9] David Irish (1700)[10] and Thomas Fallowes (1705)[11] publicized

[1] Beds. C.R.O., Francklin MSS., FN. 1060–84.

[2] Bod. Lib., Locke MSS., c. 10, ff. 106–8. (This physician has been identified as William Cole, M.D.(Oxon). *Vide* Dewhurst, K. (1962), 'A Seventeenth Century Symposium on Manic-depressive Psychosis', *Brit. J. med. Psychol. 35*, pp. 113–25).

[3] For the location of relevant references in printed sources of the seventeenth and early eighteenth centuries, the writer has drawn, in particular, upon Hunter, R.A. and Macalpine, I. (1963), *Three Hundred Years of Psychiatry 1535–1860*.

[4] Minutes of evidence 1815 S.C., p. 21. (An alternative estimate was over 300 years. Sixteenth Report (1862) C.L., p. 47.)

[5] Trosse, G. (1714), *The life of the Reverend Mr. Geo. Trosse, late Minister of the Gospel in the city of Exon, who died January 11th, 1712/3*, pp. 53–65.

[6] Anon. (1662), *Mirabilis annus secundus; or the Second Year of Prodigies*, pp. 78–9.

[7] Willis, T. (trans. Pordage, S.) (1683), *Two Discourses concerning the Soul of Brutes*, p. 206.

[8] Archer, J. (1673), *Every Man his own Doctor, compleated with an Herbal*, p. 124.

[9] B.M., C. 112, f. 9. *Vide infra*, p. 103.

[10] Irish, D. (1700), *Levamen infirmi: or, Cordial Counsel to the Sick and Diseased*.

[11] Fallowes, T. (1705), *The Best Method for the Cure of Lunaticks. With some*

their respective houses, at Guildford and Lambeth, in short publications. Such evidence suggests that the confinement of the insane in private madhouses was a well-established practice by the beginning of the eighteenth century and, during the reign of George II (1727–60), their number increased steadily. However, by this time, they had acquired a reputation for corrupt and brutal practices and increasing public concern was reflected in the publication of articles, letters and pamphlets disclosing alleged abuses. For example, in 1706, Daniel Defoe drew attention to the allegedly wrongful detention of a young woman in a madhouse supervised by Dr Edward Tyson, physician to Bethlem.[1] Such publications were to appear at intervals throughout the eighteenth and nineteenth centuries. In 1754, the College of Physicians of London was asked by Sir Cordell Firebrace, Member of Parliament for Suffolk, to consider a Bill in which it was recommended that the College should undertake the responsibility for the licensing and inspection of private madhouses. However, the College rejected the proposal, on the grounds that its implementation would be too difficult and inconvenient[2] and a further twenty years were to elapse before legislation was introduced. During this interval, further evidence accumulated of the defects ascribed to the private-madhouse system. In 1763, a Select Committee of the House of Commons was appointed, probably in response to the widespread concern aroused by an article published in January of that year.[3] The Committee's inquiry was very limited in scope, in that the investigations were confined to two London madhouses. However, attention was drawn to the practice of confining sane persons in madhouses as alleged lunatics and the Committee concluded wisely that, 'the present state of the private madhouses in this Kingdom, required the interposition of the legislature'.[4] Leave was given by Parliament for a Bill to be brought forward for the regulation of private madhouses, but it was not until 1774 that the first Act for regulating madhouses, 14 Geo. III, c. 49, finally reached the Statute-book (Plate I). In the preceding year, a similar Bill was thrown out by the House of Lords after it had been passed by the Commons. The Act of 1774 made provision for

Account of the Incomparable Oleum Cephalicum used in the same, prepared and administered by Tho. Fallowes, M.D. at his House in Lambeth-Marsh.
[1] Defoe, D. (1706), A Review of the State of the English Nation 3, pp. 327, 353–6.
[2] R.C.P.L. Lib., Annals, 23 Dec. 1754.
[3] Anon. (1763), 'A Case humbly offered to the Consideration of Parliament', Gentleman's Magazine 33, pp. 25–6.
[4] Report 1763 S.C., J.H.C., Vol. 29, p. 489.

the licensing and inspection of private madhouses within the cities of London and Westminster and within a radius of seven miles thereof, by five Commissioners appointed by the College of Physicians and throughout the rest of England and Wales by justices of the peace accompanied by a medical practitioner. In addition, a medical certificate confirming insanity was required before the confinement of non-pauper patients could take place. This Act remained in force for five years. In 1779, it was extended for a further seven years by the Act of 19 Geo. III, c. 15, and it was made perpetual, in 1786, by the Act of 26 Geo. III, c. 91. The imperfections of this legislation were numerous and contributed, to a considerable extent, to the defects of the private-madhouse system as a whole. Of particular importance was its disregard for the pauper lunatic and, from the viewpoint of this study, its failure, in the words of Sir G. O. Paul, the Gloucestershire philanthropist, in 1807, to extend more than, 'a faint influence over provincial management'[1] of madhouses.

The latter part of the eighteenth century was an important period in the history of psychiatry in this country, in that its future growth and development was being shaped by ideas and attitudes towards insanity that were part of the philosophical movement of enlightenment. The psychology of association, for example, as propounded by Locke, Hume and Hartley, exerted considerable influence on contemporary psychiatric thought and formed the basis of new systems of classification of insanity. Far-reaching advances were being made also in medical practice and thought as a whole and the concept developed of establishing charitable institutions for the care of the sick, in addition to the workhouses which existed already. Such institutions were founded first in London,[2] but the movement soon spread to provincial towns and cities.[3] The progress of this movement was dependent upon the efforts of individuals and upon public subscription and its success provides an index of the contemporary social conscience. The founding of institutions for the insane by voluntary public subscription also became an established practice during the eighteenth century. Bethel Hospital, Norwich, opened in 1713, was placed under the supervision of a governing

[1] Report 1807 S.C., p. 18.

[2] e.g. Westminster Hospital 1719, Guy's Hospital 1721 and the London Hospital 1740.

[3] *Vide* Abel-Smith, B. (1964), *The Hospitals 1800–1948*; and Poynter, F. N. L. (ed.) (1962), *The Evolution of Hospitals in Britain*.

body in 1724;[1] the wards for chronic lunatics at Guy's Hospital were opened in 1728; St Luke's Hospital, London, was opened in 1751; the Newcastle Lunatic Hospital in 1764 and the Manchester Lunatic Hospital in 1766. Other establishments followed and, in 1796, the small but subsequently renowned Retreat, at York, was opened for members of the Society of Friends. The example set in these establishments for the management and study of insanity exerted considerable influence on the way in which the specialty developed. The teaching of Dr William Battie at St Luke's Hospital exemplifies the more optimistic approach towards insanity which was developing at this period. In 1758, for example, he observed that 'madness is, contrary to the opinion of some unthinking persons, as manageable as many other distempers, which are equally dreadful and obstinate, and yet are not looked upon as incurable: and that such unhappy objects ought by no means to be abandoned, much less shut up in loathsome prisons as criminals or nuisances to the society'.[2] These public subscription hospitals, however, provided no relief for the large majority of patients, in particular the insane poor.

By the beginning of the nineteenth century, increasing alarm was being expressed about the apparently rapid increase in the incidence of insanity. Paul noted, in 1807, 'It is an observation of medical men of extensive practice, that the lunatic affection is a disease increasing in its influence in this country'.[3] John Reid (1808), a London physician, was more alarmist. 'Madness, strides like a Colossus in the country,'[4] he claimed and later that year he wrote, 'more people are mad than are supposed to be so. There are atoms, or specks of insanity, which cannot be discerned by the naked or uneducated eye.'[5] Dr Richard Powell, Secretary, 1808–25, of the Commissioners of the College of Physicians, published observations, in 1813, on the prevalence of insanity, based upon an analysis of the returns of lunatics admitted to madhouses in England and Wales and entered

[1] This institution was not typical as it was founded, built and endowed in 1713 by one person, Mrs Mary Chapman, in gratitude for the preservation of her own reason and in compassion for 'distrest lunaticks'. She died in 1724, but left instructions in her will for the constitution of a governing body under which the hospital was to continue. *Vide* Bateman, F. and Rye, W. (1906), *The History of Bethel Hospital at Norwich.*

[2] Battie, W. (1758), *A Treatise on Madness*, p. 93.

[3] Report 1807 S.C., p. 17.

[4] Reid, J. (1808), 'Report of Diseases', *The Monthly Magazine 25*, p. 166.

[5] *Ibid.*, p. 374.

in the registers kept by the Commissioners.[1] He referred to the difficulties in making an accurate evaluation of the situation, largely
because of the deficiencies in these returns. He was of the opinion,
nevertheless, that the incidence of mental derangement was increasing, principally because there was an apparent increase in the
numbers of lunatics recorded in the Town and Country Registers,
over the period 1775 to 1809. Thomas Bakewell (1815), a non-
medically qualified madhouse proprietor, referred to 'a prevailing
opinion . . . that this national opprobrium is alarmingly upon the increase'.[2] Dr George Man Burrows (1820), a noted London madhouse
proprietor, however, called upon a range of evidence to demonstrate
that insanity was not an increasing malady[3] and he suggested that the
data presented by Powell were open to a less conclusive interpretation.
In particular, he sought to explain variations in the admission
numbers put forward by Powell in terms of certain contemporary
social and economic circumstances, such as the illnesses of George
III. There can be little doubt that the repeated mental illnesses of the
King[4] had important repercussions in promoting greater awareness
and tolerance of insanity, as also did such events as the assassination,
by a lunatic, of Spencer Perceval, the Prime Minister, in the year
1812. In 1829, Sir Andrew Halliday, a physician who concerned
himself with the state of the insane, claimed that the number suffering from insanity had more than trebled in the preceding twenty
years.[5] This claim was substantiated by the returns of 1807 and 1828.
In 1807, 2,248 lunatics and idiots were revealed in England and
Wales, although Halliday personally demonstrated the total inaccuracy of these returns in the cases of two counties, Suffolk and
Norfolk. In 1828, 12,547 lunatics and idiots were accounted for and
Halliday estimated that this figure could be increased to at least
14,000 to take into account parishes which had failed to make re-

---

[1] Powell, R. (1813), 'Observations upon the Comparative Prevalence of
Insanity at Different Periods', *Medical Transactions 4*, pp. 131–59. (In 1816,
Powell presented the figures up to 1815. First Report minutes of evidence 1816
S.C., p. 79.)

[2] Bakewell, T. (1815), *A Letter addressed to the Chairman of the Select Committee of the House of Commons*, p. 4.

[3] Burrows, G. M. (1820), *An Inquiry into Certain Errors relative to Insanity*,
p. 59.

[4] He was known to have had four attacks accompanied by derangement, in
the years 1788, 1801, 1804 and 1810 respectively.

[5] Halliday, A. (1829), *A Letter to Lord Robert Seymour: with a Report of the
Number of Lunatics and Idiots in England and Wales*, p. V.

turns. Dr James Cowles Prichard (1835), an eminent psychiatric physician and a Commissioner in Lunacy from 1844 to 1848, surveyed the available evidence concerning the prevalence of insanity but remained cautious about its interpretation.[1] In 1844, the total number of persons ascertained to be insane in England and Wales, private and pauper, both in asylums and elsewhere, was 20,893.[2] The numbers continued to rise steeply during the second half of the nineteenth century, particularly in the case of pauper lunatics. Although this increase was attributed by some contemporaries to such factors as drunkenness and dissolution, it became recognized that the important factors were the greatly increased attention that the insane received, resulting in the location of cases previously unreported and the improved facilities for their treatment, which, among other effects, led to reduced mortality. This view was supported by Lord Shaftesbury,[3] in 1859, when he stated that the bulk of the increase was not made up of recent cases, but of 'old-established chronic cases, of very long standing indeed'.[4] The apparent increase in the prevalence of insanity was also related closely to changes in the size and structure of the population. During the reign of George III (1760–1820), the total population of England and Wales rose, approximately, from seven to twelve millions, and it continued to rise rapidly thereafter. The combination of this rise in the population with the widespread economic changes that accompanied the Industrial Revolution led to a vast increase in the number of paupers. The substitution of machinery for hand labour led to increasing discontent and distress, aggravated, in turn, by such factors as the Corn Law (1815), and the last five years of the reign of George III and the decade following were marked by outbreaks of rioting by the working classes. The reform movement took shape slowly, but it was not until the mid-century that many of its objectives were realized, for example, the Reform Act of 1832 and the Repeal of the Corn Laws in 1846.

By the close of the eighteenth century, workhouses and houses of correction had come to contain a variety of lunatics and idiots alongside the other inmates. This state of affairs, in turn, led to an increasing dependence on the system of contracting-out by parishes to private madhouses for the care of the more acutely disturbed or

[1] Prichard, J. C. (1835), *A Treatise on Insanity*, pp. 328–51.
[2] 1844 Report M.C.L., p. 194.
[3] Anthony Ashley Cooper, 1801–85, Lord Ashley, later 7th Earl of Shaftesbury.
[4] Report 1859 S.C. (April 1859), p. 7. (In addition, *vide* Fifteenth Report (1861) C.L., pp. 77–83.)

refractory patients. Although many parishes were reluctant to incur the expenses involved in such a system, this practice promoted the multiplication of madhouses, which, in many instances, catered largely for paupers. The custom continued, however, of supporting, from parish funds, chronic lunatics and idiots, either in their homes or boarded out. The concern about the welfare of the large numbers of the insane poor which had accumulated in houses of correction, prisons, workhouses, private madhouses and in the community culminated in the appointment of a Select Committee, in 1807, 'to enquire into the state of criminal and pauper lunatics, in England and Wales, and of the laws relating thereto'. The findings of this Committee confirmed many of the fears that had been expressed previously about the condition of pauper lunatics. The Committee observed that the treatment of paupers boarded in private madhouses depended, 'wholly upon the good conduct of the keeper . . . as, by the Act 14 Geo. III, c. 49, . . . the keepers are expressly discharged from reporting to the College of Physicians any parish-paupers whom they may take in; nor have the inspecting Commissioners considered themselves as required to examine into their situation'.[1] This defect in the Act of 1774 was not amended, however, for a further twenty years. The wretched state of the insane in parish workhouses was described by many contemporary poets. The following lines about a parish poorhouse are taken from a poem entitled 'Monkhouse Hill' and are of particular interest as they were written by Thomas Bakewell, who was later the proprietor of Spring Vale private madhouse, Staffordshire:

> 'Tis there that wasting age retires,
> To wait till painful life expires.
> Go, look within the ample space,
> Where cold damp vapours fill the place.

> There see the idiot's vacant stare,
> And th' wild maniac's frantic glare.
> Where tho' strong chains the body bind,
> No fetters can restrain the mind.[2]

The report of the 1807 Select Committee led directly to the County

[1] Report 1807 S.C., p. 6.
[2] Anon. (1807), *The Moorland Bard; or, Poetical Recollections of a Weaver in the Moorlands of Staffordshire*, Vol. I, pp. 19–20. (Although the poems were published anonymously, references to other works published by the same author indicate that the poet was Thomas Bakewell.)

Asylums Act of 1808, 48 Geo. III, c. 96. It was recommended thereby that the erection of asylums could be authorized by the magistrates of single counties or groups of counties at the expense of the county rates, to accommodate pauper lunatics maintained out of the funds of their native parishes. In the 1807 Report, a plan had been outlined for the erection, in England and Wales, of sixteen asylums for up to 300 lunatics, each catering for districts containing a population of approximately 500,000.[1] Such plans were, however, wholly unreliable because of the inadequacy of returns relating to pauper patients. The concept of a county-hospital system was not a new one and the pattern for the nineteenth-century county lunatic asylum had been established, to some extent, by the public subscription hospitals and asylums opened in the previous century. The progress of the county-asylum movement was very slow; by 1824, only nine counties had responded[2] and, in some of these cases, the county magistrates and the subscribers had joined forces. By 1844, the number of asylums erected under the Act of 1808 was only fifteen.[3] The reasons for this delay were chiefly financial. During the last quarter of the eighteenth and the first decade of the nineteenth century, county expenditure had risen steadily, principally because of the increased building, or re-building, of houses of correction, gaols, highways and bridges. As the 1808 Act was permissive in its recommendations, few counties were prepared to erect asylums at this time. This delay allowed an expansion of the private-madhouse system to take place and also fostered, perhaps inevitably, some exploitation of the situation by unscrupulous private-madhouse owners. In 1814, a Bill to repeal the Act of 1774 and make other provisions for the regulation of madhouses failed to gain the support of both houses of Parliament, either in its original or amended forms.[4] A further parliamentary Select Committee was set up in 1815 to consider institutions for the insane in England and the provisions for their regulation, shortly after the revelation of abuses and cruelties at the York Lunatic Asylum and at Bethlem, by Godfrey Higgins and Edward Wakefield respectively. A considerable volume of detailed evidence was amassed and the Com-

[1] Report 1807 S.C., p. 27.
[2] P.R., 1824.
[3] 1844 Report M.C.L., p. 209.
[4] *Vide* Beds. C.R.O., Whitbread MSS., 5073, letter, J. P. Johnson to S. Whitbread, 19 April 1814, provides an example of a madhouse proprietor's objections to clauses in the amended Bill. Whitbread, the Whig M.P. for Bedford, was a prominent lunacy reformer.

mittee issued reports in 1815 and 1816.[1] This enquiry represented the first attempt at providing a comprehensive review of institutional provisions for lunatics. The observations relating to private madhouses were based on evidence concerning a small number of provincial licensed houses as well as those in metropolitan London. One of the chief conclusions was that: 'If the treatment of those in the middling or in the lower classes of life, shut up in hospitals, private madhouses, or parish workhouses, is looked at . . . a case cannot be found where the necessity for a remedy is more urgent.'[2] But, despite the revelation of many grave defects in the condition of private madhouses and in the current legislation, the Act of 1774 was not repealed. However, an Act, 55 Geo. III, c. 46, amending the Act of 1808 was introduced in 1815. This Act provided for the borrowing of money by counties, over a period of fourteen years, in order to establish asylums. Although this gave some impetus to the county asylum movement, the private madhouse remained the principal receptacle for pauper lunatics until 1845, when the building of asylums became compulsory.

Following the 1815–16 Select Committee, several attempts were made again to bring about the reform of private madhouses. Three Bills for the regulation of madhouses were rejected by the House of Lords in 1816, 1817 and 1819, after they had passed through the House of Commons. Powerful opposition was offered to these Bills by the Lord Chancellor, Lord Eldon,[3] and the extreme Tories. In a brief review of Eldon's role at this time, Jones (1955) observed: 'His was the chief influence exerted against any attempts to increase public control over the private madhouses; he was the spokesman of those High Tories who believed that any attempt to improve the conditions of the insane was but one more aspect of the social unrest and the growth of liberal sentiments which they so greatly deplored.'[4] Eldon's intolerance was not restricted to lunacy reform, but extended to the work of 'philanthropists' in general, whom he denigrated, on one occasion, as 'men pretending to humanity but brimful of intolerance, and swollen with malignity, which they all

---

[1] In 1815, four Reports of minutes of evidence published, May–June, the page numbers running consecutively, and a Report from the Committee, published in July. In 1816, three Reports, the first being of minutes of evidence, April–June, each being numbered separately.

[2] Report 1815 S.C., p. 3.

[3] John Scott, 1751–1838, first Earl of Eldon.

[4] Jones, K. (1955), *Lunacy, Law and Conscience*, p. 111.

are'.[1] The Bills of 1816, 1817 and 1819 contained proposals for the repeal of the Act of 1774 and the establishment of a central body of full-time Commissioners, who would be responsible for the licensing and visitation of all private madhouses throughout the country. Provisions were made for increasing the safeguards against the improper confinement and maltreatment of lunatics and formal provisions were made also concerning the admission of paupers. Each of these Bills, and in particular that of 1819, would have gone a long way towards the uniform and effective control of madhouses had they reached the Statute-book. A short Act, 59 Geo. III, c. 127, was passed in 1819, 'for making provision for the better care of pauper lunatics in England'. In 1827, a further parliamentary Select Committee was appointed, this time to enquire into the provisions for pauper lunatics in the County of Middlesex, in particular within the parishes of Marylebone; St George's, Hanover Square, and St Pancras. A report was issued in the same year.[2] On the strength of the findings, which were concerned chiefly with Warburton's madhouses at Bethnal Green, the Middlesex County Asylum at Hanwell was planned and, in the following year, two Acts were passed. These were the Lunatic Asylums and Pauper or Criminals Maintenance Act, 9 Geo. IV, c. 40, concerned with county asylums (for clarity, referred to as the County Lunatic Asylums Act) and the Treatment of Insane Persons Act, 9 Geo. IV, c. 41, which applied particularly to private madhouses (referred to as the Madhouse Act). The former did little to encourage the establishment of county asylums, but the latter finally repealed the Act of 1774, after it had survived, unamended, for fifty-four years.

The Madhouse Act of 1828, whose operation was limited to three years, embodied many of the principles of the Act of 1774, with some important modifications and additions reflecting increased concern for the welfare of lunatics in confinement. Improper detention of lunatics was made more difficult, since private patients were not to be received without certificates signed by two medical men and the admission of pauper lunatics required an order signed by two magistrates, or by an overseer and an officiating clergyman of the parish, together with a medical certificate. More effective powers were given

[1] Parry-Jones, B. (1965), 'A Calendar of the Eldon-Richards Correspondence c. 1809–1822', J. Merioneth Historical and Record Soc. 5 (1), p. 50.
[2] Report 1827 S.C. on pauper lunatics in the county of Middlesex and on lunatic asylums.

regarding the licensing and visitation of private madhouses, but the county asylums and the public hospitals and asylums were exempted from inspection and lunatics confined singly were still left unprotected. Fifteen Metropolitan Commissioners, including five physicians, were to be appointed to replace the five Fellows of the College of Physicians who had acted as Commissioners under the Act of 1774. Their duties were to undertake the licensing and visitation of metropolitan private madhouses, but in the provinces these responsibilities remained in the hands of the magistrates. Lord Ashley was appointed as one of the new Commissioners and remained a prominent member of the movement for lunacy reform until his death, in 1885. An enquiry held by the House of Lords into the proposals made in the Bill of 1828 before it became law revealed substantial opposition, for many of its provisions, from those engaged in running licensed houses. Dr E. T. Monro, proprietor of Brooke House, Clapton, London, for example, suggested that the Bill would reduce the number of respectable men superintending houses as a result of their 'being liable to so many misdemeanours and so many difficulties at every step'.[1] The College of Physicians also appointed a Committee[2] to enquire into the expediency of the provisions of the 1828 Bill. The Act of 1828 was amended by 10 Geo. IV, c. 18, in 1829 and both Acts were repealed, but substantially reproduced, by the Care and Treatment of Insane Persons Act in 1832, 2 & 3 Will. IV, c. 107. By this time, a new vigour had entered the movement for improving the welfare of the insane and the spirit of the times is depicted clearly in the challenging work of W. A. F. Browne (1837),[3] superintendent of the Montrose Royal Asylum and later of the Crichton Royal Institution. Lunacy reform constituted part of the great reform and philanthropic movements of the early nineteenth century. Trevelyan (1941) has described this period as 'the age of trade unions, co-operative and benefit societies, leagues, boards, commissions, committees for every conceivable purpose of philanthropy and culture. Not even the dumb animals were left without organized protection. The nineteenth century rivalled the Middle Ages in its power to create fresh forms of corporate and institutional life, while yielding little to the eighteenth century in the spirit of self-help and personal initiative.'[4]

[1] Minutes of evidence 1828 S.C.H.L., J.H.L., Vol. 60, p. 724.
[2] 31 March–23 April 1828.
[3] Browne, W. A. F. (1837), *What Asylums were, are, and ought to be.*
[4] Trevelyan, G. M. (1941), *History of England*, p. 617.

In this social climate, the application of humane and enlightened methods in the treatment of the insane, based on the disuse of mechanical bodily restraint, became an increasingly important issue. The use of such methods had been pioneered before this time, but the non-restraint system did not become fully established until the experiments of Robert Gardiner Hill at the Lincoln Asylum, in 1838, and John Conolly at the Middlesex County Lunatic Asylum at Hanwell, had demonstrated, conclusively, that total abolition of restraint was practicable on a large scale. Subsequently, as part of 'moral treatment', non-restraint became adopted enthusiastically in new asylums and constituted part of the frame of reference by which the older establishments, in particular the private madhouses, were judged.

The Poor Law Amendment Act of 1834, 4 & 5 Will. IV, c. 76, represented an attempt to remedy some of the problems which were being created at this time, by the large numbers of both sick and able-bodied paupers. It was hoped that able-bodied pauperism would be reduced by curtailing outdoor relief, whilst those who needed relief, namely the aged, children and the sick, could be admitted to the workhouse, where conditions for the able-bodied were to be 'less eligible' than those of the poorest-paid labourer outside. It was enacted also that parishes should be grouped into unions and that union workhouses should be substituted for parish poorhouses. In addition, the detention of dangerous lunatics and idiots in workhouses for longer than fourteen days was prohibited. However, this latter provision was rarely adhered to, partly because the cost of maintaining a lunatic in a private madhouse or in a county asylum was often up to twice as much as that charged in a workhouse, and also because the statutory provisions were ambiguous in the case of non-dangerous lunatics. Although the policy, theoretically, was to curtail outdoor relief, in practice, the inadequacy of local provisions for outdoor medical relief continued to lead to many paupers being relegated to the already overcrowded workhouses. The dilemma in which many parishes and unions were placed, with regard to the disposal of their pauper lunatics, is reflected in the Annual Reports of the Poor Law Commissioners. Despite the widespread concern that was expressed, however, the parishes were suspicious of proposals for the erection of asylums by the magistrates, who would exercise supervisory powers. In 1838, in evidence before the Select Committee on the Poor Law Amendment Act, it was even suggested, by an Assistant Poor Law Commissioner, that unions should be united to establish and to maintain lunatic asylums, distinct from county asylums,[1] but this plan never came to fruition.

The Lunatic Asylums Act of 1842, 5 & 6 Vict., c. 87, extended the powers of the Metropolitan Commissioners to include the provinces and they were directed to visit and inspect all the public and private asylums throughout England and Wales, with the exception of Bethlem. Their report was presented to the Lord Chancellor in 1844 and it contained the first comprehensive survey of provincial private licensed houses. D. H. Tuke (1882) referred to it as 'the Doomsday Book of all that concerns institutions for the insane at that time'.[2] Many of the recommendations made in this report were later embodied in the Lunatics Act of 1845, 8 & 9 Vict., c. 100. This Act replaced the Metropolitan Commissioners by the Board of Commissioners in Lunacy.[3] The Commissioners in Lunacy constituted a permanent, central, supervising body whose statutory duties included the visitation and inspection of provincial private licensed houses. It now became compulsory for all the counties and principal boroughs in England and Wales to make provision for their insane poor and the majority of the county asylums were built in the next twenty years, thereby bringing to fruition one of the key objectives of the lunacy reformers. The views of their leader, Lord Ashley, were expressed decisively in a speech made in 1845: 'Our present business . . . is to affirm that poor lunatics ought to be maintained at the public charge. I entertain . . . a very decided opinion that none of any class should be received for profit; but all, I hope will agree that paupers, at any rate, should not be the subjects of financial speculation.'[4] His views about private madhouses did not change and, in 1859, he stated: 'I feel strongly that the whole system of private asylums is utterly abominable and indefensible.'[5] The erection of county lunatic asylums led to the progressive withdrawal of pauper lunatics from private licensed houses and to the closure of the pauper departments in such houses. However, despite the careful planning of county asylums to meet the estimated demands, they became overcrowded rapidly and additional accommodation had to be built every few years in the great majority of asylums. In a few areas,

[1] Fifth Report 1838 S.C. on Poor Law Amendment Act, pp. 10–11.
[2] Tuke, D. H. (1882), *Chapters in the History of the Insane in the British Isles*, p. 178.
[3] The Lunacy Commissioners were replaced, in 1913, by the Board of Control.
[4] H.P.D., Vol. LXXXI, 6 June 1845, H.C., col. 194.
[5] Report 1859 S.C. (April 1859), p. 14.

ironically, the private licensed houses were called into service again when the county asylum became overfull. J. T. Arlidge (1859), a psychiatric physician, described the way in which the newly-established asylums were 'besieged by unheard of applicants for admission'.[1] He drew attention to factors operating, both within asylums and in the community, which tended to diminish the curability of insanity and to lead to a multiplication of chronic lunatics.[2] As the century progressed, it became increasingly apparent that the county asylums were not going to fulfil the promise of the early county-asylum movement. The era of the large-scale institutionalization of lunatics and idiots was taking shape and, in general, the 'moral management' of patients blurred into a kindly, but essentially custodial, régime, which precluded individual study and treatment of patients. As a result of the lack of adequate accommodation in county asylums, pauper lunatics in some districts continued to be placed in the custody of proprietors of private licensed houses. This was particularly the case in borough parishes, where administrative problems led to delays in agreement being reached between the Visitors of county asylums and the officials of boroughs which did not possess their own asylums. In addition, parishes often declined to enter into contracts with county asylums, one of the reasons being that, so long as the pauper lunatics were admitted to licensed houses, the whole control remained with the Boards of Guardians, whereas this control would be lost to the magistracy if the lunatics were placed in county asylums. In some areas, the magistrates displayed persistent reluctance to make proper provision for pauper lunatics in accordance with the Act of 1845. Under these circumstances, little change could take place in the prevailing conditions in workhouses, in many of which lunatic wards were established and continued in use for many years.

Three amending Acts were passed in 1853; the Lunacy Regulation Act, 16 & 17 Vict., c. 70; the Lunatics Care and Treatment Amendment Act, 16 & 17 Vict., c. 96, and the Lunatic Asylums Amendment Act, 16 & 17 Vict., c. 97. Under 16 & 17 Vict., c. 96, Bethlem Hospital was brought into line, for the first time, with other asylums, by being placed under the jurisdiction of the Commissioners in Lunacy and being registered as a hospital. The format of the admis-

---

[1] Arlidge, J. T. (1859), *On the State of Lunacy and the Legal Provision for the Insane*, p. 7.
[2] *Ibid.*, pp. 31–124.

sion documents was amended and an important provision was made, which empowered proprietors of private licensed houses, with the consent of the Commissioners, to accommodate, as a boarder, any patient desiring to remain after his discharge and also any relative or friend of a patient. The Lunatic Asylums Amendment Act repealed the several Acts then in force respecting county and borough asylums and re-enacted a large number of their clauses. The compulsory obligations upon the justices to provide asylums continued and this obligation was transferred from the Quarter Sessions to the county and borough councils by the Local Government Act, 1888, 51 & 52 Vict., c. 41. Its provisions included the requirement that all paupers were to be examined quarterly to locate lunatics suitable for confinement in the county asylums, a recommendation which served to increase, further, the overcrowding of these asylums.

By this period a greater consistency had become discernible in the nomenclature relating to the various types of asylums. Private madhouses or licensed houses were becoming known increasingly as private asylums, in contrast to county asylums, which were referred to as public asylums, whilst registered hospitals, supported by voluntary contributions, constituted the third group. Even before this time, in 1820, Burrows had preferred the term 'asylum' to 'madhouse', pointing out that it was then more generally used.[1] In 1858, E. T. Conolly noted that, even at that time, the 'odious term "madhouse"' was still used occasionally. He suggested that the term private asylum should be substituted for it, as the name madhouse 'must always seem an opprobrious epithet, only suited to the horrible ideas formerly deservedly associated with such places.'[2]

The insane members of the upper and middle classes of society were afforded no substantial aid by the establishment of county asylums, since private accommodation was only exceptionally provided in them.[3] Asylums which were subject to visitation by the local magistrates were clearly unpopular with the upper classes. E. J. Seymour (1859), M.D., F.R.S., observed that the families of

[1] Burrows (1820), *op. cit.*, p. 243.
[2] Conolly, E. T. (1858), *Suggestions for the Amendment of the Laws relating to Private Lunatic Asylums*, pp. 4–5.
[3] In 1844, of the 4,400 patients confined in county asylums, 245 were private, distributed in seven out of the total of fifteen asylums. 1844 Report M.C.L., p. 209. By 1852, the number of private patients in county asylums had only increased to c. 268, distributed in ten of the thirty-one asylums. Seventh Report (1852) C.L., Appendix B, pp. 44–112.

some lunatics would even send the patients abroad to avoid such inspection and the consequent risks of local publicity.[1] Public opinion was, therefore, strongly in favour of separate institutions for the educated and for the uneducated classes. In some districts, the magistrates even considered plans for the establishment of a separate asylum to meet the needs of this section of the community, but no such institutions ever came into being.[2] Henry Monro (1852),[3] physician to St Luke's Hospital and proprietor of Brooke House, Clapton, was one of those who advocated the establishment of self-supporting asylums for those who could not afford the charges of proprietary asylums, but such proposals were not acted upon. Instead, the private licensed houses and the registered hospitals continued to provide the necessary accommodation, the bulk of the patients being confined in the former.

The opening of county asylums on a widespread scale led to changes both in the character and the range of accommodation offered by private asylums. As had been anticipated for some time, the large-scale transfer of paupers from private to county asylums, without any likelihood of further pauper admissions, forced the proprietors to close down departments in their houses which catered for an 'inferior class' of paying patients and to concentrate attention upon patients from the wealthier classes. The principal objects of concern, therefore, became those persons who were neither wealthy enough to resort to a good private asylum nor so destitute as to claim the privileges of a pauper and be received into a county asylum.[4] The expenses incurred by prolonged confinement, either as a single lunatic or in a private asylum, could reduce the lunatic and his family

---

[1] Seymour, E. J. (1859), *A Letter to the Right Honourable The Earl of Shaftesbury on the Laws which regulate Private Lunatic Asylums*, p. 8.

[2] Amongst unlisted lunacy papers in the North Riding of Yorkshire C.R.O., was discovered a leaflet, dated 11 February 1852, and entitled, *Prospectus of an Institution proposed to be erected near York, adjacent to the estate of the North and East Ridings Lunatic Asylum, for the Cure, Care, Rational and Useful Occupation and Entertainment of the Insane from the Upper and Middle Classes of Society, under the Superintendence of the Committee of Visitors of the North and East Ridings Asylum.*

[3] Monro, H. (1852), *Articles on Reform in Private Asylums*, p. 15.

[4] *Vide* Dickson, T. (1852), *Observations upon the Importance of establishing Public Hospitals for the Insane of the Middle and Higher Classes*; Anon. (1850), *Familiar views of Lunacy and Lunatic Life*, p. 164 (this work has been attributed to J. Conolly); Gaskell, S. (1860), 'On the Want of Better Provision for the Labouring and Middle Classes when attacked or threatened with Insanity', *J. Ment. Sci.* 6, pp. 321–7.

to pauperism. Although pauperization was much dreaded, there is little doubt that many people whose social position was above that of the pauper were thrown on to the parish in order to ensure the benefits of treatment. Alternatively, in some cases, private arrangements were made, with parish officials, in order to obtain admission to county asylums for persons who did not rightfully qualify as paupers,[1,2] the expenses being wholly or in part reimbursed by friends or relatives. An additional factor which made it more difficult for the lower-middle classes to find cheap accommodation in private asylums was the disuse of mechanical restraint. The use of moral treatment necessitated the employment of additional attendants, of a higher calibre than formerly, and this was accompanied, inevitably, by higher maintenance charges. By the last quarter of the nineteenth century, the character of many of the institutions founded by public subscription had changed. These establishments derived their income from legacies, occasional charitable donations, from interest on investments and from the reception of paying patients. In the past, the payments of the latter had been sufficient to subsidize the admission of poorer patients. However, it was now observed that fewer subsidized admissions were, in general, being allowed and that profits were being used to provide accommodation designed to attract the higher classes and not to relieve the middle classes. The Commissioners in Lunacy recorded, on many occasions, their concern that more provision for the accommodation of middle-class patients, at low or moderate rates, was not being made by those very institutions which had been founded, originally, as 'charities for the insane'. The total accommodation provided by these hospitals was never large and expansion took place slowly and only a small number of new establishments were opened in the second half of the nineteenth century. Under these circumstances, the private asylums remained indispensable, despite the hostility that their continued existence and their prosperity aroused amongst the more zealous reformers.

In 1859, a Select Committee of the House of Commons was appointed to consider the efficacy of the lunacy legislation and its final Report was published in July 1860. In 1858, widespread press

Vide Arlidge (1859), *op. cit.*, p. 37.

[2]Of local interest is a circular, dated 1850, issued by the Visitors of the County Lunatic Asylum at Littlemore, Oxfordshire, drawing attention to the fact that patients were being admitted who were not strictly paupers. Berks. C.R.O., Q/AL. 6.

publicity had attended two commissions of lunacy,[1] which had aroused public concern about the possibility of the incarceration of the sane upon the false imputation of insanity. However, the Select Committee uncovered no evidence which effectively substantiated this fear. At this time, numerous proposals were made for the modification of the situation, many of which were considered by J. C. Bucknill, in his Presidential Address, in 1860, to the Association of Medical Officers of Asylums and Hospitals for the Insane, to be 'so wild that they would themselves seem to furnish plausible evidence that there are more people out of asylums than there ought to be'.[2] A provision of the Irremoveable Poor Act of 1861, 24 & 25 Vict., c. 55, allowed the cost of maintenance of pauper lunatics in county asylums, licensed houses and registered hospitals, to be transferred from the funds of individual parishes to a common union fund. Naturally, this provision fostered the removal of chronic lunatics from their parishes to the county asylums. In some areas, however, particularly the more remote districts, large numbers of paupers continued to be disposed of singly, in order to save the expense of maintenance in an asylum. An Act 'to amend the Law relating to lunatics', 25 & 26 Vict., c. 111, was passed in 1862. This Act consolidated previous legislation with several additions, including the granting of power to licensed-house proprietors to receive, as voluntary boarders, persons who had been patients within the preceding five years. This provision was not extended to include other types of asylum and its introduction was a remarkable and somewhat paradoxical feature, as late-nineteenth-century lunacy legislation was based on the concept that formal orders of admission were the only means of keeping track of every lunatic in every asylum. However, there had been considerable pressure applied, by such persons as Samuel Gaskell, Commissioner in Lunacy 1849 to 1866, to allow voluntary confinement, in order that early treatment could be facilitated.

The first sixty years of the nineteenth century were notable, therefore, for the great activity of the legislature, although, by the end of this time, it must have been difficult to have a precise understanding of the lunacy laws. The possibility of illegal detention again caused considerable public disquiet in the last few decades of the century. The Lunacy Law Reform Association was founded in 1873 and its

[1] *Vide infra*, p. 237.
[2] Bucknill, J. C. (1861), 'Presidential Address', *J. Ment. Sci.* 7, p. 13.

objectives were fourfold; to focus public attention on the defects of existing lunacy laws; to assist those wrongfully incarcerated in public or private asylums; to improve the treatment of all lunatics and to secure the gradual substitution of public for private asylums.[1] In 1877, a parliamentary Select Committee was set up to enquire into the workings of the lunacy laws, with particular emphasis on the security afforded against the violation of personal liberty. Also in the same year, a Committee was appointed by the *Lancet* to report on the care and cure of the insane.[2] However, neither of the 1877 Committees found substantiated evidence of serious abuses and, it would appear that, by this time, overtly ill-managed private asylums had ceased to exist and that the majority of those remaining were running uneventfully. Pressure for the reform of the private-asylum system continued, nevertheless, and often took the form of proposals for its entire abolition. It was closely associated with the concern felt for the insane of the middle classes and criticism was centred around the principle of profit on which the system was based. The Commissioners recognized that 'the licensed houses supply at present a social want . . . their abolition, without the substitution of other and better establishments, would assuredly multiply cases of illegal charge and consequent neglect and ill-treatment of lunatics, and would also lead to the clandestine removal of many such persons to foreign parts'.[3] They observed that the public had not shown any disposition, during previous years, to increase the number of lunatic hospitals founded by voluntary subscription and suggested that asylums for private patients built with public funds, would not be popular. The personal attention and privacy that was possible in private asylums, particularly in the smaller ones, was much valued by the wealthier classes and, undoubtedly, the replacement of such facilities, in the event of the compulsory closure of private asylums, would have presented considerable financial and practical difficulties. In 1881, C. Lockhart Robertson, the Lord Chancellor's Visitor in Lunacy, criticized the Commissioners for placing endless impediments in the way of licensing new private asylums in the metropolitan district in the preceding years. He observed that the monopoly which had been created in this way had not raised the metropolitan asylums

[1] An advertisement for the Association included in *The Bastilles of England* (1883) by L. Lowe, late Hon. Sec. of the Association.

[2] Granville, J. M. (1877), *The Care and Cure of the Insane, being the Reports of the Lancet Commission on Lunatic Asylums.*

[3] Thirty-third Report (1879), C.L., p. 111.

to a higher standard than those in the provinces where 'free trade in lunacy' prevailed.[1] Robertson suggested that only time and competition would show which type of institution for the insane would gain public approval and confidence and this view was supported by others. H. C. Burdett (1891), who wrote extensively on hospitals and their administration, recommended state competition with the private asylums by establishing private departments in all county and borough asylums. If the accommodation offered was of a high standard and the charges lower than in private asylums, the middle-class private asylum would disappear, leaving only the first-class establishments, which would probably become '"homes" for the harmless cases whose friends were able to pay high rates . . . managed in all respects as private houses or country hotels'.[2] This latter observation reflects a change in role which, by this time, had already taken place.

The Lunacy Act of 1890, 53 Vict., c. 5, did not introduce new powers to close private asylums, but it restricted further expansion of the system by stating that no new licences were to be granted except under certain specified circumstances and the enlargement of existing houses was prohibited. In addition, before the magistrates could issue licences, the proposed private asylum had to be inspected by the Commissioners. The Act itself was comprehensive in its coverage of every aspect of lunacy legislation and was a triumph for the legalistic concept of mental illness, although this view was to impede the development of mental treatment services until the Mental Health Act of 1959. Despite the restrictions of the Act of 1890, however, in 1926 there were still fifty-five private licensed houses (thirty-six in the provinces), licensed for a total of over 3,500 patients. The 1926 Royal Commission on lunacy and mental disorder observed that, as had been the case with other Select Committees in the past, the Commission was confronted with a great diversity of opinion on the propriety of recognizing private asylums. It was satisfied that the private asylums met a real and legitimate public demand and even proposed the withdrawal of the restriction on new licences, so as to terminate the anomalous situation under which a limited number of licensed houses enjoyed a monopoly. There was no evidence to suggest that wrongful detention of lunatics occurred particularly in licensed

---

[1] Robertson, C. L. (1881), 'Lunacy in England', *J. Psychol. Med. & Ment. Path.* (New Series) *VII*, pp. 185–6.

[2] Burdett, H. C. (1891), *Hospitals and Asylums of the World*, Vol. I, p. 148.

houses and the Board of Control, the British Medical Association and the Medico-Psychological Association were satisfied with the situation, despite the adverse reports given by some witnesses, who had themselves been treated in private asylums. Finally, the Commission observed: 'There remains the fundamental objection to a system under which a conflict between duty and interest may arise in consequence of private profit being derived from the care and treatment of the insane, as a result of which licensed houses are liable to be regarded with disfavour and suspicion.'[1] Similar observations had been made for over two centuries.

The administrative functions of the Board of Control, which had been reorganized by the Mental Treatment Act of 1930, were transferred to the Minister of Health by the National Health Service Act of 1946, 9 & 10 Geo. VI, c. 81. The Minister became the licensing authority in the metropolitan area, but the justices of the peace retained their duties in every county or Quarter Sessions borough in the provinces. The Royal Commission on the law relating to mental illness and mental deficiency, 1954–7, made recommendations for the rationalization of the registration and inspection of registered hospitals and licensed houses and, in particular, expressed the view that 'the licensing of provincial licensed houses by justices of the peace is an anachronism'.[2] Subsequently, under the Mental Health Act of 1959, 7 & 8 Eliz. II, c. 72, licensed houses, together with registered hospitals, had to be registered by county and county borough councils under the Public Health Act of 1936 and they became known as mental nursing homes. In this capacity, several former private licensed houses are still operating at the present day, for example, Grove House, Church Stretton (established 1853); Ticehurst House, Sussex (1792); Bailbrook House, Bath (1831); Wyke House, Isleworth (1826); Northumberland House, London (1840) and Cliffden, Teignmouth, Devon (originated as Kenton House, 1869).

[1] Report of Royal Commission on lunacy and mental disorder, 1926, p. 135.
[2] Report of Royal Commission on the law relating to mental illness and mental deficiency, 1957, p. 279.

3

◇◇

The Madhouse System:
the Range and Development
of its Provisions

◇◇

The number of provincial private madhouses,
their geographical distribution and lifespan

OFFICIALLY documented information about the number of private madhouses, their capacity, distribution and proprietors, is not available prior to 1774. The Country Register,[1] the sole surviving copy of which commences in 1798, constitutes the earliest surviving list of provincial private madhouses, although, in some areas, records relating to individual houses extend back to 1774. This Register is probably almost complete, but it is known that no returns were made by some private licensed houses and that unlicensed houses did receive patients.[2] The names of forty-two proprietors are given in the Register, together with information regarding the admission of 1,788 patients. An estimate of the number of houses in use in 1802 and 1810, based on material extracted from the Register, is included in Table 1, which, in conjunction with Table 2, displays the total number of provincial private licensed houses at intervals from 1774 to 1900, the figures for metropolitan houses being added to afford a comparison. In many cases the figures refer to the number of individual, named houses and not to the number of licences issued. This fact may account for some of the variation in the numbers, and it must be recognized that, for the early part of the century, the accuracy of the figures quoted cannot be relied upon. The Report of

---

[1] *Vide* Appendix A, p. 296.   [2] *Vide* Powell, *op. cit.* p. 151.

TABLE 1 *Number of provincial and metropolitan private licensed houses, 1774–1841*[a]

Date	Provincial licensed houses	Metropolitan licensed houses	Total licensed houses	Source of data
1774		16		Treasurer's Account Book, 1774–1828
1802	22			Country Register, 1798–1812
1807	28	17	45	Report 1807 S.C.
1810	33			Country Register
1813		33		P.R., 1825
1815	38	34	72	Minutes of evidence, 1815 S.C.
1819	49[b]	40	89	P.R., 1819 (a)
1821		40		P.R., 1825
1824		47		P.R., 1825
1825	58			P.R., 1826
1828		48		Treasurer's Account Book
1831	68	38	106	P.R., 1831
1837	83*	34**	117	*P.R., 1838 **Report (1838) M.C.L.
1841	90† (38 receiving paupers)	33‡	123	†P.R., 1842 ‡Report (1841) M.C.L.

[a] It is necessary to note at this juncture that, in this and subsequent Tables, the dates of the appropriate sources are quoted in cases when the precise dates of the data presented are not available.

[b] Including Ticehurst Asylum, Sussex, which was placed by mistake in the return for public hospitals and lunatic asylums, P.R., 1819 (a), p. 3. (*Vide* Burrows (1820), *op. cit.*, p. 292).

the 1807 Select Committee included lists from the Town and Country Registers of the names and places of abode of those who kept 'houses for the admission of lunatics'[1] and similar ones were included in the Report of the 1815 Select Committee.[2] These latter lists

[1] Report 1807 S.C., pp. 25–6.   [2] Minutes of evidence 1815 S.C., pp. 165–6.

were compiled by Powell, who stressed again their unreliability, because unlicensed madhouses clearly did exist. As an example, he referred to William Rickett's house at Droitwich, Worcestershire, which had never been licensed or visited by the magistrates, who had displayed total indifference towards their duties in this respect.[1] Parliamentary Returns relating to private licensed houses provide an invaluable source of information about the number, the location, the amount of accommodation and the proprietors of these establishments during the first half of the nineteenth century. Returns of

TABLE 2 *Number of provincial and metropolitan private licensed houses, 1844–1900*

| Date | Provincial licensed houses | | | Metropolitan licensed houses | | | Total licensed houses |
	Receiving only private patients	Receiving paupers	Total	Receiving only private patients	Receiving paupers	Total	
1844	55	45	100	36	3	39	139
1847	54	42	96	36	9	45	141
1848			98			47	145
1849	62	37	99	39	8	47	146
1850	56	35	91	39	6	45	136
1855	63	25	88	36	5	41	129
1860	59	14	73	35	5	40	113
1870	60	4	64	39	5	44	108
1880	56	5	61	30	5	35	96
1890	55	3	58	28	5	33	91
1900	44	2	46	19	5	24	70

Source of data: 1844 Report M.C.L.; Further Report (1847) C.L.; Third Report (1848) C.L. and subsequent Annual Reports C.L.

particular importance, in this respect, were published in 1819, 1826, 1831, 1838 and 1842. In the appendix of their 1844 Report, the Metropolitan Commissioners included a list of all private licensed houses, their proprietors, the number of patients confined and the weekly charges made for pauper lunatics.[2] This practice was continued in subsequent reports of the Commissioners and the data provided in these statistical appendices became increasingly more elaborate and detailed. The greater part of the numerical information

[1] Minutes of evidence 1815 S.C., p. 169. *Vide infra*, p. 264.
[2] 1844 Report M.C.L., pp. 211–13.

discussed in this chapter has been extracted from the above-mentioned sources.

It is evident from Tables 1 and 2 that the number of provincial private licensed houses rose steadily throughout the first half of the nineteenth century, the peak being reached, as far as can be ascertained, in 1844 and being maintained for some five years. Subsequently, the number declined, with a sharp decrease in the number of pauper establishments as pauper lunatics and idiots became absorbed by the newly opened county asylums. This decrease, however, was offset, to some extent, by a consolidation in the position of private licensed houses receiving private patients, a state of affairs which was maintained until the close of the century.

The total number of licensed houses in England and Wales declined slowly during the first half of the twentieth century. By 1938 there were still thirty-one provincial private licensed houses out of the total of fifty houses in the whole country.[1] In 1959, shortly before the Mental Health Act came into operation there were twenty licensed houses in England and Wales, together licensed for a maximum of 970 patients. Twelve of these houses were situated in the provinces and they catered for 527 private patients and thirty-six Health Service patients.[2]

The private licensed houses for which there are known to be surviving MSS. are listed, according to counties, in Appendix B. Naturally these lists do not represent a comprehensive register of all the houses licensed. The apparently high number of houses in certain counties is explicable, in certain cases, by the fact that proprietors moved from one house to another within the same locality, transferring the licence and the patients, and, in addition, by the brief, even ephemeral, lifespan of some houses. The geographical distribution of provincial licensed houses, according to the counties in which they were situated, is displayed in Table 3, at selected intervals from 1807 to 1900. It can be observed that the increase in the number of licensed houses was associated with their more widespread geographical distribution and, in the period 1807 to 1844, the number of counties containing private licensed houses rose from sixteen to thirty-two. This numerical increase was associated also with a relative concentration of houses in certain parts of the country. The most notable areas, in this respect, were Co. Durham, Lancashire,

---

[1] *Local Government Manual and Directory*, 1938, p. 282-4.
[2] Forty-sixth Report (1960) Board of Control, pp. 6, 8.

Gloucestershire, Hampshire, Warwickshire, Somerset and the East and West Ridings of Yorkshire. The spread of private licensed houses in this way appears to have been related, principally, to the higher density of the population in the area and to the presence, or lack of, other licensed houses or alternative types of establishments for lunatics in the vicinity. In addition, various other local factors usually played an important part.

The distribution of private licensed houses, according to lists published in 1844, illustrates many of the factors which influenced the spread of houses. In that year, Lancashire, the largest county in England (population in 1841 census, 1,717,413) contained seven private licensed houses, of which only one catered for paupers, namely Haydock Lodge, which was opened, in fact, in 1844. This situation was probably due to the fact that there had been a county asylum at Lancaster since 1816. There were, in addition, two public-subscription asylums, one of which, the Liverpool Lunatic Asylum, accommodated paupers. By 1844, the county asylum was very over-crowded, the resident population having risen from 160, in 1816, to 611 in that year[1] and, therefore, the opening of Haydock Lodge was timely. A similar situation prevailed in the West Riding of Yorkshire (population, in 1841, 790,751), where a county asylum for pauper lunatics had been opened at Wakefield, in 1818. In 1844, the three licensed houses receiving paupers in the county provided little accommodation for paupers. In the East Riding of the county, however, there was no county asylum and four of the six private licensed houses in this area received paupers, one of which, the Hull and East Riding Refuge, contained ninety-three pauper lunatics. The concentration of private madhouses in and around the city of York was undoubtedly fostered by the influence of the York Retreat, especially during the early decades of the nineteenth century, when the reputation of the Retreat was particularly high. The Tukes had stressed the advantages of treating the insane in the surroundings of a country retreat and, in the vicinity of York, it became a particularly common practice to name private madhouses a 'Retreat' or a 'Refuge', for example, Cottingham Retreat, Sculcoates Refuge and Southcoates Retreat. This practice was adopted, to a lesser extent, elsewhere, for example, Heigham Retreat, Norwich and Clapham Retreat, London. Somerset was the sixth largest county in England and Wales (population, in 1841, 454,446) and, in 1844, private

[1] 1844 Report M.C.L., pp. 90, 209.

TABLE 3 *Distribution of provincial private licensed houses according to counties (figures in brackets refer to houses receiving paupers)*[a]

County	1807	1815	1819	1825	1831	1837	1844	1854	1870	1900
Bedfordshire	0	0	0	0	0	1	1	1	1	2
Berkshire	0	1	0	0	0	0	0	0	0	0
Buckinghamshire	0	0	0	0	0	0	1	0	0	0
Cheshire	0	0	0	0	0	0	0	0	1	0
Derbyshire	0	0	0	0	0	1	1 (1)	0	1	1
Devon	0	0	1	2	1	3	3 (2)	2 (1)	2	2
Dorset	1	1	1	2	3	2	2	1	0	0
Durham	0	1	1	4	5	5	5 (5)	5 (5)	2	2
Essex	0	0	0	2	3	4	2 (1)	2	2	1
Glamorgan	0	0	1	0	0	0	1 (1)	1 (1)	1 (1)	0
Gloucestershire	2	1	1	3	3	6	7 (2)	4 (1)	5	2
Hampshire	0	2	2	2	3	5	5 (4)	2 (2)	1	2
Herefordshire	0	0	0	2	2	2	2 (2)	1 (1)	0	0
Hertfordshire	3	1	1	1	1	1	1	2	2	1
Kent	1	1	1	1	2	1	3 (1)	3	3	3
Lancashire	2	4	5	6	5	4	7 (1)	6	4 (1)	5 (1)
Leicestershire	1	1	2	2	2	2	1	0	0	0
Lincolnshire	2	3	4	2	2	2	1	2	0	0
Norfolk	3	3	2	2	2	4	4	4 (1)	2	2
Northamptonshire	0	0	0	0	0	0	0	1	1	0

34

Northumberland	1	0	0	0	0	2	2 (1)	2 (1)	0	0
Nottinghamshire	0	0	0	0	0	0	0	1	0	0
Oxfordshire	1	1	2	2	2	2	3 (1)	2 (1)	0	0
Pembrokeshire	0	0	0	0	0	0	0	1 (1)	0	0
Shropshire	1	1	1	3	0	3	2	2	2	4
Somerset	0	1	3	3	4	3	4 (2)	5 (1)	6	3
Staffordshire	1	2	3	2	1	3	3 (1)	3 (1)	2	2
Suffolk	0	0	0	0	1	0	3 (1)	4	3	0
Surrey	3	3	4	3	2	2	2	3	2	2
Sussex	1	1	1	1	3	3	3	3	2	4
Warwickshire	1	3	4	4	4	5	5 (2)	5 (1)	5	1
Wiltshire	3	3	5	6	5	7	7 (6)	6 (3)	4 (1)	4 (1)
Worcestershire	1	1	1	1	1	1	1 (1)	1 (1)	1	0
Yorkshire										
N. Riding	0	0	0	0	3	0	1 (1)	0	1	0
E. Riding	0	1	0	0	5	5	6 (4)	4 (2)	2	0
W. Riding	0	0	0	0	0	3	7 (3)	1	5 (1)	2
City of York	0	2	3	4	3	1	4	8 (4)	1	1
Total	28	38	49	58	68	83	100 (45)	88 (28)	64 (4)	46 (2)

[a] Essex and Surrey, at times, contained additional houses situated within seven miles of the city of London, which, therefore, were not licensed by county magistrates.

Source of data: Reports S.C. 1807 and 1815; P.R., 1819 (a), 1826, 1831, 1838; 1844 Report M.C.L., and Reports C.L., 1854, 1870 and 1900.

licensed houses constituted the only type of establishment for the insane in this county. It is notable that, in Somerset, the number of licensed houses which catered for private patients increased during the second half of the nineteenth century. At least eighteen licensed houses existed at one time or another during the century and these were located around Taunton and in the Bristol–Bath region. Included in the latter area was Brislington House, which was one of the foremost private licensed houses in the country. It is interesting to note, also, that five of the Gloucestershire licensed houses were to be found clustered in that part of the county which adjoined Bristol.

In a few areas, the spread of licensed madhouses was centred on a single parish. Thus, in 1825, all four licensed houses in Co. Durham were at Gateshead, whilst in Warwickshire, three of the four houses were at Henley-in-Arden. These circumstances still prevailed in 1844 and did not escape the notice of the critics of the private-madhouse system. For example, Richard Paternoster (1841) referred to Gateshead as, 'a whole parish devoted to the trade in lunacy, containing on a moderate calculation one hundred and forty patients' and he described Henley-in-Arden as, 'a peaceful country village fattening on the spoils of humanity'.[1] The Gateshead private licensed houses provided for a large number of pauper lunatics drawn from a wide area in which there were no county asylums. The subsequent development of the provisions for lunatics in the Gateshead–Newcastle area is referred to later in this chapter. The tradition for keeping private madhouses in Henley-in-Arden was a long-established one. William Roadknight's madhouse at Henley-in-Arden was the first Warwickshire madhouse to be licensed, in 1774.[2] By 1796, the number of licensed houses in this parish had risen to three. One of these, Thomas Burman's house, which was opened in 1795, remained a family concern until the mid-nineteenth century. Perhaps the best example, however, of the existence, over a long period of time, of a number of madhouses within a single district, is provided by the situation prevailing at Hoxton, London, during the seventeenth, eighteenth and nineteenth centuries. The Hoxton madhouses comprised Hoxton House, Whitmore House and Holly House, and A. D. Morris (1958) has made them the subject of a short, but detailed, booklet,[3] the only

---

[1] Paternoster, R. (1841), *The Madhouse System*, pp. 78, 80. *Vide infra*, p. 228.
[2] Warwicks, C.R.O., Q.S. 24/a/I/6, accounts of Clerk of Peace.
[3] Morris, A. D. (1958), *The Hoxton Madhouses*.

one to have been devoted exclusively to madhouses. In Wiltshire, the situation must have been influenced, substantially, by the Finch family, who owned three houses in that county in 1826, two of which, Laverstock House and Fisherton House, were noted establishments. Members of the Finch family are known to have kept private madhouses elsewhere in the provinces and also in London; for example, W. C. Finch kept two houses in London, Kensington House and a house in King's Road, Chelsea, in 1831.[1] It seems likely that the presence of one or more madhouses in a single neighbourhood fostered the establishment of others in that area. Some of those who worked in private madhouses, naturally, wished to set up their own establishments after they had gained experience. Conolly (1855) drew attention, in a rather cynical fashion, to the fact that:

Clever and cunning subordinates, in private asylums, often become inspired by the wish to set up for themselves ... They pursue a well-considered course; ingratiate themselves with the friends of the patients, and are profoundly obsequious to the Commissioners, or to the Visiting Magistrates; and ... having got a licence for a house of their own, defy the claims of duty and honour, and triumph with the power given to them to trade in lunatics.[2]

The calculation, with any precision, of the lifespan of individual private madhouses would necessitate, in the majority of cases, lengthy and detailed research. However, it is encouraging to record that it has been possible to accumulate information concerning the history of a considerable number of private madhouses. The first attempt to provide a comprehensive list of the opening dates of private madhouses was that published in 1844[3] and the information given, at this time, concerning provincial licensed houses is analysed in Table 4. In the ten instances in which the date of opening was not given precisely, the dates provided related either to the date of the commencement of the surviving records, or to the date when the current or previous proprietor took over the establishment. For example, J. Mercer of Portland House, Halstock, Dorset, replied simply to the request for information: 'Succeeded my aunt, Miss B. Mercer, April 1839, and my late mother,' and the proprietors of Lea Pale House, Stoke, near Guildford, Surrey, stated: 'The records

[1] P.R., 1831, p. 2.
[2] Conolly, J. (1855), 'Fourth Notice of the Eighth Report of the Commissioners in Lunacy', *Asylum J. Ment. Sci. 1*, p. 183.
[3] Statistical Appendix to 1844 Report M.C.L. (Details presented as part of a statement of returns from each licensed house.)

furnish a statement from August 1803. The house has been used as an asylum for above a century.'[1] Such returns suggest that the accuracy of many other replies cannot be relied upon, and, in many instances, this has been shown definitely to be the case. Thus, the respective dates of opening given for the houses at Hook Norton and Witney are 1814 and 1842 and these are both incorrect. Hook Norton was first licensed in 1775 and, probably, had been functioning as a private madhouse since *c.* 1725, whilst Witney was opened in 1823. Similarly, Kingsdown House, Box, Wiltshire, was recorded as having been established in December 1841, although, as has been noted previously, there is some evidence that it was a madhouse in *c.* 1615.

TABLE 4   *Dates of opening of provincial private licensed houses in operation in 1844 (figures in brackets refer to houses receiving paupers)*

Date of opening	Number of licensed houses
Before 1800	5 (3)
1800–	4 (1)
1810–	3 (2)
1820–	11 (7)
1830–	30 (15)
1840–1844	16 (7)
Precise date not given	10 (4)
No return made	19 (5)
Total	98[a]

[a] The total number in 1844 was, in fact, 100, as there were two licensed departments at both Hook Norton and Ticehurst.

Since Kingsdown House remained open until November 1947 its recorded lifespan of over 330 years is considerably longer than that of any other private madhouse known to the writer. Provincial private licensed houses indicated, in 1844, as having been established during the eighteenth century were those at Fonthill Gifford, Wiltshire (1718); Fishponds, near Bristol, Gloucestershire (1760)[2];

[1] Statistical Appendix to 1844 Report M.C.L., pp. 105, 137.

[2] It was stated that in 1760, 'patients removed from another house opened in 1738' were transferred to Fishponds. Statistical Appendix to 1844 Report M.C.L., p. 167. For further details, *vide*, Phillips, H. T. (1970), 'The Old Private Lunatic Asylum at Fishponds', *Bristol Medico-Chirurgical J. 85*, pp. 41–4; and Robinson, B. and Hudleston, C. R. (1938), 'Two Vanished Fishponds Houses', *Trans. Bristol & Gloucester Archeol. Soc. 60*, pp. 238–59.

Belle Grove House, Newcastle upon Tyne (1766); Droitwich Lunatic Asylum, Worcestershire (1791) and Ticehurst Asylum, Sussex (1792). In the metropolitan area, three houses were described clearly as having been founded in the eighteenth century, namely Brooke House, Clapton (1759); Beaufort House, Fulham (1758) and Whitmore House, Hoxton ('nearly a century', i.e. *c.* 1750). Although the opening date of Hoxton House was stated as not known, another source claimed that it had been open since 1695.[1] Despite the inaccuracies of the returns, however, the sharp rise which appeared to take place in the number of new licensed houses in the fourth decade of the century is notable and corresponds to an equivalent rise in the total number of licensed houses. This degree of correlation is, perhaps, predictable, as the returns relating to the more recently established houses were more likely to be accurate.

The widespread erection of county asylums led, naturally, to the closure of many private licensed houses in the fifth and sixth decades of the nineteenth century. Establishments catering predominantly or solely for private patients, however, were largely unaffected and many well-established houses continued, successfully, throughout the century. Seventeen of the forty-five provincial private licensed houses still open in 1910 had been in operation in 1844.[2] Well-known houses which survived this period were Brislington House; Ticehurst Asylum; Laverstock House; Fisherton House; Haydock Lodge; West Malling Place, Kent; Fairford Retreat, Gloucestershire and Plympton House, Devon. Approximately one-half of the thirty-one provincial private licensed houses open in 1938 had been functioning for nearly a century and some for a much longer period.

The capacity of provincial private licensed houses and the numbers of patients admitted and discharged

Unfortunately, no lists have survived giving the total number of lunatics for whose reception each provincial madhouse was licensed, prior to 1838, when this information was included in a Parliamentary Return. Further returns, in 1842 and 1854, furnished these details, and later they were included regularly in the statistical summaries of the Commissioners' Annual Reports. With regard to metropolitan houses, the surviving Treasurer's Account Book provides information

---

[1] Fourteenth Report (1860) C.L., p. 21. *Vide* Hunter & Macalpine (1963), *op. cit.*, p. 790.   [2] Sixty-fourth Report (1910) C.L., pp. 547–50.

as to whether a licence was issued for the reception of less or more than ten patients, during the period 1774 to 1828. In 1815 and 1816, Powell quoted the figures for metropolitan houses and in 1816, for example, nine houses were licensed for less than ten patients and twenty-seven for a number in excess of ten.[1] Quarter Sessions records would provide, in some areas, a source of information regarding provincial houses, but, in general, a detailed search of such material would be impractical on a large scale, because of the frequently incomplete nature of the records and the considerable amount of material that would require handling and sorting. Consequently, in the absence of more precise information, the best available index of the relative sizes of licensed houses and of the capacity of individual houses, is furnished in returns recording the total number of patients in each house at a particular time.

Table 5 sets out the relevant information concerning the distribution of provincial licensed houses, during the period 1819 to 1870, according to the number of patients confined or according to the number of patients each house was licensed to receive, the figures for 1837 and 1841 being based largely on data of the latter type. It is apparent that, in the particular years for which details are available, the greater number of provincial houses contained up to approximately twenty-five patients. However, it is likely that many houses contained fewer patients at the time a return was made than they were actually licensed to receive. For example, the Workhouse Asylum, at Stoke Damerel, Devon, was licensed for the reception of 100 patients in each year from 1837 to 1841, but it did not contain more than thirty-four patients during this time.[2] Further, the figures for 1837 and 1841 suggest that the pattern of the distribution of houses would be different if all the figures were based on the number of patients for which the houses were licensed. It is shown that the number of the larger establishments increased up to the mid-century and then declined. The figures for 1841 and 1844 demonstrate clearly that the larger establishments were those which catered chiefly for paupers, usually accompanied by a smaller number of private patients. These facts are illustrated also in Table 6, which lists the provincial licensed houses containing, or licensed to receive, 100 or more patients, during the period 1819 to 1870. In addition, it is interesting to note that a small number of houses were licensed to receive precisely ninety-nine patients; for example, in 1842,

[1] First Report minutes of evidence 1816 S.C., p. 75.   [2] P.R., 1842, p. 8.

40

cular time or for whose reception the houses were licensed

Date	Number of patients						Total licensed houses	Comments
	< 5	6–25	26–50	51–100	101+	Not known		
1819	10	27	8	2	1	1[a]	49	[a] Details for two licensed parts of Laverstock House not given separately.
1825	11	27	12	5	2	1[b]	58	[b] West Derby, Liverpool.
1831	14	32	9	10	2	1[c]	68	[c] Bailbrook House, Somerset, licensed but not yet opened.
1837	4	29	28	19	3	0	83	Figures based largely on number for which houses licensed; 17 houses received paupers.
1841 (a) Priv. patients only	5	29	11	7	0	0	52	Figures based largely on number for which houses licensed.
(b) Paupers received	0	8	9	17	4	0	38	
1844 (a) Priv. patients only	12	32	5	2	0	4[d]	55	[d] No details for 3 houses; joint figures for 2 licensed parts of Ticehurst.
(b) Paupers received	3	7	13	14	7	1[e]	45	[e] No figures for Haydock Lodge.
1854 (a) Priv. patients only	13	35	10	3	0	0	61	
(b) Paupers received	0	7	11	4	5	0	27	
1870 (a) Priv. patients only	15(2)	26(29)	15(22)	4(6)	0(1)	0	60	Bracketed figures refer to number of houses within category, according to number each was licensed to receive.
(b) Paupers received	0(0)	0(0)	1(1)	1(0)	2(3)	0	4	

Source of data: P.R., 1819 (a), 1826, 1831, 1838, 1842; 1844 Report M.C.L. and Reports C.L., 1854 and 1870.

41

TABLE 6 *Provincial private licensed houses containing, or licensed to receive, 100 or more patients (figures in brackets refer to the number of pauper lunatics)*

Date	Private licensed house	Number of patients
1819	Droitwich Lunatic Asylum, Worcs.	102
1825	Droitwich Lunatic Asylum	112
	Laverstock House, Wilts.	103
1831	Brislington House, Somerset	124
	Laverstock House	120
1837	Brislington House	110 (20)
	Laverstock House	125 (30)
	Fisherton House, Wilts.	100 (60)
	Kingsdown House, Wilts.	139 (89)
1841	Workhouse Asylum, Stoke Damerel, Devon	100[a]
	Kingsdown House	140 (87)
	Belle Vue House, Devizes, Wilts.	100 (85)
	Fisherton House	100 (70)
	Laverstock House	150 (50)
	Fiddington House, Wilts	175 (135)
	Droitwich Lunatic Asylum	100 (70)
1844	Fairford Retreat, Glos.	140 (119)
	Dunston Lodge, Co. Durham	100 (77)
	Laverstock House	126 (35)
	Fisherton House	112 (90)
	Kingsdown House	137 (101)
	Belle Vue House	156 (148)
	Fiddington House	180 (144)
	Hull and East Riding Refuge, Yorks.	106 (93)
	Haydock Lodge, Lancs.	200 (160)*
1854	Bensham, Co. Durham	160 (139)
	Dunston Lodge	120 (93)
	Vernon House, Glam.	146 (131)
	Fairford Retreat	105 (67)
	Fisherton House	214 (172)
1870	Vernon House	120 (54)
	Haydock Lodge	250 (170)
	Brislington House	105
	Fisherton House	616 (502)

[a] Class of patient not specified in return, but undoubtedly all paupers.

Source of data: P.R., 1819 (a), 1826, 1831, 1837, 1842; 1844 Report M.C.L. and Reports C.L., 1854, 1870; Report C.L. re Haydock Lodge Lunatic Asylum, 1847, p. 3.*

Duddeston Hall and the Hull and East Riding Refuge.[1] It seems very likely that this number was chosen to preclude the necessity of having a resident medical attendant as would have been obligatory with 100 patients or more under the Act of 1828, 9 Geo. IV, c. 41. The largest provincial private licensed houses for private patients alone, in 1844, were Ticehurst Asylum (fifty-nine patients), Brislington House (ninety) and High Beech, Essex (forty-one). By 1854, Laverstock House (seventy-four) patients had joined this list.

Throughout the greater part of the nineteenth century, the metropolitan licensed houses included a number of very large establishments, the largest, as in the provinces, being those which received paupers as well as private patients. In 1815, there were 486 patients at Miles' house[2] (Hoxton House), three-quarters of them being paupers; at Talbot's house, Bethnal Green, there were 360 patients, including about 230 paupers and at Rhodes' house, Bethnal Green,[3] the 275 patients included about 215 pauper lunatics.[4] In 1831, five licensed houses contained over 100 patients, Hoxton House accommodating 546 patients, including 440 paupers.[5] The three establishments receiving paupers in 1844, namely Peckham House, Hoxton House and Warburton's Red and White Houses at Bethnal Green, contained, 251, 396 and 562 patients, respectively.[6] The largest metropolitan establishment receiving private patients only was Pembroke House, Hackney, in which ninety-five patients were confined in the four separately licensed premises which the house comprised. In 1870, the five licensed houses receiving paupers all contained over 300 patients and the number at Pembroke House had increased to 135. The largest metropolitan house in that year was Grove Hall, Bow, licensed for 452 patients, but Fisherton House, Wiltshire, was licensed, at that time, for 616 patients. During the period 1878 to 1890, Fisherton House was licensed to receive 672 patients, including 542 pauper or criminal lunatics,[7] making it the largest private licensed house ever known in this country. In[8] 1844,

---

[1] P.R., 1842, pp. 29, 35.   [2] i.e., Sir Jonathan, son of John Miles.
[3] These two houses were owned by Th. Warburton, but were referred to commonly by the names of their superintendents, or as the White and Red Houses respectively. From c. 1850 they became known as Bethnal House.
[4] Minutes of evidence 1815 S.C., pp. 75, 81.   [5] P.R., 1831, pp. 2–3.
[6] 1844 Report M.C.L., p. 211.
[7] Wilts. C.R.O., Q.S. lunacy records, accounts of Clerk of Peace.
[8] Taken over by the Ministry of Heath in 1954, this house remains in use as a mental hospital: the Old Manor, Salisbury.

eight of the fifteen county asylums erected under the Act of 1808 contained over 200 patients, the largest being those at Hanwell, Middlesex (975 patients) and at Lancaster Moor, Lancashire (611). There were 355 patients at Bethlem Hospital, but only three other public asylums or hospitals out of the ten in existence contained over 100 patients: those at Lincoln, York and Northampton.[1]

The details recorded in the Country Register can be used to provide an approximate guide to the relative sizes of provincial licensed houses, during the first decade of the nineteenth century, if a comparison is made of the total number of admissions to each house over a given period. In the case of eighteen of the forty-two licensed houses named in the Register, the period for which admissions were recorded was ten years or over. No admissions were reported from one house and, at three houses, all the admissions recorded took place during a single month. Of the houses with recorded admissions covering a period of ten years or more, Cox's house at Fishponds, Gloucestershire, would appear to have been the largest, with 183 admissions in the period October 1801 to November 1812. The house of William Finch at Laverstock, Wiltshire, had 162 admissions from December 1801 to November 1812. Thomas Arnold's house at Leicester received 142 patients in the period December 1801 to October 1812 and there were ninety-six admissions to James Johnson's house at Shrewsbury between October 1801 and November 1812. The admission rates at Hook Norton (fifty-six patients admitted in the period October 1801 to October 1812) and at the Willis's house at Greatford, Lincolnshire (forty-six patients, December 1801 to December 1812) are representative of those of many of the smaller houses. An analysis of the details regarding admissions to Hook Norton, extracted from the Country Register, is displayed in Table 7. The small scale on which such a licensed house operated at this period is apparent and it can be seen that its business was essentially local, since the preponderance of its patients were residents of Oxfordshire. In some cases, the number of recorded admissions is very small, for example, only eleven admissions took place at William Terry's house, Sutton Coldfield, Warwickshire, from January 1793 to July 1812. Of houses at which the recorded admissions covered a period of less than ten years, the highest admission rates were at Thomas Burman's house at Henley-in-Arden, Warwickshire (forty-six patients, December 1808 to Novem-

[1] 1844 Report M.C.L., pp. 209–10.

ber 1812); Samuel Newington's house at Ticehurst, Sussex (ninety-seven patients, April 1802 to December 1812) and at Thomas Bakewell's house, Spring Vale, Staffordshire (forty-one patients, October 1808 to December 1812). Eight patients were admitted during the same number of months at John Beal's house at Gate Helmsley, York (March 1812 to October 1812), and at Walton Lodge, Liverpool, twenty-one patients were admitted in November to December 1812. When viewed as a whole, average admission rates of one

TABLE 7 *Number of patients admitted to Hook Norton, 1801–12, as recorded in the Country Register*

Date	Males	Females	Total patients	Formerly resident in Oxfordshire
5 Oct.–31 Dec.				
1801	1	2	3	2
1802	4[a]	0	4	2
1803	3	1	4	1
1804	2	1	3	3
1805	0	3	3	2
1806	2	6	8	5
1807	0	0	0	
1808	2	2	4	4
1809	4[a]	3	7	6
1810	2	2	4	2
1811	6	5	11	8
1 Jan.–8 Oct.				
1812	2	3	5	5
Total	28	28	56	39

[a] Sex of one patient unclear in MS. and assumed to be male.

patient every one to two months were maintained at only thirteen of the houses whose recorded admissions covered a period of twelve months or more.

Scattered references to the number of lunatics confined in individual madhouses and to the number admitted annually, during the late-eighteenth and the early part of the nineteenth century, are to be found in a variety of sources other than the Country Register. For example, 402 patients were admitted to the Newcastle upon Tyne

Lunatic Hospital during the period July 1764 to July 1817[1] and, according to the proprietor, 619 cases were admitted to the Droitwich Lunatic Asylum, Worcestershire, during a period extending, probably, from the time of its opening in 1792 until 1816.[2] It is of interest to note that only two admissions to the latter house were recorded in the Country Register and these were in April 1802. This fact emphasizes the unreliability of the Register as a source of information about the total number of the insane in provincial madhouses and the total annual number of admissions. In addition, the value of

TABLE 8   *Number of patients admitted to private licensed houses, 1775–1824, as recorded in the Country and Town Registers*

Date	Patients admitted to provincial licensed houses	Patients admitted to metropolitan licensed houses	Total patients	Aggregate for 5-year periods from 1775
1775	153	253	406	1,783
1780	108	258	366	1,893
1785	115	299	414	1,892
1790	148	283	431	2,292
1795	110	344	454	2,242
1800	138	339	477	2,463
1805	110	313	423	2,271
1810	177	367	544	3,657
1815	307	543	850	
1815–1824			7,904	

Source of data: (i) For period 1775 to 1815, First Report minutes of evidence 1816 S.C., p. 79; (ii) for period 1815 to 1824, P.R., 1826.

data derived from the Country Register is severely limited by the fact that the returns, which were required to be recorded, related only to non-pauper patients. Table 8 displays the total number of patients admitted annually to provincial and metropolitan licensed houses, according to the entries made in the Country and Town Registers, the details being derived from two contemporary printed sources. The total number of recorded admissions rose sharply between 1810 and 1815 and, throughout the period 1775 to 1815, the number recorded in the Town Register was greater than that in the

[1] Newcastle upon Tyne City Lib., L.042.L.Tr.dy 51, account of patients at the Lunatic Hospital Newcastle upon Tyne (printed).
[2] First Report minutes of evidence 1816 S.C., p. 45.

Country Register, indeed, in some years it was up to three times greater. Hunter and his colleagues (1956) suggested that this difference could be accounted for, 'by the greater vigilance of the London Commissioners in ensuring accurate returns; by the greater number of wealthy persons living in London; by diminished tolerance of mental abnormality in a large city; and by a greater number of private madhouses in the metropolis, to which patients came from the country'.[1] The incompleteness and inaccuracy of the provincial returns were probably the most relevant factors and the available evidence, in fact, indicates that there was not a greater number of private licensed houses in the metropolitan areas as compared with the provinces (Table 1).

The Parliamentary Return of 1831 stated the number of patients in each licensed house and the number discharged or deceased during the previous year, but the admissions were not enumerated. The aggregate of the figures given for the number of patients resident in each provincial house at various, generally unspecified, dates, is 1,742, and this figure is certainly unreliable. The number of patients discharged, in 1830, was 717 and deaths amounted to 159.[2] The Statistical Appendix to the 1844 Report of the Metropolitan Commissioners in Lunacy furnishes the first detailed and comprehensive admission statistics relating to the majority of private licensed houses. In this Appendix, the returns are displayed, generally, under six headings: (1) a general table of admissions, including re-admissions, since the opening of the establishment, with separate figures for the five-year period, 1839 to 1843; (2) the number of deaths, discharges, removals, suicides and attempts at suicide over similar periods; (3) the average number of patients resident during each year and the proportions per cent, upon such average numbers, of the annual cures and deaths; (4) admissions during the previous five years relative to the form of insanity; (5) admissions during the previous five years relative to hereditary predisposition to, and exciting causes of, insanity; (6) the causes of death during the previous five years. In addition, details are given regarding the number and condition of the patients in each licensed house on 1 January 1844. The Eighth Report (1854) of the Commissioners in Lunacy contained a similar

---

[1] Hunter, R. A., Macalpine, I. and Payne, L. M. (1956), 'The Country Register of Houses for the Reception of "Lunatics", 1798–1812', *J. Ment. Sci.*, *102*, p. 862.
[2] The figures for discharges and deaths in Wiltshire were amalgamated and have been included as discharges, so the total figures are not necessarily accurate.

set of statistics for the five-year period, 1849 to 1853, excluding items (4), (5) and (6) above. Thus, for the two periods 1839 to 1843 and 1849 to 1853, a fairly detailed picture of the activity of individual houses may be obtained.[1] The wide variation in the content of the returns, however, renders it difficult to make more than a few general deductions. In some cases, the returns published in 1844 refer to a considerable number of admissions, for example, there was a total of 1,015 admissions to Ticehurst Asylum during the period 1792 to 1843 and, at Fiddington House, Wiltshire, 1,005 admissions from 1816 to 1843.[2] The numbers of re-admissions at these two houses were 132 and 201 respectively and, in general, re-admissions constituted from one-tenth to one-fifth of the total admissions. There was a significant difference in the turnover of patients in houses receiving private patients only from those receiving paupers. This diversity is in keeping with the observations that have been made regarding the capacity of these two types of establishment and it is illustrated by the details for 1843. At only two establishments, out of the forty-five houses in the former category, for which statistical returns were made, were there twenty or more recorded admissions. Four houses, in fact, had no admissions in that year. However, twenty-three of the forty-one houses receiving paupers which made returns had twenty or more admissions. The original tables of statistics for Brislington House, Somerset, and Duddeston Hall, Warwickshire, as published in 1844, are given in Appendix E, as representative of widely differing types of establishment. In addition, the figures are given for Hook Norton for the periods 1839 to 1843 and 1849 to 1853.[3]

Provisions for the various categories of the insane

Males and females

The proportion of male and female patients received in private madhouses was likely to be influenced, to a large extent, by the proprietor's personal predilections and, to a lesser degree, by the lay-out of the madhouse premises, as strict segregation of the sexes

[1] Statistics for the periods 1854 to 1858 and 1859 to 1863 were given, respectively, in Fifteenth Report (1861) C.L., pp. 137–236, and in Eighteenth Report (1864) C.L., pp. 293–306.

[2] Statistical Appendix to 1844 Report M.C.L., pp. 139, 199.

[3] These tables are numbered with roman numerals and are distinguished in the text by the suffix 'A'.

had to be maintained in mixed houses. These features are illustrated in the case of the houses at Hook Norton and Witney.[1] Many of the smaller houses receiving private patients were licensed for patients of one sex only and several proprietors are known to have maintained separate licensed premises for the two sexes. For example, Dr S. G. Bakewell's houses, Stretton House and Grove House, Shropshire, were situated about a mile apart and accommodated male and female patients respectively.[2]

Despite the various local factors which influenced the distribution of the sexes in licensed houses, the analysis of data from several sources reveals some consistent trends in the pattern of this distribution. According to Powell (1813) the admissions recorded in the London Register during the period 1804 to 1808, comprised 1,128 males and 1,000 females.[3] The return of 1819[4] revealed that the males outnumbered considerably the females in metropolitan licensed houses. According to returns submitted to the Commissioners of the College of Physicians, the total number of patients admitted to private madhouses, in the decade 1815 to 1824, comprised 4,461 males and 3,443 females.[5] The return of 1831 indicated a similar balance between the sexes in the provincial houses and also revealed the fact that female paupers outnumbered the male paupers in metropolitan licensed houses. This finding was displayed in 1844, in the statistics presented by the Metropolitan Commissioners,[6] but, at this time, there was only a slight excess of females amongst the paupers in provincial licensed houses. In both the provinces and the metropolitan district, male private patients outnumbered the females in this class. By this time, there was a marked preponderance of females amongst the paupers in county asylums, a fact which was thought to reflect the higher recorded incidence of female pauper lunatics as a whole. This disproportion of the sexes amongst pauper lunatics in asylums increased during the second half of the nineteenth century and came to be attributed, in part, to the lower mortality-rate among women than among men. Most writers in the first half of the nineteenth century had been of the opinion that insanity was more prevalent amongst women than men, but J.

[1] *Vide infra*, p. 161.   [2] Sixteenth Report (1862) C.L., pp. 30–1.
[3] Powell, *op. cit.*, p. 153.   [4] P.R., 1819(a).   [5] P.R., 1826, p. 15.
[6] 1844 Report M.C.L., p. 185. (In provincial licensed houses, the numbers of male and female private patients were 748 and 678 respectively, and the numbers of paupers were 947 and 973 respectively.)

Thurnam (1845) sought to refute this view.[1] He reviewed the proportions of the sexes amongst all the patients admitted to British asylums from their opening up to the beginning of 1844, his figures being derived largely from the Statistical Appendix to the 1844 Report of the Metropolitan Commissioners. Thurnam demonstrated that in both provincial and metropolitan licensed houses there had been an excess (approximately 30 per cent) of male private patients over females. Amongst the paupers, males outnumbered the females in provincial houses, although this was not the case in London. This balance in the distribution of the sexes remained largely the same until approximately the last two decades of the century, when the proportion of females increased. In 1890, for example, both female paupers and female private patients were in the majority in licensed houses, registered hospitals and county asylums, the disproportion being particularly striking in the latter.

Pauper lunatics and private patients

Returns regarding the admission of pauper lunatics were not required to be made under the provisions of the Act of 1774 and, consequently, little information exists about the number of madhouses receiving parish-maintained patients during the period when this Act was in force. In only a single instance, and then probably only as a result of ignorance of the statutory requirements, was the admission of a pauper recorded in the Country Register. This admission occurred at William Crook's house at Laycock, Wiltshire. In some areas, surviving Quarter Sessions lunacy records furnish information about the number of paupers accommodated in individual private licensed houses. For example, in 1809, John Blount's house at Warwick contained one male pauper out of the total of eight lunatics in the house and the five patients at Edward Price's house at Southam, Warwickshire, included three male paupers.[2] Parliamentary Returns in 1819 and 1826 contained no separate references to pauper lunatics, with the exception, in the latter return, of a description of the provisions for pauper lunatics in the licensed departments of the houses of industry at Oswestry and Shrewsbury, Shropshire.[3] After 1828, returns were required relating

[1] Thurnam, J. (1845), *Observations and Essays on the Statistics of Insanity*, pp. 145–55.
[2] Warwicks, C.R.O., Q.S. 24/a/I/6, Minutes V.M.
[3] P.R., 1826, pp. 6–7.

to paupers in private licensed houses. A further source of information concerning the reception of paupers is provided by parochial pauper lunatic returns. Although first required by an Act of 1815, few returns have survived for the period pre-1828. Buckinghamshire returns, for example, for the period 1831 to 1835, provide information regarding the confinement of pauper lunatics at Warburton's houses in Bethnal Green, London and at Miles's house, Hoxton, London.[1] In Berkshire, similar returns for Reading parishes in 1838, reveal that five lunatics were confined at Warburton's houses in Bethnal Green.[2] The Parliamentary Return of 1831 included details of the number of paupers in metropolitan licensed houses, but not in the case of provincial houses. The Parliamentary Return of 1838 included a statement concerning the numbers and sex of the patients for whose reception the houses were licensed and, in many instances, the number of paupers the house was licensed to receive was quoted. The return of 1842, with a few exceptions, furnishes details concerning the class of patient each provincial house was licensed to receive. The number of houses stated clearly as receiving paupers in 1841 was thirty-eight (Table 1) and it is likely that the correct figure was slightly greater than this. A definitive list of houses receiving paupers was provided, for the first time, in the 1844 Report of the Metropolitan Commissioners in Lunacy and, subsequently, the Annual Reports of the Commissioners provided this information (Table 2).

The increase in the number of private licensed houses during the fourth decade of the nineteenth century was, to a large extent, related to the need to accommodate pauper patients, whose number, in asylums of all types, increased astronomically during the second half of the century. The county and borough lunatic asylums played the main part in accommodating this increase, although, initially, private licensed houses made an important contribution. According to the Parliamentary Return of 1837, private licensed houses accommodated over one-third of the pauper lunatics in England and Wales who were confined in asylums, in that there were 1,491 paupers in licensed houses and 2,780 in county lunatic asylums.[3] The distribution of the total accommodation available for pauper patients in 1842 is displayed in Table 9. The returns which furnish this information indicate that, in that year, forty-two houses in England and Wales,

---

[1] Bucks, C.R.O., Q.S. lunacy records.
[2] Reading Publ. Lib., Reading Q.S. records, box 168.
[3] P.R., 1837, p. 2.

TABLE 9 *Accommodation available for pauper lunatics in England and Wales in 1842 (counties containing no accommodation not listed)*

County	Number of pauper lunatics in county	Number for whom accommodation available		Number without accommodation
		County asylums; public asylums/ hospitals	*Private licensed houses*	
Bedfordshire	135	180	0	0
Chester	296	110	45	141
Cornwall	297	129	0	168
Derbyshire	216	0	24	192
Devon	611	0	100	511
Dorset	227	113	0	114
Durham	210	0	297	0
Essex	325	0	2	323
Glamorgan	155	0	36	119
Gloucestershire	498	190	125	103
Herefordshire	147	0	48	99
Kent	478	300	12	166
Lancashire	1,102	629	0	473
Leicestershire	244	130	0	114
Lincolnshire	296	73	0	223
Middlesex	1,619	1,000	560	59
Norfolk	470	292	27	151
Northamptonshire	269	181	0	88
Northumberland	321	0	58	263
Nottinghamshire	261	125	0	136
Oxfordshire	192	0	74	118
Pembrokeshire	105	18	0	87
Salop	291	0	94	197
Somerset	572	0	73	479
Southampton	448	0	207	241
Staffordshire	452	185	30	237
Suffolk	361	180	16	165
Surrey	591	360	210	21
Warwickshire	406	0	60	346
Wiltshire	382	0	442	0
Worcestershire	284	0	60	224
Yorkshire				
E. Riding	187	0	173	14
N. Riding	167	0	40	127
W. Riding	1,027	420	15	592
City of York	38	0	13	25

Source of data: 1844 Report M.C.L., pp. 238–43 (based on Poor Law Returns for 1842.)

outside the counties of Middlesex and Surrey, were licensed for the reception of a total of 2,071 pauper lunatics and there was provision for 3,255 paupers in provincial county asylums and in public asylums and hospitals. Provincial licensed houses, therefore, provided nearly 40 per cent of the total accommodation available at this time, and the contribution made by metropolitan houses was approximately the same. It is shown, in Table 9, that in certain areas, licensed houses made particularly important contributions, notably, Devon, Co. Durham, Gloucestershire, Oxfordshire, Salop, Southampton, Wiltshire and the East Riding of Yorkshire. With the exception of Gloucestershire, these counties did not contain county asylums. In 1843, there were still eleven English counties and ten in Wales, in which there were no asylums at all for the reception of pauper lunatics.[1]

Table 10 displays some of the available information relating to the number of patients in provincial and metropolitan licensed houses during the period 1807 to 1841. The marked difference between the figures for 1837 and 1841 and the preceding ones is attributable largely to the fact that the totals for these two years were calculated on the basis of the number of patients each house was licensed to receive. According to the relevant sources, the total numbers in all asylums in the years 1819, 1826, 1829 and 1831 were 3,701, 4,729, 6,237 and 5,320 respectively. The remainder of the century is covered in Table 11, which sets out, in addition, the number of pauper and private patients in licensed houses and the total number of patients in all asylums. The reliability of the returns for the early part of the century is questionable, as they contain a number of obvious omissions. In 1828, Burrows described the returns of 1819 as 'very defective and inaccurate' and claimed that those made subsequently were so incorrect that they provided no useful index of the incidence of insanity.[2] Nevertheless, returns for the first half of the nineteenth century, when taken in conjunction, do delineate the prevailing trends of the period. The highest number of patients known to have been confined, at any one time, in provincial houses was in 1848, when there was a total of 3,949 patients in these establishments. In 1844, over one-half of the total number of lunatics confined in private licensed houses were paupers, who represented

[1] 1844 Report M.C.L., p. 243.
[2] Burrows, G. M. (1828), *Commentaries on the Causes, Forms, Symptoms, and Treatment, Moral and Medical, of Insanity*, p. 509. (In 1820, Burrows published his own revised versions of the 1819 returns. Burrows (1820), *op. cit.*, pp. 287–93.)

over 37 per cent of the paupers resident in all types of lunatic asylums in England and Wales. As far as can be established, from the returns published by the Commissioners, the highest number of paupers accommodated in provincial houses was reached in 1847 (2,332 paupers) and, in the case of metropolitan houses, in 1849 (1,960 paupers). During the period 1844 to 1853, the paupers in provincial licensed houses outnumbered the private patients and this was also the case in the metropolitan houses, with the exception of

TABLE 10   *Number of patients in private licensed houses, 1807–41*

Date	Provincial licensed houses	Metropolitan licensed houses	Total in licensed houses
1807	104 paupers	110 paupers (Middlesex)	
1813		1,385	
1816		1,433	
1819	963[a]	1,622	2,585
1821		1,703	
1825	1,321	1,761	3,082
1829	1,703	2,031	3,734
1831	1,742	2,345 (966 paupers)	4,087
1837	3,362*		1,491 (pauper lunatics and idiots)†
1841	3,929 (1,643 paupers)		

[a] Inclusive of forty patients at Ticehurst Asylum.
Source of data: Report 1807 S.C., P.R., 1819(a), 1825, 1826, 1831, 1837†, 1838*, 1842. Details for 1829, Halliday (1829), *op. cit.*, pp. 25, 56.

the year 1844. Subsequently, the number of paupers in private licensed houses declined sharply, as more county and borough asylums were opened. In 1844, there were 4,244 paupers in county and borough asylums. In 1853, this number was 9,966 and, by 1880, it was 38,395, the total number in private licensed houses in the latter year being only 1,141.

The total number of private patients in asylums increased only slowly during the second half of the nineteenth century. The reports of the Commissioners reveal that the greatest number of private

TABLE 11 *Number of patients in private licensed houses, contrasted with the total number in all types of asylums, 1844–1900*

Date	Provincial licensed houses			Metropolitan licensed houses		Total in licensed houses	All types of asylum		Total in all asylums
	Private	Pauper	Total	Private	Pauper		Private	Pauper	
1844	1,426	1,920	3,346	973	854	5,173	3,790	7,482	11,272
1847	1,530	2,332	3,862	1,103	1,664	6,629	4,065	9,767	13,832
1848			3,949	3,081		7,030			13,876
1849	1,576	2,218	3,794	1,177	1,960	6,931	3,759	10,801	14,560
1850	1,557	2,229	3,786	1,120	1,825	6,731	3,774	11,305	15,079
1854	1,533	1,000	2,533	1,206	1,141	4,880	4,429	15,026	19,455
1860	1,606	750	2,356	1,342	602	4,300	4,927	18,790	23,717
1870	1,478	726	2,204	1,666	1,034	4,904	5,924	29,989	35,913[b]
1880	1,554	533	2,087	1,854	608	4,549[a]	7,152	41,127	48,279[c]
1890	1,397	582	1,979	1,641	927	4,547[a]	8,364[d]	53,621	61,985[c]
1900	1,313	357	1,670	1,457	461	3,588[a]	9,142[d]	73,721	82,863[b]

[a] Including provincial and metropolitan licensed idiot establishments.
[b] Including Naval and Military Hospitals & State Criminal Asylum.
[c] Including India Asylum, otherwise as 1870.
[d] Including all criminal patients.

Source of data: 1844 Report M.C.L.; Further Report (1847) C.L.; Third Report (1848) C.L. and subsequent Annual Reports C.L.

patients in provincial private licensed houses was attained in 1863 (1,706 patients), although figures at this time were amplified slightly by the fact that some of the criminal patients at Fisherton House were included as private patients. The total number did not fall below 1,600 until 1869. The peak in the case of metropolitan houses was not reached until 1879. It is significant that, in 1844, more than 63 per cent of the total number of private patients confined in all types of asylums in England and Wales were in private licensed houses and, by 1850, the proportion had increased to approximately 70 per cent. Subsequently, however, the relative contribution of the licensed houses decreased slowly. By 1880, the proportion of the total which was confined in private asylums had fallen to approximately 47 per cent, but the private asylum still constituted the most important single type of institution, with the registered hospitals ranking next in importance and catering for nearly 38 per cent of the total.

The provisions for paupers in private licensed houses underwent greater changes during the course of the nineteenth century than did those for private patients and, consequently, displayed a wider variation in the type of accommodation available. The rapid increase in the number of pauper lunatics, the resultant demand for accommodation and the delays in the implementation of legislation relating to county and borough asylums had particular repercussions on the provisions made within the private-madhouse system for paupers. Naturally, not all madhouse proprietors wished to take in paupers, since the presence of a pauper department would tend to lower the tone of a high-class establishment. Some proprietors, quite apart from those who kept houses noted for their aristocratic clientele, placed great emphasis upon the high social calibre of their patients. For example, in 1826, Mr Preston Hornby, the proprietor of Dunnington House in the East Riding of Yorkshire, made the somewhat arrogant, but revealing, statement: 'I only admit a certain number of patients into my establishment and these are persons of distinction.'[1] Social class, however, was not always the principal criterion for admission. Certain establishments were proud of the wide variety of clinical disorders which they received. For example, in 1817, the Newcastle-upon-Tyne Lunatic Hospital was reputed to cater for the cure of the insane, the incurable and for cases of every description

[1] E.R. Yorks. C.R.O., QAL. 3/25, letter, Hornby to John Lockwood, Clerk of Peace, 21 April 1826.

of mental derangement drawn from the poor-houses, not excluding dying patients, when they became too difficult to manage at the poor-house.[1] Some proprietors had strong views about the range of clinical conditions they were prepared to accept. Thus, T. Bakewell pointed out, in 1815, that his small establishment at Spring Vale was, 'intended solely for the purposes of cure, and not the reception of those that are deemed incurable'.[2]

Large numbers of pauper lunatics and idiots were accumulating in workhouses by the beginning of the nineteenth century. There were unlicensed lunatic wards in numerous workhouses, but in some areas the directors of workhouses obtained licences for sections of their establishments to accommodate local pauper lunatics. Thus, the Oswestry and Shrewsbury houses of industry were licensed in 1821;[3] by 1831, part of the Carisbrooke poor-house, Isle of Wight[4] and, by 1837, the workhouse at Stoke Damerel, Devonport,[5] had also been licensed. As far as can be ascertained, very few of the private mad-houses opened in the early nineteenth century were purpose-built. Houses known to have been so designed were the Red House, Bethnal Green, London;[6] Brislington House, Somerset;[7] Gate Helmsley, near York;[8] Northwoods, Gloucestershire;[9] Springfield House, Bedford[10] and Dunston Lodge, Co. Durham.[11] It follows that the majority of private licensed houses were premises adapted in various ways for the purpose of accommodating lunatics. The degree of adaptation undertaken depended both upon the enterprise of the proprietor and on the capital sum invested. Since prospective medical proprietors were, in general, unlikely to possess large sums of money, opportunists with capital to spare, but with no other

[1] Newcastle upon Tyne City Lib., L.042.L.Tr.dy.51, Account of patients at the Lunatic Hospital, Newcastle upon Tyne.

[2] Bakewell, T. (1815), *op. cit.*, p. 9.

[3] P.R., 1826, p. 6. (In 1825, five lunatics were confined at the Oswestry house of industry, and, in 1826, there were eleven lunatics at the Shrewsbury house of industry, at Kingsland. The latter was closed in 1853.)

[4] P.R., 1831, p. 6. (twenty-six pauper lunatics were confined in this house, which was closed in 1853.)

[5] P.R., 1842, p. 8. (In 1837 there were twenty-eight patients in this house, which was licensed for the reception of 100 patients.)

[6] Minutes of evidence 1815 S.C., p. 18.　　　[7] *Vide infra*, p. 112.

[8] N.R. Yorks. C.R.O., Q.S. lunacy records, Minutes M.C.L., 12 Sept. 1842; and 1844 Report M.C.L., p. 43.

[9] Sixteenth Report (1862) C.L., p. 18. (Opened 1833. Built by Dr H. H. Fox, son of E. L. Fox.)

[10] *Ibid.*, p. 8. (Opened 1837.)　　　[11] *Ibid.*, p. 13. (Opened 1831.)

qualifications, were in a position to exploit the situation. Country mansions and similar large premises, often of imposing appearance, were used, not infrequently, to accommodate lunatics and it was the pauper patients who generally fared worst in such establishments. Whilst the private patients resided in the mansion, often with the proprietor and his family, the paupers, in some instances, were accommodated in the converted stables and outbuildings. This was the case, in 1844, at a number of houses[1] including Lainston House, Winchester; Bailbrook House, Bath;[2] Plympton House, Devon and Duddeston Hall, near Birmingham.[3] This arrangement was known to have been adopted also at Haydock Lodge, Lancashire and the Commissioners in Lunacy, in 1847, gave an interesting account of the conversions made in the outbuildings of this house and of the difficulties involved.[4]

Once a county asylum was established, withdrawal of pauper patients belonging to parishes within the county, who had been confined in private licensed houses, took place on a large scale. The early years of the sixth decade of the nineteenth century saw the closure of many pauper lunatic departments of private licensed houses and, by 1860, the official plan was to discourage the further reception of paupers into licensed houses. However, overcrowding occurred in most county asylums within a short time of their opening and, in many areas, paupers continued to be admitted to private licensed houses, either directly or transferred from a county asylum. Such was the demand for pauper lunatic accommodation that some licensed houses re-opened their pauper departments. The history of Haydock Lodge illustrates, effectively, several of these points. The establishment (Plate II) was opened in January 1844, licensed for 160 paupers and forty private patients, at a time when the county asylums of Lancashire, Cheshire, Staffordshire, Leicestershire and the West Riding of Yorkshire were 'crowded to their utmost limits'.[5] Two years later, Haydock Lodge was licensed for 400 paupers and fifty private patients. In 1847, following a detailed enquiry into the management of the establishment, the Commissioners claimed that

---

[1] 1844 Report M.C.L., pp. 41–2.

[2] This house was intended originally as a residence for George IV, when he was Prince of Wales, but was never occupied by him.

[3] Formerly the villa of a banker, in the suburbs of Birmingham.

[4] Further Report C.L. re Haydock Lodge Lunatic Asylum, March 1847, pp. 6–7.

[5] *Ibid.*, p. 3.

'the revocation or non-renewal of the licence ... would be a most unwise and mischievous proceeding'.[1] The principal reason for this decision was that: 'At this moment, every considerable lunatic asylum, both public and private, in which pauper patients are received, is full to overflowing; and if Haydock Lodge were to be at once shut up, a body of pauper lunatics not less than 340 in number ... all utterly unfit to be at large, would be instantly turned adrift, and thrown back upon the already overcrowded workhouses, or left in hopeless neglect and destitution to roam as outcasts through the country, to the terror and injury of the whole community'.[2] The asylum was closed in 1851, but a year later it was re-opened and, in 1854, the house was re-licensed to receive paupers, in order to meet the urgent need for pauper accommodation, which was not being fulfilled by the three existing county and borough asylums.[3] An interesting insight into the contemporary attitude towards the re-opening of the pauper department at Haydock Lodge is incorporated in the weekly minutes of the Chester Board of Guardians in which Haydock Lodge, by reason of its antiquity, was described as 'the next best receptacle to the Cheshire Asylum'.[4] There are, in fact, many examples of the important part that private licensed houses, in certain areas, continued to play in the management of paupers, until well into the second half of the nineteenth century. Thus, in 1848, twenty pauper lunatics were transferred to Hook Norton from the Gloucestershire County Asylum and, from 1850 onwards, paupers were admitted to Hook Norton from various London unions. Vernon House, Briton Ferry, Glamorgan, took paupers from the Monmouthshire County Asylum at Abergavenny, in 1867-9, and from unions in Yorkshire and Herefordshire, in 1870-3.[5] In the period 1850 to 1860, the bulk of borough pauper lunatics were largely unprovided for in borough or county asylums and they were still being sent to private licensed houses. In their Report of 1856, the Commissioners in Lunacy quoted the situation existing in Portsmouth and in Southampton as examples. In these areas, union with the neighbouring county asylum had been turned down by the Visitors of the county asylum, but the contract they had offered to the boroughs had been rejected because it was cheaper to send patients to a large metropolitan licensed house, namely Camberwell House (11s. per week), than to

[1] *Ibid.*, p. 15. [2] *Ibid.* [3] Ninth Report (1855) C.L., p. 24.
[4] Chester City R.O., TC/WP/834, Minutes, Chester Board of Guardians, 24 Aug. 1854.
[5] Glam. C.R.O., Q.S. L/VH. 13.

the county asylum (13s. per week).[1] Such arrangements virtually severed the patient's contact with his relatives and friends, whilst the borough and parish authorities made only annual visits.

By the end of the 1860s, fourteen provincial licensed houses still received paupers and the location and size of these establishments, in 1859, is displayed in Table 12. The list of houses includes several large establishments and, in four cases, over 100 paupers were accommodated. In the metropolitan district, five licensed houses

TABLE 12 *Provincial private licensed houses receiving paupers in 1859*

Private licensed house	Number of paupers confined	Total number confined
Bensham, Gateshead, Co. Durham	73	95
Gateshead Fell, Co. Durham	88	94
Dunston Lodge, Gateshead, Co. Durham	126	161
Vernon House, Glam.	194	212
Fairford House, Glos.	25	77
Portland House, Hereford.	3	19
Haydock Lodge, Lancs.	162	205
Infirmary Asylum, Norwich, Norfolk	75	75
Fisherton House, Wilts.	117	330
Fiddington House, Wilts.	29	29
Dunnington House, Yorks.	19	44
Gate Helmsley Retreat, Yorks.	28	55
Claxton Grange Retreat, Yorks.	7	22
Grove Hall, Acomb, Yorks.	7	23

Source of data: Fourteenth Report (1860) C.L., pp. 110–17.

catered for paupers at this time. These five houses were all large establishments and the following list presents the number of paupers accommodated, together with the total number confined, indicated in brackets; Bethnal House, 314 (455); Grove Hall, 173 (359); Camberwell House, 247 (318); Hoxton House, 213 (312); and Peckham House, 188 (317).[2] In the case of the provincial houses, the size of Vernon House, Briton Ferry, Glamorgan, is explicable by the

[1] Tenth Report (1856) C.L., pp. 6–7.
[2] Fourteenth Report (1860) C.L., pp. 108–9.

fact that the county asylum for this part of South Wales was not opened until 1864, although an asylum in the neighbouring county, Monmouthshire, had been opened in 1851. The existence of three large private licensed houses catering for paupers in the Gateshead area was the result of similar circumstances, although here the situation was more complex. The development of the institutional provisions for the insane in the Newcastle–Gateshead region is discussed in some detail, at this point, because it illustrates, clearly, the way in which the private licensed-house system was exploited in areas where the magistrates were unwilling, for financial reasons, to implement the official policy of erecting a county or borough lunatic asylum.

As early as 1686, there is evidence of the existence in Newcastle of a small private madhouse owned by Dr William Luck.[1] In 1765, the first plans were laid for a public asylum at Newcastle and, in 1767, the 'Hospital for lunaticks for the counties of Northumberland, Newcastle upon Tyne and Durham' was opened.[2] It was built with funds raised by public subscription, including an annual payment from the Newcastle Common Council.[3] Within a few years, however, it was taken over by Dr John Hall, to whom the hospital was licensed as a private licensed house, known as the Newcastle upon Tyne Lunatic Asylum. Hall, who was a prominent Newcastle physician, had quarrelled with the governors of the Lunatic Hospital, prior to its inauguration, over the question of the provisions for private patients and, in 1766, he opened his own madhouse, St Luke's House, in Newcastle.[4] The Newcastle Corporation continued to make an annual subscription of ten guineas towards the running costs of the Newcastle Lunatic Asylum, despite the fact that it was classified as a private licensed house. In 1824, after the death of the proprietor, the Corporation claimed to be the sole surviving proprietor and took

[1] Newcastle upon Tyne City Archives Dept., L.A. I/1–2, Deed of Bargain and Sale, 1 and 2 June 1686.
[2] The printed 'Rules' for this asylum, c. 1767, provide interesting information about the role of the governors, physician, surgeon, secretary, matron, keepers, nurses and servants. Newcastle upon Tyne City Lib., L.042.L.Tr.
[3] Brand, J. (1789), *The History and Antiquities of the Town and County of the Town of Newcastle upon Tyne*, Vol. 1, pp. 421–2. Mackenzie, E. (1827), *A Descriptive and Historical Account of the Town and County of Newcastle upon Tyne including the Borough of Gateshead*, p. 525.
[4] Hall, J. (1767), *A Narrative of the Proceedings Relative to the Establishment etc. of St. Luke's House.* (In 1795, St Luke's House was taken over by Dr R. Steavensen and re-named Belle Grove Retreat.)

possession of the asylum, principally because of its concern about the way in which it had been conducted.[1] Major reconstruction was undertaken and a medical superintendent appointed. The entire management of the asylum rested with this physician, who was required to pay interest on the sum of £4,390 which had been spent in the refurbishing of the establishment. This licensed house accommodated the Newcastle pauper lunatics until 1855, when the proprietor closed it in order to open his own establishment, Dinsdale Park Retreat, Co. Durham. Subsequently, the Newcastle Magistrates contracted their pauper lunatics to be admitted to two private licensed houses, at Bensham, Gateshead, and at Gateshead Fell, both in Co. Durham, and, in addition, paupers were admitted to the Durham County Asylum at Sedgefield. These contracts expired, finally, in 1864 but, as no preparation had been made yet for the erection of a borough asylum in Newcastle, the buildings of the now disused licensed house at Bensham were rented to house pauper lunatics. After further delay, a borough asylum was established at Gosforth in 1869.

A further example is provided by the state of affairs in North Wales. The union of the North Wales counties preparatory to establishing a joint county asylum was delayed because the Anglesey and Caernarvonshire Magistrates felt that existing contracts with Haydock Lodge, Lancashire, afforded adequate and undoubtedly cheaper accommodation for parish patients. Agreement between the magistrates was precipitated, however, by the disclosure of defects in the management of Haydock Lodge in 1846,[2] and the joint county asylum for the five North Wales counties was opened, at Denbigh, in November 1848.

The tendency to make use of existing local provisions as a temporary and economical measure can be seen also in other parts of the country. In 1849, for example, the Hull Borough Magistrates took over a former private licensed house, the Hull and East Riding Refuge,[3] and named it the Hull Borough Asylum. Although conditions

[1] Newcastle upon Tyne City Archives Dept, L.A. I/4, Report of Committee of the Common Council on lunatic asylums, 23 June 1824.

[2] U.C.N.W. Lib., Caernarvon and Denbigh Herald, 21 Nov. 1846.

[3] This establishment was formerly licensed to Richard Casson, surgeon. In 1839, the licences for two licensed houses owned by Casson, the Sculcoates Refuge and Southcoates Retreat, were given up. The former was renamed by Casson the Hull and E. Riding Refuge, and the latter continued under a different proprietor. *Vide* Tuke, D. H. (1889), *The Past and Present Provision for the Insane Poor in Yorkshire*, p. 15; also the *Hull Advertiser*, 7 May 1814, p. 2.

at the Refuge had been unsatisfactory for some time, it is significant that little in the way of improvements were carried out by the magistrates, when they assumed control of the establishment.[1] Similarly, the only provision made by the magistrates of Norwich for their pauper lunatics was to license part of the union workhouse for their reception, namely, the Infirmary Asylum. These premises, intended originally for old and infirm paupers, were never adequate and the management of lunatics appears to have been poor.[2] The Visitors displayed limited concern for making this establishment 'a fit and sufficient building for the reception of pauper lunatics'.[3] In 1860, in accordance with the recommendations of the Commissioners, renewal of the licence was refused by the justices, although this decision was reversed shortly afterwards. However, the Recorder of Norwich refused his sanction on legal grounds and the patients were retained at the house illegally.[4] The Corporation of Norwich evaded their duty to build an asylum for many years until, in 1874, legal proceedings taken by the Secretary of State against the Corporation made it compulsory. The new borough asylum was opened at Hellesdon in 1880.

The use of the public subscription asylum at Newcastle as a private licensed house was not a unique occurrence and a further example is provided in the case of the Hereford Lunatic Asylum. This establishment was erected and furnished with funds raised by voluntary contributions in 1797, but, in 1802, a licence was granted to a physician and a surgeon to run it, jointly, as a private licensed house. As early as 1799, the governors of Hereford Infirmary, under whose auspices the asylum had been established, had considered leasing it to 'individuals of the faculty' and, by 1801, they had decided that it 'could not be continued on its then present footing'.[5] The arrangements made regarding the asylum are described in a document of 1806, from which the following extract is taken:

A person from Bethlehem Hospital . . . conducted it on a salary for the Committee during two or three years. At length they deemed it more conducive to the interests of the Institution and of the public, that the

[1] Seventh Report (1852) C.L., pp. 8–10.

[2] *Vide* Eighth Report (1854) C.L., pp. 21–3; Ninth Report (1855) C.L., pp. 22–23 and Tenth Report (1856) C.L., p. 16.

[3] Norfolk and Norwich R.O., Norwich Q.S. records, Proceedings of the Committee of Visitors of the Infirmary Asylum, 1854–6.

[4] Fifteenth Report (1861) C.L., pp. 43–4.

[5] Hereford C.R.O., Q/ALL/1–2.

management should be placed in the hands of a physician and surgeon belonging to the Infirmary who offered their services without a salary, one of whom was required to be resident at the asylum, and the whole conduct was to remain as before, subject to the inspection and control of the Committee of Governors. The house is regularly licensed as a public receptacle for lunatics by the magistrates ... the patients vary in number from three to twenty; they only pay a common price for their board, and the public liberality supplies them gratis with proper rooms, the attendances of a physician and surgeon, nurses and other servants together with all the medicines which their cases may require. The establishment remains open to subscriptions or donations.[1]

An illustration of the reverse process is provided in the history of Abington Abbey, Northampton. This private licensed house was opened, in 1845, by Dr T. O. Prichard, who had been the first superintendent, 1838–45, of the Northampton Lunatic Asylum. In 1848, his son, Thomas Prichard, who had taken over the house on his father's death, registered it as a public hospital, for thirty-two patients, namely Abington Abbey Retreat.[2] However, in 1853, it was re-licensed as a private asylum[3] and Prichard remained as proprietor until 1877.[4]

Criminal, naval, military and chancery lunatics

There are occasional references to the confinement in madhouses, during the eighteenth century, of lunatics who had committed criminal acts. For example, William Perfect (1787) described the confinement for life in his house at West Malling, Kent, of a man who had murdered his mother.[5] The Criminal Lunatics Act of 1800, 39 & 40 Geo. III, c. 94, which was passed shortly after an attempt on the life of George III, made the first provision for the detention of persons as criminal lunatics, but no formal arrangement for their accommodation was made, other than in gaols. Following the Act of 1808, criminal lunatics were to be confined in the county lunatic

[1] Hereford C.R.O., Pateshall MSS., Statement of the case re exemption from payment of window duties for which the house was liable. (In 1840 this asylum was licensed for thirty-six patients including twenty-four paupers. It was closed in 1853.)

[2] Third Report (1848) C.L., Appendix I, p. 8.

[3] Eighth Report (1854) C.L., p. 8. *Vide infra*, p. 111.

[4] Subsequently, the asylum was carried on by other members of the Prichard family, until its closure in 1892. Northampton R.O., X.3323–6. (Abington Abbey now houses a local history museum.)

[5] Perfect, W. (1787), *Select Cases in the Different Species of Insanity, Lunacy, or Madness, with the Modes of Practice as adopted in the Treatment of Each*, pp. 196–203.

asylums, but, in areas where this was not possible, the alternatives were gaols, houses of correction, private madhouses or Bethlem.[1] The cost of maintenance of such persons had to be met by the parish of legal settlement.[2] It was not uncommon practice, during the early part of the nineteenth century, for dangerous insane persons to be confined in the county house of correction or gaol, even though they were not criminals.[3] No lists are available of the number and distribution of criminal lunatics in private licensed houses prior to 1837, when this information was furnished in a Parliamentary Return. In their 1844 Report, the Metropolitan Commissioners provided comprehensive information[4] and, subsequently, the details

TABLE 13 *Number and distribution of criminal lunatics confined in asylums, 1837–70*

Date	Provincial licensed houses	Metro-politan licensed houses	Bethlem Hospital	Other asylums	Total criminal lunatics
1837	17 (F.H.[a]1)	17	55	49	138
1843	39	22	87	76	224
1847	64 (F.H.7)	40	111	122	337
1851	97	27	105	158	387
1855	153 (F.H.119)	29	106	246	534
1860	220 (F.H.196)	23	128	365	736
1864	287 (F.H.276)	23	113	95[b] 399[c] 7[d]	924
1870	66 (F.H.61)	2	1	595 (460[b])	664

[a] Fisherton House.   [b] Broadmoor (all females on 1 Jan. 1864).
[c] Asylums.   [d] Hospitals.
Source of data: P.R., 1837; Fourteenth Report (1860) C.L., Appendix H, p. 155 (details for 1843–60) and Reports C.L. 1864, 1870.

[1] A criminal establishment for males and females was opened as part of Bethlem in 1816 and continued in use until 1864.
[2] E.g. the Order by the Buckinghamshire Magistrates, in 1828, to the overseers of Aylesbury to pay the County Treasurer seven shillings per week for the maintenance of a criminal lunatic in Aylesbury Gaol. O.C.R.O., QSL. X/1/A.
[3] E.g. of the fifty-six lunatics confined in gaols and houses of correction in England and Wales, only twenty-five were designated as criminals. P.R., 1824, pp. 5–10.
[4] Statement of criminal lunatics, April 1843, in 1844 Report M.C.L., Appendix G, p. 274 and Statistical Appendix, pp. 6–11.

were made available annually in the reports of the Commissioners in Lunacy. The number and distribution of criminal lunatics in asylums during the period 1837 to 1870, is displayed in Table 13. The Oxfordshire records for 1828 to 1857 include references to only two criminal lunatics, both being detained at Hook Norton. These were John Jennings (confined April 1842 till his death in November 1843) and John Stockley (confined December 1844 to October 1854), who was removed to another private licensed house, namely Fisherton House, near Salisbury, Wiltshire.

Fisherton House, which was owned by members of the Finch family, played a very important part in the accommodation of criminal lunatics during the second half of the nineteenth century. Largely because of the overcrowding of the Bethlem criminal lunatic buildings, official arrangements were made, in 1850, for the reception, in special wards at Fisherton House, of a number of harmless criminal lunatics from Bethlem and from asylums in other parts of the country. The order for the transfer of criminal lunatics had to be signed by the Secretary of State. The number of criminal lunatics confined at Fisherton House reached considerable proportions (Table 13) and, in fact, the criminal wards at this asylum constituted virtually a state establishment. Even in 1862, a year before the State Institution at Broadmoor was opened, extensions were being made at this asylum for the accommodation of an increased number of criminal lunatics[1] and in the succeeding years their number declined only slowly; for example, in December 1867, the 527 inmates at Fisherton House included 225 criminals.[2] By 1872, however, its reception of criminal patients had ceased. As an example of the cost of maintenance, the terms, per person, in 1852, were eleven shillings and sixpence per week.[3]

The majority of the pauper departments of private licensed houses were unsuitable for the detention of criminals and, consequently, escapes and assaults on other patients and attendants occurred. The Metropolitan Commissioners recorded, in 1844, that a criminal lunatic had escaped from Plympton House, Devon, for the third time and had not yet been re-captured, and at Moor Cottage, Nunkeeling, Yorkshire, a patient had escaped three times and had

[1] Wilts. C.R.O., Q.S. lunacy records (county asylum).
[2] Twenty-second Report (1868) C.L., p. 43.
[3] Beds. C.R.O., LSM. 9, correspondence re transfer of criminal lunatics from Bedford Lunatic Asylum to Fisherton House, 14 Aug. 1852.

attempted both to murder the attendants and to set fire to the asylum.[1] At Gateshead Fell, Co. Durham, a 'maniac' was kept hand-cuffed permanently, after he had escaped from the house, murdered his wife and child and had been re-admitted as a criminal lunatic.[2] The Commissioners expressed the view that there was no objection to the confinement of cases of minor misdemeanour in licensed houses, but the situation was wholly different in cases 'of an atrocious character, calculated to render the party dangerous, and an object of dread and disgust to those around him, such as murder, arson, and unnatural offences'.[3] In April 1843, provincial private licensed houses contained thirteen criminal lunatics who had committed 'atrocious offences', out of a total of fifty confined in asylums in England and Wales. These thirteen lunatics comprised seven murderers, four who were guilty of malicious cutting, stabbing or shooting; one whose offence was arson and one person guilty of 'detestable crime'.[4] A further ten such cases were confined in metropolitan licensed houses. The need for the separate accommodation of criminal lunatics was stressed, repeatedly, by the Commissioners during the period 1850 to 1860. It was not until 1863, however, that the State Criminal Asylum was opened, at Broadmoor, under the provisions of an Act passed in 1860, 23 & 24 Vict., c. 75.

In addition to the use of a specific private licensed house for the accommodation of criminals, it is of interest to note the official use of licensed houses for naval and military lunatics. From 1791 and possibly earlier, formal arrangements had been made by the Admiralty for the confinement of insane officers and seamen of the Royal Navy at Hoxton House, London.[5] In 1812, Dr John Weir, Inspector of Naval Hospitals, revealed the unsatisfactory nature of accommodation and treatment at this establishment, recommending the erection of a hospital specifically for naval lunatics.[6] An enquiry into their management was conducted by the 1815 Select Committee, which confirmed the existence of exceedingly bad conditions. At this time, the naval contingent at Hoxton House comprised fourteen

---

[1] 1844 Report M.C.L., pp. 197–8.   [2] *Ibid.*, p. 198.   [3] *Ibid.*, p. 196.
[4] *Ibid.*, p. 275.   [5] *Vide* Morris, *op. cit.*
[6] Report to the Commissioners of Transports, 13 Nov. 1812, 'Remarks on the management of such officers, seamen, and marines, belonging to His Majesty's Naval Service, and of such prisoners of war, as are admitted into the house of Messrs Miles & Co. of Hoxton, for the cure of mental derangement.' In Papers relating to the management of insane officers, seamen, and marines, belonging to His Majesty's Naval Service, 1814.

officers and 136 seamen and marines. In 1818, part of the Naval Hospital at Haslar was set apart for the accommodation of insane officers and seamen.

Fort Clarence, Chatham, was opened, in 1819, as a military asylum. There were plans to build a new and larger asylum, but these were not fulfilled at this time. In 1846, the Naval Hospital at Great Yarmouth was converted for the reception of military lunatics and re-named the Royal Military Lunatic Asylum, but, in 1854, it was taken over again as a hospital for sailors. The sixty-nine soldiers and five women then confined were transferred to a private licensed house, Grove Hall, Bow, which was owned by Edward Bias and the nineteen officers were admitted to Coton Hill Asylum, a registered hospital at Stafford.[1] Grove Hall was opened by Bias in 1844 and it developed into a large establishment with accommodation for several hundred patients. By 1860, the number of military lunatics at this house had reached 118.[2] The governmental decision to use the facilities offered by a private licensed house, together with that to transfer criminal lunatics to Fisherton House, seems paradoxical in view of the official attitude towards licensed houses and, not unnaturally, it aroused much strong feeling. Thus, in a leading article in the Asylum Journal, in 1855, the following observations were made:

While the Legislature has been emptying licensed houses, Government has been filling them. While the former has been removing the insane poor from the custody of the speculators, the latter has been farming out all the insane patients who are charged upon its funds ... The ratepayers of the county of Essex having placed their pauper lunatics under the care of Mr. Bias, of Grove Hall, the Legislature interferes, and compels them to build a county lunatic asylum at great cost, to which the Essex lunatics are moved. The vacancies so created are speedily filled up by the intervention of government. ... If it is cheaper for Government to farm out its insane soldiers to Mr. Bias, and its insane criminals to Mr. Finch, and thereby save the cost of buildings and of official staffs, it was also cheaper to the counties and boroughs to farm out their insane dependants to the keepers of those licensed houses which are now closed to them by the operation of Acts of Parliament.[3]

It was noted, however, after listing the deficiencies of Grove Hall,

[1] Robertson, C. L. (1856), 'The Military Lunatic Hospital', *Asylum J. Ment. Sci. 2*, pp. 31–40.
[2] Fourteenth Report (1860) C.L., p. 31.
[3] Editorial (1855), 'The Want of a Military Lunatic Asylum', *Asylum J. Ment. Sci. 1*, p. 177.

that 'Mr Bias has conducted his asylum with such liberality, and has displayed so much judgement in his selection of men skilful and devoted to their duties as medical attendants, that he has deserved and enjoyed the marked favour of the Commissioners in Lunacy'.[1] It is interesting to note, in addition, that insane soldiers of the East India Company were confined in another metropolitan licensed house, Dr Williams's establishment, Pembroke House, Hackney.[2]

Another category of the insane which was confined in private licensed houses was composed of 'chancery lunatics', i.e., persons who had been found lunatic by inquisition. During the eighteenth century, a non-statutory procedure had evolved, whereby the relatives or heirs of a wealthy, or landed, alleged lunatic could petition the Lord Chancellor to enquire into the case, with a view to preventing the dissipation of the lunatic's fortune. The Lord Chancellor could issue a writ '*de lunatico inquirendo*', following which the case could be heard before a jury. If the case of lunacy was upheld, the estates would pass into the supervision and protection of the Crown. Records relating to this procedure have survived in many areas, for example, those concerning the inquisition of John Howard, held at Leicester in 1790,[3] and of William Jones of Southwell in 1832.[4] The procedure was somewhat simplified and placed on a statutory basis by an Act of 1833, 3 & 4 Will. IV, c. 36. Under the Lunatics' Property Act of 1842, 5 & 6 Vict., c. 84, two Commissioners in Lunacy were appointed to supervise estates and these persons were designated Masters in Lunacy by the Act of 1845, 8 & 9 Vict., c. 100. Further modifications were made by an Act of 1853, 16 & 17 Vict., c. 70. The number and distribution of persons found lunatic by inquisition in the period 1844 to 1870, is displayed in Table 14. The role of the private licensed house, particularly in the provinces, with regard to chancery lunatics was, clearly, an important one. The records relating to the two Oxfordshire private licensed houses contain evidence of only a single patient who had been found lunatic by inquisition. This person was a seventy-year-old spinster from Henley-on-Thames, who was admitted to Witney in March 1842 and died there, in May 1851.[5]

[1] *Ibid.*, p. 178. [2] Robertson, C. L. (1857), 'The Military Lunatic Hospital,' *Asylum J. Ment. Sci. 3*, p. 273; and Fourteenth Report (1860) C.L., p. 54.
[3] Bod. Lib., MS. Eng. Misc., b.69 (195, 196, 200). (John Howard (1765–99) was the only son of John Howard, the philanthropist and prison-reformer. The inquisition was held four months after his father's death in January 1790.)
[4] Nottingham Publ. Lib., M.1735 (MS.).
[5] O.C.R.O., QSL. I/11/343, Frances E. Sadler.

TABLE 14 *Number and distribution of persons found lunatic by inquisition and confined in asylums*

Date	Provincial licensed houses	Metropolitan licensed houses	County and borough asylums	Hospitals	Total
1844	116	80	7	14	217
1847	119	89	10	18	236
1849	112	103	6	15	236
1850	120	96	5	17	238
1860	117	127	13	36	293
1870	164	195	12	81	452

Source of data: 1844 Report M.C.L.; Further Report (1847) C.L. and subsequent Annual Reports C.L.

A contemporary return, however, indicates that there was a male patient in this category confined in the private department at Hook Norton,[1] but no manuscript proof of this has been discovered.

Idiots and children

No special establishments for idiots or children were included within the private-madhouse system in the first half of the nineteenth century. W. C. Ellis (1815) observed that he had never seen a patient under the age of puberty in a public asylum or a private madhouse.[2] However, there is evidence, in Oxfordshire and elsewhere, of the confinement of young teenage patients in madhouses. Perfect (1791) described, in detail, the case of an eleven-year-old boy, whom he treated at home, without admission to his madhouse at West Malling, Kent.[3]

The development of establishments for idiots in the second half of the nineteenth century demonstrates a further variation in the application of the licensed-house system. A small school for idiot children was opened in Bath in 1846 and, in the following year, the

[1] Statistical Appendix to 1844 Report M.C.L., p. 11.
[2] Ellis, W. C. (1815), *A Letter to Thomas Thompson, Esq., M.P.*, p. 30. (Thomas Thompson was M.P. for Midhurst, 1807–18.)
[3] Perfect, W. (1791), *A Remarkable Case of Madness, with the Diet and Medicines used in the Cure.*

'Idiot Asylum', Park House, Highgate, London, was opened by the Reverend Dr Andrew Reed, with the support of John Conolly.[1] The fact that Park House was essentially a training establishment posed the problem of whether or not it fell within the jurisdiction of the Commissioners in Lunacy but, finally, it was classed as a registered hospital.[2] In 1850 a branch of this establishment was opened at Essex Hall, Colchester.[3] The latter was closed in 1858, all the patients having been removed when the Idiot Asylum at Earlswood, Surrey, was opened. In the following year, however, Essex Hall was re-opened, under the title of the Eastern Counties Asylum, as a charitable institution supported by public subscription but licensed (thirty patients), nevertheless, as a private asylum.[4] The reason for this somewhat paradoxical situation was that registration as a lunatic hospital would have made it necessary to have a resident medical superintendent, whereas this was not so in private licensed houses for up to 100 patients. This manoeuvre was employed by two other charitable institutions for idiots. The Western Counties Idiot Asylum, Starcross, Devon, was opened in 1864, and the Commissioners decided, not without some difficulty, that existing lunacy laws did not apply to it as the object was training and there was an upper age limit of fifteen years.[5] In fact, it was certified as a school by the Poor Law Board in 1865, so that Boards of Guardians could send children there, but ten years later it was licensed as a private asylum (forty patients).[6] In 1868, Dorridge Grove, Knowle, a Warwickshire private licensed house was converted into the Midland Counties Idiot Asylum, but it remained a licensed house (twenty patients) despite the fact that it was now supported by public subscription,[7] even after new buildings were opened in 1874. The situation was well recognized by the Commissioners, who encouraged the formation of institutions for the care and training of idiots and imbeciles, whilst pressing for new legislation to cater for them. In 1865, a small licensed establishment, Downside Lodge, Bath, was opened for idiots (six patients) and during the last quarter

---

[1] Anon. (1848), *The Asylum for Idiots.*

[2] Fourth Report (1849) C.L., p. 9.

[3] *Vide* Anon. (1853), *Cretins and Idiots. A Short Account of the Progress of the Institutions for their Relief and Cure.*

[4] Sixteenth Report (1862) C.L., p. 14.

[5] Nineteenth Report (1865) C.L., p. 47.

[6] Thirtieth Report (1876) C.L., pp. 61–2.

[7] Twenty-ninth Report (1875) C.L., pp. 49–50.

of the nineteenth century, therefore, there were four provincial licensed houses catering solely for idiots.[1] These were registered as idiot establishments under the Idiots Act of 1886[2] and, by the end of the century, all, with the exception of Downside Lodge, had become registered hospitals.

Provisions for the insane in Wales

In 1844, the Metropolitan Commissioners in Lunacy drew attention to the very neglected state of the insane poor in Wales.[3] Halliday (1827) had observed that 'Wales, in proportion to the population has very few lunatics and the same remark holds good with regard to the Celtic tribes in other portions of the empire'.[4] However, Poor Law returns of 1843 revealed 1,177 pauper lunatics in Wales and the proportion per cent to the population, 1·10, was the same as that in England.[5] Over 1,000 of these paupers were boarded out or at large in the community and there is evidence that many of them were confined under deplorable conditions. Of those in institutions, ninety were in union workhouses, thirty-six in county asylums and forty-one in English private licensed houses. According to Powell, in 1815, no returns from licensed houses had ever been received from any part of Wales[6] and the first reference to an asylum in Wales was in 1819, when it was indicated that there was a private licensed house in Glamorgan run by Thomas Hobbes.[7] At that time, this house contained three patients, but no records relating to it have been discovered. In 1822, the town gaol at Haverfordwest, Pembrokeshire, was appropriated for the reception of the insane and declared a county asylum under the provisions of the Act of 9 Geo. IV., c. 40. It could accommodate only a small number of patients (seventeen in 1844) and, at the time of their first visit, the Metro-

---

[1] In addition, there was a small house, Haldon View, Topsham, Exeter, which was opened in 1886 and closed two years later.

[2] In the metropolitan area, at this time, two houses catered for idiots, namely, Normansfield, Hampton Wick, and Colville, Lower Norwood, but only the former was registered under the Idiots Act. In January 1887, idiots in licensed houses numbered 461 (319 in provincial houses) out of a total of 1,582 in all hospitals and licensed houses. Forty-first Report (1887) C.L., pp. 144–53.

[3] 1844 Report M.C.L., pp. 199–203, and Supplemental Report for Wales, 1844.

[4] Halliday, A. (1827), *A General View of the Present State of Lunatics, and Lunatic Asylums, in Great Britain and Ireland, and in some other Kingdoms*, p. 16.

[5] 1844 Report M.C.L., Appendix F.

[6] Minutes of evidence 1815 S.C., p. 166.   [7] P.R., 1819 (a), p. 6.

politan Commissioners found it to be totally unfit for the reception of lunatics. The Country Register provides evidence of the fact that, in the early years of the nineteenth century, a small number of Welsh patients were treated in private madhouses in the English border counties, such as J. Johnson's house at Shrewsbury and J. Squires's house, Walton Lodge, Liverpool.[1] In 1843, a private licensed house, Vernon House, was opened at Briton Ferry, Glamorgan, for pauper and private patients and this establishment was not closed until 1895.[2] Another private licensed house was opened, in 1851, at Amroth Castle, Tenby, Pembrokeshire. However, conditions at this house were never satisfactory and the licence was withdrawn in 1856.[3] The first county asylum to be built in Wales was that at Denbigh, Denbighshire, which catered for the five North Wales counties and which was opened, after the considerable delays referred to previously, in 1848. Before the opening of this asylum, it had been customary to send a considerable number of pauper lunatics from North Wales to Haydock Lodge. One of the complaints about the facilities at Haydock Lodge had been that there was an insufficiency of Welsh-speaking attendants and other staff, relative to the number of Welsh paupers confined in the house.[4] However, in 1846, the superintendent, Charles Mott, claimed that there had never been more than four patients, at one time, who could not speak English and that, at that time, there were eight Welsh-speaking attendants or servants for the thirty-six Welsh paupers.[5] At Vernon House, in 1847, nearly all the eighty-six pauper lunatics were Welsh, but there were no Welsh-speaking attendants.[6]

---

[1] E.g. at James Johnson's house, during the period Oct. 1801–Nov. 1812, thirteen of the ninety-six admissions came from Wales.
[2] Glam. C.R.O., Q/S. L/VH. 1–15.   [3] *Vide infra*, p. 256.
[4] *Vide infra*, p. 277.
[5] Returns re Haydock Lodge Lunatic Asylum, 1846.
[6] Further Report (1847) C.L., p. 105.

4

◇◇◇

The Private-Madhouse Proprietor[1]

◇◇◇

I T was not until the mid-eighteenth century that medical men began to take an active interest in the institutional care of the insane, although the treatment of insanity had been included within their province by a few physicians in preceding centuries. The second half of the eighteenth century saw the emergence of professionalism and specialism in medicine in general; a process that was linked, closely, with the foundation of hospitals in London and the provinces. In the field of mental illness, the methods adopted at the small number of new lunatic hospitals, such as St Luke's Hospital, in London, and the Manchester Lunatic Hospital, played an important part in raising standards in the treatment of insanity. The assumption of medical responsibility for the insane, however, was a slow process, particularly in private madhouses, and the 'mad-doctor' had little social or professional status. Owing to these circumstances, the keepers of madhouses[2] in the eighteenth century formed an essentially heterogeneous group, not uncommonly including clergymen, and quack-

---

[1] In this book, the term 'proprietor' has been used generally, as it was in the contemporary source-material, to signify the owner and licensee of a madhouse. The licensed proprietor himself often used to act as superintendent but these three positions could be combined in other ways or held by separate individuals.

[2] The term 'keeper' was often used, at this period, to denote both the master of a madhouse and a person attending the lunatics, but it came to be replaced by 'superintendent' with regard to the person in charge of an establishment (e.g. Burrows (1820), *op. cit.*, p. 243).

doctors who specialized in treating the insane flourished, e.g. Irish, Fallowes and Thomas Warburton. The selection of the Reverend Dr Francis Willis to treat George III in 1788 was, therefore, an event of considerable importance in the history of medical madhouse proprietors and of 'mad-doctors' in general. It brought some professional respectability to the 'trade in lunacy' and demonstrated that the treatment of insanity required special skills and experience not necessarily possessed by the most eminent physicians of the day. Macalpine and Hunter (1969) emphasized that Willis 'made his mark in medical history for propagating the notion that insanity was curable',[1] removing, thereby, 'the excuse for neglect which therapeutic pessimism had fostered for centuries'.[2]

Francis Willis (1718–1807), the son of a Lincoln clergyman, became a physician relatively late in life (M.D. Oxon. 1759), although he had had a long-standing inclination towards medicine. After initially studying theology at Oxford (M.A. Oxon. 1740), he took Holy Orders and practised as a clergyman. For a time, he was Vice-President of Brasenose College, Oxford. In 1749, he married and settled at Dunston, Lincolnshire. In 1769, he was appointed one of the physicians to the Lincoln Hospital and, by this time, he had established a reputation for treating mental illness, using his home at Dunston as a madhouse. Willis had rented this property for some years, at a nominal sum, from his friend, Lord le Despencer and, by 1770, he wished to own it permanently. However, Despencer would not agree to the sale of the property and a protracted quarrel ensued, lasting until 1776, when it culminated in legal proceedings being taken by Despencer against Willis.[3] In a letter to Despencer, Willis wrote of his concern for the future of his sons, which, he claimed, would be prejudiced, 'as I intend to bring up my second and youngest son to physick, if I did not look forward with hopes of leaving them in possession of an accustom'd House for wrongheads, with proper conveniencys for their reception. I must own I have flatter'd myself I might have one day promis'd myself that sort of comfort in a long lease here, but as that is all over, I am resolv'd as I possibly can get a piece of ground convenient in the neighbourhood to build me con-

---

[1] Macalpine, I. and Hunter, R. (1969), *George III and the Mad-business*, p. 269.

[2] *Ibid.*, p. 276.

[3] For details *vide* Bod. Lib., MSS. D. D. Dashwood (Bucks), B. 19/3–6, correspondence Willis to Despencer, etc., 1758–78.

veniency by degrees.'[1] Willis finally left Dunston and opened a madhouse at nearby Greatford (Gretford) in 1776.[2] The documentary evidence concerning this quarrel certainly portrays Willis as a determined,
rather unscrupulous person, a characterization that is essentially in
keeping with one contemporary view of him during the treatment of
the King. He was called to treat George III in 1788, when, as he stated
later, he had had twenty-eight years experience of looking after some
thirty lunatics annually.[3] Following the King's recovery, in the following year, Willis received a reward of £1,000 a year for twenty-one
years and his son, Dr John Willis (1751–1835), who had assisted him,
received £650 a year for the rest of his life. John and his brother
Robert Darling (1760–1821) treated the King again in 1801.[4]
By this time, the fame and prosperity of the Willis family was established and the list of the patients admitted between 1801 and
1812, as recorded in the Country Register, indicates that their
private licensed house attracted a fashionable and noble clientele.
John and Robert Darling Willis both attended the King during
his final illness, 1810–11. A second licensed house was opened at
Shillingthorpe, in the neighbouring parish, in c. 1816. In 1830, it was
licensed, for thirty patients, to John Willis and his nephew, Francis
Willis junior (1792–1859). The house at Greatford was closed in
1838, but Francis Willis continued at Shillingthorpe until his
death.[5]

Another physician who attended George III in 1788–9 was
Anthony Addington, M.D. Oxon., F.R.C.P., who, like Francis
Willis, had had experience as a madhouse proprietor. In his evidence
before the 1788 Committee, which examined the physicians attending the King, Addington referred to the private madhouse he had
opened at Reading in 1749 and which he continued to run until 1754,
when he moved to London. He built this house adjoining his own
private residence and it was capable of accommodating eight to
ten patients at one time.[6]

[1] *Ibid.*, B.19/3/3, letter, Willis to Despencer, 25 Nov. 1770.

[2] *Ibid.*, B.19/6/14, letter, Thomas Sandon to Despencer, 18 March 1776.

[3] Report from the Committee appointed to examine the physicians who had
attended His Majesty, during his illness, 1788, p. 9.

[4] For an account of the part played by the Willis family during the King's illnesses *vide* Trench, C. C. (1964), *The Royal Malady*, pp. 93–142; and Macalpine
and Hunter, *op. cit.*

[5] R. Gardiner Hill became proprietor in 1860 and the house was closed in 1863.

[6] Report from the Committee appointed to examine the physicians who have
attended His Majesty, during his illness, 1788, p. 13.

Medical and lay proprietors

Few details are available concerning those medical men who kept madhouses in the mid-eighteenth century. Several well-known physicians, who had an especial interest in insanity, are known to have owned houses, for example, William Battie (1703–76),[1] physician to St Luke's Hospital and John Monro (1715–91),[2] physician to Bethlem Hospital. Further examples are provided by Dr John Hall, whose career at Newcastle has been referred to previously, and Nathaniel Cotton (1705–88) M.D. Cotton opened a house at St Alban's, which was known as the 'Collegium Insanorum', in *c.* 1745, after working previously in association with Dr Thomas Crawley, who had kept a madhouse at Dunstable.[3] The changeover from non-medical to medical proprietorship and superintendence of private madhouses which began to take place in the late-eighteenth and early-nineteenth centuries is displayed clearly in the history of those private madhouses whose management passed from members of one generation to the next within the same family. Examples are provided by the Finch family at Laverstock House, Wiltshire (1830);[4] the Bakewells at Spring Vale, Staffordshire (1835),[5] and, to a lesser extent, by the Harris family at Hook Norton (1785);[6] in each case, an approximate date of transition is given in brackets. It has not been possible to prove conclusively which of the forty-two proprietors named in the Country Register were medical men. They included, however, a number of established physicians, such as Francis Willis, Thomas Arnold, M.D. Edin., F.R.C.P. Edin.; Joseph Mason Cox, M.D. Leyden; Edward Long Fox, M.D. Edin., L.R.C.P. and William Perfect, M.D. St Andrews. A Parliamentary Return of 1819[7] indicates only eight proprietors as being a 'Dr' or possessing an M.D. and it is not possible to compile, from this type of source, a

[1] House at Wood's Close, Clerkenwell, London, previously run by James Newton. (For further details re this madhouse, *vide* Hunter and Macalpine (1963), *op. cit.*, pp. 200–1.)

[2] Brooke House, Clapton, London, which remained in the Monro family until the late-nineteenth century and was not closed until 1940, when it was damaged by enemy action.

[3] *Vide* Hill, B. (1967), ' "My Little Physician at St Alban's." Nathaniel Cotton 1705–1788', *Practitioner 199*, pp. 363–7; and Hunter, R. A. and Wood, J. B. (1957), 'Nathaniel Cotton, M.D., Poet, Physician and Psychiatrist', *King's Coll. Hosp. Gazette 36*, p. 120. Also pamphlet *On Madness* by T. Crawley, Beds. C.R.O., X.125/68.

[4] *Vide infra*, p. 116.   [5] *Vide infra*, p. 93.   [6] *Vide infra*, p. 133.
[7] P.R., 1819(a).

comprehensive list of medically trained private licensed house proprietors until 1831, when this information was required by a further Parliamentary Return. At this time, of the sixty-eight provincial licensed houses named, forty-four had proprietors who were described as medically or surgically qualified. The proportion was similar in 1844, despite the overall increase in the number of licensed houses. Sixty-one of the 100 provincial licensed houses now had, as proprietors, medical men, that is, persons described as surgeons or possessing an M.D. It has to be borne in mind, however, that the Medical Registration Act was not passed until 1858 and also that an M.D. degree could be obtained, at certain universities, without attendance. In 1854, of the eighty-eight provincial licensed houses, sixty-eight had one or more medical proprietors. According to Lord Shaftesbury, in 1858, forty-nine of the seventy-seven provincial licensed houses had a resident medical officer and in thirty-three cases this person was the proprietor. Twenty-four of the thirty-seven metropolitan licensed houses had a resident medical officer who, at fifteen of these houses, was also the proprietor.[1] By 1870, thirty-eight of the sixty-four provincial licensed houses were licensed to medical proprietors.

During the late-eighteenth and for the greater part of the nineteenth century, it was not unusual for medical private-madhouse proprietors and medical officers to have held appointments previously at either county asylums or public hospitals or vice versa and, consequently, considerable inter-change of staff took place between the various types of establishment. It was fairly common practice for visiting physicians to county asylums to keep their own private licensed houses[2] and a few medical superintendents of county and borough asylums also owned private establishments. For example, in 1855, the proprietor of Field House, Hull, F. W. Casson, surgeon, was also the resident medical superintendent of the Hull Borough Asylum.[3] Arnold, the proprietor of Belle Grove Asylum, Leicester, was the chief instigator in the founding of the Leicester Lunatic Asylum and became its first physician in 1794. A number of examples exist of notable persons who practised, initially, in private madhouses before moving to other establishments. One such example is furnished by the career of Sir William Charles Ellis (1780–1839), M.D.

[1] Report 1859 S.C. (April 1859), p. 32.
[2] *Vide* Editorial (1855), 'Visiting Physicians to County Asylums', *Asylum J. Ment. Sci. 1*, p. 35.   [3] Ninth Report (1855) C.L., p. 24.

St Andrew's, M.R.C.S., who worked at the Refuge, Hull, founded by Dr J. Alderson in 1814, before becoming superintendent of the West Riding County Asylum in 1818. In 1838, after a seven-year period as superintendent of the Middlesex County Asylum at Hanwell, he became resident director and physician at Denham Park, Uxbridge, and, for a short period before he died he owned Southall Park, a private licensed house in Middlesex. To quote another example, Sir William Charles Hood (1824–70), M.D. St Andrew's, F.R.C.P. Lond., a former resident physician of Fiddington House, Market Lavington, Wiltshire, became, in 1851, the first resident physician in charge of the male department of the Middlesex County Asylum at Colney Hatch, and, from 1852 to 1862, he was medical superintendent of Bethlem Hospital. Similar exchanges were made by non-medical staff also, for example, George Wallet, the steward of Bethlem in 1815, was formerly the superintendent of Dr Rees's madhouse, Hackney, London.[1]

It is significant that there are numerous instances of superintendents and medical officers of public hospitals and county asylums who, subsequently, owned private licensed houses. Thus, John Harris, the first proprietor of Springfield, a licensed house opened at Bedford in 1837,[2] had been the medical superintendent of the Bedfordshire County Asylum. T. O. Prichard, who established Abington Abbey, Northampton, in 1845, had been the first superintendent, 1838–45, of the Northampton Lunatic Hospital and his son, Thomas Prichard, was for a period the medical superintendent of the Glasgow Royal Lunatic Asylum. Robert Gardiner Hill, after leaving the Lincoln Asylum in 1840, was co-proprietor of several licensed houses including Eastgate House, Lincoln, and Earl's Court House and Wyke House, London. Richard Mallam, one of the proprietors of Hook Norton, is recorded as having obtained experience in the treatment of insanity at the Oxford Lunatic Asylum before taking over the licensed house.[3]

John Conolly's contact with the private-madhouse system started when he acted as Medical Visitor to the Warwickshire licensed houses during the years 1824 to 1828.[4] He had an interest in several houses after his retirement from the superintendency of the Hanwell

---

[1] Minutes of evidence 1815 S.C., p. 35.
[2] Springfield remained open until 1963.
[3] O.C.R.O., QSL VII/3, Minutes V.M., 25 March 1843.
[4] Warwicks. C.R.O., Q.S. 24/a/I/6.

Asylum in 1844. It is significant that Conolly claimed that he was authorized to speak on behalf of the proprietors of licensed houses when he gave evidence before the 1859 Select Committee and he admitted to being favourably disposed towards private asylums.[1] From 1845 until 1866, he used his own residence, Lawn House, Hanwell, as a small, select asylum for up to six ladies and, in 1848, he is recorded as being one of the co-licensees of Wood End Grove, Hayes, Middlesex.[2] His brother, Dr William Conolly, was proprietor of Castleton House, Cheltenham, from 1835 to 1849, before moving to Hayes Park licensed house, Middlesex. When he, in turn, retired in 1852, his son-in-law, Charles Fitzgerald, continued the work, but ran into financial difficulties in 1859, whereupon Conolly and his son, E. T. Conolly, took over the licence until 1861. It is of interest to note that a third ex-superintendent of the Hanwell Asylum at this time, J. G. Millingen (1782–1862), became the co-proprietor of a licensed house, York House, Battersea, on his resignation from Hanwell in 1839. Similarly, Dr Thomas Dickson, having resigned the medical superintendency of Cheadle Hospital, Manchester, in 1858, opened his own private licensed house, Wye House, Buxton.[3] A number of proprietors are known to have been attendants at various establishments previously but it is difficult to estimate the size of this group. A typical illustration is provided by the career of Mr Gillett, proprietor of a licensed house at Taunton, Somerset, of whom Edward Wakefield, a London land-agent and Quaker philanthropist, in evidence before the 1815 Select Committee, claimed that he 'bragged of having been a keeper at Bethlem, and was sent from that hospital to Exeter Asylum, from whence he came to keep this house for himself'.[4] A similar example is provided in the case of Isaac Taylor, who, in 1839, was taken into partnership by Henry Mannering to run Grove Hall, Acomb, York, and, in 1840, assumed sole charge of the establishment. Previously, Taylor had been, for fifteen years, one of the head keepers at the York Asylum.[5] It was not uncommon practice for experienced attendants to be the resident superintendents of private licensed houses. In addition, a few proprietors are known to have

---

[1] Report 1859 S.C. (April 1859), pp. 165, 177.
[2] Third Report (1848) C.L., pp. 3–4.
[3] Sixteenth Report (1862) C.L., p. 9.
[4] Minutes of evidence 1815 S.C., p. 22. (Gillett's successor at Fivehead House, W. E. Gillett, was qualified as a surgeon and apothecary and moved, in 1828, to Fairwater House, Somerset.)
[5] York City Lib., Q.S. lunacy records, K.124.

been employed, formerly, as druggists, such as Stephen Terry, proprietor, in 1837, of Bailbrook House, Bath.[1]

In the return of 1831, eight women were listed as the sole proprietors of provincial private licensed houses.[2] This number was unchanged by 1844, but ten years later eighteen out of the eighty-eight provincial houses had a female proprietor[3] and, by 1870, the proportion was thirteen out of sixty-four. In many instances, the women were the widows or daughters of former proprietors. The transfer of licences to relatives was, in fact, permitted by law, but it aroused concern at a time when it was clearly the policy of the Commissioners in Lunacy to promote the medical element, in contra-distinction to the lay element, in the care of the insane in private establishments. Sir J. C. Bucknill (1857), editor of the *Asylum Journal of Mental Science*, observed:

If insanity is a disease requiring medical treatment, ladies cannot legally or properly undertake the treatment ... Physicians or surgeons to whom licenses are granted are not necessarily more speculative in the maladies of their patients than any other class of medical men who invest money in their professional pursuits. ... But with laymen and ladies the medical treatment of insanity is out of the question, and a license granted to them becomes merely a permission to speculate upon the profits of their maintenance. It is a remnant of the olden times when safe custody was everything, and medical treatment deemed absurd, or even an interference with the decrees of Providence. ... If private interests ... are to override public ones, the widow of a clergyman ought on the same principle to hold the rectory of her departed husband, and manage the parochial duties by means of curates.[4]

In fact, a distinction had been drawn between the treatment of the insane in madhouses kept by medical and lay proprietors, at intervals since the late-eighteenth century. William Pargeter (1792), a physician who had a particular interest in insanity, stated clearly that the treatment was superior in madhouses kept by medical men or clergymen and that abuses were not permitted in these establishments, whereas the other keepers were often ignorant, illiterate and of low integrity. In the latter category, there were included 'men, who have just pecuniary powers sufficient to obtain a licence, and set themselves up keepers of private madhouses, alluring the public in an advertise-

---

[1] P.R., 1838, p. 6.   [2] P.R., 1831.
[3] The proportion of female proprietors was even higher in the metropolitan area, where approximately one in four of the houses was licensed to women.
[4] Bucknill, J. C. (1857), 'Tenth Report of the Commissioners in Lunacy to the Lord Chancellor', *Asylum J. Ment. Sci. 3*, pp. 19–20.

ment, that the patients will be treated with the best medical skill and attention ... when at the same time, they are totally devoid of all physical knowledge and experience and in other respects extremely ignorant, and perhaps illiterate'.[1] Similarly, Burrows (1820) distinguished two kinds of madhouses: 'in the one, nothing more is professed, unless especially required, than kind usage and safe custody; while, in others, the means of cure are professed, and sometimes very efficaciously employed: the first are commonly under the superintendence of unprofessional persons, the second are generally under that of a member of the faculty.'[2] Burrows reiterated these views in evidence before the 1828 Select Committee of the House of Lords and his remarks reflect the widespread view that lay proprietors were more likely to be corrupt and avaricious than their medically trained colleagues. Nevertheless, there are many examples of lay persons of apparent integrity who kept well-conducted madhouses, in both the eighteenth and nineteenth centuries, and their contributions cannot be disregarded. In addition to the distinction drawn between the treatment offered by medical and lay proprietors, there was, also, dissension within the ranks of medical men concerning the suitability of surgeons and apothecaries to treat insanity. Metropolitan medical proprietors were generally physicians and they tended to view provincial proprietors with some disdain, as they were often surgeons or apothecaries.

There can be little doubt that many of those who kept madhouses must have been wholly unsuited to their task, although they were able, nevertheless, to make a good living. Thomas Bakewell, a successful non-medical private-madhouse proprietor, had little respect for the qualifications of many contemporary proprietors. In 1809, he observed:

It is doubtful, whether many of those that keep madhouses, are qualified for the important purpose. I know of two, whom I have been told began business without any information but what they got from me: if so, they began with a very small stock of knowledge indeed; for one of them had all the information he acquired from me, before I was eleven years of age; and the other, in a single conversation: and neither of these men, either by nature or education, seemed fitted for anything above a common labourer.[3]

[1] Pargeter, W. (1792), *Observations on Maniacal Disorders*, pp. 124–5.
[2] Burrows (1820), *op. cit.*, pp. 22–3. (He advocated the adoption of the French custom whereby such houses were referred to, respectively, as Maisons de détention and Maisons de santé.)
[3] Bakewell, T. (1809), *The Domestic Guide in Cases of Insanity*, pp. 100–1.

In a later publication, Bakewell disarmingly blamed the pecuniary interests of the masters of madhouses for the abuses which occurred.[1] In particular, he blamed some proprietors for leaving the patients in the care of servants and, he noted, 'as well might a Wellington depute his charge to a subaltern in the day of battle'.[2] Other writers echoed these observations. Thus, Dickson (1852), resident super-intendent of the Manchester Royal Lunatic Asylum, claimed that, under the screen of worthiness and success created by some private madhouse proprietors, others had worked 'with no more fitness for the task than would enable them to perform the duties of a common boarding house'.[3] In addition to the considerable body of evidence which has been accumulated relating to negligent and unscrupulous proprietors and which will be considered in detail in Chapter 8, information has been discovered concerning instances of drunken-ness and mental disorders on the part of certain proprietors. Thus, J. S. Paget, the proprietor of Belle Grove Lunatic Asylum, Newcastle upon Tyne, in 1837,[4] and Miss Catherine Taylor, who owned Hessle House, Yorkshire, in 1847,[5] were both shown to be drunkards by special committees of enquiry convened by the Visiting Magis-trates. The most severe case discovered concerning the psychiatric disturbance of a proprietor was that of Dr James Pownall. From 1839 on, he had repeated attacks of 'mania' and extreme violence and in the course of the next twenty years, he was admitted six or seven times to metropolitan or provincial licensed houses. In 1853, he became the proprietor of a licensed house, Northfield House, Calne, Wilt-shire, although it was known that he suffered from mental disorder. In 1854, one of the Visitors reported to the Commissioners in Lunacy that Pownall was unfit to be in charge of the establishment after he had struck and shot a patient.[6] Subsequently, Pownall became a patient at another private asylum and Northfield House was closed. In 1859, following a period of treatment in Northwoods Asylum, Gloucestershire, he murdered the servant girl of a Gloucestershire surgeon, with whom he was lodging, by cutting her throat with a razor.[7]

[1] Bakewell, T. (1815), *op. cit.*, p. 10.   [2] *Ibid.*, p. 54.
[3] Dickson, *op. cit.*, p. 25.
[4] Minutes V.M., 13 June 1837. In the custody of the Medical Superintendent, St Nicholas's Hospital, Newcastle upon Tyne.
[5] E.R. Yorks. C.R.O., QAL. 3/35.   [6] P.R.O., M.H.50, Minute Book C.L., Vol. 7, 3 May and 19 June 1854.
[7] Fourteenth Report (1860) C.L., pp. 91–7.

The private-madhouse proprietor as a speculative 'tradesman'

The available evidence certainly suggests that owning a private mad-house could be lucrative and some of this evidence is now considered. In 1770, Willis regarded 'an accustom'd House for wrongheads' as a very desirable proposition to leave to his sons.[1] Thomas Bakewell's writings indicate that ignorant, illiterate proprietors could, nevertheless, prosper financially. Andrew Duncan, junior (1809), Professor of Medical Jurisprudence at Edinburgh, observed that: 'Few speculations can be more unpleasant than that of a private mad-house, and it is seldom if ever undertaken, unless with the hope of receiving large returns on the capital advanced.'[2] Ellis (1815) referred to those proprietors, who, 'finding it a very lucrative concern, have wished to involve it in great mystery'[3] and to foster false beliefs about insanity in order to conceal and protect their interests. Similarly, Halliday (1827) referred to 'the mystery which was made to hover round the precincts of a madhouse'[4] and he condemned those proprietors 'who have realized immense fortunes as wholesale dealers and traffickers in this species of human misery'.[5] In 1829, he observed, with reference to Middlesex: 'The keeping of madhouses has long been a gainful trade in this county, and many have realized very large fortunes by the confinement of their fellow-creatures.'[6] Conolly (1830) stated that although, in some parts of the country 'many respectable, well-educated and humane individuals' devoted their time and talents to the care of the insane, 'the prospect of certain profit' attracted the ignorant and uneducated and those who were 'capable of no feeling but a desire for wealth'.[7] Under the supervision of such persons, Conolly asserted that: 'The patients are transmitted, like stock in trade, from one member of the family to another, and from one generation to another; they come in youth to the father, they linger out their age with the son.'[8] Dickson (1852) claimed that two-thirds of those who kept private licensed houses did so because they constituted profitable pecuniary speculations.[9] He referred also

---

[1] *Vide supra*, pp. 75.

[2] Duncan, A., jun. (1809), 'Observations on the General Treatment of Lunatics, as a Branch of Medical Police', in Duncan, A., sen. (ed.), *Observations on the Structure of Hospitals for the Treatment of Lunatics*, p. 18.

[3] Ellis, *op. cit.*, pp. 6–7.   [4] Halliday (1827), *op. cit.*, p. 7.

[5] *Ibid.*, p. 10.   [6] Halliday (1829), *op. cit.*, p. 25.

[7] Conolly, J. (1830), *An Inquiry concerning the Indications of Insanity*, p. 13.

[8] *Ibid.*   [9] Dickson, *op. cit.*, p. 24.

to the practice of prolonging the detention of convalescent patients by mercenary proprietors who were vulnerable to the influence and bribery of relatives and nominal friends of patients. In 1856, Conolly expressed the view that: 'An excessive desire of gain had been, more than cruelty, the general cause of those gradually accumulating evils which had brought disgrace on many of the old institutions', and that those proprietors who were bent on making a fortune had resisted bitterly any changes which interfered with their plans.[1] Such remarks and imputations, however, have to be seen in perspective, as a desire for financial reward on the part of madhouse proprietors did not, necessarily, involve the exploitation of the insane. Indeed, the continued success and prosperity of private establishments, particularly those receiving private patients, depended, to a large extent, on the personal reputation of the proprietor and the public confidence he held. An editorial note, in the *Journal of Psychological Medicine* in 1852,[2] made the following timely observation:

The self-same charge, may . . . be brought against the managers of public asylums [i.e. county asylums]; they have an exchequer to maintain; they have an interest in keeping up the full complement of patients in the house; they must keep their revenue up at par; and to satisfy the grumbling rate-payers, they must have their contracts cut down to the most transparent shaving; they also must exhibit a satisfactory amount of receipts upon their balance-sheet. They, therefore, have a 'personal interest', as the learned baron calls it, in taking charge and keeping pauper lunatics, quite as strong as might be supposed to actuate any unworthy proprietor of a private lunatic asylum.[3]

The expense involved in opening a private licensed house, with adequate facilities for recreation and occupation and in keeping it running properly must not be overlooked. Little manuscript information has survived regarding these costs and such facts as are available are incomplete and isolated. For example, Brislington House, near Bristol, which was opened in 1806, is known to have cost the truly

[1] Conolly, J. (1856), *The Treatment of the Insane without Mechanical Restraints*, pp. 136–7.

[2] Editorial (1852), 'Baron Alderson's "Charge" against Private Lunatic Asylums', *J. Psychol. Med. & Ment. Path.* V, pp. 399–401. This editorial by Forbes Winslow was a refutation of the outspoken denunciation of all private asylums made, from the Bench, by Baron Alderson, in 1852, during the trial at the Central Criminal Court of Henry Baker, who had kept an unlicensed house in Lambeth.

[3] *Ibid.*, p. 401.

remarkable sum of £35,000 to build.[1] A deed of co-partnership between the proprietors of Denham Park, Uxbridge, Buckinghamshire, in 1838, indicates that a sum of approximately £2,500 had been laid out for 'the purchase of furniture, carriages, horses and other goods and things', and at that time, the capital and joint stock was £4,000.[2] The cost of adapting premises adequately for use as an asylum, involving attention to the water supply, heating, ventilation and drainage, must have been considerable in the case of large and expanding establishments, such as Haydock Lodge in the period 1844 to 1846. Returns recording routine expenditure at the latter establishment were published as part of a report of the Commissioners in Lunacy in 1847 and provide a detailed picture of the outgoing expenses. During the winter months, for example, approximately twenty tons of coal per week were used and the outlay on coal, during the period August 1845 to April 1846, was £171. In the course of a similar period, the bills for butcher's meat totalled £1,191. In 1844, the expenditure on wine and brandy was £139 as compared with only £81 for medicines.[3]

There is evidence which suggests that certain proprietors were remarkably charitable, in that they admitted some patients at especially low rates or allowed patients to remain in their houses without receiving any form of payment. In 1785, Arnold announced in an advertisement[4] that, for the relief of impoverished non-pauper patients, he had opened part of his establishment as a 'charitable asylum' for the reception of ten persons 'on the reduced terms, of eight shillings per week; being the sum, or nearly, which is usually required in the general lunatic asylums already established at York and Manchester'. In addition, he offered to receive two other patients 'free of all expence whatever'. In 1844, the Visitors to Denham Park commented on 'a circumstance highly creditable to the establishment that a patient named Querios, whose father it appears has lately died, having no means to provide for his maintenance here, yet the proprietors . . . have continued to keep him without any remuneration'.[5] Many other examples of this kind could be quoted and, even in 1926, the Royal Commission on lunacy and mental disorder referred to

[1] Minutes of evidence 1828 S.C.H.L., J.H.L., Vol. 60, p. 710.
[2] Bucks. R.O., BRA., 833.
[3] Further Report C.L. re Haydock Lodge Lunatic Asylum, March 1847 (Appendix VI), pp. 28–30.
[4] Leicester Publ. Lib., *The Leicester Journal*, 7 May 1785.
[5] Bucks. R.O., Q.S. lunacy records, Minutes V.M., 22 Jan. 1844.

the fact that in private asylums there were 'instances of patients being accommodated . . . at rates which can not be remunerative or even for nothing, where the only reason for keeping them is philanthropy'.[1] In 1847, the Commissioners in Lunacy declared that many proprietors were 'entitled to great credit' for 'expending large sums of money, with little or no prospect of immediate return',[2] in order to improve their premises in accordance with current requirements, despite the diminished incentive to do so occasioned by the erection of county and other asylums. Conolly spoke up for private asylum proprietors when he gave evidence before the 1859 Select Committee and, writing in the *Journal of Mental Science* in 1861, he stated the case for the proprietors, with considerable vigour, as the following excerpt demonstrates:

Full credit is given to the officers of public asylums for the poor . . . But the proprietors and physicians of private asylums, following these public examples, and at great expense modifying their houses so as to afford the rich all the advantages happily enjoyed by the pauper lunatic, have been treated with no consideration whatever. They are simply regarded as the keepers of boarding houses, eager for gain, and careless as to the means. Although the majority of them are men of liberal education, and many of them of rank in their profession, they are regarded by law as dishonest tradesmen, and have to apply for a licence, to be renewed yearly, after the manner of public-house keepers, and proprietors of tea-gardens and dancing rooms; a degradation that is very generally complained of, and might most easily be removed.[3]

In 1859, W. G. Campbell, one of the Commissioners in Lunacy, gave a warning that any legislation which tended to degrade or reflect extreme suspicion on licensed-house proprietors, would injure the cause of reform by discouraging medical men of integrity from undertaking the work.[4]

The form and content of advertisements for many private madhouses in the late-eighteenth and first half of the nineteenth centuries, designed primarily to attract patronage, effectively substantiate the essential commercialism of their proprietors and the subject of printed advertisements in general will be discussed in greater detail in Chapter 5. Increased attention was focused on the commercial aspects of running a private licensed house, in the mid-nineteenth century, when it became known that large sums of money were paid,

[1] Report of Royal Commission on lunacy and mental disorder, 1926, p. 130.
[2] Further Report (1847) C.L., p. 63.
[3] Conolly, J. (1861), 'Licences and Certificates', *J. Ment. Sci.* 7 (No. 37), p. 133.
[4] Report 1859 S.C. (Aug. 1859), p. 47.

in some instances, for the goodwill of an establishment at the time of its purchase by a new proprietor. This was the case in 1854, when it was stated that a certain Dr James Baillie had purchased Grove Place, Nursling, Hampshire. At this time, the Commissioners considered that: 'A payment of this nature ... offers a strong temptation to those who purchase to curtail the comforts and accommodation of the patients committed to their charge, in an attempt to reimburse themselves out of the profits of the asylum.'[1] In 1858 Dr Forbes B. Winslow, President of the Association of Medical Officers of Asylums and Hospitals for the Insane, himself the owner of two metropolitan private asylums, criticized current advertisements which were often couched 'in the glowing, fanciful, poetical, and flowery language of the auctioneer'.[2] He condemned the practice whereby asylums and their inmates were 'brought into the market and offered for sale, like a flock of sheep, to the highest bidder, in a manner calculated to destroy all public confidence and trust, in the honesty, integrity, and even common respectability of those connected with similar institutions'.[3] In addition, he described the 'liberal percentages and bonuses', which proprietors were prepared to pay to medical practitioners who patronized their houses. Winslow quoted the following advertisement from a current weekly journal as an illustration of this practice: 'Insanity.—Twenty per cent. annually on the receipts will be guaranteed to any medical man recommending a quiet patient of either sex, to a first class asylum, with the highest testimonials.'[4] The restriction to 'quiet' patients reflected the change which took place in the nature of the clientele accepted at many licensed houses during the second half of the nineteenth century. By the last quarter of the century, the lists of houses included in the Annual Reports of the Commissioners in Lunacy indicated which houses were prepared to accept only 'quiet and harmless cases' and, in 1880, for example, eight provincial licensed houses fell into this category.

During the period under consideration, the laws regulating the way in which licences for keeping private asylums could be obtained were, undoubtedly, inadequate. There was no provision for inquiry into the character of the applicants and, as Conolly observed in 1849,

---

[1] Ninth Report (1855) C.L., pp. 20–1. (This statement was contradicted in the next report and the licence was not renewed.)

[2] Winslow, F. B. (1858), 'Presidential Address', *J. Ment. Sci. 4*, p. 10.

[3] *Ibid.*   [4] *Ibid.*

'their previous occupation and education is immaterial to the success of their application'.[1] The concern of the Commissioners in Lunacy for this deficiency, however, is reflected in the questions, published in 1859, which they put to prospective licensees.[2] These questions were designed to explore the applicant's experience, especially medical, and his fitness to be entrusted with the planning and management of an asylum and the care of the insane. It was not until 1862 that the first statutory provisions were made for a house to be inspected before it was licensed. In 1858, John Conolly's son, E. T. Conolly, a barrister, published detailed recommendations for the amendment of existing procedures prior to the granting of licences.[3] By 1860, the official policy, as stated by the Commissioners, was not to issue new licences other than to medical men or other persons of high character and reputation. But the problem was not resolved easily. There was an indisputable public demand for accommodation in private asylums and, although medical practitioners were the most suitable persons to run such establishments, they were not always in the best position financially to open a house and carry it on with propriety. Even in 1815, Ellis had referred to the reluctance on the part of those established medical men, who founded private madhouses, to give up their practices for the uncertain success of running an asylum and, instead, they tended to place 'servants' in charge of their houses.[4] The employment of resident medical officers compensated, to some extent, for the existence of lay proprietors but, naturally, the medical officer could not be a free agent and this could lead to divided responsibility, which, in turn, would further prejudice good management. It is likely that many of the defects of the private-madhouse system stemmed from the practice whereby a single proprietor owned a number of houses, but resided in none of them; instead, delegating managerial responsibility to superintendents, whose prime concern was to fulfil the requirements of their employer.

The Association of Medical Officers of Asylums and Hospitals for the Insane was founded in 1841 and the first number of its journal, the *Asylum Journal*, was published in 1853. Each list of new members included a small number of private licensed-house proprietors and staff from whose ranks twelve presidents were chosen during the

[1] Conolly, J. (1849), *A Remonstrance with the Lord Chief Baron*, p. 34.
[2] Thirteenth Report (1859) C.L., pp. 58–9.
[3] Conolly, E. T., *op. cit.*, pp. 9–17.   [4] Ellis, *op. cit.*, pp. 22–3.

nineteenth century. Richard Mallam, proprietor of the licensed houses at Hook Norton, was an early member and, in 1855, the 121 ordinary members included at least thirty who were associated with provincial licensed houses.[1] Mallam appears to have been a regular attender at meetings of the Association and it is of interest to note that, in 1849, Mallam and W. M. Bush, of Sandywell Park, Gloucestershire, were the only licensed-house proprietors amongst those members of the Association who published a congratulatory letter to Samuel Gaskell, on his appointment as a Commissioner in Lunacy.[2] Dr Harrington Tuke, proprietor of the Manor House, Chiswick, and son-in-law of John Conolly, was, for a period, one of the auditors of the Association and, in 1859, he drew attention to the 'distinct line of demarcation between the medical officers of public asylums and the proprietors of private asylums'.[3] Tuke and others, including Sir Charles Hastings,[4] sought to erase this distinction, but this was difficult to accomplish. One of the failings of the private-madhouse system was that it never achieved any effective corporate organization or identity, especially at a time when a whole range of philanthropic movements were flourishing. Public and professional recognition of private asylums, their proprietors and staff might have been facilitated if closer identification with county asylums and with hospitals for the insane had been achieved. But, as the second half of the nineteenth century advanced, psychiatry became an increasingly isolated speciality centred almost entirely on the county asylums and the prospects of closer integration became more remote.

Published works of private-madhouse proprietors

It is significant that the principal printed contributions of private-madhouse proprietors were made during the late-eighteenth and the early-nineteenth centuries. They were, essentially, the isolated products of the enterprise and interests of individuals, whose combined contribution was, for a time, influential. Important contributions were made by Arnold, Perfect, Cox, Hallaran and Burrows. Thomas Arnold

[1] (1855), 'Officers for the Year 1854–55 and Ordinary Members', *Asylum J. Ment. Sci. 1*, pp. 223–4.

[2] (1850), 'Congratulatory Address to Samuel Gaskell, Esq., F.R.C.S.E.', *J. Psychol. Med. & Ment. Path. III*, pp. 139–40.

[3] (1860), 'Statistics of Asylums' (a discussion at Annual Meeting of the Association), *J. Ment. Sci. 6*, p. 22.

[4] *Vide* Hastings, C. (1860), 'Presidential Address', *ibid.*, p. 4.

(1742–1816) was a notable eighteenth-century psychiatric physician. His chief works were concerned with the causes, treatment and classification of insanity and they were commended widely, both in England and abroad. His work, *Observations on the Nature, Kinds, Causes and Prevention of Insanity, Lunacy or Madness*, published in 1782, was particularly well known. Arnold's theoretical concepts were advanced and were based upon the association psychology of Locke and Hartley.[1] Hunter and Macalpine (1963) observed that, 'Arnold's attention to clinical detail and his thorough historical survey set an entirely new standard of scientific scholarship in psychiatric literature'.[2] In addition to the evidence of his considerable learning, it is clear that he was held in high esteem, both in private and public life, within his own locality. One of his obituaries contained the tribute that 'in his public character, he always proved himself an unshaken friend of civil and religious liberty, and the anxious promoter of every design which tended to ameliorate distress. In a word, he was an enlightened ornament of his native town'.[3] William Perfect (1737–1809), owner of a private-madhouse at West Malling, Kent, lacked the academic abilities of Arnold, but his published work was based upon his own practical experience and very detailed clinical observations and provides a valuable account of contemporary therapeutic practice in private madhouses. His work, *Methods of Cure, in Some Particular Cases of Insanity . . . and Nervous Disorders*, first published in 1778, ran into seven editions under varying titles. The edition published in 1787 was entitled, *Select Cases in the Different Species of Insanity . . . with the Modes of Practice as adopted in the Treatment of Each*.

Joseph Mason Cox (1763–1818) M.D. Leyden, of Fishponds private madhouse, near Bristol, was the most distinguished member of a family which kept madhouses for several generations. In 1788, Cox took over the management of the madhouse which his grandfather, Joseph Mason, had kept on the same site at Fishponds from 1760 until his death in 1779.[4] At this time, Cox stated, in a newspaper

---

[1] *Vide* Hoeldtke, R. (1967), 'The History of Associationism and British Medical Psychology', *Med. Hist. 11*, pp. 46–65.

[2] Hunter and Macalpine (1963), *op. cit.*, p. 469.

[3] (1816), 'Obituary; with Anecdotes of Remarkable Persons', *Gentleman's Magazine 86* (part ii), p. 378.

[4] *Vide supra*, p. 38. (Until 1788, Mason's married daughters, Elizabeth Cox and Sarah Carpenter, continued the asylum. Following Mason Cox's death, the asylum was run by his cousin, George Gwinnett Bompas, surgeon, until he died in 1847, when his son, Dr Joseph Carpenter Bompas took over. *Vide infra*, p. 275.)

advertisement, that he proposed 'to confine his practice solely to cases of insanity, hypochondriasis, and other chronic nervous affections: these disorders having been the peculiar object of his studies and observation for several years past at the Universities of Edinburgh, Paris and Leyden'.[1] His writings reveal a scholarly and humane approach towards the insane and his *Practical Observations on Insanity*, first published in 1804, was described by D. H. Tuke (1882) as 'the best medical treatise of the day on insanity'.[2] Cox introduced, for the first time, the concept of 'medical jurisprudence as connected with diseased intellect' and, incidentally, he described at length the use he made of the circulating swing in maniacal disorders. W. S. Hallaran (1765–1825), M.D. Edin., senior physician to the South Infirmary and to the Lunatic Asylum, Cork, owned a private madhouse at Cittadella, Cork. He wrote, like Cox and Perfect, from an extensive personal experience. In his work, *An Enquiry into the Causes producing the Extraordinary Addition to the Number of Insane, together with Extended Observations on the Cure of Insanity*, which was published in 1810, Hallaran claimed that the book was offered to overcome the difficulty that was experienced widely in obtaining practical information on the management of insanity. G. M. Burrows (1771–1846), M.D. St Andrew's, F.R.C.P. Lond., was one of the most noteworthy authors of works on insanity in the first half of the nineteenth century. He owned a small madhouse in Chelsea from 1816 to 1823 and, subsequently, until 1843, he was proprietor of the Retreat at Clapham. He published a number of books on insanity and on contemporary legislation, but it was his *Commentaries on the Causes, Forms, Symptoms, and Treatment, Moral and Medical, of Insanity*, published in 1828, that brought him recognition. This treatise was detailed and comprehensive and received widespread approval. In the course of it, Burrows made frequent reference to the works of Cox and Hallaran and also to the prevailing psychiatric views and developments in France. It incorporated the first report in English of the investigations of Bayle and Calmeil in France, which led to the definition of general paralysis. Burrows had considerable interest in the legal status of the medical profession and, as chairman of the Association of Apothecaries and Surgeon-Apothecaries, he was the main

[1] Gloucester City Lib., Gloucestershire Collection R.19753, the *Gloucester Journal*, 25 Aug. 1788, p. 2.
[2] Tuke, D. H. (1882), *op. cit.*, p. 513.

driving force in securing the passing of the Apothecaries' Act in 1815.

Thomas Bakewell (1761–1835), proprietor of Spring Vale, Staffordshire, achieved modest prominence, despite the fact that he was not medically qualified. He had started his working life as a weaver and for many years he was the manager of a tape mill. Bakewell's uncle and his grandfather had both kept a madhouse before him and Bakewell opened Spring Vale in 1808. In 1815, he gave evidence before the Select Committee of the House of Commons and published, that same year, a letter addressed to the Chairman of that Committee containing 'Remarks on the Nature, Causes and Cure of Mental Derangement'. Bakewell had published, in 1809, *The Domestic Guide in Cases of Insanity*, in which he reviewed the concept of insanity, its causes, symptoms and treatment. He recommended that this work be read by the clergy and by the general public[1] and, in an introductory advertisement, he claimed that the book was written 'from the honest impulse of wishing to be found useful by his fellow creatures, and from a full conviction that such a work is wanting'.[2] He noted that the work would not have the disadvantage of being too learned in style and added: 'The reader has my full liberty to call me illiterate, provided he does not pronounce me ignorant.'[3] Bakewell had, without doubt, considerable literary flair and his work has a refreshingly informal and practical quality. The *Domestic Guide*, in particular, provides a useful source of information about the small madhouse in the early nineteenth century. Samuel Glover Bakewell (1811–66), succeeded his father as proprietor of Spring Vale, which was sold in 1840, the asylum being removed to the Oulton Retreat.[4] Subsequently, he moved to Shropshire in 1853 where he ran The Retreat and The Grove House, Church Stretton, until his death.[5] He had studied medicine at Edinburgh and chose insanity as the subject of his dissertation, in Latin, for the degree of M.D. in 1833. This work was published, that same year, as *An Essay on Insanity*, and he dedicated it to his father who had made it 'the

[1] *Vide* advertisement for *The Domestic Guide* in *The Moorland Bard*, a collection of poems published in 1807, and written by Bakewell earlier in his life. Many of these poems reveal his longstanding interest in insanity.

[2] Bakewell, T. (1809), *op. cit.*, p. vi.

[3] *Ibid.*, p. xi.

[4] Bowers, W. H. and Clough, J. W. (1929), *Researches into the History of the Parish Church and Parish of Stone, Staffordshire*, p. 288.

[5] The Grove House remains open at the present day as a registered mental nursing home.

principal object of his life to ameliorate the condition of lunatics'. The younger Bakewell relied heavily, in this work, on his father's practical experience at Spring Vale which, he claimed, could 'boldly challenge comparison, in regard to the proportion of cures effected in it, with any existing in any part of the world, or with the private success of any practitioner, however eminent'.[1]

Matthew Allen (1783–1845), M.D. Aberdeen, was the proprietor of licensed houses at High Beech, Essex, from 1825 till 1845.[2] He published a number of books on insanity and also a series of essays and sermons, but his literary contribution is difficult to evaluate. In a recent study by Barnet (1965),[3] it is suggested that the essays and sermons were, essentially, an elaboration of work by Allen's father, a Wensleydale clergyman. It was to Allen's care that John Clare, the poet, was committed from 1837 to the time of his escape in 1841 and it is notable that his literary friends included Thomas Carlyle and Alfred Lord Tennyson. Allen's academic qualifications were meagre and his style was rather flamboyant. Many of his ideas, however, were ahead of his time. In his, *Essay on the Classification of the Insane*, published in 1837, he recommended the use of voluntary confinement in order to facilitate early treatment, together with the use of parole and voluntary boarding by convalescent patients. He claimed to be the first to advocate a mild system of management, as the following extract, from a letter written in 1841, to Cyrus Redding, a well-known journalist, demonstrates:

I am extremely sorry that I was in Town when you called on Friday, as I should liked very much . . . to have had an opportunity of showing and explaining to you the plan and treatment which I have pursued for now more than 20 years and which I could have proved to you that I was the first who carried out a system of kindness and liberality about which others who have been to imitate it, have made so much puff and fuss in puffing themselves off while in my quiet and retired way have been altogether overlooked by the press and as I am satisfied that you required nothing more than the facts of the conviction of all this to put the public right on these matters.[4]

In a further letter to Redding,[5] Allen expressed his feelings in a more

---

[1] Bakewell, S. G. (1833), *An Essay on Insanity*, p. 54.

[2] High Beech Asylum remained open until 1859.

[3] Barnet, M. C. (1965), 'Matthew Allen, M.D. (Aberdeen) 1783–1845', *Med. Hist. 9*, pp. 16–28.

[4] Northampton Publ. Lib., Clare MSS. 51, letter, Allen to Redding, 21 April 1841.

[5] *Ibid.*, 25 May 1841.

embittered and near-paranoid tone. In 1833, he published a self-vindicating account of the events which had led up to his appearance in court in the previous year, charged with the non-payment of fees; a charge that, in fact, was not proved against him.[1]

Other authors who were connected with private madhouses in the capacity of proprietor or medical officer, during the course of the late-eighteenth and the first half of the nineteenth centuries, include the following, in each case the date of their principal literary contribution[2] and the names of madhouses to which they were attached being given in brackets: Benjamin Faulkner (1789, proprietor, Little Chelsea, London); Francis Willis, junior (1823, proprietor, Shillingthorpe House, Lincolnshire); John Burdett Steward (1845, proprietor, Southall Park Asylum, Middlesex; formerly physician to Droitwich Lunatic Asylum, Worcestershire); Henry Monro (1850, proprietor, Brooke House, Clapton, London); Daniel Noble (1853, medical officer, Clifton Hall Retreat, Manchester); George Robinson (1859, proprietor, Bensham Asylum, Co. Durham). A small number of medical men associated with private licensed houses wrote theses on topics related to insanity. For example, J. Mason Cox's M.D. thesis at Leyden in 1787 was concerned with mania and John Warburton (son of T. Warburton and later proprietor of Whitmore House, Hoxton) submitted a dissertation *On Insanity* for the M.B. degree of Cambridge, in 1815.[3] S. G. Bakewell's work has already been mentioned.[4] In addition, a number of original contributions were made by such persons as C. M. Burnett, M.D. (Westbrook House, Alton, Hampshire) and J. S. Bushnan, M.D., F.R.C.P.E. (Laverstock House, Wiltshire) to contemporary psychiatric journals, namely the *Asylum Journal of Mental Science* and the *Journal of Psychological Medicine and Mental Pathology*. The latter was edited alone, during the period 1848 to 1858, by F. B. Winslow, M.D., D.C.L., who was the proprietor of two private licensed houses, namely Sussex House and Brandenburgh House, Hammersmith, London. Winslow wrote extensively on a wide range of psychiatric subjects and what may be considered his principal work, *On Obscure Diseases of the Brain, and Disorders of the Mind*, was published in 1860. Not unnaturally, much of his writing was partisan, tending to favour private-madhouse proprietors.

---

[1] Allen, M. (1833), *Allen versus Dutten*.
[2] Full title quoted in the Bibliography.
[3] R.C.P.L. Lib., 329/MSS. 61 (WAR).   [4] *Vide supra*, p. 93.

5

Some Contemporary Descriptions of Nineteenth-Century Private Licensed Houses

◇•◇

D URING the first half of the nineteenth century, the range of accommodation available in private licensed houses was extremely varied. As a result, it is difficult to describe the structure and pattern of life in a typical establishment. Instead, the available information has to be used to provide a picture of private madhouses in general, supplemented, wherever possible, by more detailed sketches of individual houses, which illustrate the conditions prevailing at a particular period in their history. Contemporary descriptions of licensed houses during the nineteenth century, in particular the first half of the century, are, unfortunately, not numerous and data used to provide more detailed accounts usually have to be gleaned from a wide variety of sources; in only a few instances has it been possible to corroborate the facts derived from a single source.

Manuscript material has provided very few detailed descriptive accounts of individual houses. The value of such material as does exist emerges, however, when the scattered details and fragmentary items of information from various sources are pieced together. The reports of the Visiting Magistrates and Commissioners in Lunacy provide the main body of such material. Prior to 1842, when the Metropolitan Commissioners first visited provincial licensed houses, the Visiting Magistrates' Minutes were, in general, not detailed. Subsequently, however, the details included regularly, in particular by the Commissioners, allow a fairly clear impression to be obtained of individual establishments; the type of accommodation offered; the clientele catered for; the attitudes of the proprietors and staff; the range of facilities for recreation and employment; the diet; the religious activities and the therapeutic régime. From 1828 onwards, the surviving plans of private licensed houses aid the reconstruction of a more precise picture of these establishments. The account, given in Chapter 6, of the private licensed houses at Hook Norton and Witney, demonstrates the extent to which surviving records can be employed. Neither of these houses had any particular claim to fame but each is broadly typical of many other English provincial private licensed houses in the nineteenth century. The house at Witney was a small establishment, opened in the third decade of the century and catering primarily for middle-class patients; whilst that at Hook Norton exemplifies an establishment, with roots in the eighteenth century, which was expanded in the fourth decade of the nineteenth century to accommodate a greatly increased number of pauper lunatics.

A representative example of late-eighteenth century Visitors' Minutes is provided by those made in 1776, following the inspection of William Roadknight's house at Henley-in-Arden, Warwickshire. After a preamble about the statutory provisions for licensing and the appointment of Visitors and after listing the names of the patients (seven females and one male) the report continues:

And we also report that we found the said house and the apartments of all the lunaticks neat and in good condition and the lunaticks themselves furnished with proper accommodations and under due care and management and that for the confinement of each lunatick there appears to be an order in writing duly made out under the hand and seal of a physician, surgeon or apothecary.[1]

The observations were no more precise in entries made twenty years later and the same formula was used in the reports on all three licensed houses in the county. Even during the period when Dr John Conolly was a Medical Visitor to the Warwickshire licensed houses, little meaningful information was included and the observations made were brief and couched in very general terms.[2] Minutes signed by Dr James Cowles Prichard, when acting as a Medical Visitor to the Gloucestershire private licensed houses, 1826–8, were similarly brief. The principal observation in these particular minutes was

[1] Warwicks. C.R.O., Q.S. 24/a/1/6, Minutes V.M., 16 April 1776.
[2] *Ibid.*, 1824–8.

usually: 'Nothing was remarked in the state of the house or of the patients that requires to be noticed.'[1]

Several exceptions have been discovered, however, to the general tendency on the part of early-nineteenth-century Visitors' Minutes to be stereotyped and lacking in detail. One such exception was provided by the relatively lengthy report made by the Gloucestershire Visitors in October 1816, following their inspection of Cox's house, at Fishponds, near Bristol.[2] This particular report provides an illustration of the repercussions of the publicity attached to the findings of the 1815–16 Select Committee, which had the effect of increasing the diligence of the Visitors, although the improvement, unfortunately, was often only shortlived. In their Minutes, the Visitors noted:

Not till we had known the proceedings in Parliament concerning madhouses did we consider it our duty to do more than to ascertain whether the individuals confined were in a state of mental derangement. This is the reason that the minutes taken at our inspections have not before been accompanied by observations.[3]

The Visitors went on to state that, subsequently:

we met with no delay, as we generally had done on former occasions (for the purpose we presume of putting the patients and their apartments in order) in proceeding to an immediate inspection tho' it was evident that our visit had not been expected.[4]

The ensuing account of Fishponds in fact, provides one of the most detailed descriptions available of a provincial madhouse at this period.

The house contained fifty-seven patients and, as was generally the case at this establishment, there was a preponderance of men over women. There were nine 'servants' (i.e. attendants), five of whom were male; in addition, two ladies had their own female servants in personal attendance. Six patients (one man and five women) were under restraint, the apparatus in use being the strait-waistcoat, manacles, handcuffs, leglocks, wire-masks, various types of straps and a 'great chair'.[5] Twenty-one patients were receiving some form of medical treatment. The classification and separation of patients according to their condition and behaviour was minimal, apart from the segregation of idiots from the others. The Visitors reported only a

[1] Glos. R.O., Q/AL. 39, Minutes V.M., 23 Jan. 1826, entry made following the inspection of Ridgeway House, Stapleton, kept by Nehemiah Duck, surgeon.
[2] Glos. R.O., Q/AL. 39, Minutes V.M., 11 Oct. 1816.
[3] *Ibid.*   [4] *Ibid.*   [5] Presumably a restraining chair.

single 'outrageous' patient, whose 'cries could be distinctly heard in a large part of the men's cells ... as well as in the court'. The accommodation included three sitting-rooms for the men and two for the women and, although those on the ground floor were gloomy and damp, these rooms were clean. Only three of the bedrooms contained more than one bed and, as far as could be seen, there was only one patient per bed. Outside, there was a large walled garden for the women to exercise in, and a courtyard for 'the worst description of patients'. The men had a shrubbery, a walled flower garden and a similar courtyard, the latter being for the use of the most disturbed patients. It was reported that the women occupied themselves at needlework, but there was no reference to the employment of the men, who amused themselves with card games, culvers, backgammon, chess and draughts. Slipper and shower baths were in use but there was only one pump. The Visitors received no complaints from the patients, but they did make reference to the use of restraint, 'confinement' (probably solitary) and the circular swing as punitive measures; the principal inducement for good behaviour being increased personal liberty.

Many of the accounts of individual houses given in printed sources are concerned with the abuses and defects perpetrated in them and the evidence derived from this type of source will be described, therefore, in Chapter 8. Descriptions of houses which figured in evidence given before various Select Committees fall into this category chiefly. However, the Commissioners in Lunacy did include short accounts of all metropolitan and provincial licensed houses in their reports of 1860[1] and 1862[2] respectively. These accounts are of considerable interest and, generally, each comprises a brief description of the asylum, details concerning the licensees, remarks on the previous history of the house, especially if it had been unfavourable and observations on its current state. Nevertheless, it follows that the number of sources whose main content is descriptive rather than condemnatory is very limited, with regard to provincial private-madhouses. One example of such a source is provided by a pamphlet, published anonymously in 1860, in which a visit to Laverstock House, Wiltshire, is described[3] and the content of this pamphlet will

[1] Fourteenth Report (1860) C.L., pp. 18–60.
[2] Sixteenth Report (1862) C.L., pp. 8–52. (A further review was included in the Twenty-sixth Report (1872) C.L., pp. 31–48.)
[3] Anon. (1860), *Our Holiday at Laverstock House Asylum.*

be referred to later. Nineteenth-century autobiographies sometimes provide an interesting source of anecdotal details about madhouses, for example, J. Hollingshead (1895) referred to Whitmore House and Hoxton House, Hoxton.[1] Interesting information may be gleaned, nevertheless, from accounts of houses which were incorporated in certain works whose primary purpose was the denunciation of the private-madhouse system, as, for example, J. T. Perceval's descriptions of his stay at Brislington House and at Ticehurst Asylum during the period 1831 to 1834.[2] Amongst accounts of metropolitan licensed houses, those by Paternoster (1841) of Finch's house, Kensington; Brooke House, Clapton and Blacklands House, Chelsea, may be singled out for their detailed quality, although their context was one of fierce censure of the madhouse system. The following is an extract from Paternoster's description of Brooke House, which was owned at that time by Henry Monro, M.D., F.R.C.P.:

It is licensed for fifty patients, who are under the charge of the Misses Pettingal, Dr Monro residing in Cavendish-square, and going only occasionally to Clapton to give general orders and arrange accounts . . . The present number of patients . . . is males-16, and females 20. The house is an old fashioned dilapidated place, to which a modern front has been attached, which fails to give any idea of what the interior is. The situation is low and damp, and devoid of any prospect. Immediately behind the house is a grass-plot, of about thirty paces square, surrounded by a high wall. This, with the exception of the gravel walk round it, was entirely under water. Beyond was an extensive kitchen-garden in which the female prisoners . . . were allowed to walk . . . Not one foot of pleasure garden, no flowers, no shady walks, no seats, nothing whatever pretty or agreeable.[3]

Paternoster stated that he was informed that attempts to drain the ground had been made at great expense. In the corner of the 'green swamp' was, 'a gloomy-looking building of about seven feet square' which was 'a cell for the refractory'. In the female section, Paternoster noted that individual rooms led out of 'long galleries, some looking into a small court-yard, surrounded by buildings, and some into the green swamp where the male prisoners are allowed to walk round and round. They were most wretchedly furnished with old-fashioned latticed windows, letting the wind in so as to defy all attempts at keeping them warm . . . and with thick iron bars outside, which would effectually prevent escape.'[4] Many metropolitan

[1] Hollingshead, J. (1895), *My Lifetime*, Vol. I, pp. 2, 5, 6.
[2] Perceval, J. T. (1838 and 1840), *A Narrative of the Treatment experienced by a Gentleman, during a State of Mental Derangement*.
[3] Paternoster, *op. cit.*, p. 9.   [4] *Ibid.*, p. 30.

licensed houses suffered, in contrast with provincial houses, from the lack of adequate ground-space around the establishment. For example, at Spring Vale, Staffordshire (Plate III), regarded by its proprietor, T. Bakewell, as a model madhouse, there were extensive pleasure grounds and waste lands attached to the house, together with an airing ground for the male patients, measuring, approximately, sixty feet by twenty feet, which was called 'Bethlem' as, in the words of Bakewell, 'it is considered a sort of punishment to be put there, and they [i.e. the patients] are only there in case of behaving amiss'.[1]

In 1856, Conolly contrasted the 'new system in private asylums' with that prevailing earlier in the century. At that time, madhouses

were generally distinguishable from all the houses in the neighbourhood by their dismal appearance: their exterior was as gloomy as their interior was dirty. Heavy gates, a neglected shrubbery, windows heavily barred, doors clumsily locked prepared the visitor for rooms which, although rooms of reception, had an air of cold discomfort and shabby finery.[2]

He acknowledged, however, that, by the time of writing, most private asylums no longer had the outward appearance of places of confinement. Earlier on, in 1850, an anonymous author, possibly Conolly, provided a graphic description of what he termed 'an ordinary middle class establishment of the present day'.[3] The author described an imaginary visit to one such establishment, which, undoubtedly, bore resemblance to many contemporary provincial houses. The writer suggested that it was likely to be a large brick-built mansion, once the residence of a wealthy merchant or banker, then used perhaps as a school until it was taken over by a medical man for use as an asylum. The accommodation would be arranged according to the fees charged, there being three classes of paying patients. Two guineas per week would be the fee if use of the comfortable parlour was required; one guinea per week was charged for more crowded conditions and the lowest rate would be fifteen to sixteen shillings per week. The author suggested that the bedrooms would be very much after the fashion of a ladies' boarding school, with white dimity curtains and chintz hangings at the windows. There would be a garden, perhaps an orchard and a meadow for outdoor exercise and recreation.

---

[1] Minutes of evidence 1815 S.C., p. 122.
[2] Conolly, J. (1856), *op. cit.*, p. 138.
[3] Anon. (1850), *Familiar Views of Lunacy and Lunatic Life*, p. 158.

Printed advertisements for private madhouses

Printed advertisements constitute an interesting and rewarding source of information about private-madhouses. Such advertisements can be divided into the following categories: advertisements appearing in newspapers, journals and books; handbills, leaflets, brochures and reports; advertisements in medical directories and in works on insanity written by the proprietors of private madhouses, in order, to a lesser or greater extent, to publicize and recommend their own establishments. The latter category includes works by Irish,[1] Fallowes,[2] Faulkner[3] and T. Bakewell.[4] J. G. Millingen (1840) contemptuously disregarded the importance of such works, which he described as 'merely verbose prospectuses of private establishments ... [containing] an ad captandum collection of cures'.[5] Although this statement may be true in the case of the early-eighteenth-century writers, publications by later authors, such as T. Bakewell, showed greater balance and less bias and are, therefore, of some value as source material.

Advertisements for private madhouses in newspapers and journals date, at least, from the beginning of the eighteenth century. One of the earliest advertisements of this kind was that for a madhouse at Clerkenwell, London, which appeared in *Post Boy* in 1700, and an extract from this advertisement reads as follows:

In Clerkenwell-Close, where the figure of mad people are over the gate; liveth one, who by the blessing of God, cures all lunatick distracted or mad people, he seldom exceeds 3 months in the cure of the maddest person that comes in his house, several have been cur'd in a fortnight, and some in less time; he has cur'd several from Bedlam and other mad-houses in and about this city, and has conveniency for people of what quality soever. No cure—no money.[6]

The principle of the 'money refund guarantee' was a popular one and another good example is afforded in the advertisement for

---

[1] Irish, *op. cit.*   [2] Fallowes, *op. cit.*

[3] Faulkner, B. (1789), *Observations on the General and Improper Treatment of Insanity.* (Faulkner's madhouse at Little Chelsea, London, was unique, in that it was run as a 'free house', where the patients were attended by their own physicians and the proprietor provided only board, lodging and the attendants.)

[4] Bakewell, T. (1809), *op. cit.*

[5] Millingen, J. G. (1840), *Aphorisms on the Treatment and Management of the Insane*, p.v.

[6] *The Post Boy*, No. 741, 1700. Cited by Tuke, D. H. (1882), *op. cit.*, pp. 92–3.

Joseph Mason's house at Turvey's Corner, Fishponds, near Bristol, in 1740:

This is to give notice that Dr. Joseph Mason . . . undertakes to cure Hypochondriacs, Mad and Distracted People, with great success . . . No Cure, No Pay. Boarding excepted . . . N.B. He will undertake to cure the King's Evil. No Cure, No Pay, if the Bones be not foul.[1]

A search of provincial newspapers for the last two decades of the eighteenth century yields many advertisements and this method of advertising continued during the first half of the nineteenth century, though it was later accompanied by the use of other, and more appropriate, media for publicity, for example, the medical directories. The advertisement for the private madhouse at Hook Norton, which appeared in *Jackson's Oxford Journal* in 1778, is reproduced in Figure 4. The majority of nineteenth-century newspaper advertisements contain few precise details, but the emphasis placed on certain aspects of management, particularly early in the century, reflects, clearly, the attitudes and requirements of the public and the extent of its suspicion of the private-madhouse system. Attempts were made, consistently, to convince the public both of the integrity and high ideals of the proprietor and of the humanity of the treatment, which, it was emphasized, would be directed, indisputably, towards the restoration of the patient.[2] Thus, an advertisement for Sculcoates Refuge, Hull, at the time of its opening in 1814, states categorically: 'In this Institution every attempt consistent with humanity, will be made to restore the patient. No coercion, no restraint, but what is absolutely necessary to protect the attendant, and to prevent self-destruction, will ever be employed', and the overall mode of treatment was likened to that practised at the York Retreat.[3] An advertisement of 1823, for the licensed house at Fairford, Gloucestershire, is typical of many at this time and is, therefore, quoted in full:

Establishment for Insane Persons, by Alexander Iles.

A. Iles begs to inform the public, and those persons who may be disposed to commit to his charge individuals of both sexes suffering under mental

---

[1] Gloucester City Lib., *Gloucester Journal*, 25 Nov. 1740.

[2] Even in *c.* 1674, these sentiments were expressed by Newton in an advertisement for his madhouse at Clerkenwell: ''Tis not more my own than others good I aim at; nor do I seek more to cure the rich for reward than the poor gratis, but I labour by all means to cure both, rather than keep either in my house for advantage'. B.M., C. 112, f. 9.

[3] Kingston-upon-Hull Central Lib. (Local history), *Hull Advertiser*, 7 May 1814, p. 2.

LUNATICS.

HAYDOCK LODGE LUNATIC ASYLUM,

(Near Newton Railway Station, half-way between Liverpool and Manchester.) Under the Superintendence of Mr. MOTT, late one of her Majesty's Poor Law Assistant Commissioners.

The healthy situation and eligibility of HAYDOCK LODGE are too well known in the county of Lancaster, and adjoining counties, to need remark.

The noble mansion stands within a spacious park, secluded from the public sight, and is connected with suitable attached and detached buildings, and large walled gardens. It is surrounded by about 370 acres of land, in a ring-fence. The establishment affords facilities for recreation, healthful and interesting employment, superior to those attainable in any similar Asylum in England, or indeed in Europe.

It is conducted upon the system of non-restraint and kind moral treatment, so successfully employed by Dr. Connolly, and now followed at the Hanwell Middlesex County Asylum, forming a most gratifying contrast with the cruel and disgraceful treatment Pauper Lunatics were formerly subject to.

The Medical Department is under the direction of the eminent Physicians, Dr. R. Baron Howard, of Manchester, and Dr. James Vose, of Liverpool, with the constant attention of an experienced resident Surgeon.

The most experienced Keepers and Nurses have been engaged, of known humanity and good temper, to insure to the Patients the kindest and most careful treatment.

Bowls, books, and amusing periodicals, are provided for recreation.

The dietary has been fixed under the sanction of the Medical Officers of the Establishment; and will be varied, under their direction, as circumstances may require.

Haydock Lodge is about a mile-and-a half from the Newton Station, forming a junction of the railways from Birmingham, Lancaster, Leeds, &c.; thus affording a ready conveyance from the surrounding districts of Lancashire, Cheshire, the West Riding of Yorkshire, and Westmoreland, and from all parts of England, having access to the great railroads.

Careful Keepers and Nurses will be sent to take charge of Patients to the Asylum, on application for that purpose.

Forms for the admission of Pauper Patients, with proper certificates for the Medical Officers, may be had at the Asylum.

A large portion of the Establishment and of the Grounds, is set apart and furnished for the reception of PRIVATE PA-TIENTS.

₊ The charge for Maintenance is SEVEN SHILLINGS PER WEEK; a rate of charge which the cheapness of provisions in the neighbourhood, and the largeness and advantageous situation of the establishment renders possible; and which is so low as to reimburse in a few weeks the cost of travelling of a patient from any part of England or Wales.

Figure 1 Advertisement for Haydock Lodge Lunatic Asylum, Lancashire, in the *Caernarvon and Denbigh Herald*, 1844

104

affliction, that at his establishment the utmost attention will be paid to their comfort, health, and safety, without resorting to the unfeeling mode of confinement in irons, or severe treatment. Those whose malady will admit of liberty of person will be allowed the free use and enjoyment of large gardens, and such recreations as they may be disposed to engage in, under the superintendence of proper guardians. Terms in proportion to the care and attention each individual may require.[1]

As the century progressed, the advertisements tended to become more verbose and more flamboyant and that for Haydock Lodge Lunatic Asylum, in 1844,[2] illustrates this point well (Figure 1).

A *Medical Register*, edited by S. F. Simmons,[3] was published in 1779 and appeared in a number of editions. The first consecutive medical directories in this country were published in 1845[4] and, from the outset, the annual directory was used as a medium for advertisement by a small number of licensed houses. Thus, in the 1845 *Medical Directory of Great Britain*, three houses were advertised; ten houses were named in the *London and Provincial Directory* for 1847 and fourteen in the 1851 edition. In the course of the ensuing discussion, the content of the advertisements appearing in the 1845, 1847 and 1851 medical directories is reviewed, in order to illustrate the principal characteristics of advertisements printed in this source. These advertisements, like those in newspapers, provide little precise information about individual houses and their chief value lies in the composite picture that they afford of the more publicity-seeking, mid-nineteenth-century private licensed houses. In some cases, biographical details relating to the proprietors, their families and the staff are provided and, occasionally, there is reference to the history of the establishment. A large part of most of these advertisements is taken up by an account of the licensed house, its site and grounds, the type of accommodation available and the facilities for recreation. It is significant that, in many cases, it is stressed that the premises possessed the character of a gentleman's residence, a feature that became increasingly important during the second half of the century, when private asylums catered primarily for the middle and upper classes. Indeed, in most cases, the advertisements emphasize the fact

---

[1] Bod. Lib., N.G.A., Oxon. a4, *Jackson's Oxford Journal*, No. 3653, 3 May 1823, p. 3.

[2] U.C.N.W. Lib., *Caernarvon and Denbigh Herald*, 11 May 1844.

[3] 1750–1813, physician to St Luke's Hospital, 1781–1811, and owner of a private madhouse.

[4] *The Medical Directory of Great Britain and Ireland*, 1845. *The London Medical Directory*, 1845–7. *The London and Provincial Medical Directory*, 1847 on.

that the establishments were particularly suitable for patients from these social classes. Francis Willis, proprietor of Shillingthorpe House, Lincolnshire (1847), went beyond this, stating that his house was 'exclusively adapted for persons moving in the upper ranks of society' (Figure 2). Private apartments were offered for the wealthier classes; for example, at Fishponds, Gloucestershire (1847), separate cottages were provided in the grounds to ensure a high degree of

SHILLINGTHORPE HOUSE,
NEAR STAMFORD, LINCOLNSHIRE.

THIS ASYLUM for the INSANE was established by the celebrated Dr. Francis Willis, who had the happiness of restoring his Majesty George the Third from the serious malady with which he was afflicted, in 1788.

It is now conducted by his grandson, Dr. Francis Willis, Fellow of the Royal College of Physicians, in the style of a country gentleman's residence.

It is exclusively adapted for persons moving in the upper ranks of society.

The Invalids are separately provided for in their own private apartments, and do not associate with each other, unless they are capable of joining Dr. Willis's family.

The numbers are very limited.

Figure 2 Advertisement for Shillingthorpe House, Lincolnshire, in the *London and Provincial Medical Directory*, 1847

privacy, a practice that was quite widely adopted at this time. Clearly, the trend was to maintain, wherever possible, the atmosphere of a private dwelling. If well enough, the patients could be treated in the manner of guests of the family of the proprietor or superintendent. Thus, at the Oulton Retreat, Staffordshire (1845), owned by S. G. Bakewell, quiet and convalescent patients were allowed to attend prayers with the proprietor's family and it was stated that: 'The ladies usually occupy the same apartments with Mrs Bakewell [i.e. the proprietor's mother] and her daughters and are accompanied by them in walks and drives.' There is evidence in some reports of the Commissioners and Visiting Magistrates that the advertised claims to treat patients in a 'domestic' setting were, in fact, realized in a number of licensed houses.

The qualifications and experience of the proprietor or superintendent of the house are mentioned in most advertisements appearing in medical directories, and brief reference is made, in a few instances, to the past achievements of the establishment. Thus, S. G. Bakewell referred, in 1845, to the success of his father, Thomas Bakewell, in the period before the asylum was transferred from Spring Vale. Thomas Allis, the non-medical superintendent at Fern Hail, Osbaldwick, York (1851), was recommended as having been, for more than eighteen years, superintendent of the Friends' Retreat, where he had 'directed the moral treatment of the patients'. The attendants also receive their share of recommendation in these advertisements. In addition to the term attendant, it is interesting to note that they were referred to, variously, as carefully selected 'companions, whose liberal education and moral temperament are in every way calculated to alleviate suffering and facilitate recovery' (Westbrook House, Hampshire, 1845); as humane, respectable 'servants' (Fishponds, 1847); and as 'superintendents' (Laverstock House, Wiltshire, 1847), where, it was claimed, there were forty such persons of 'humanity and experience'.

The existence of extensive and attractive gardens and pleasure grounds was a feature that was stressed in most of these advertisements. Thus, the Oulton Retreat (1845) was described as 'beautifully situated in a retired and healthy neighbourhood; on a warm and sheltered, but elevated site, commanding a cheerful and extensive prospect', and there was, in addition, a small farm attached to the premises. Typical forms of the amusements supplied included books, music, indoor games such as bagatelle and, out-of-doors, bowling, and the use of a carriage. There are many references to provisions for religious activities, always according to the Church of England,[1] and there were private chapels at the larger houses, such as Fishponds and Laverstock House (1847). There are very few references to the methods of treatment employed and, in some instances, a great deal is left to the imagination of the reader. Thus, at Castleton Lodge Retreat, Leeds (1845), it was stated that:

Mental occupation is encouraged by every possible means—every opportunity being embraced and cultivated which can have a tendency to conciliate the esteem and gain the confidence of the patient, always avoiding the subject of mental aberration ... all circumstances are ... strictly

---

[1] The only establishment known to the writer whose patients were restricted to members of a particular denomination was St George's Retreat, Burgess Hill, near Brighton, opened in 1870 for Roman Catholics.

attended to which will have a tendency to impart pleasure and content-ment.

Presumably, such a description was aimed at indicating the humane system employed and this is confirmed by the comment that the patients seemed 'kindly treated', which had formed part of a report by the Commissioners in Lunacy and which was quoted in the ad-vertisement. It was claimed that moral treatment had been adopted at the Fairford Retreat, Gloucestershire (1851), 'when it was both unpopular and unprofitable to do so, but it has since reaped a rich reward in the number of its cures and in the happiness of its in-mates'. The subject of mechanical restraint was either avoided or referred to in veiled terms. At Westbrook House (1845), treatment was effected 'with the least possible display of direct control, and an entire absence of severity'. At Castleton Lodge in the same year, 'every appearance of restraint' was avoided as far as possible, 'especially in mild or incipient cases'. The use of medical treatment received little attention, but at Fishponds (1847) its value was stressed, since it was believed, at this house, that insanity was depen-dent upon physical disorders of the nervous system. The establish-ments which employed a form of advertisement having such a wide circulation were prepared, clearly, to receive patients from any part of the country. Thus, it was claimed with regard to Castleton Lodge (1845) that 'experienced attendants can be sent for patients of either sex to any part of the Kingdom'. Similarly, it was stated, in a news-paper advertisement, that the geographical position of Haydock Lodge Lunatic Asylum afforded 'a ready conveyance from the sur-rounding districts . . . and from all parts of England, having access to the great railroads'[1] (Figure 1).

Finally, with regard to this category of printed advertisements, reference must be made to those which were printed, occasionally, on the fly-leaves of medical and other books. An example of this practice is afforded by the advertisement for Castleton Lodge Retreat, which appeared, in 1838, in an edition of a medical work by the proprietor, Samuel Hare, surgeon.[2]

The proprietors of many private licensed houses issued handbills, leaflets and brochures to publicize the achievements and advantages of their establishments. For example, in 1817, an *Account of Patients*

---

[1] U.C.N.W. Lib., *Caernarvon and Denbigh Herald*, 11 May 1844.
[2] Hare, S. (1838), *Practical Observations on the Causes and Treatment of Curvatures of the Spine.*

at the Lunatic Hospital Newcastle upon Tyne, for the period 1764 to 1817, was published.[1] The date suggests that this report was prepared in response to an enquiry into the affairs of the establishment by the Newcastle Common Council, an investigation which itself was prompted by publicity given to the findings of the 1815–16 Select Committee. Simple statistics were given to demonstrate that the cure rate at this house equalled that in better-known establishments. In 1830, a prospectus was issued, concerning Ticehurst Asylum, Sussex, entitled *Views of Messrs. Newington's Private Asylum for the Cure of Insane Persons, Ticehurst, Sussex.*[2] It comprises copies of recent Visitors' Minutes, lithographic views of the asylum, ground plans and a map of the premises and pleasure grounds, but it included no information about the types of patient received or the mode of treatment. A brochure about Haydock Lodge was issued in *c.* 1845 and included a view of the impressive mansion (Plate II). A similar type of illustrated brochure was printed for Brislington House.[3] In keeping with the rather elaborate descriptions of the asylums, the illustrations in these brochures and other contemporary engravings generally portrayed the establishments in a characteristically romanticized style, emphasizing the idyllic grace and peacefulness of the setting. A view of Spring Vale, dated 1838, is a representative example (Plate III). An interesting leaflet by Samuel Millard, surgeon, proprietor of Whitchurch Asylum, Herefordshire, appeared in 1840.[4] Millard was anxious to encourage the referral of local pauper lunatics to his house and he attempted to demonstrate that the most effective and economical way of treating lunatics was in private licensed houses, such as his own establishment. The statistics quoted by Millard are referred to in a further section. The livelihood of many proprietors depended upon the reception of a full complement of pauper lunatics. In an advertisement of July 1851, Mrs Gowland, the proprietress of Wrekenton Lunatic Asylum, Co. Durham, expressed, 'her sincere thanks to the public and to the parochial and Union authorities who have so kindly patronized her establishment'[5] (Figure 3).

The forms of advertisement that have been considered, naturally,

[1] Newcastle upon Tyne City Lib., L. 042, L.Tr.dy 51.
[2] E. Sussex C.R.O., QAL/1/2/E.2, 1830.
[3] The brochures for Haydock Lodge Institution and Brislington House are by courtesy of Dr R. A. Hunter.
[4] Hereford Asylum, later called Portland House. R.O., Q/ALL/98.
[5] Durham C.R.O., *Durham County Directory* (Hagar & Co.), 1851.

WREKENTON
LUNATIC ASYLUM.

ESTABLISHED. IN THE YEAR 1825.

PROPRIETRESS:
MRS. GOWLAND.

SUPERINTENDENTS:
MALE DEPARTMENT—MR. JOHN GOWLAND.
FEMALE DEPARTMENT—MRS. FLECK.

Mrs. Gowland returns her sincere thanks to the public and to the parochial and Union authorities who have so kindly patronized her establishment.

She can confidently refer to the official visitors who regularly inspect the house and the condition of the inmates as a sufficient guarantee for the judicious treatment of those whose misfortune has rendered such an asylum necessary for their condition.

The dietary table for the Patients is of the most generous description, and their health and contentedness afford the best evidence of the success of the arrangements made for their security and improvement.

The house is situated on an elevated site in the parish of Gateshead, and commands an extensive prospect over the Team Valley. There is a farm of land attached to the establishment, whereon those patients who are sufficiently well to go at large, can receive healthy exercise and recreation.

This Asylum was established twenty-six years ago by Mrs. Gowland and her late husband, and from that long experience she can speak confidently of her successful arrangements.

THE TERMS ARE EXCEEDINGLY MODERATE.

Wrekenton, July, 1851.

Figure 3 Advertisement for the Wrekenton Lunatic Asylum, Co. Durham, in the *Durham County Directory*, 1851

provide no impartial information about the licensed houses concerned and this lack of objective information must have made it difficult for those members of the public who were obliged to select a private madhouse for the accommodation of relatives or friends. It is likely that the advice of a physician was relied upon, although this trust could be abused, as proprietors often made private arrangements with physicians to recommend their establishments. One contemporary commentator drew attention to the injurious effects which exaggerated, flamboyant advertisements had on the public and professional reputation of proprietors and he noted: 'If a man imagines that by investing £300 or £400 a-year in puffing advertisements, he will escape from his legitimate insignificance, and fill his asylum with patients, he will find, to his cost, that he has much overrated both the credulity of the public and profession.'[1] Thirty years earlier, in an attempt to remedy the deficiency of impartial information, Burrows (1820) advocated the publication of regular returns, with annual reports, to provide a clear, comparative statement of the therapeutic results in every asylum in the country.[2] T. Prichard, M.D., F.R.C.P. Edin., M.R.C.P. Lond., proprietor of Abington Abbey, Northampton, from 1845 to 1877, recommended that greater publicity be given to the achievements of private licensed houses and stressed the need to allow the general public to have the opportunity to compare the results of treatment in licensed houses with those in other types of establishment. In 1859, he wrote:

We [i.e. proprietors of private asylums] should invite enquiry, publish correct statements of our proceedings, and give the public an opportunity of comparing our success in the treatment of insanity with that met with in public establishments. Had we done this hitherto, much that has been lately written to our disparagement would never have been published; or, if published, could have been readily refuted by a simple reference to facts.[3]

Such ideas were expressed in a series of reports relating to Abington Abbey, which Prichard addressed chiefly to the Visiting Magistrates. Prichard's sensitivity about the shortcomings of private licensed houses and their proprietors provides a clue to the reasons which lay behind his decision to change the status of the establishment in 1848.

[1] Editorial (1852), 'Private Asylums', *J. Psychol. Med. & Ment. Path. V*, p. 160.
[2] Burrows (1820), *op. cit.*, p. 279.
[3] Prichard, T. (1859), *Statistical Report of Cases of Insanity treated in Abington Abbey, Northampton*, pp. 7–8.

The surviving records provide no clarification, as they date only from 1853. Prichard was clearly an ambitious man and he may well have resented running a private licensed house in Northampton, where, previously, his father had superintended the public subscription asylum so competently. His reports certainly represented a serious attempt by a private licensed house proprietor to allow his own house to compete on even terms with public establishments. However, his recommendations were not, in fact, adopted by more than a few licensed houses and the importance which Prichard attached to statistics was criticized strongly, in 1860, by Bucknill in the *Journal of Mental Science*.[1]

Four better-known provincial licensed houses

A series of notes is now given relating to four prominent provincial licensed houses. These cannot be comprehensive in either their descriptive or historical content, but seek to depict some aspects of the conditions which prevailed at these houses at specific periods, together with some relevant biographical and historical details.

(1) Brislington House, near Bristol, Somerset

This establishment was one of the most reputable provincial licensed houses in the early-nineteenth century and was, undoubtedly, the finest of the small number of purpose-built houses. Fortunately, there are numerous references to the establishment in contemporary printed sources, and some MS. material relating to it has survived also. The amalgamation of information from these sources allows a relatively detailed picture of the establishment to be constructed. Edward Long Fox (1761–1835), M.D. Edin., started building this house in 1804, and it was completed by 1806.[2] Brislington House was situated not far distant from the small Quaker madhouse at Cleeve Hill, Downend, near Bristol, which Fox ran during the period 1794 to 1806, and it is interesting to note that there was considerable local opposition to the building of the new asylum. Fox was a leading physician in Bristol and the West of England and was on the staff of the Bristol Royal Infirmary from 1784 to 1816. He was among the first licensed-house proprietors to practise humane methods of treat-

---

[1] Bucknill, J. C. (1860), 'Annual Reports of Lunatic Asylums', *J. Ment. Sci.* 6, pp. 509–11.

[2] Minutes of evidence 1828, S.C.H.L., J.H.L., Vol. 60, p. 710.

ment based upon the abolition of restraint, and he was certainly the first to do so on as large a scale as was practised at Brislington House. His achievements, in this respect, seriously rival those of Samuel Tuke. A biographical sketch by one of his grandsons describes how he was commanded, on an unspecified date,[1] to Windsor to see, in consultation, George III, and was requested to take charge of the King, although he declined to do so.[2] In 1828 he was called to give evidence before the Select Committee of the House of Lords and, in the following year, he gave up the management of the establishment to two of his sons, Drs F. K. and C. J. Fox. In 1836, following their father's death, they carried out extensive alterations and wrote a pamphlet[3] on the house. Further major reconstruction was carried out later, in 1850. During the first half of the nineteenth century, the average number of patients confined at Brislington House was in the region of ninety and a small number of pauper patients was received until 1838.[4] Brislington House remained open until 1951, under the management of successive members of the Fox family[5] and the building is now used as a nurses' hostel.

According to the first printed notice for Brislington House, Fox built a new house because, although conditions at Cleeve Hill 'were as good as any he had seen (and he had visited the most celebrated in the nation) he was satisfied that they were improvable'.[6] The following description of Brislington House, in its early years, is based on accounts of c. 1806,[7] 1809[8] and 1836.[9] The institution comprised a series of eight houses which were connected at the basement level and were so designed as to provide the optimum degree of classifica-

[1] 1811, according to Macalpine and Hunter, *op. cit.*, p. 327.
[2] Fox, A. (1906), 'A Short Account of Brislington House, 1804–1906', B.H.Q.N.C.N., p. 5. (This item by courtesy of Mrs E. M. Fox, Swiss Cottage, Brislington House, who was the last proprietor, 1947–51.)
[3] Fox, F. K. and C. J. (1836), 'History and Present State of Brislington House, near Bristol'. Reprinted in B.H.Q.N.C.N., pp. 16–23.
[4] *Vide* Table IX^A. (From 1835 to 1837, the house was licensed for 110 patients, including twenty paupers. P.R., 1838, p. 6.)
[5] For details of the Fox family, *vide* (i) Fox, A., *op. cit.*, (ii) Fox, *Genealogical Memoranda relating to the Family of Fox, of Brislington*, 1872.
[6] Reprint of notice re Brislington House, B.H.Q.N.C.N., p. 1.
[7] *Ibid.*, pp. 1–3.
[8] Fox, E. L. (1809), 'An Account of the Establishment of an Asylum for lunatics lately erected near Bristol', in Duncan, A. sen. (ed.), *Observations on the Structure of Hospitals for the Treatment of Lunatics*, pp. 71–7.
[9] Fox, F. K. and C. J., *op. cit.*

tion. The upper storeys of the centre building were partitioned into two sections, each with separate access and there were two large houses on each side of the building. In this way, three classes of accommodation were provided for male and female patients. In addition, there was a small building on each side for the physically sick of both sexes. Those patients who paid most occupied the centre house, where the living-quarters of Fox and his family were sited. Patients in each class had a separate court for exercise and all the patients had separate bedrooms. 'Detached apartments' were provided for each class, in order to accommodate noisy and violent patients and there were also other houses on the estate, where wealthy patients could 'pursue any style of living and expense', attended by their own servants and one attendant appointed by the proprietor. It was noted, in 1836, that, 'many of the houses and cottages in the neighbouring parishes are also fitted up and appropriated to this purpose, and are more particularly adapted for those patients whose cases do not require . . . a separation from their own family circle'. Fire risk was taken into account during the planning and, wherever possible, iron was substituted for wood.[1] Heating was provided by guarded open fires, with warm-air flues in some areas to protect 'the more furious who discard clothing'. There were provisions for 'warm and other baths'; there was a fives court; a room set aside for religious services and, outside, a bowling green. Fox, who was a Quaker, appears to have been the first proprietor to have introduced regular religious observances, according to the Church of England, paying a salary to the local parish clergyman, who officiated at the asylum chapel. His primary intention in so doing was to reproduce within the establishment, whenever possible, patterns of normal social activity. On the basis of the example set at Brislington House, according to Fox, Lord Robert Seymour recommended that a similar practice should be adopted at Bethlem Hospital.[2]

In 1812, the establishment was praised by Paul, despite the fact that he was a strong advocate of public asylums. Paul observed that the facilities afforded at Brislington House were 'probably not exceeded by any thing to be found in the best constructed public buildings for the purpose in England: and . . . it must be admitted,

---

[1] The M.C.L. noted, in 1844, that they knew of only two private licensed houses where the building was designed to be fire proof; most public hospitals were not constructed in this way. 1844 Report M.C.L., p. 14.

[2] Minutes of evidence 1828 S.C.H.L., J.H.L., Vol. 60, p. 714.

that a lunatic patient, placed under the care of Dr. Fox, has the advantage of great skill and experience in the treatment of his disease'.[1] Wakefield, in 1815, described the house as 'delightfully and cheerfully situated',[2] a fact supported by a number of nineteenth-century writers, including the diarist, the Reverend Francis Kilvert. In his diary, in 1874, following a visit to an aunt who was confined at Brislington House, Kilvert wrote: 'Brislington Asylum is a fine palatial-looking building very beautifully situated on the high ground between Keynsham and Bristol.'[3] In 1815, it was surrounded by a twelve-foot wall, but mounds of earth had been raised in the centre of the grounds as vantage points for the patients, without danger of their escape. At that time, there were seventy resident patients and twenty-eight attendants. According to Wakefield, little or no coercion was used and the benefits of occupation, amusement and exercise were stressed. Some female patients had silver pheasants and doves in their courtyard and greyhounds were kept for the patients' amusement. J. W. Rogers (1816), an apothecary, in his work concerning the defects of private madhouses, used the example set by 'the noble and extensive establishment of Dr Fox' to illustrate the fact that the brutal treatment of lunatics in madhouses was unnecessary. Rogers commented that:

The order here observed, the excellence of the food, the healthful cleanliness, and, above all, the humanity which is invariably exercised are truly admirable, and reflect the highest honor on the worthy and enlightened founder. In this asylum when coercion appears necessary, the patient is rather coaxed than frightened into compliance, so that of the numerous patients restored, we never find any one alarmed at the thought or sight of his keeper, but on the contrary impressed with a strong sense of gratitude for the kindness, he has experienced.[4]

The only adverse account of the establishment was provided by J. T. Perceval in 1838 and again in 1840. Writing of his experiences as a patient at Brislington House, from January 1831 to May 1832, he claimed that he was exposed to much degradation and ill-treatment at that 'madhouse, for to call that, or any like that, an asylum, is cruel mockery and revolting duplicity'.[5]

[1] Paul, G. O. (1812), *Observations on the Subject of Lunatic Asylums*, p. 55.
[2] Minutes of evidence 1815 S.C., p. 21.
[3] Plomer, W. (ed.) (1964), *Kilvert's Diary*, pp. 264–6. Entry for 2 Nov. 1874.
[4] Rogers, J. W. (1816), *A Statement of the Cruelties, and Frauds which are practised in Mad-houses*, p. 26. (*Vide infra*, p. 244.)
[5] Perceval (1838), *op. cit.*, p. 91. (*Vide infra*, p. 230.)

(2) *Laverstock House, near Salisbury, Wiltshire*

The date of opening and the early history of this establishment is not known. In 1779, in an advertisement for his house, William Finch stated that for many years he had had 'great success in curing people disordered in their senses' and that 'every person he has had charge of, has, with the blessing of God, been cured and discharged from his house perfectly well'.[1] In 1799, the establishment was taken over by Finch's medically qualified grandson, also named William Finch. The number of admissions to the asylum recorded in the Country Register, during the period 1801 to 1812, suggest that Laverstock House was, at that time, one of the largest provincial licensed houses. The asylum housed over 100 patients throughout the first half of the nineteenth century. Paupers were being received in 1815 and the peak number of paupers which the house was licensed to receive was reached in 1841, when provision was made for fifty paupers and 100 others.[2] Subsequently, the size of the pauper department decreased and it was closed in 1851. The number of private patients which were accommodated diminished slowly during the second half of the century, the licence being for seventy in 1890. The asylum remained in the hands of the Finch family until 1854, when it was continued for a year by J. W. F. Noyes before being taken over by John Warwick, surgeon. In 1858, Dr Bushnan[3] became the proprietor of the establishment, which was not closed until 1955. It is noteworthy that a complete register of patients for the period 1797 to 1955 is still extant.[4]

A printed handbill for the house, headed 'Insanity' and dated 26 December 1807, has survived, and its contents are reproduced in full:

The care of those afflicted with this most distressing of all human calamities must naturally be an object of the greatest solicitude to their relatives and friends. It may therefore be satisfactory to them to be informed, that an establishment many years well known for superior care and attention to patients, in a situation combining every requisite for domestic comfort (the house on a healthy eminence, with many acres of garden and pleasure ground, for the exercise and amusement of the patients, besides every possible advantage from the most skilful medical assistance). Arrange-

[1] Salisbury City Lib., *Salisbury and Winchester Journal*, 8 Feb. 1779.

[2] Wilts. C.R.O., Q.S. lunacy records, accounts of Clerk of Peace, 1828–90.

[3] J. S. Bushnan, M.D., F.R.C.P.E., late Senior Physician at the Metropolitan Free Hospital.

[4] Wilts. C.R.O., Q.S. lunacy records (private asylums).

ments have been made by which the proprietors are enabled to offer apartments and accommodations for persons of the first rank, and for all others, on terms at least as moderate as at any other asylum.

I beg leave further to assure the public, that the great success which has attended the management of this asylum, and the consequent public patronage, far from relaxing my professional exertions, shall operate as an additional stimulus to my efforts for the relief of those labouring under diseased intellect. W. Finch, Surgeon.

P.S.—Patients are attended by Mr F. at their own houses; and careful and experienced servants sent in cases which will not admit of a removal.[1]

This licensed house was not purpose-built but it would appear that extensive modifications had rendered it well adapted for use as an asylum. In 1815, Dr Richard Fowler, the Medical Visitor to the Wiltshire licensed houses, considered that it was as well arranged for the reception and cure of patients 'as attention to private interest will in human nature permit' and he described it as 'infinitely the best private establishment'[2] he had ever seen. Wakefield praised the admirable way in which the house was conducted and, with regard to the management of patients, he observed: 'In this establishment I saw all that Tuke has written realized; and no words in which I can describe it . . . can characterize it in too high terms.[3] Finch appeared as a witness before the 1815 Select Committee and again, in 1828, before the Select Committee of the House of Lords.

The details given in 1815 before the Select Committee, by Finch, Wakefield and Fowler, included a description of a mound raised in the grounds, as at Brislington House, which enabled the patients to be amused by views of the surrounding countryside. There were two houses within 500 yards of the main building which provided privacy for wealthier patients, and nine acres of pleasure grounds for 'superior' patients, with about an acre for the paupers. Strict segregation of patients was maintained according to sex and social status. Finch stressed the value of classification, exercise and employment and very little personal restraint was resorted to. A medical case-book was being kept by him in 1815 and he had also devised medical certificates with attached questionnaires requesting remarkably detailed information. A second copy of Finch's handbill, previously referred to, and dated 1805, included a reference to these forms, which he considered: 'Having too frequently witnessed the

---

[1] Wilts. C.R.O., Britford parish records, 499/27.
[2] Minutes of evidence 1815 S.C., p. 48.　　[3] *Ibid.*, p. 22.

inefficiency of Lunatic Certificates, . . . as most consistent with the Act of Parliament, as well as most satisfactory to the parties concerned.'[1] This questionnaire was a forerunner of the type of document required for private patients after the Madhouse Act of 1828. Like Fox, Finch strongly advocated participation in religious activities and, in 1828, he claimed to be one of the foremost, if not the first, to propose 'spiritual assistance' for patients, although he had reservations about allowing 'patients going indiscriminately to places of worship, particularly where their hallucinations turn in religious points'.[2] In the 1829 Annual Report of the Wiltshire Clerk of the Peace, it was noted that Divine Service was performed every Sunday, 'in a chapel fitted up for the purpose in the garden . . . and which the Visitors report as a very neat and commodious building'.[3]

In 1860, an account was published of a visit, by some fifty medical persons, to the asylum, where they were entertained by the proprietor, Dr Bushnan.[4] The overall picture given was of a spacious, well-conducted asylum catering for the middle and upper classes and the accommodation, recreational facilities, dietary and treatment were described in glowing terms. The mode of classification adopted was 'that necessitated by the stages of the patient's disease and by the social position to which each belongs'[5] and not by the amount of the payment made. With regard to the asylum itself, the anonymous author wrote, 'standing in its own grounds . . . partly hidden from public view by rich umbrageous foliage, Laverstock Asylum, with its extensive gardens, lawns, pleasure grounds and shrubberies all kept in the most perfect order, presents a picture of cheerful retirement and comfort'.[6] Unfortunately, however, there is evidence that during the course of the next few years the management of the establishment deteriorated sharply. In 1865, the Commissioners in Lunacy stated that the house had 'fallen into the hands of a new and non-medical proprietor, who apparently regards it as a money speculation only; and the comforts of the patients have consequently been neglected to a shameful extent'.[7] The Visiting Magistrates threatened not to re-

---

[1] Wilts. C.R.O., Britford parish records, 499/27.

[2] Minutes of evidence 1828 S.C.H.L., J.H.L., Vol. 60, pp. 722–3.

[3] Wilts. C.R.O., Q.S. lunacy records (private asylums), Annual Report (1829) of Clerk of Peace.

[4] Anon. (1860), *Our Holiday at Laverstock House Asylum.*

[5] *Ibid.*, p. 60.   [6] *Ibid.*, p. 57.

[7] Nineteenth Report (1865) C.L., p. 17. (New proprietor not named but co-licensees were Drs Bushnan and S. L. Haynes.)

new the licence unless improvements were made but, subsequently, the reports were more favourable.

(3) *Ticehurst Asylum, Sussex*

This establishment is known to have been opened, in 1792, as a small house for under twenty patients, although it is possible that its history can be traced further back. Subsequently, for more than a century, it was managed by consecutive members of the Newington family.[1] Samuel Newington's house was included (1802–12) in the Country Register and also in the list of houses furnished by Powell before the 1815 Select Committee. In the Parliamentary Return of 1819,[2] however, Ticehurst Lunatic Asylum was included in the list of hospitals and asylums and not amongst the licensed houses; it being indicated, clearly, that there were no private licensed houses in Sussex at that time. Burrows (1820) attributed this circumstance to an error in classification[3] and this explanation seems tenable. Ticehurst was recorded again as a licensed house in the Parliamentary Return of 1826. In the return of 1831, it was indicated that two separate parts of the establishment were licensed, namely, Ticehurst House (later known as Highlands), catering for a few patients only, all of whom had separate apartments, and Ticehurst Asylum, which provided accommodation for about sixty patients. Parish patients were not received. At a later period, a number of other houses were added to the establishment. Throughout the nineteenth century, Ticehurst held a high reputation as an asylum for the wealthier classes and, indeed, in 1900, it was described as 'the Mecca of private asylums', by Dr David Bower, the proprietor of Springfield House, Bedford.[4] Ticehurst remains in active operation, at the present day, as a registered mental nursing home.

In the early-nineteenth century, the houses were set in extensive grounds, covering some fifty acres and these were beautifully laid out, probably in 1816, when the proprietor had utilized the services of the large numbers of local men unemployed after the battle of

---

[1] Newington, H. H. and A. (1901), 'Some Incidents in the History and Practice of Ticehurst Asylum', *J. Ment. Sci. 47*, pp. 62–72. (This paper, by the medical superintendents, was read at the meeting of the S.E. division of the Medico-Psychological Association held at Ticehurst, 10 Oct. 1900.)

[2] P.R., 1819(a).

[3] Burrows (1820), *op. cit.*, p. 292.

[4] (1901), Discussion, meeting of S.E. division of Medico-Psychological Association, *J. Ment. Sci. 47*, p. 73.

Waterloo. By 1900, the estate covered over 300 acres. A brochure, dated 1830,[1] included a series of views of the asylum (Plate IV); the aviary, with its gold and silver pheasants; the bowling green; buildings such as the pagoda and the summer house in the pleasure grounds and several secluded houses on the estate. Groundplans of this time show that the amenities included a music room and a reading room. A serious fire destroyed much of the old asylum in 1852, but, subsequently, spacious new buildings were erected, later known as Ridgeway House. The Visitors' and Commissioners' Minutes for the period 1828 to 1864[2] suggest that the establishment was consistently well conducted. In 1842, it was noted that many patients had separate rooms and their own attendants, whilst, in other cases, two or more patients shared the same parlour and bedrooms. The sexes were always kept quite distinct. There were fifty-two 'domestic servants', of whom nearly forty were in 'exclusive attendancy on the patients'. Little coercion was employed, for example, in 1845, one female patient was wearing 'slight linen bracelets' to prevent injury to other persons. It is clear that the facilities of the establishment were designed chiefly to satisfy the requirements of the upper or educated classes. In 1862, for example, it was recorded by the Commissioners that:

Several of the patients, who are persons of wealth and station, keep their own carriages and horses, with separate servants. The proprietors have also carriages for the use of the patients, and they keep a pack of beagles ... which are a source of great amusement to many of the inmates ... Sociable meetings are promoted ... Lectures on interesting subjects are also delivered frequently.[3]

Despite his great animosity towards the private-madhouse system, Perceval credited Charles Newington with 'humane intentions, and an anxious desire to prevent any gross abuse of their power by his servants; united, however, with a great deal of erroneous conceit'.[4] Perceval's confinement at Ticehurst was a happier experience than the preceding period which he had spent at Brislington House and he commented, particularly, on the increased personal privacy and freedom granted to him, which, to a large extent, must have been

[1] E. Sussex C.R.O., QAL/1/2/E.2, 1830.
[2] E. Sussex C.R.O., QAL/1/3/E.10–14. (Other surviving MS. material preserved at this R.O. includes licensing documents, 1829–1937; registers of patients, 1828–45, and admission and discharge documents, 1832–1928.)
[3] Sixteenth Report (1862) C.L., p. 39.
[4] Perceval (1840), *op. cit.*, p. xix.

rendered possible by his improved mental state. The descriptive content of Perceval's narrative provides a useful corroboration of the impression of Ticehurst derived from other sources.

The fire of 1852 took place a few days before the death of Charles Newington, who had been resident proprietor since 1811. The Visiting Magistrates had high regard for Newington, 'whose life was devoted to the care of those afflicted beings whose infirmities it was his constant effort to relieve and whose amiable, conscientious and benevolent disposition was such as ever to endear him to those who had the advantage of his acquaintance'.[1] The Commissioners in Lunacy observed that he had taken

a lead in practically improving the treatment and condition of the insane, by introducing . . . a milder and more kindly system of management, by allowing them a far greater degree of personal freedom, in the enjoyment of exercise and recreation out of doors, than had been theretofore permitted, and by gradually but steadily diminishing the use of instrumental restraint to an extent which of late years has almost amounted to its abolition.[2]

A progressive policy was maintained by Charles Newington's sons, for example, in 1864, the step was taken to rent houses at St Leonard's for convalescent patients. A member of the Newington family, H. Hayes Newington, F.R.C.P. Edin., was President of the Medico-Psychological Association in 1889.

(4) *Droitwich Lunatic Asylum, Worcestershire*

This licensed house was opened in 1791 by William Ricketts, surgeon and remained in use until 1871. During the first half of the nineteenth century, the asylum housed up to 100 patients, the majority being paupers. The largest number of residents recorded in the surviving records was in 1848, when, on one occasion, there were 104 patients, including seventy-one paupers.[3] The pauper department was closed in 1852, when the county asylum was opened at Powick, near Worcester. Subsequently, the accommodation for private patients was improved; increased provision was made for 'second and third-class patients'[4] and, for some years, the number of resident patients remained in the region of thirty. William Ricketts gave evidence

[1] E. Sussex C.R.O., QAL/1/3/E.12, Minutes V.M., 8 July 1852.
[2] Seventh Report (1852) C.L., p. 20.
[3] Worcs., R.O., BA.710.b.125. 1(i), Minutes V.M., 22 June 1848.
[4] Advertisement, Droitwich Lunatic Asylum, *London and Provincial Medical Directory*, 1852.

before the 1816 Select Committee and, in the following year, he was succeeded as proprietor by his sons, W. H. and M. Ricketts, both of whom were surgeons. In 1828, W. H. Ricketts appeared as a witness before the Select Committee of the House of Lords and the content of his evidence suggests a person of considerable experience and integrity. He expressed well-defined views on the proposed legislation then passing through Parliament and, throughout, displayed considerable interest in the well-being and treatment of the insane. In 1843, Charles Hastings (1794–1866) M.D., became a co-proprietor of the asylum with M. Ricketts and it is interesting to note that, for some years previously, he had been the Medical Visitor to the establishment. Hastings was a well-known Worcestershire physician and was knighted in 1850. He was the founder of the British Medical Association and, in 1859, he was the President of the Medico-Psychological Association.[1]

It was disclosed, in 1815, that the house had never been licensed or visited by the Worcestershire Magistrates.[2] Subsequently, the Member of Parliament for the county, W. H. Lyttleton, visited the house and reported his findings to the Select Committee of 1816 and, later, Ricketts himself was called to give evidence. Despite the lack of formal licensing and proper inspection, it appears that the house had been well run, nevertheless. In a letter addressed to a member of the Select Committee, Lyttleton described the asylum as 'a large building, retreating a good distance from the street, with a court before and a spacious garden behind, open to the country'.[3] At this time, there were over ninety patients, approximately half of whom were paupers, drawn chiefly from Birmingham, with which town the proprietor had a long-standing contract. The admission rate was 30 to 35 patients per annum. The treatment employed and the estimated cure rates are discussed in Chapter 7 and it suffices to note that Ricketts stressed the desirability of the early treatment of insanity, chiefly by medical means and accompanied by as little restraint as possible. J. B. Steward (1845), M.D., F.R.C.P. who was formerly physician to the asylum, claimed that the non-restraint system was first introduced there in 1833, although, subsequently, restraint continued to be used selectively.[4] The range of accommodation

[1] *Vide* Hastings, C. (1860), 'Presidential Address', *J. Ment. Sci. 6*, pp. 3–13.
[2] Minutes of evidence 1815 S.C., p. 169.
[3] First Report minutes of evidence 1816 S.C., p. 44.
[4] Steward, J. B. (1845), *Practical Notes on Insanity*, pp. 88–9.

offered and the terms for maintenance were described in a printed advertisement, in the form of a leaflet, which Ricketts submitted to the 1816 Select Committee and part of which is now reproduced for the interesting details it incorporates:

1st. Separate apartments, four guineas per week—those who pay this price have the best apartments; each male is allowed a man, and each female a woman servant, and every proper indulgence suitable to their disorder. Three guineas per week—the treatment in all respects the same, except having a separate servant.

2nd. Associated apartments, two guineas per week, having convenient rooms allotted them. The above classes dine with the family, when their cases will admit of it.

3rd. The Lodges. These are detached buildings, with wards for each sex and courts for air and exercise; of this department there are three classes: 1st. One guinea and a half per week, are more nicely dieted and lodged than the undermentioned. 2nd. Pay 25 shillings per week. 3rd. class, one guinea per week; not allowed tea.

There are two detached squares for pauper lunatics of both sexes, who pay fourteen shillings per week, and one guinea entrance . . . No patient is taken for less than a quarter of a year, but should one be removed for any cause whatever before that time, the quarter must be paid for. The same rule observed in case of death. Curable patients, after the first quarter, are charged only for the number of weeks; but a week entered upon, the whole is reckoned.

All patients find for their own use two pair of sheets, and four towels, pay the sum charge for one week as entrance, and five shillings per quarter for servants . . . No patient can be admitted until Mr. Ricketts had visited them, that it may be ascertained if it is proper to receive them, for which visit a reasonable fee is expected.[1]

In company with most other contemporary licensed houses, Droitwich suffered from having rambling, non-purpose-built premises.[2] Nevertheless, in 1844, the Metropolitan Commissioners included Droitwich Asylum amongst the best-conducted provincial houses licensed to receive paupers;[3] at a later period, however, the principal adverse comments about the establishment related to the accommodation for paupers. The Commissioners, in 1849, described this accommodation as 'so indifferent as well as so incurably defective, that we are glad to be informed that as soon as the county asylum is opened, the house will cease to be used as a receptacle for

[1] Leaflet, 'Droitwich Medical Lunatic Asylum . . . Terms of admission for insane patients, under the care of Mr. Ricketts, and son, surgeons, Droitwich, Worcestershire.' First Report minutes of evidence 1816 S.C., p. 45.
[2] Worcs. R.O., BA.323. s. 125, plan of asylum, 2 April 1836.
[3] 1844 Report M.C.L., p. 41.

that class of patients, an intention which we trust will be rigidly adhered to'.[1] The years following the closure of the pauper department saw a gradual improvement in the overall conditions and by 1862, the Commissioners were able to state that: 'As at present conducted, the establishment affords fair accommodation for persons of small means, although the situation of the house, which is in the town of Droitwich and close to the salt works, is far from cheerful.'[2]

The cost of maintenance and treatment in private madhouses

The charges made for lunatics in private madhouses, naturally, varied very widely, according to the type of accommodation occupied and the services rendered. This variation is reflected particularly in the charges made for private patients. Examples are now given which are illustrative of some of the charges made, the terms for private patients being considered first.

In 1761, a weekly charge of three to five guineas was made at Nathaniel Cotton's house, St Alban's.[3] At St Luke's House, Newcastle upon Tyne, the annual charge, in 1767, for diet, washing and lodging was £20[4] and at Turlington's house, Chelsea, London, in 1763, the annual payments ranged from £20 to £60.[5] In a letter written in 1787, the terms at Mr Stroud's house, near Bilstone, Staffordshire, were stated to be two-guineas entrance fee and £30 a year, but, at Mr Chadwick's house, Lichfield, the charges were lower, that is to say, 'one guinea entrance, £17 for the first year, to find him board, medecines, washing and attendance, and if he does not find him troublesome, the second year at £14'.[6] The house in Islington, London, at which Charles Lamb's sister, Mary, was confined, in 1796, after she had murdered her mother, contained accommodation at about £50 per annum, which was less expensive than that occupied

[1] Worcs. R.O., BA.710.b.125. 1(i) Minutes C.L., 21 Nov. 1849.
[2] Sixteenth Report (1862) C.L., p. 49.
[3] Linnean Society, London, Pulteney MSS. Cited by Hunter and Macalpine (1963), op. cit., p. 425.
[4] Hall, op. cit.
[5] Report 1763 S.C., J.H.C., Vol. 29, p. 488.
[6] Archives Dept., Glyn Mills & Co., London, letter, Thomas Mottershaw of Derby to Henry Mutton, 4 July 1787, re William Key, a lunatic born in 1768. Key was admitted to St Luke's Hospital, London, in 1789, at a cost of £13 per annum and remained there until his death in 1805. (The Country Register names Samuel Proud as the proprietor of the house at Bilstone.)

by Mary, who had a room and a servant to herself.[1] At Thomas Arnold's house, Leicester, the charges for John Howard, during the period 14 August 1789 to 12 November 1791, amounted to over £606.[2] A Warwickshire solicitors' collection contains papers (1793–1827) relating to the costs of maintenance and treatment of a Miss Dorothy Croft at Thomas Burman's house, Henley-in-Arden and the following details have been extracted from this source.[3] In 1795, Burman wrote: 'My general terms are one guinea/week for board and medecines, the patient finding their own linen and washing. If any person chuses a servant constantly to attend on them, board and wages are separately considered.' The accounts detail the costs of various items of treatment. Thus, on 6 October 1794, the charges for bleeding and deobsturient pills were both one shilling and the cost of eleven purging pills and ten purging draughts, prescribed between January and July 1798, was £1 8s. Other items mentioned include 'nervous mixtures', 'fever pills' and, in October 1797, one box of 'detergent pills', which cost three shillings. Details are not available regarding the charges made for private patients at Hook Norton and Witney and there is only limited information available relating to other asylums during the first half of the nineteenth century. The terms, already quoted, for the several classes of patient at the Droitwich Lunatic Asylum in 1816, are representative, probably, of those charged for similar accommodation in better-known madhouses, during the early-nineteenth century. The charges ranged from one to four guineas per week, and the latter rate corresponds with that charged for Perceval, during his stay at Brislington House. In the words of Perceval himself, the sum of 300 guineas was paid 'for his being manacled and beaten, strangled and insulted, and groomed at Dr. Fox's'.[4] The terms at a typical middle-class establishment in 1850 have been quoted already as ranging from 15s. to two guineas per week, depending upon the type of accommodation required. Evidence extant relating to charges at a number of similar establishments, in various parts of the country, in the mid-nineteenth century, substantiates this estimate.[5] Some licensed houses provided

---

[1] Letter, Charles Lamb to S. T. Coleridge, 3 Oct. 1796. Cited in Lucas, E. V. (ed.) (1905), *The Works of Charles and Mary Lamb*, Vol. 6, pp. 45–6.

[2] Bod. Lib., MS. Eng. Misc. b.69(192).

[3] Warwicks. R.O., Campbell, Brown & Ledbrook papers, CR.556/691.

[4] Perceval (1840), *op. cit.*, p. xx.

[5] e.g. terms quoted for a range of houses in Yorkshire varied from 14s. to two guineas per week. Manchester Royal Lunatic Hospital Committee Book, 1845–

accommodation for private patients at terms which were suitable for persons of limited means. In *c.* 1845, attention was drawn to the need for provisions of this kind by the proprietor of Haydock Lodge, where 'the lowest classes of private patients' were accommodated in a separate part of the establishment, the weekly charges being 8s. 6d.[1]

In the case of paupers, generally, inclusive weekly charges were fixed, in order to allow contracts to be made with their parishes and unions. The basic rate for paupers at Brislington House in 1812, was about 13s. per week, although when incidental charges, such as those for clothing and washing, were added the average weekly cost amounted to 17s. 6d. or 18s.[2] The contents of bills sent to the overseers of Britford, Wiltshire, in 1808 and 1809, by Finch of Laverstock House, indicate that the weekly charges, without medicines, were 12–14s.[3] and this scale applied to paupers in 1815.[4] At Kingsdown House, Box, in 1814, the terms for men were 25s. a week.[5] This figure was considerably higher than that for women, as the proprietor believed that men required more coercion, which necessitated the employment of more male attendants. Bakewell's annual charge for paupers at Spring Vale, at this time, was £40.[6] The introduction of the non-restraint system led, inevitably, to increased expenses, because the replacement of relatively cheap apparatus for restraint and security, by an increased establishment of attendants, who were of a higher calibre than formerly, was costly. However, the competition for contracts between rival houses created a need to keep charges as low as possible. In the fourth decade of the century, a number of provincial houses are known to have been charging about 10s. a week for paupers, a sum that was moderate enough to satisfy some parish officials.[7] By 1843, the average weekly cost for the maintenance, clothing and treatment of English pauper lunatics in private licensed houses was 8s. $11\frac{1}{2}$d., compared with 7s. $6\frac{3}{4}$d. in the county asylums.[8] The charges in both types of asylum were much greater than the average weekly cost for pauper lunatics in the com-

---

1846. Examined by courtesy of the medical superintendent, Cheadle Royal Hospital *Vide infra.*, p. 254.

[1] Brochure for Haydock Lodge Institution, *c.* 1845, pp. 2–3.

[2] Paul, *op. cit.*, p. 55.   [3] Wilts. C.R.O., Britford parish records, 499/27.

[4] Minutes of evidence 1815 S.C., p. 50.

[5] Minutes of evidence 1815 S.C., p. 21.   [6] *Ibid.*, p. 122.

[7] e.g. at Fairford, Glos., P.R., 1830, p. 40. (Cf. at this time, the weekly charge for paupers at St Luke's Hospital was 6s.)

[8] 1844 Report M.C.L., Appendix F.

munity, which was 2s 7¼d. Naturally, this factor made parish officers reluctant to send their paupers to lunatic asylums until they were unmanageable elsewhere.[1] The average charges for Oxfordshire paupers in various private licensed houses in 1837, were 8s. 6d. for male and female idiots; 9s. for male lunatics and 9s. 2d. for female lunatics;[2] and at Hook Norton, in 1844, the charges, which excluded the cost of clothing, were similar.[3] The fact that no minimum sum was fixed, below which licensed houses would not be permitted to take pauper patients, undoubtedly fostered the continuance of the merely custodial confinement of lunatics, in overcrowded conditions, with little in the way of curative measures. This was particularly the case in the metropolitan area, where local competition was more intense and more unscrupulous than in the provinces. In 1845, Lord Ashley realistically summed up the situation in the following way:

How is it possible that the proprietor of the house should out of 8s. a week give the patient everything that is required—full diet, ample space of house and grounds, all the expensiveness of the non-restraint system, and realize in the remainder an adequate return for himself and his family? The thing is next to impossible, and ought not to be attempted.[4]

Nevertheless, in the county asylums, costs were kept as low as possible and the constant drive for greater economy by their management committees was assisted by the admission of greater numbers of patients than had been anticipated and by the relative overcrowding that ensued. Thus, at the Oxfordshire County Lunatic Asylum, the weekly charge in 1848 was 11s.[5] but, by 1851, it had been reduced to 8s.[6] and it even reached 7s. 6d. in 1853,[7] despite the rise in the prices of provisions and labour.

[1] In Oxfordshire in 1830, the weekly costs for the maintenance of insane paupers, both in the community and in asylums, ranged from 4d. to 15s., the average being 5s. 1d. P.R., 1830, p. 87.

[2] P.R., 1837, p. 4.   [3] 1844 Report M.C.L., p. 213.

[4] H.P.D., Vol. LXXXI, 6 June 1845, H.C., col. 194.

[5] Report of Committee of Visitors of Littlemore Asylum, 1848, p. 4.

[6] Ibid., 1851, p. 7.   [7] Ibid., 1853, p. 10.

6

The Private Licensed Houses
at Hook Norton and Witney

Provisions for the insane and the incidence of insanity in Oxfordshire

OXFORDSHIRE provides a particularly good region in which to study the history of institutions for the insane in the eighteenth and nineteenth centuries, because representative examples of all the various types of institution were contained within the county. There were the private licensed houses, at Hook Norton (*c.* 1725–1854) and at Witney (1823–57); a public subscription asylum, the Oxford Lunatic Asylum, opened in 1826; and, a county asylum, which was opened at Littlemore, near Oxford, in 1846. In addition, as was the practice throughout the country, lunatics were confined in workhouses, houses of correction and singly in their own homes or boarded out and, occasionally, criminal lunatics were confined in the gaols.

The Oxford Lunatic Asylum, now the Warneford Hospital, was founded, as an entirely independent institution, with funds raised by public subscription and received substantial support from the colleges, the city and from prominent Oxford residents. It was intended that the asylum should cater for the upper and middle classes and 'those who, though poor, were not paupers; those who, though above poverty, were far from affluence; and those who, though blessed with sufficiency to meet the ordinary calls upon their resources, were unable to satisfy the pressing demands of this burthensome calamity'.[1] The maintenance payments for this latter group

[1] Thomas, V. (1827), *An Account of the Origin, Nature and Objects of the Asylum on Headington Hill, near Oxford*, p. 5.

could be supplemented or paid out of a charity established by the governors and trustees, into which were paid the profits made in the reception of the 'superior' patients. The first moves to found this asylum were made in 1812 by the governors of the Radcliffe Infirmary, Oxford,[1] who planned initially to build it on a site close to the Infirmary, as had been the practice in other cities, such as Manchester, Liverpool and Leicester. In accordance with the recommendations of the Report of the 1807 Select Committee and the County Asylum Act of 1808, consideration was given to the suggestion that the proposed asylum should be associated with an establishment for pauper lunatics, as, for example, had been the case at Nottingham. Agreement could not be reached, however, in the negotiations between the governors and the magistrates and this was a contributory factor in postponing the opening of the asylum, on its present site in Headington, until 1826.[2] The pauper lunatic asylum for the counties of Oxfordshire and Berkshire, in conjunction with the city of Oxford and the boroughs of Abingdon and Reading was not opened until 1846 and was built at the expense of the county rates. No reference to local private madhouses have been discovered in the surviving records relating to the establishment of these two asylums.

During the first half of the nineteenth century, Oxfordshire was essentially an agricultural county and the university city of Oxford constituted its largest urban area. The population of Oxfordshire in the 1841 census was 14,330 and it ranked as one of the smaller English counties. Witney was a flourishing market town at this time and was noted for the manufacture of blankets.[3] The town was situated some twelve miles west of Oxford. Its population in 1821, including a few surrounding hamlets, was 4,784.[4] Hook Norton was described, in 1830, as 'a large village, in the parish of its name, and in the same hundred as Chipping Norton, about five miles from that town. Here is a large church with a fine steeple, two chapels and a meeting place

[1] Bod. Lib., G.A. Oxon. 629, Minutes of proceedings relative to a proposal for establishing a lunatic asylum in the vicinity of Oxford by voluntary contributions, 1814.

[2] Known originally as Oxford Lunatic Asylum; from 1828 as Radcliffe Asylum and, from 1843, as Warneford Lunatic Asylum. (*Vide Brief History of the Warneford Hospital, compiled for the Committee of Management*, 1926.)

[3] *Vide* Giles, J. A. (1852), *History of Witney*; and Monk, W. J. (1894), *History of Witney*.

[4] Pigot and Co.'s *London and Provincial New Commercial Directory*, 1830, p. 661.

for dissenters.'[1] The village of Hook Norton was situated near the edge of the county abutting upon Warwickshire and it was some twenty-five miles from Oxford. The population in 1821, 1831 and 1841, was 1,351, 1,506 and 1,422 respectively.

Information concerning the number of pauper lunatics in Oxfordshire, at intervals from 1807 to 1863, is presented in Table 15. It has been pointed out previously that early estimates were grossly unreliable, in part because numerous parishes failed to make the appropriate returns. Nevertheless, the changes in the distribution of the lunatics are of some interest and the contents of this Table do reflect the development of institutional provisions for this section of the community.

TABLE 15 *Number and distribution of Oxfordshire pauper lunatics, 1807–63*

Date	Number and distribution of pauper lunatics	Source of data
1807	22 in, 'poor houses, houses of industry or workhouses'.	Report 1807 S.C. p. 11.
1828	146 (65 lunatics and 81 idiots).	O.C.R.O., QSL.IV, Annual Returns of pauper lunatics.
1829	177, comprising 17 in public asylums, 20 in private madhouses, 140 at large or with relatives.	Halliday (1829), *op. cit.* p. 55.
1830	155 (65 lunatics and 90 idiots), including 14 in asylums.	P.R., 1830.
1835	171 (79 lunatics and 92 idiots).	O.C.R.O., QSL.IV, Annual Returns of pauper lunatics.
1837	186, including 2 in county asylums and 46 in private licensed houses.	P.R., 1837.
1843	201 (90 lunatics and 111 idiots), comprising 5 in county asylums, 66 in private licensed houses, 62 in workhouses, 68 elsewhere.	1844 Report M.C.L., Appendix F.
1863	416, comprising 266 in county asylums, 9 in registered hospitals or licensed houses, 80 in workhouses, 7 in lodgings, 54 residing with relatives.	Eighteenth Report (1864) C.L., p. 202.

[1] *Ibid.*, p. 643.

Hook Norton and Witney

The private madhouse at Hook Norton was established, as far as can be ascertained, in *c.* 1725. In *Jackson's Oxford Journal* of 10 October 1778, there appeared a notice for the sale by auction at the Sun, Hook Norton, of:

A freehold convenient house; now in the occupation of Mrs. Harris, tenant at will, (late in the possession of the noted Minchings, of Hook Norton deceased), fitted up in a most excellent manner for the reception of lunaticks. Upon the ground floor, kitchen, parlour, apothecary's shop, wood-house and stable, and a garden thereto adjoining, a back-yard with a large pair of gates and is fit for a surgeon or apothecary.[1]

From the *Journal* of three weeks later, it is clear that Mrs Harris reversed her decision to auction the establishment. Under the heading of 'A House for Lunaticks' there appeared an advertisement[2] in which she announced her decision to keep on the business, 'which her late mother kept with a distinguished reputation for upwards of half a century' and stated that she had a proper licence and that she would be assisted by her son, who was a surgeon and apothecary (Figure 4).

Apart from a passing reference in an anonymous letter,[3] as yet unauthenticated, to a house, situated in the Oxford parish of St Clement's, which took in lunatics and in which the poet William Collins (1721–59) was said to have been confined in 1754, there is no evidence of other private madhouses in Oxfordshire in the eighteenth century. In 1823, the only other privately owned madhouse known to have existed in the county was opened at Witney. *Jackson's Oxford Journal* again provides information regarding the opening of this establishment and, on 12 April 1823, the following advertisement appeared:

To Parents and Guardians. EDWARD BATT, surgeon, etc. having been solicited to open a house for the reception of persons labouring under diseases of the mind, begs to state that he has now accommodation for patients of that description, near to his residence, in Witney, Oxfordshire. Terms and other particulars may be known on application to him.[4]

[1] Bod. Lib., N.G.A. Oxon. a4, *Jackson's Oxford Journal*, 10 Oct. 1778, No. 1328, p. 3.
[2] Bod. Lib., N.G.A. Oxon. a4, *Jackson's Oxford Journal*, 31 Oct. 1778, No. 1331, p. 3. [3] Anon. (1781), 'Memoirs of the Life of William Collins, the Poet', *Gentleman's Magazine 51*, p. 11.
[4] Bod. Lib., N.G.A. Oxon. a4, *Jackson's Oxford Journal*, 12 April 1823, No. 3650, p. 3.

At least three private dwelling houses in Oxford were used to accommodate single lunatics. In 1848 'a decided lunatic' was found confined irregularly at Samuel Cox's house in Headington,[1] and later there are references to Aries's House at Marston and Harris's house in the Cowley Road.[2]

The private madhouse at Hook Norton was licensed for the first time by the magistrates at the Epiphany Quarter Sessions 1775.[3] The

A HOUSE for LUNATICKS.

THIS is to inform the Public in general, and the Friends of Persons difordered in their Senfes in particular, That Joanna Harris, Daughter of the late Mrs. Sarah Minchin, deceafed, of Hook-Norton, Oxfordfhire, intends keeping on the Bufinefs, which her late Mother kept with a diftinguifhed Reputation for upwards of Half a Century.— She, the faid Joanna Harris having been an Affiftant to her Mother for upwards of 30 Years, and having for feveral Years paft had the Management of it herfelf, and having now a proper Licence according to Act of Parliament for the fame, the Friends of her prefent Boarders, and all Others who may have Occafion for her Affiftance, are hereby informed, that they may depend upon the utmoft Tendernefs being ufed, that fuch unhappy Cafes will admit of, by their humble Servant,

JOANNA HARRIS.

N..B. Her Son, who is a Surgeon and Apothecary, is an Affiftant to her in the above Bufinefs.

Figure 4 Advertisement for the house at Hook Norton, in *Jackson's Oxford Journal*, 1778

licence was granted to Joanna Harris, who was recorded as 'having entered into a recognisance herself in the sum of one hundred pounds and William Harris of Hook Norton also in one hundred pounds upon condition that the said Joanna Harris do and shall keep a good rule and order and be of good behaviour during the continuance of the said licence'.[4]

The Hook Norton parish records[5] reveal that there were several medical men in the Minchin (Minching) family during the eighteenth

[1] P.R.O., M.H.50. Minute Book C.L., Vol. 3, 13 April, 19 June 1848.

[2] Twentieth Report (1866) C.L., pp. 39–41. (The case was quoted of Miss E.S. who was accommodated without a certificate in these houses. E.S. has been identified by the writer as Elizabeth Simms, a patient at Hook Norton, 1852–4, and at Witney, 1854–7.) [3] O.C.R.O., QSM.1/3, Sessions Minute Book. [4] *Ibid.*

[5] In the parish chest, Hook Norton, examined by courtesy of the vicar.

century and it is likely that the madhouse was originally part of an apothecary's establishment. The following list presents the names of the persons to whom the house was licensed from 1775 to 1854 and includes the duration of their tenure of the licence and brief biographical details, the latter being compiled from a variety of sources, including parish registers, land tax assessment returns and directories.

1775–84	Joanna Harris, widow (d. 1784). Her father may have been an apothecary, but no records relating to him have been traced.
1785–1815	James Harris (1753–1815), son of Joanna, surgeon and apothecary.[1]
1816–22	Eliza Harris (d. 1822), widow of James.
1823–24	Henry Harris (1799–1824), son of James and Eliza. Not medically qualified.
1825	Mabel Harris, widow of Henry.
1826–42	Henry Tilsley (d. 1858), member of a prominent Chipping Norton Family,[2] one of whom, in 1783, was recorded as being a surgeon.[3] Qualified as M.R.C.S. January 1821. Ceased to reside full-time at the asylum in 1841 and moved to Chipping Norton, where he died subsequently.
1843–54	Richard Mallam (1811–89). Qualified as an apothecary in 1832 and as M.R.C.S. in 1833. Worked for a period at the Oxford Lunatic Asylum. Following the closure of Hook Norton, he continued to live at Bridge House and acted as a union medical officer for a number of years, before he retired to Kidlington, Oxfordshire, where he died.

Henry Tilsley and Richard Mallam both had assistants, with whom they shared the management of the houses at Hook Norton. In October 1842, Tilsley referred to one Thomas Pearce Beavan, who was 'an experienced legally qualified surgeon and apothecary', and

---

[1] Neither James Harris nor any member of the Minchin family could be traced in the admission records of the Society of Apothecaries for the eighteenth century. This finding is not unexpected for, until the introduction of the licence of the Society in 1815, its membership was drawn almost exclusively from inhabitants of the city of London. The assistance of the Librarian, Guildhall Library, London, is acknowledged hereby.

[2] For other references to the family *vide* O.C.R.O., Farant and Sinden MSS., Far VII/1.

[3] Simmons, S. F. (ed.) (1783), *The Medical Register*, p. 102.

who resided with him in the private house.[1] By this time, Tilsley was not resident full-time at the house and, presumably, Beavan acted as medical superintendent. Beavan, who came from Banbury, qualified as a surgeon and apothecary in 1839. Two weeks prior to the reference to Beavan, Tilsley mentioned Edmund Cruso, who had been resident superintendent and planned to remain in that position, but had been taken seriously ill.[2] Cruso had qualified as an apothecary in 1829. In January 1845, the admission notice of a pauper lunatic was signed by a B. Sharp, assistant to Mallam,[3] but the MSS. contain no other reference to this person.

The private licensed house at Witney was under the supervision of successive members of a well-known Witney family named Batt, which was notable for possessing medical men in five successive generations. As far as can be ascertained, the proprietors were resident at the house throughout the period, with the exception of the period 1842 to 1849, when Miss Jane Batt acted as resident superintendent on behalf of the proprietor, her nephew E. A. Batt. An abbreviated genealogical table of the Batt family, in which the proprietors of the asylum are indicated, in chronological order, by roman numerals is presented below.[4]

The first licence was granted to Edward Batt in 1823[5] and, following his death four years later, his wife, Rebecca, continued as proprietor and resident superintendent until 1842. Upon her death, Augustine William's son,[6] Edward Augustine, a local surgeon like his father, became proprietor (Plate V) but for the first seven years he was not resident at the asylum and lived at his home on Church Green, Witney, while the asylum was managed by his aunt. Following her death, Edward Augustine and his family moved to the asylum. His wife, Eliza, played an active part in the management of the female patients and, after her husband's death, she continued to run the licensed house until it was closed down in 1857. Remarks in a number of printed works bear witness to the standing of the Batt family in the Witney neighbourhood. Preserved in the Witney parish church are several memorial tablets to successive members of

[1] O.C.R.O., QSL.X/1/C, letter, Tilsley to Clerk of Peace, 23 Oct. 1842.
[2] O.C.R.O., QSL.X/1/C, letter, Tilsley to Clerk of Peace, 23 Oct. 1842.
[3] O.C.R.O., QSL.1/15.
[4] Published with the consent of the late Dr B. E. A. Batt, Burford, Oxon.
[5] O.C.R.O., QSM.II/5, Sessions Minute Book.
[6] Augustine William Batt lived at The Hill, High Street, Witney, a fine house which now forms part of the West Oxfordshire Technical College.

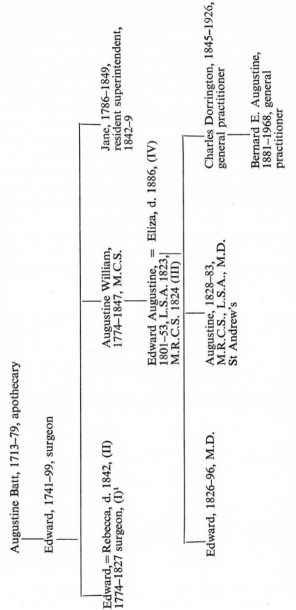

The Batt family of Witney

Augustine Batt, 1713–79, apothecary

Edward, 1741–99, surgeon

Edward, = Rebecca, d. 1842, (II)
1774–1827 surgeon, (I)[1]

Augustine William,
1774–1847, M.C.S.

Jane, 1786–1849,
resident superintendent,
1842–9

Edward, 1826–96, M.D.

Edward Augustine, = Eliza, d. 1886, (IV)
1801–53, L.S.A. 1823,
M.R.C.S. 1824 (III)

Augustine, 1828–83,
M.R.C.S., L.S.A., M.D.
St Andrew's

Charles Dorrington, 1845–1926,
general practitioner

Bernard E. Augustine,
1881–1968, general
practitioner

[1] Qualification as surgeon not corroborated. Not traced in lists of Royal College of Surgeons of England.

135

the family and the reredos of the church was, in fact, erected in memory of Augustine Batt by his fellow townsmen. In addition, a marble monument in the church, depicting, significantly, the Good Samaritan, is dedicated to the memory of Edward Augustine Batt in 'gratitude for the services of a life of incessant and unwearied devotion to the alleviation of bodily suffering'.

The Witney private licensed house was situated in the centre of the town on the west side of the High Street. Surviving plans of the establishment are sufficiently detailed to allow the present Field House, 33 High Street, which is now the Reading Room of the Christian Science Society, together with the adjoining ironmonger's shop, to be identified as the major part of the original asylum. This identification has been corroborated by information given by members of long-established Witney families. Much of the original building is remarkably well preserved and the lay-out of the garden is little changed. A large, coloured plan of the house in 1828[1] shows that, at that time, it was a low-roofed, two-storeyed building attached on either side to neighbouring properties and that it possessed a considerable area of ground at the rear. There were separate quarters for male and female patients, the men being accommodated in a detached 'asylum for gentlemen', a building which still stands, although fast becoming derelict. In his application for a licence in 1842, accompanied by a groundplan, E. A. Batt stated that the men and women were separated by two boundary walls, of more than ten feet high, at a distance of thirty-five yards apart[2] (Figure 5). The 1828 plans included areas demarcated as the Paupers' Court Yard, the Ladies' Court Yard and Gardens and Pleasure Grounds. Detailed dimensions are given for the accommodation, which comprised, in the case of the 'Ladies' Asylum', the dining-room, kitchen, two bedrooms and the paupers' room on the ground floor. There were seven bedrooms on the first floor, a sitting-room and a room probably for the confinement of acutely disturbed patients, known as the 'Dark Room', which measured $9'9'' \times 7'0'' \times 7'6''$. During the lifespan of the establishment, many structural changes were carried out. In 1846, an additional room was built on the first floor and plans of the premises in 1849, 1853 and 1854 indicate other proposed alterations.[3] These alterations included the erection, in 1849, of an arcade 'for exercise in wet weather and shade in summer'. In 1853, the premises

[1] O.C.R.O., QSL.III/2.   [2] O.C.R.O., QSL.V/1.
[3] O.C.R.O., QSL.III/2 (includes all the plans for Witney.)

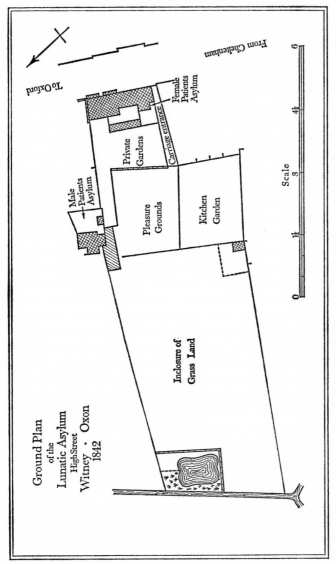

To Oxford

From Cheltenham

Ground Plan
of the
Lunatic Asylum
HighStreet
Witney · Oxon
1842

Male
Patients
Asylum

Female
Patients
Asylum

Carriage entrance

Private
Gardens

Pleasure
Grounds

Kitchen
Garden

Inclosure of
Grass Land

Scale

0   1½   3   4½   6

Figure 5   Groundplan of the house at Witney, 1842

137

were extended considerably by the appropriation of two neighbouring houses and, in 1854, improvements were made to the drainage and two water closets were provided for the patients and staff.

The following reference to the Hook Norton asylum was made in a history of that village, published in 1928:

The fine old house near the tite[1] formed part of the asylum and was used for the staff, the paying patients and the kitchen. The poorer patients, and those who were in a dangerous condition were housed in the redbrick part now cottages . . . Mr. Richard Mallam had also a licensed asylum for paying patients at Bridge House.[2]

It has been possible to identify the building referred to as Bridge House as the original asylum and it stands in fine condition and still inhabited at the present day. The external appearance of this house resembles closely that shown in a sketched elevation plan dated 1834.[3] The first available ground and elevation plans are for 1828 and, in the intervening six years, considerable structural alterations had taken place. In 1828, the asylum comprised a two-storeyed, thatched house, with two short single-storeyed wings projecting at the front and rear (Plate VI). In the following year various modifications were made, including the construction of 'privies' in the garden. In 1831, an attic storey was added to the main building, which was re-fronted and a slate roof was added. The new storey allowed the number of patients accommodated to be increased from eighteen to twenty-one. The apartments for the men and women were unconnected and the garden was divided into areas for male and female patients by palisading, which was over four feet high. In 1842, Tilsley discontinued taking female patients of the upper class and, subsequently, the garden was for the sole use of the male patients.[4] The house described as being near the tite has been identified as the establishment which Tilsley purchased in 1835, 'exclusively for patients of an inferior class'.[5] This addition made possible the accommodation of a greatly increased number of pauper lunatics, together with a small number of paying patients of 'an inferior class' to those in the Bridge House. The latter was referred to in the records as the 'Lower House' and the new premises as the 'Upper House', because

---

[1] A local term for the place where water collects.
[2] Dickins, M. (1928), *A History of Hook Norton*, p. 180.
[3] O.C.R.O., QSL.III/1.
[4] O.C.R.O., QSL.X/1/C, application for renewal of licence, 29 Sept. 1842.
[5] O.C.R.O., QSL.I/4, letter, Tilsley to Clerk of Peace, written on the admission form of a patient, August 1835.

of their respective situations in relation to the stream which runs through the village. Tilsley hoped that the new establishment could be included with the original house under one licence.[1] In fact, this was the case until 1842, when, at the Michaelmas Sessions, separate licences for the houses were applied for and granted. This change in the licensing arrangements was related probably to the Act, 5 & 6 Vict., c. 87, passed in August of that year, which enacted that two Metropolitan Commissioners were to visit each provincial licensed house at least once every six months. It may well have been recognized that the Commissioners might challenge the propriety of including two separate establishments, over 100 yards apart, under a single licence. Certainly, in other parts of the country, the proposed visits by the Metropolitan Commissioners are known to have caused quite a stir. The building of the Upper House was pulled down a few years ago, but the red brick cottages remained and were still inhabited until demolition took place very recently. They were known as the Asylum Cottages by a few of the older inhabitants of Hook Norton and, indeed, some of the upper rooms incorporated what was described by Dickins as 'a small opening in the wall through which food could be passed or a watch kept on a violent patient'.[2] A groundplan of the Upper House in 1835 shows that the main building was three-storeyed and had been adapted for use as an asylum by its division into three sections, each of which included a ground-floor sitting-room, a first-floor chamber and an attic. The large garden at the rear was surrounded by a wall, twelve feet high, and divided into two courts by a brick wall of eight to fifteen feet in height. In the male court, there was a partly twin-storeyed building (referred to above as a row of redbrick cottages) which incorporated three 'strong-rooms'.[3] A new 'strong-room' and a sitting-room in the female court were included in the plan of 1840 (Figure 6). Considerable further alterations and additions had been made by 1841 and the groundplan[4] for that year has additional interest in that it distinguishes the accommodation allotted to three classes of pauper patients, although the criteria for their classification are not known. This process of repeated structural modifications is typical of what took place, continuously, in the majority of non-purpose-built

[1] O.C.R.O., QSL.X/1/A, letter, Tilsley to Clerk of Peace, 2 Oct. 1835. (Tilsley stated that he had no doubt that the Clerk of the Peace would 'use his influence' on his behalf.)
[2] Dickins, *op. cit.*, p. 180.　　[3] For acutely disturbed patients.
[4] O.C.R.O., QSL.III/1 (includes all the plans for Hook Norton.)

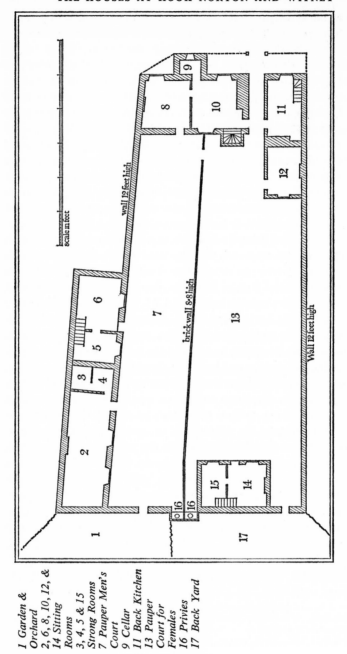

Figure 6 Groundplan of the Upper House (Paupers) Hook Norton, 1840

1 Garden &
  Orchard
2, 6, 8, 10, 12, &
  14 Sitting
  Rooms
3, 4, 5 & 15
  Strong Rooms
7 Pauper Men's
  Court
9 Cellar
11 Back Kitchen
13 Pauper
  Court for
  Females
16 Privies
17 Back Yard

licensed houses, particularly those which increased their provision for paupers in the third and fourth decades of the nineteenth century.

The Witney madhouse was licensed, originally, for up to ten patients, but when Rebecca Batt took over in 1827 the number was increased to up to twenty-five patients, including not more than six paupers. The practice of taking paupers, however, was discontinued in 1832. Subsequently, the house remained licensed for the reception of up to twenty patients, although the records indicate that the number actually resident never reached this level. In the surviving records, the largest number recorded was in 1829, when there were sixteen patients.[1] The number of men accommodated, as far as can be ascertained, was never greater than four and, in 1854, when Eliza Batt took over the establishment, the male department was closed.

The madhouse at Hook Norton was licensed in 1775 for the reception of up to ten patients and the surviving licensing documents indicate that this remained the case until 1817, when Eliza Harris was granted a licence to receive ten or more patients. In 1819, she indicated in a letter that, at that time, there were fourteen residents, nine men and five women and she added 'most of them are placed with me for life having had every assistance, but in vain'.[2] She claimed, in the same letter, that she was able to accommodate comfortably up to twenty persons in the house and she noted also that 'in the last three years I have had about fifty under my care'. The number of inmates did not alter appreciably during the next decade, but, by 1835, the structural alterations which had been undertaken allowed up to thirty patients to be accommodated, including twelve paupers. Following the acquisition of new premises, the Upper House, there was a sharp increase in the number of patients who could be received in the two houses. At first, the Upper House accommodated fifty paupers and ten 'inferior' patients and the Lower House, thirty private patients. By 1842, the two houses were licensed for a total of ninety patients (fifty men and forty women) including seventy paupers and the records suggest that the numbers of resident patients kept well up to the numbers which the houses were licensed to receive. It was in 1842 that Tilsley discontinued the admission of 'upper class' female patients and his successor, Mallam, continued the practice of only receiving male private

---

[1] O.C.R.O., QSL.VII/6, Minutes V.M., 29 Jan. 1829. (Four paupers and twelve 'superior patients'.)

[2] O.C.R.O., QSL.X/1/C, return, Eliza Harris to Clerk of Peace, 12 March 1819.

patients at the Lower House. During the proprietorship of Mallam, the number of patients which the two houses were licensed to receive was further increased to ninety-eight. However, in 1846, the county asylum was opened and, in the course of that year, all the Oxfordshire paupers confined at Hook Norton, totalling thirty-four were transferred to that establishment. Thereafter, no paupers from Oxfordshire were admitted to Hook Norton, but the pauper section remained open until 1853, the pauper lunatics now being drawn from areas where county asylums had not been erected or where they were already overcrowded, principally the London area. It is of interest to note that, in 1847, twenty paupers were transferred to Hook Norton from the Gloucester County Lunatic Asylum because of over-crowding;[1] this is an instance of a not uncommon practice during the early part of the second half of the nineteenth century. This latter factor led also to the admission to Hook Norton of one pauper lunatic from Gloucestershire and this particular patient's history is given in Case (5), Appendix D. This case is of interest, also, in that it allows the tracing of previous admissions to the Radcliffe Asylum, Oxford and his transfer from Hook Norton to the Oxfordshire County Asylum at Littlemore. In 1851, the average number of resident patients at Hook Norton was still over sixty, but, subsequently, the numbers dwindled, until the closure of the establishment in 1854.[2]

The accommodation, general conditions and the management of patients

The main source of information about the general conditions, the activities of the patients and their management in these two establishments is provided by the reports of the Visiting Magistrates and of the Visiting Commissioners. Unfortunately, no Visitors' Minutes have survived for the period before 1829 and, consequently, the account of conditions at Hook Norton and Witney relates chiefly to the second quarter of the nineteenth century. The number of visits made annually to each house is displayed in Table 16. Two major deficiencies in the system of visitation and inspection by the Visiting Magistrates

---

[1] O.C.R.O., QSL.II/3, 99–118. (Transfer occurred 20 Sept. 1847. Thirteen of these patients returned to Gloucester County Asylum in July 1849. In the interim, five others had died and two had been discharged.) *Vide* P.R.O., M.H.50, Minute Book C.L., Vol. 2, 4, 17, 30 Sept., 8 Oct., 1847.

[2] *Vide* Appendix E, Table VIII.

An act for regulating madhouses.

WHEREAS *many great and dangerous abuses frequently arise* **Preamble.**
from the present state of houses kept for the reception of luna-
ticks, for want of regulations with respect to the persons keeping such
houses, the admission of patients into them, and the visitation by proper
persons of the said houses and patients : And whereas the law, as it
now stands, is insufficient for preventing or discovering such abuses ;
may it therefore please your Majesty that it may be enacted ;
and be it enacted by the King's most excellent majesty, by and
with the advice and consent of the lords spiritual and temporal,
and commons, in this present parliament assembled, and by the
authority of the same, That from and after the twentieth day **After Nov. 10,**
of *November,* one thousand seven hundred and seventy-four, if **1774, if any**
any person or persons, in that part of *Great Britain* called *Eng-* **person conceal**
land, the dominion of *Wales,* or town of *Berwick upon Tweed,* **lunatick with-**
shall, upon any pretence whatsoever, conceal, harbour, enter- **out licence,**
tain, or confine, in any house or place, kept for the reception of **he shall for-**
lunaticks, more than one lunatick, at any one time, without **feit 500l.**
having such licence for that purpose, as is herein-after directed,
(except such lunaticks as are committed by the lord high chancellor of *Great Britain,* or lord keeper, or commissioners for the
custody of the great seal for the time being), every such person
shall, for every such offence, forfeit and pay the sum of five
a hundred pounds.

XXIII. And be it further enacted, That the justices of the **Justices to**
peace, at any general quarter sessions of the peace, to be holden **grant licences**
for any such county or place, are hereby authorised and requir- **at general**
ed to grant licences to such person and persons as shall apply for **quarter ses-**
sions ; and re-
that purpose, such person or persons paying for each licence the **ceive for every**
sums following; (that is to say), for each and every house, **house keeping**
wherein there shall be kept any number of lunaticks, not ex- **not exceeding**
ceeding ten, the sum of ten pounds, and no more; and for each **10 lunaticks,**
and every house, wherein there shall be kept above the number **10 l. ; and for**
above that
of ten lunaticks, the sum of fifteen pounds, and no more; and **number 15 l.**
that no one licence shall authorise any person or persons to keep
more houses than one for the reception of lunaticks, nor shall
any such licence be granted for any longer term than for one
year ; and the said justices shall, at the time of granting such licences as aforesaid, nominate and appoint two justices of the
peace for the said county, and also one physician, to visit and inspect all such houses as shall be licensed by such justices as aforesaid ; and the said justices and physicians, so nominated and appointed, or any two of them, whereof the physician to be one,
may, and are hereby authorised and impowered to visit, in the
day time, every house so licensed, within the county where
such house or place shall be so licensed, as often as they shall
think fit.

XXIV. And be it further enacted, That the said justices and **Justices, at vi-**
physician, so nominated, or such of them as shall visit any licensed **sitations, to**
house as aforesaid, may at every visitation, if they think neces- **make minutes**
of the conditi-
sary, make, or cause to be made, minutes, in writing, of the **ons of houses,**
state and condition of every house which they shall visit, as to the
b care of the patients therein, and all such other particulars as

Plate I Extracts from the Act for regulating madhouses, 1774
(*a*) Preamble to the Act   (*b*) Licensing duties of the justices
of the peace

Plate II (*above*)   Haydock Lodge Institution, Lancashire, taken from a brochure, *c.* 1845

Plate III (*below*)   A view of Spring Vale Asylum, Staffordshire, 1838

Plate IV   Ticehurst Asylum, Sussex, taken from a brochure, 1830

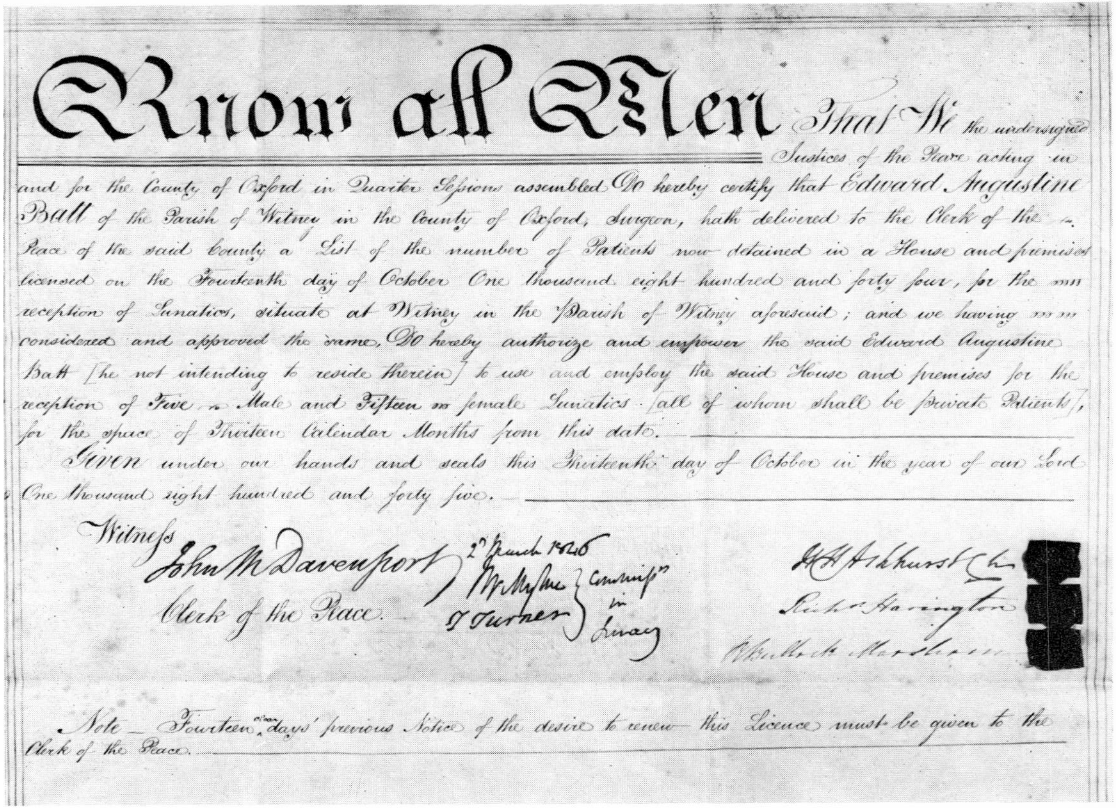

Know all Men That We the undersigned Justices of the Peace acting in and for the County of Oxford in Quarter Sessions assembled Do hereby certify that Edward Augustine Batt of the Parish of Witney in the County of Oxford, Surgeon, hath delivered to the Clerk of the Peace of the said County a List of the number of Patients now detained in a House and premises licensed on the Fourteenth day of October One thousand eight hundred and forty four, for the reception of Lunatics, situate at Witney in the Parish of Witney aforesaid; and we having considered and approved the same, Do hereby authorize and empower the said Edward Augustine Batt [he not intending to reside therein] to use and employ the said House and premises for the reception of Five Male and Fifteen female Lunatics [all of whom shall be private Patients], for the space of Thirteen Calendar Months from this date.

Given under our hands and seals this Thirteenth day of October in the year of our Lord One thousand eight hundred and forty five.

Witness John M Davenport
Clerk of the Peace.

2d March 1846
W. Mylne
J Turner
Commissrs in Lunacy

J H Ashhurst Chn
Richd Harington
W Bullock Marsham

Note – Fourteen clear days' previous Notice of the desire to renew this Licence must be given to the Clerk of the Peace.

Plate V
Licence granted to E. A. Batt, surgeon, of Witney, October 1845; signed by the Commissioners in Lunacy on visiting the house in March 1846

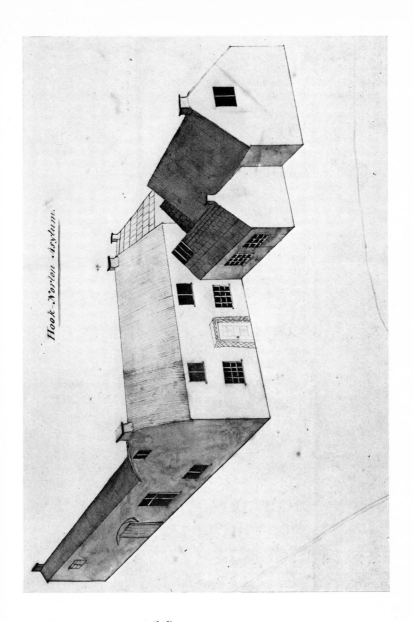

Plate VI A sketch of Hook Norton Asylum, submitted, with an accompanying groundplan, to the Oxfordshire Quarter Sessions in October 1828, as required by the Madhouse Act of 1828

(copy)

THE

TWO MEDICAL CERTIFICATES,

FOR SUPERIOR PATIENTS,

To be delivered to Mrs. Batt upon the admission of Lunatics and others of unsound mind into the Asylum kept by her at Witney, Oxfordshire, according to 9 Geo. IV. c. xli. sect. 30. 51.

PARTICULARS*.

1. The name of the Patient is ..... *Sarah S. Jackson*
2. The age of the Patient is *48*
3. The Patient's place of residence is .. *Newbury. Berks:*
4. The former occupation of the Patient was
5. The Asylum in which the Patient has been before confined is ..... } *Hope - House, Amelia Smith*
6. Has the Patient been found Lunatic or of unsound mind under a Commission issued by the Lord Chancellor or Lord Keeper or Commissioner of the Great Seal? ..... }
7. The Christian and Surnames of the Person by whose authority I have examined this Patient are ..... } *William Boys Greenham Berks Trustee*
8. As to the relationship or circumstances of connection between these parties, I am given to understand and believe, that . }
9. If special circumstances have prevented the obtaining of the certificates and signatures of two medical Practitioners, state those special circumstances, in order to the correction of the irregularity, within seven days after the Patient's admission. }

CERTIFICATE, No. I.

I the undersigned, having ascertained to the best of my ability the above particulars, hereby certify, that I separately visited, and personally examined, the above named *Sarah S. Jackson* on the *eleventh* day of *Jan.* in the year *1832* and that the said *S. S. Jackson* is of unsound mind, and proper to be confined in your Asylum.

† Signed .... *John Fawtin Surgeon & Apothecary*

* These particulars are to be set forth without any abbreviations of words.
† Please to add Physician, Surgeon, Apothecary, as the case may be.

Plate VII A medical certificate for a private patient admitted to Witney in January 1832, using a form issued by Mrs Rebecca Batt in accordance with the Madhouse Act of 1828

Gentlemen——   Kingsdown Decr 2d 1749

According to yr Request when I was to wait on you
Concerning John Porter, this is to inform you of his Disorder,
its much worse than a Raving madness & more difficult to Cure
he being in a Sullen Morose way, insomuch that he in some interval
will neither take his medicines or Eatables, nor put on his Clothes
or off, without much adoe with him, I believe need no more at present
but that I shall do the best I can for his recovery,

                    I am Gentle: yr most Obedt.
                to Command Jas Jeffery

P.S. he need a Shirt & a pair
of Stockings wch was at ye Chaple
de plaisters for him but a Couple Shirts
more are wanting,

One Milion of Money Due to the King of Great
Britan Which I John Rundle must pay my Self at My
Safe Being at Prusia...

I Hope my Son is in Good Helth John Rundle

Prince Ferdinand.. Prince of Brunswick..

I Hope all My Horce and Foot Soldiers be of Good
Spirits in Doing their Duty and Ready to Wait on
on their King. When I Come home to Prusia..

Plate VIII (*above*) A letter concerning a lunatic from James Jeffery,
owner of the madhouse at Kingsdown, Box, Wiltshire, to the
Trowbridge Parish Overseers, 1749

Plate IX (*below*) Extract from a letter of John Rundle, a pauper
lunatic at the Kingsdown madhouse, to his son, *c.* 1765

THE

TRADE OF LUNACY

OR,

AN APPROVED RECEIPT,

To make a Lunatic, and seize his Estate.

WATCH for some season of vexation, and then, by proper insinuations and a pitying tone of voice, work up the patient to a due pitch of passion; then lay on blisters; and before his agitation of spirits has time to subside, hurry him away violently to a mad-house, so denominated, that is to say, one of the graves of mind, body, and estate, much more dreadful than the Bastille and Inquisition. There, as an

Plate X "Goodman goaded to madness." An illustration from *Valentine Vox* by H. Cockton (1840)

Plate XI "The trade of lunacy." Part of a pamphlet, *Address to Humanity*, by W. Belcher, 1796

TABLE 16 *Number of visits per annum by the Visitors and Commissioners to Hook Norton and Witney (figures in brackets refer to visits which did fulfil the statutory requirements)*

Date	Witney		Hook Norton	
	Magistrates	*Commissioners*	*Magistrates*	*Commissioners*
1829	1		2	
1830	0		0	
1831	0		1	
1832	0		0	
1833	5 (1)		3 (2)	
1834	2		2 (1)	
1835	4		1	
1836	2		0	
1837	3		0	
1838	2		0	
1839	3		0	
1840	3		0	
1841	3		1	
1842	3	?[a]	1	1
1843	3	?	2	1
1844	2	?	2	2
1845	3	1	3 (2)	1
1846	4	2	2	2
1847	5	2	1 (1)	2
1848	4	3	5 (2)	3
1849	3	1	3 (2)	1
1850	5	2	3 (1)	2
1851	4	2	3	2
1852	4	2	3	2
1853	3	2	2 (2)	2
1854	4	3	1	2
1855	6	2	Closed	
1856	3	2		
1857	4	1		

[a] Probably visited by Metropolitan Commissioners during October 1842, when Hook Norton was inspected for the first time.

are demonstrated clearly, namely, the failure to comply with statutory requirements in terms of the frequency of visits and of the proper constitution of the visiting group. These deficiencies will be discussed in greater detail in Chapter 8.

In general, the premises at Hook Norton and Witney appear to have provided a consistently satisfactory level of comfort and convenience and to have been maintained in a clean and orderly state. The domestic arrangements, the heating, ventilation and sanitation received no consistently adverse comments. Reports about Witney often stressed the cleanliness and neatness which prevailed, and the way in which the house was conducted was praised. Early reports by the Visitors refer to the commodious nature of the premises and to the effective separation of the different categories of patient. In 1846, the Commissioners observed: 'the house is clean and in the best order and its condition and management reflect great credit on the lady[1] who resides in and personally superintends it.'[2] By 1848, terms such as 'exceedingly creditable' were being used although, in 1853, shortly before the closure of the male departments, the premises used by two male patients were reported as being in a neglected and dilapidated state. As was the case at Witney, the reports of the Visitors to Hook Norton were generally complimentary about the accommodation and atmosphere and this was particularly the case during the proprietorship of Mallam. On the occasion of their first visit to Hook Norton in 1842, the Metropolitan Commissioners made no adverse comments about the pauper or private departments. The full minutes made by the Metropolitan Commissioners at this time are reproduced, as they illustrate the type of report which was to establish a more uniform pattern for reporting by the Visiting Magistrates:

We have today officially visited the two houses situated at this place, which are comprised in Mr. Tilsley's house, have seen and spoken to all the persons who are now confined in them, and have inspected and examined the different apartments, outbuildings and yards which are occupied by them or appropriated to their use.

The inmates are at present 85 in number, of whom 16 are private and 69 are pauper patients: Of the former 13 are males and 3 females. Of the latter 34 are males and 35 females. Generally speaking they were in a tranquil and contented state at the time of our visit and one only, a man who was in the habit of tearing his clothing and striking at his companions, was under personal restraint. Such restraint, however, is very little resorted to; Mr. Tilsley having endeavoured as much as possible to get rid of it.

[1] Miss Jane Batt.
[2] O.C.R.O., QSL.VII/4, Minutes C.L., 2 March 1846.

Although there are, as he conceives certain violent cases in which it cannot be entirely dispensed with consistently with the safety and advantage of the patients themselves.

The certificates which were examined were correct and the different books required by the two acts of parliament (including the Patients' Book) appear to have been regularly kept and filled up. Such suggestions as the Visiting Magistrates have from time to time made in their reports for the better arrangements of the premises and the patients seem to have met with the attention from the proprietor and to have led to various alterations and improvements.

Pains have been taken to classify and arrange the patients according to their comparative degrees of quietness and convalescence and the separation of the sexes is complete.

The rooms and yards were clean and in good order and the sitting rooms warm and comfortable and the general character of the pauper establishment with reference as well to the physical comforts of the inmates, as the condition of the apartments in which they are lodged was creditable and satisfactory. We tasted the food provided for the paupers, which was of good quality and supplied in abundance. There are three male and as many female attendants employed in that branch of the establishment.

The house in which nearly all the private patients reside was clean, well ventilated and in good order and they appeared in general to be contented and cheerful. A considerable number of the pauper men work in the garden and adjoining grounds and also at Mr. Tilsley's farm. They likewise amuse themselves at skittles and other games. Of the pauper women one or two occupy themselves in spinning and many of them knit and sew and are employed in cleaning the rooms and in other household work.

Prayers are read regularly to such of the patients as are in a fit state to join in them and some of them occasionally go to the Parish Church with the attendants.[1]

In 1846, following their visit to Hook Norton, the Commissioners reported that: 'We have been much pleased with the result of our visit and . . . consider both of the establishments in a very creditable and satisfactory condition.'[2] Only occasional remarks were made about possible improvements in such aspects as ventilation, heating or furnishing. Comments on the insufficiency of the bedding for paupers at Hook Norton during the winter months were made on a few occasions. In January 1847, however, the Commissioners regarded as sufficient 'a pair of sheets, an under blanket and two upper blankets . . . particularly as the patients are allowed to keep their own clothes and during the severe weather they are all placed on

[1] O.C.R.O., QSL.X/1/C, Minutes M.C.L., 18 Oct. 1842. (On this occasion, the Commissioners were J. W. Mylne and Dr Thomas Turner.)
[2] O.C.R.O., QSL.VII/5, Minutes C.L., 3 March 1846.

their beds at night'.[1] The clothing of patients at both Hook Norton and Witney appears not to have attracted any adverse comments.

The dietary

The Visiting Magistrates and the Commissioners generally recorded a comment about the patients' food. It was reported often that they had tasted the food and, invariably, it was found to be of good quality and ample in amount. The pauper dietary at Hook Norton in 1844[2] and 1847[3] is available, but there are no details of the dietary at Witney.

The pauper dietary at Hook Norton, in 1847, is summarized as follows:

Breakfast
Males   6–7 oz. bread; 1 quart boiled milk or broth.
Females 5–6 oz. bread; $1\frac{1}{2}$ pints boiled milk or $\frac{1}{2}$ pint of coffee.

Supper
Males   5–6 oz. bread; $1\frac{1}{2}$ oz. cheese; $\frac{3}{4}$ pint table beer.
Females 4 oz. bread and butter; $\frac{1}{2}$ pint tea.

Dinner
Males   *Sunday*: 4 oz. meat cooked free from bone; 8 oz. batter pudding, baked under the meat; 12 oz. potatoes; $\frac{3}{4}$ pint table beer.
Monday and Thursday: 1 pint rice pudding made with suet and milk; 4 oz. bread; 1 oz. cheese; $\frac{3}{4}$ pint table beer.
Tuesday and Friday: 6 oz. meat cooked free from bone; 3 oz. bread; 12 ozs. potatoes or other vegetables; $\frac{3}{4}$ pint table beer.
Wednesday: 16–18 ozs. suet pudding; $\frac{3}{4}$ pint table beer.
Saturday: 8 oz. bread; 3 pints soup.

Females *Sunday*: 3 oz. meat cooked free from bone; 8 oz. pudding baked under the meat; 10 oz. potatoes; $\frac{1}{2}$ pint table beer.
Monday and Thursday: $1\frac{1}{4}$ pints rice pudding made as stated; $\frac{1}{2}$ pint table beer.
Tuesday and Friday: 5 oz. meat cooked free from bone; 3 oz. bread; 12 oz. potatoes or other vegetables; $\frac{1}{2}$ pint table beer.
Wednesday: 14–16 oz. suet pudding; $\frac{1}{2}$ pint table beer.
Saturday: 6 oz. bread, 2 pints soup.

The soup is made with the liquer the meat is boiled in, the day previous with the bones, and a shin or ox cheek, also meat liquer from private house about six or eight pints of peas, and an abundance of vegetables and herbs. In winter the soup is given twice in the week. Fresh mutton or beef are

---

[1] O.C.R.O., QSL.VII/5, Minutes C.L., 21 Jan. 1847.

[2] 1844 Report M.C.L., Appendix E, p. 266. (The pauper dietaries at twenty provincial licensed houses were given.)

[3] O.C.R.O., QSL.X/1/C, letter, Mallam to Clerk of Peace, 26 April 1847, enclosing the dietary, by direction of the C.L.

used on Sunday or Tuesday. On Friday the beef has been salted one week. In the fruit season it is often used in the suet puddings. Lettuces, radishes or onions are often given with the supper in the summer. The patients who work in the garden are allowed bread and cheese and beer extra, also women who are actively employed. Two sorts of vegetables are usually giveni n the summer.

This diet table was typical of the majority published in the 1844 Report of the Metropolitan Commissioners. It was customary for the female portion to be smaller than that for the men and, also, for extra allowances to be made to those patients who worked; such allowances were given often in the form of an extra meal in the late morning. In 1842, at Fairford, Gloucestershire, it was recorded that, 'Such of the patients as labour have ale and table beer mixed, and, occasionally, meat for their breakfast; and are, moreover, allowed small quantities of tobacco and snuff'.[1] Similar allowances were made at Duddeston Hall and Fisherton House and the Dietary Table for the paupers at Laverstock House, in 1847, included the statement: 'Patients who work are allowed 2 extra pints of beer with snuff and tobacco and have their meals in the kitchen with the servants.'[2]

The treatment of patients

Mechanical restraint

During the period covered by the surviving records, the treatment of patients at Hook Norton and Witney does not appear to have been unduly harsh. In 1778, Joanna Harris stated that she used only great tenderness in the handling of lunatics placed in her charge.[3] (Figure 4). The Visiting Magistrates observed, in 1833, that at Witney, 'the treatment of the patients has uniformly been conducted on principles of assiduity, caution, kindness and due attention to the wants both intellectual and bodily of the unfortunate inmates . . . the system of active treatment and the opportunities for recreation are both admirably conducive to the restoration of lost faculties'.[4] Later, they noted that 'the tedium of necessary confinement was alleviated by the invigorating effect of exercise in a large and airy close and garden'.[5] Similar remarks were made concerning the treatment of

[1] 1844 Report M.C.L., p. 263.

[2] Wilts. C.R.O., Q.S. lunacy records (private asylums).

[3] Bod. Lib. N.G.A. Oxon. a4, *Jackson's Oxford Journal*, 31 Oct. 1778, No. 1331, p. 3.

[4] O.C.R.O., QSL.VII/6, Minutes V.M., 20 June 1833.

[5] O.C.R.O., QSL.VII/6, Minutes V.M., 27 June 1833.

patients at Hook Norton. In addition, in 1830, it was noted in a directory that the asylum was 'most ably conducted by Mr. Henry Tilsley, surgeon, whose humanity to his unfortunate inmates has secured to him the respect and regard of all who know him and especially those connected with his patients'.[1] A similar comment was made in the 1842 edition of this directory and the picture of Tilsley, obtained from various sources, is certainly that of a kindly person, who was greatly interested in the welfare of his patients and the running of his establishment. Mechanical restraint of patients was used, to some extent, at both houses throughout the period 1828 to 1855; its use being discontinued for the last two years of the lifespan of Witney. The surviving records indicate clearly that the Visiting Magistrates and Commissioners approved of instrumental restraint in cases of extreme violence, when the safety of attendants or other patients was endangered. The usual forms employed were those involving the use of leather straps and belts, to confine the patient to the bed or chair or to fasten the hands to a waist-strap. Linen muffs, cuffs and gloves and strait-waistcoats were used at both houses and there is one reference to hobbles at Witney and to the use of a wrist-lock at Hook Norton. In general, it appears that the restraint was applied for short periods, when the patient was particularly violent or dangerous. Restraint of troublesome patients at night, but not during the day, is often described and this practice was related, undoubtedly, to the reduced number of attendants on duty at night. The principal reasons given for its use included dangerous and destructive tendencies, the tearing of clothing and bedding and violence associated with epilepsy. The first references to the use of the term 'seclusion' were in 1844, at Hook Norton[2] and, in 1854, at Witney.[3]

Mechanical restraint does not appear to have been employed excessively, at any time, at Hook Norton. On the occasion of their first visit to the house, in 1842, the Metropolitan Commissioners observed that one man, 'who was in the habit of tearing his clothing and striking at his companions', was under restraint, but it was added that 'such restraint . . . is very little resorted to, Mr. Tilsley having endeavoured as much as possible to get rid of it. Although there are,

---

[1] Pigot and Co.'s *London and Provincial New Commercial Directory*, 1830, p. 643.

[2] O.C.R.O., QSL.VII/5, Minutes M.C.L., 9 Oct. 1844.

[3] O.C.R.O., QSL.VII/4, Minutes C.L., 19 Jan. 1854.

as he conceives, certain violent cases in which it cannot be entirely dispensed with consistently with the safety and advantage of the patients themselves'.[1] This view appears to have been shared by Tilsley's successor and restraint continued to be used only in a limited and selective way at the asylum until its closure. The maximum number of patients recorded as being under restraint at any one time was in 1846, when the number was five and, generally, there were only one or two patients restrained. Frequently, no patients were being restrained at the time of inspection, although, according to the official visitors, there was evidence in the weekly Medical Journal that restraint was employed at times. The Commissioners were of the opinion that Mallam's use of restraint was judicious[2] and they stressed that it was employed sparingly and always with his sanction.

At Witney, the use of mechanical restraint featured more prominently, principally during the last five years of its lifespan. It is interesting to note that the first positive reference to the use of restraint, at this house, was made in 1846, although, in the previous year, the Visiting Magistrates had made such ambiguous comments as, 'no unnecessary restraint or severity is practised'.[3] The following is a typical comment made by the Visiting Magistrates regarding the use of restraint at Witney: 'The female patients are all in an excited state and two of them under restraint both confined to chairs with straps round their waists. The hands of one were confined with a muff. We are informed by the attendants they are liberated in the course of the day to take exercise out of doors.'[4] Earlier, the Commissioners had recommended that such constant restraint should be reduced during the day, when the patient was 'under the eye of her attendant'. 'Filthiness of habits' and a 'disposition to destroy ... personal and bed linen' were quoted, upon a number of occasions, as reasons for the use of restraint. In 1850, the Visitors expressed their approval of the use of restraint after witnessing a violent attack by a patient on a female attendant, 'whose patience and forbearance were exemplary'.[5] By 1851, the Commissioners were becoming more critical of the regime at Witney and, in that year, recommended the removal of mildewed straps, staples and padlocks from beside the

[1] O.C.R.O., QSL.X/1/C, Minutes M.C.L., 18 Oct. 1842.
[2] Cf. views expressed by Mallam in 1854. *Vide infra*, p. 179.
[3] O.C.R.O., QSL.VII/2, Minutes V.M., 31 July 1845.
[4] *Ibid.*, 4 March 1847.
[5] O.C.R.O., QSL.VII/4, Minutes V.M., 3 Jan. 1850.

beds of male patients. In 1853, the Commissioners criticized the fact that 'one lady is generally fastened at night by a belt and that occasionally she wears cuffs . . . one of the male patients is always fastened at night by a belt and strap which is fastened to a staple in the wall near his bed, and that another male patient has very frequently been restrained by a belt and cuffs lately' and they disapproved of 'so large an amount of mechanical coercion in an asylum containing only ten patients'.[1] In 1855, it was recorded that six of the nine women in the house were 'fastened', three of them repeatedly. The Commissioners expressed grave concern and recommended that all instruments of restraint should be withdrawn from the control of the 'nurses' and not be used without the express consent of the medical attendant.[2] At the 1855 Michaelmas Sessions, Eliza Batt's licence was granted for a four-month period only, pending further reports by the magistrates. Subsequently, she discontinued the use of any form of mechanical restraint and her full licence was re-granted in 1856, following favourable reports by the Visitors.[3] It is interesting to read, in her application for the renewal of her full licence, the statement that, since her husband's death in October 1853, she had spent upwards of £500 improving the asylum 'in accordance with the tastes and requirements of the present day'.[4] She was referring, probably, to some of the changes and recommendations recorded by the Commissioners in November 1855, when the following observations were made:

The wall surrounding the yard fronting the general sitting room . . . has been taken down and the space covered with turf and ornamental planting. The heavy fire guards and iron works have also been removed and the partition forming a dark room on the ground floor taken down and the room itself taken into the adjoining room.

Suggestions were made for the gardens, 'where exercise . . . may be . . . substituted for restraint or seclusion during periods of excitement. The yard adjoining the cottage should be planted and ornamented and objects of interest placed in the rooms.'[5]

'Moral management'

The principles of moral management of patients appear to have been adopted at both houses, although this was more clearly the

[1] O.C.R.O., QSL.VII/4, Minutes C.L., 24 June 1853.   [2] *Vide* P.R.O., M.H. 50, Minute Book C.L., Vol. 7, 11, 18 July 1855.   [3] *Vide* O.C.R.O., QSL.X/1/E.   [4] *Ibid.*, letter, Eliza Batt to Oxfordshire Magistrates, 13 Dec. 1855.   [5] O.C.R.O., QSL.VII/4, Minutes C.L., 9 Nov. 1855.

case at Hook Norton. Provisions were made for the 'classification' of patients, in addition to the usual separation of private and pauper patients and of the sexes, but reference to such provisions were not made by the Visitors before 1842. In that year, the Metropolitan Commissioners observed, with regard to Hook Norton, that 'pains have been taken to classify and arrange the patients according to their comparative degrees of quietness or convalescence'.[1] Later, reference was made to the separation of the violent and dirty patients from the others. It is likely that classification of patients was not a difficult problem at Witney, where a small number of patients, principally middle-class women, were housed in a relatively commodious establishment. The occupation of patients by means of manual work appears, primarily, to have been a requirement for the paupers. At Hook Norton, the male paupers were employed in the yards, gardens and attached grounds. In 1844, Mallam was reported to have purchased additional land, to be 'broken up' for the employment of patients.[2] The difficulties of finding suitable outdoor occupation for the men in wintertime are mentioned. The women were employed in general household work, needlework, spinning and lace-making. At Witney, there are a few references to the use of gardening as an occupation for the male patients, but in view of the type of patient accommodated at this house, occupation was equated generally with recreation. It emerges from the Visitors' and Commissioners' reports, after 1844, that facilities for recreation were adequate at Hook Norton and Witney, prior to this time, detailed descriptions of provisions were not recorded and, in fact, the earlier reports suggest little awareness of its importance. The recreational facilities provided were typical of those employed in most licensed houses and included indoor amusements, such as bagatelle, billiards, draughts and chess, together with the use of musical instruments, books, newspapers and literary periodicals 'of an amusing character'. Suitable patients were encouraged to take exercise in the gardens and courtyards and, at Witney in 1856, a small aviary was built for the amusement of the patients. It was not unusual for birds to be used in this way, particularly doves, silver pheasants and various cage-birds. Another similar example is afforded in the records of the house at Fonthill Gifford, where, in 1832, there was 'a canary and other

[1] O.C.R.O., QSL.X/1/C, Minutes C.L., 18 Oct. 1842.
[2] This land may have been the area of land in Hook Norton once referred to as 'Madman's Close', but now known as Mallam's Close.

singing birds for the gratification of those who are attached to such domesticated living objects'.[1] A good deal of liberty was allowed to convalescent and non-acutely disturbed private patients, who tended to be treated as members of the proprietor's household, a practice that was common in the smaller licensed houses. In 1828, Tilsley noted that: 'Patients not requiring absolute restraint are allowed to walk in the village and fields accompanied by proper attendants.'[2] Subsequently, at both houses, certain patients appear to have been allowed similar freedom. On one occasion, a Witney patient was even allowed to attend the Great Exhibition held in London in 1851[3] and, subsequently, the Visitors noted that 'he expressed himself much gratified with the indulgence and the Visitors consider it has been beneficial to him'.[4]

Considerable attention was paid to religious activities at both Hook Norton and Witney. The general rule was for daily prayers to be read by the proprietor, a member of his family, or one of the attendants. Visits were made, at varying intervals, by the parish incumbent, and a small number of patients were allowed to attend the parish church. Such arrangements clearly depended a good deal on the enthusiasm of the local clergyman. It was noted, frequently, that religious observances were only appropriate for patients who were likely to benefit from them, although, apparently, all patients were allowed access to the Bible and to religious tracts.

Very few complaints by the patients are recorded in the minutes of the Visitors or Commissioners, indeed, on several occasions, it is reported that the patients expressed appreciation of the kindness with which they had been treated. In 1850, one of the male patients at Witney complained that he had not received his proper allowance of pocket money, but an enquiry by the Visitors revealed no foundation for this complaint.[5]

Medical treatment and the general health of the patients
The medical treatment of patients was the responsibility of the medical attendant, in the absence of a medically qualified proprietor or superintendent. Statutory provisions concerning the appointment

---

[1] Wilts. C.R.O., Q.S. lunacy records (private asylums), Minutes V.M., 7 Nov. 1832.
[2] O.C.R.O., QSL.X/1/B, letter, Tilsley to Clerk of Peace, 2 Oct. 1828.
[3] The Great Exhibition of the industries of all nations, at the Crystal Palace.
[4] O.C.R.O., QSL.VII/2, Minutes V.M., 11 Dec. 1851.
[5] O.C.R.O., QSL.VII/2, Minutes V.M., 12 Sept. 1850.

and the visiting requirements of a medical attendant were first made in 1828. These applied when the resident proprietor or superintendent was not a medical man and, consequently, the Witney licensed house required a medical attendant during the periods 1828 to 1849 and 1853 to 1857. During the first period, when Rebecca Batt ran the asylum, her brother-in-law, Augustine William, a well-established local surgeon, acted as medical attendant. During the period 1842 to 1849, Jane Batt acted as resident superintendent on behalf of her medically qualified nephew. Following his death, Eliza Batt was assisted by her son, Augustine, who was medically qualified. At Hook Norton, there was an unbroken succession of resident medical superintendents from 1826 onwards. Very little information relating to the forms of medical treatment employed is to be found in surviving manuscript material. Fortunately, however, a printed account dating from 1847 has survived of the remedies and opinions of Mallam. His views correspond fairly closely with those of the majority of medical officers of asylums at that time and they will be referred to in detail in Chapter 7.[1] The bodily health of patients at the time of admission is also discussed in the same chapter,[2] a notable finding being evidence to suggest that many paupers were admitted in a poor physical state. It is of interest to note that neither of the houses was affected by the Asiatic cholera epidemics of the mid-nineteenth century.[3] In the 1849–50 outbreak, 454 patients in asylums in England and Wales were infected and 311 of these died. Provincial licensed houses affected, at this time, were Kingsland Asylum, Shrewsbury; Vernon House, Glamorgan; and Wrekenton Asylum, Gateshead. At Vernon House, nine of the 151 patients were infected and eight of them died.[4] In August 1850, an outbreak of erysipelas occurred amongst the pauper patients at Hook Norton, particularly those from London, who appear to have been generally unhealthy. There was one death attributed to this condition but Mallam was praised by the Visitors for his efforts to combat infection by fumigation, ventilation, great cleanliness and dietary changes, such as 'substituting porter for beer to invigorate the constitutions of the inmates'.[5]

The attendants

The Oxfordshire records suggest that the attendants treated the

[1] *Vide infra*, p. 194.   [2] *Vide infra*, p. 216.
[3] Fifth Report (1850) C.L., Appendix (C) Cholera, pp. 29–49.
[4] *Ibid.*, p. 48.   [5] O.C.R.O., QSL.VII/3, Minutes V.M., 13 Aug. 1850.

patients in a kindly fashion and did not misuse their position, but the evidence is sparse. There is record of only a single instance in which a patient was ill-used by an attendant and this occurred at Hook Norton, in 1851, when a female attendant struck a patient. The Visiting Magistrates enquired into the incident and reported that

as there was no serious injury we consider the loss of her situation a sufficient punishment. Mr. Mallam having very properly discharged her and a reprimand having been given her by ourselves and she herself having expressed great contrition, we do not consider it necessary to recommend any further steps to be taken.[1]

Unfortunately, there is very limited information regarding the role and number of attendants at Hook Norton and Witney. The number of attendants per patient was inevitably lower in houses catering principally for paupers. Thus, at the pauper establishment at Hook Norton, the Upper House, in 1842, three male and three female attendants looked after seventy paupers.[2] By January 1854, when Hook Norton was licensed for a total of sixty-eight patients, there were only fifteen resident patients, with two male and two female attendants.[3] At Witney, in 1854 to 1855, the proportion of attendants to patients varied from four to ten, to four to six. The staff at Witney, at this time, comprised four resident attendants, a cook and a house-maid, the duties of the latter two being divided between the patients and Mrs Batt and her family. One of the attendants was male and he received a salary of £15 a year. The other three comprised the head nurse, who had been at the asylum for over fourteen years and received a salary of £21 10s. a year; the second nurse, who received £8 10s.; and the under nurse, at £6 a year.[4] In 1842, the Upper House at Hook Norton was superintended by one John Blea, an experienced attendant, who had managed it previously for seven years. Many attendants are named in the course of the records but little or no biographical details are given. The terms 'attendant', 'nurse' and 'keeper' did not indicate any difference in role or status, apart from the fact that women were generally referred to as nurses. The duties of an attendant appear to have been primarily custodial and, in addition to the maintenance of general observation, these duties involved activities such as, accompanying patients in their exercise

---

[1] *Ibid.*, 10 Oct. 1851.
[2] O.C.R.O., QSL.X/1/C, Minutes M.C.L., 10 Oct. 1842.
[3] P.R., 1854(a), p. 29.
[4] O.C.R.O., QSL.X/1/E, letter, Eliza Batt to Clerk of Peace, 19 Oct. 1855.

and recreation both in and outside the asylum; attending to their personal needs and cleanliness and the application of mechanical restraint. There is virtually no information about the personal relationship between the patients and the staff, although this must have been close at a small establishment such as that at Witney. It was at Witney that the strange circumstance is recorded of a female attendant sleeping, by night, in the same room as a male patient, who was 'addicted to disgusting habits, especially in the presence of females',[1] and the history of this patient is detailed in Case (4), Appendix D.

The custodial duties appear to have been carried out effectively, in that only two patients are known to have escaped from the Oxfordshire madhouses during the period 1828 to 1857. In October 1843, Thomas Parsloe, a pauper lunatic, described by Mallam as 'incoherent . . . and harmless as respects himself and others', evaded his keeper at Hook Norton, scaled the boundary wall and escaped. He was not recaptured for three days.[2] In June 1845, Robert Taylor, who had been deluded for several years, escaped from Witney. However, 'being soon missed his attendant started in pursuit of him and overtook him at a village about three miles from this place and brought him back to the asylum'.[3] Only two deaths by suicide occurred at these houses during the period for which records are available and, in one of these cases, the suicide attempt had been made prior to admission. Ann Watson, a pauper admitted to Hook Norton in June 1836, died nine days later, 'from the effects of a severe wound of the throat extending into the trachea committed by herself before admission'.[4] In June 1838, Anne Wheeler, a forty-seven-year-old spinster, committed suicide at Witney by 'hanging herself to a bed's post'.[5]

Details relating to admissions and discharges

Statistical information relating to the Hook Norton and Witney licensed houses may be derived from the following sources:

(1) The Country Register, 1798–1812. Admissions to Hook Norton

[1] O.C.R.O., QSL.VII/4, Minutes C.L., 24 June 1853.
[2] O.C.R.O., QSL.X/1/C, letters, Mallam to Clerk of Peace, 21 & 22 Oct. 1843.
[3] *Ibid.*, letter, E. A. Batt to Clerk of Peace, 26 June 1845.
[4] O.C.R.O., QSL.I/5.   [5] O.C.R.O., QSL.I/7.

in the period October 1801 to October 1812 are recorded. This information has been referred to in Chapter 3.[1]

(2) The Parliamentary Return of 1831. The number of patients in each house was given, together with the number discharged or deceased during 1830. Rebecca Batt's original return has survived.[2] At Witney, from 4 January to 28 February 1831, six women and a man were admitted and, in the same period, nine women and two men were discharged and one woman died. The twelve patients resident at the time of the return comprised four incurable men, seven incurable women and one woman who was curable. According to the Return, three men and three women were discharged from Hook Norton in 1830 and one man died.[3]

(3) The Statistical Appendix to the 1844 Report of the Metropolitan Commissioners in Lunacy. The statistics were intended to cover the period 1839 to 1843, but, in the case of Witney, they date from October 1842, which date was given, erroneously, as the date of opening of the asylum, but, in fact, it was the date when Edward Augustine took over the asylum from Rebecca Batt.

(4) The Eighth Report (1854) of the Commissioners in Lunacy, Appendix H. This source provides admission and discharge statistics for Hook Norton, 1849–53, and a statement of the average annual numbers and of the number of resident patients on the first of January in each of these years.

The relevant tables for Hook Norton included in sources (3) and (4) are presented in Appendix E, principally to allow comparison with the findings derived from the surviving records.

(5) Admission and discharge documents and registers of patients, relating to Hook Norton and Witney, amongst the Oxfordshire Quarter Sessions lunacy records. An exhaustive study of this material was carried out and details concerning the extraction, coding and analysis of the data derived from this source are given in Appendix C. General statistics are presented below and those concerned with clinical aspects and the outcome of treatment are given in Chapter 7.

Statistical data derived from the Oxfordshire MSS.

The primary purposes of the statistical study of admissions and discharges, during the period 1828 to 1857, were, firstly, to make the

---

[1] *Vide supra*, p. 44.   [2] O.C.R.O., QSL.X/1/B, return, 1 March 1831.
[3] *Ibid.*, 28 Feb. 1831.

fullest possible use of surviving records, in order to illuminate the functioning and role of the two Oxfordshire licensed houses; and secondly, to investigate both the potential value and the limitations of this wholly unexplored source as research material for the study of insanity and its management in the first half of the nineteenth century. The limitations of such a study are considerable and, with regard to many of the findings, only broad interpretations are possible. During the particular period covered by the Oxfordshire records, three legislative changes produced alterations in the format of the admission and discharge documents. The development and modification of these documents is discussed in Appendix A, and clarification is given in Appendix C of the respective dates following which certain items of information became legally necessary. The details required on the documents introduced in 1828 (Plate VII) and in 1832 were only rudimentary and, as a result, the items of information which, theoretically, should be available for all patients in the Oxfordshire series are, in fact, limited to those concerned with the dates of admission and discharge, the sex, legal status and place of abode. Clearly, the study of a consecutive series of admissions after 1845 would be much more rewarding. This variation in the content of the documents leads to difficulties with regard to the presentation of the extracted data and, in many cases, is sufficient to preclude any decisive statistical interpretations. It was decided that, for the purposes of this study, the simplest mode of presentation would be, generally, in terms of the total number of admissions. In addition, separate reference is made to the findings of the study of a group of patients, whose first admission to Hook Norton or Witney constituted, as far as can be ascertained, their first admission to any asylum. The patients included in this group had to fulfil two criteria on their first admission during the period of study; firstly, that the attack precipitating admission was stated clearly to be the first attack of insanity and, secondly, that they were stated as having had no previous period of confinement.

Annual admissions and discharges and the frequency of admission of patients in the survey-period
A complete series of consecutive admissions to Hook Norton and Witney is available for the period 24 August 1828 to 11 May 1856,[1]

---

[1] O.C.R.O., 1828–32, QSL.VI/3; 1832–45, QSL.I/1–15; 1845–56, QSL.II/1–12.

referred to henceforth as the survey-period.[1] During this period, a total of 745 admissions took place to the two establishments, comprising 634 to Hook Norton and 111 to Witney. The group of first admissions numbered eighty-six patients and comprised seventy-one admitted to Hook Norton (fifty-three paupers) and fifteen to Witney, during the period 1845 to 1856.

The annual admission and discharge figures for each licensed house are set out in Table 17. It is significant that minor discrepancies only are revealed by a comparison of the published statistics for Hook Norton, in the periods 1839 to 1843 and 1849 to 1853, (Tables I[A], II[A], VI[A] and VII[A]) with the figures derived from the MS. source. In the Statistical Appendix to the 1844 Report of the Metropolitan Commissioners, the only details given for Witney related to the twelve months from October 1842. During this year, seven admissions were recorded, with two discharges and one death.[2] The turnover of patients at Witney was consistently small and in one year, 1841, there were no admissions or discharges. At Hook Norton, however, although the number of private patients admitted per annum remained fairly consistent, never exceeding eleven (the number admitted in 1840), the admission of paupers rose considerably following the opening of the Upper House, in 1835. The aggregates of both the admissions and discharges for each quarter of the year are displayed in Table 18. At both houses, the greatest number of admissions took place in the period April to September, in particular, during the third quarter of the year. This finding is in keeping with several contemporary nineteenth-century observations. For example, at Bethlem Hospital, 1846–53, the largest aggregate of admissions was during the second quarter, followed by the third quarter.[3] At Hook Norton, the number of discharges was considerably greater during the period July to September, but this was not the case at Witney.

The 745 admissions to the two Oxfordshire licensed houses related to 604 individual patients, comprising 523 patients admitted to Hook Norton and eighty-one to Witney at the time of first admission during the survey-period. Table 19 summarizes the information

---

[1] Actually delineated by the first admission to take place under the Act of 9 Geo. IV, c. 41 (passed 15 July 1828) and the final admission to Witney. The last of the corresponding discharges took place on 19 Oct. 1857, when the house at Witney closed.

[2] Statistical Appendix to 1844 Report M.C.L., p. 130.

[3] Hood, W. C. (1855), *Statistics of Insanity*, pp. 78–83.

TABLE 17 *Annual admissions and discharges to Hook Norton and Witney (pauper admissions and discharges are given in brackets)*

Year	Admissions				Discharges			
	Hook Norton		Witney	Total	Hook Norton		Witney	Total
24 Aug.								
1828	3	(2)	1	4	0		0	0
1829	4	(1)	8 (1)	12	6	(3)	5	11
1830	7	(4)	7 (1)	14	5	(3)	8 (2)	13
1831	14	(9)	7	21	7	(4)	3	10
1832	21	(12)	6	27	15	(10)	5	20
1833	12	(5)	3	15	12	(3)	2	14
1834	11	(7)	2	13	6	(4)	3	9
1835	21	(16)	3	24	9	(5)	0	9
1836	24	(16)	5	29	11	(4)	5	16
1837	35	(29)	3	38	19	(16)	3	22
1838	44	(40)	3	47	43	(37)	4	47
1839	43	(33)	1	44	30	(23)	1	31
1840	42	(31)	1	43	39	(31)	4	43
1841	41	(34)	0	41	33	(26)	0	33
1842	34	(31)	6	40	45	(34)	3	48
1843	22	(19)	3	25	19	(15)	2	21
1844	28	(27)	1	29	31	(28)	1	32
1845	33	(29)	3	36	25	(22)	4	29
1846	34	(29)	4	38	60	(55)	4	64
1847	45	(38)	5	50	22	(18)	6	28
1848	16	(12)	3	19	22	(14)	3	25
1849	24	(17)	3	27	39	(32)	2	41
1850	32	(27)	2	34	27	(21)	4	31
1851	24	(16)	1	25	28	(24)	2	30
1852	15	(11)	4	19	44	(36)	4	48
1853	4	(1)	6	10	18	(15)	6	24
1854	1	(1)	11	12	15	(10)	8	23
1855	Closed		4	4	Closed		7	7
1856			5	5			6	6
1857			0	0			3	3
Not known					4	(4)	3	7
Total	634 (497)		111 (2)	745	634 (497)		111 (2)	745

TABLE 18   *Aggregates of the admissions and discharges in each quarter*

Quarter	Admissions			Discharges		
	Hook Norton	Witney	Total	Hook Norton	Witney	Total
Jan.–March	132	24	156	144	20	164
April–June	172	31	203	122	27	149
July–Sept.	188	36	224	221	31	252
Oct.–Dec.	142	20	162	143	30	173
Not known	0	0	0	4	3	7
Total	634	111	745	634	111	745

concerning the frequency of admission of patients to these houses during the survey-period. The great majority of the patients, namely 522, were admitted once only during this period and this number comprised 457 to Hook Norton and sixty-five to Witney. Amongst the twenty-three patients who were admitted three or more times, seventeen were Hook Norton patients, eleven of these being paupers. The patient admitted eight times was a middle-aged female pauper, for whom there is little clinical information, as only one of her admis-

TABLE 19   *Frequency of admission of patients during the survey-period* (*Hook Norton and Witney combined*)

Frequency of admission	Number of patients	Total admissions
1	522	522
2	59	118
3	9	27
4	5	20
5	3	15
6	2	12
7	2	14
8	1	8
9	1	9
Total	604	745

sions took place after 1845. The case history of the patient admitted nine times is given in Case (3), Appendix D.

Legal status and sex
Data relating to the legal status and sex of the patients are summarized in Tables 20 and 21. Admissions of pauper lunatics consti-

TABLE 20 *Legal status*

Legal status	Hook Norton	Witney	Total admissions
Pauper lunatic	497	2	499
Private patient	137	107	244
Not known	0	2	2
Total	634	111	745

tuted over three-quarters of the total admissions to Hook Norton during the survey-period and the bulk of these admissions took place from 1837 to 1847 (Table 17). At Witney, only two patients known to be paupers were admitted during the survey-period and the status of two others was unclear in the MS. although they were likely to have been private patients. At this house, there was a significant difference in the distribution of the sexes, as male admissions

TABLE 21 *Sex (pauper admissions given in brackets)*

Sex	Hook Norton	Witney	Total admissions
Male	316 (227)	20 (1)	336 (228)
Female	318 (270)	91 (1)	409 (271)
Total	634 (497)	111 (2)	745 (499)

constituted less than one-quarter of the total. Despite the popular mid-nineteenth-century view that insanity was more prevalent amongst women than amongst men, it is likely that the preponderance of female patients at Witney was due to the fact that, during twenty-five of the thirty-four years of its lifespan, the proprietor or superintendent was a woman. Females outnumbered the males amongst the admissions of pauper lunatics to Hook Norton, but

161

there were nearly twice as many admissions of male private patients as there were of females. The latter finding was related, in part, to the fact that, from 1842, the policy at Hook Norton was not to receive female private patients. In the group of first admissions, female patients outnumbered the males at both licensed houses.[1] A slightly higher number of pauper lunatic admissions took place by order of parochial officials, including the officiating clergyman, than by order of the justices of the peace. The involvement of the officiating clergyman was restricted by the Act of 1845, which recommended that an order should be made by him only if the patient was too ill to be taken before a magistrate and, in fact, after 1845 the majority of orders for the admission of paupers to Hook Norton were made by magistrates.

Age, marital status, religion and occupation
Tables 22–5 display the admissions by age-groups, marital status, religion and occupation respectively. The average age of the admissions to Hook Norton and Witney were very similar, being forty-

TABLE 22   *Age groups*

Age group (years)	Hook Norton	Witney	Total admissions
< 20	8	3	11
20 –	59	11	70
30 –	63	25	88
40 –	62	19	81
50 –	42	17	59
60 –	40	10	50
70 –	23	2	25
80 –	1	0	1
90 +	1	0	1
Not known	27	22	49
Not applicable	308	2	310
Total	634	111	745

five and forty-four years respectively. The average age of the eighty-six patients in the group of first admissions was forty-three years. Amongst the patients aged less than twenty years at the time of

[1] Cf. general discussion re distribution of sexes in licensed houses. *Vide supra,* p. 48.

TABLE 23 *Marital status*

Marital status	Hook Norton	Witney	Total admissions
Single	105	43	148
Married	142	28	170
Widowed	28	12	40
Not known	20	5	25
Not applicable	339	23	362
Total	634	111	745

admission, the youngest were two sixteen-year-old boys. At Hook Norton, a greater proportion of the total admissions, for whom details are available, were married than single, although this was not the case at Witney, where there were forty-three admissions of single persons, thirty-two of whom were women (Table 23). The study of first admissions also indicated that married patients were more numerous than the unmarried at Hook Norton, but not at Witney. The great majority of the admissions, for whom details in respect of religious persuasion are available, were members of the Church of England (Table 24), especially if those described by the ambiguous term 'Protestant' are included.

In view of the high intake of pauper lunatics at Hook Norton, the largest occupational category, naturally, was that which comprised labourers and servants (Table 25). Similarly, at Witney, which always catered essentially for the upper and middle classes, 'gentlefolk' formed the largest group. It is interesting to note the low figure for

TABLE 24 *Religion*

Religion	Hook Norton	Witney	Total admissions
Church of England	98	30	128
'Protestant'	37	9	46
Nonconformist	28	2	30
Roman Catholic	9	0	9
None	3	1	4
Others	1	0	1
Not known	30	8	38
Not applicable	428	61	489
Total	634	111	745

TABLE 25 *Occupation*[a]

Occupation	Hook Norton	Witney	Total admissions
Professional and other educated persons	15	6	21
Farmers	23	14	37
Occupied in retail trade	29	10	39
Occupied in handicrafts or manufacture	43	0	43
Agricultural labourers	7	0	7
Labourers and servants	98	3	101
Gentlefolk and persons without occupation	22	38	60
Not known	62	37	99
Not applicable	335	3	338
Total	634	111	745

[a] Female patients or dependants, without specified occupation, were classified according to the occupation of husband or father, if available.

persons actually specified as 'agricultural labourers', in view of the wholly rural surroundings of Hook Norton. It is recorded, however, that on 1 January 1844, the 'class of life' and previous occupation of the seventy paupers resident at Hook Norton was as follows: agricultural, thirty-nine; artisan, nine; and other, twenty-two.[1] For the purposes of comparison, the occupations of the 493 patients admitted to the Oxford Lunatic Asylum, during the period 1826 to 1844, are now quoted: clergymen, sixteen; members of other professions, fifty-nine; wives and children of professional men, thirty-two; farmers, their wives and children, seventy-seven; tradesmen, their wives and children, 205; and servants, 104.[2]

Previous place of abode and history of previous confinement outside the survey-period

Private licensed houses, naturally, had no specific catchment areas

[1] Statistical Appendix to 1844 Report M.C.L., p. 11.
[2] Register of patients, 1826–44. By courtesy of the Warneford Hospital, Oxford.

from which patients were drawn. The concept of such an area came into being with the establishment of county asylums and, initially, it was only applicable to paupers. The distribution of Oxfordshire pauper lunatics at the time of the opening of the Oxfordshire County Asylum, illustrates the fact that Hook Norton had not served as the asylum for all the pauper lunatics in the county, who needed confinement. Thus, during the first five months following its opening, the county asylum received a total of fifty-seven paupers from eight asylums outside the county and thirty-four from Hook Norton.[1] However, the admissions from Oxfordshire to both Hook Norton and Witney greatly outnumbered those from any other county (Table 26). It has been shown previously (Table 7) that in the years

TABLE 26 *Previous place of abode, given by counties*

Previous place of abode	Hook Norton	Witney	Total admissions
Oxfordshire	254	81	335
Warwickshire	148	0	148
Gloucestershire	75	1	76
Northamptonshire	46	4	50
Buckinghamshire	36	1	37
London (including Middlesex)	29	0	29
Berkshire	13	14	27
Worcestershire	22	3	25
Other English counties	6	2	8
Elsewhere	4	1	5
Not known	1	4	5
Total	634	111	745

1801 to 1812 the majority of the admissions made to Hook Norton were drawn from Oxfordshire.[2] The geographical position of Hook Norton, however, led to the reception of a considerable number of patients, especially paupers, from Warwickshire and Gloucestershire, although both of these counties contained private licensed houses at this period. This finding supports the view that

[1] Register of patients, 1846–53, Oxfordshire & Berkshire County Asylum, Littlemore.
[2] *Vide supra*, p. 45.

paupers were admitted, generally, to the establishments situated nearest to their parishes and that they were sent further afield only if these establishments were full or if substantially cheaper accommodation could be found elsewhere, in, for example, one of the large metropolitan licensed houses.

A summary is presented, in Table 27, of the details concerning

TABLE 27   *Previous confinement in asylums as stated on first admission during the survey-period*

Previous place of confinement	Hook Norton	Witney	Total patients
Hook Norton	4	1	5
Witney	0	5	5
Other licensed house(s)	18	6	24
Public asylum(s) and hospital(s)	23	3	26
County asylum(s)	22	1	23
More than one type of establishment	6	2	8
No previous confinement	126	32	158
Not known	60	29	89
Not applicable	264	2	266
Total	523	81	604

previous confinement of patients in asylums, as stated at the time of their first admission to Hook Norton or Witney during the survey-period. It was not possible to estimate the number of previous admissions of individual patients. According to the available data, approximately one-half of the total number of patients, for whom details are available, admitted to Hook Norton and Witney had no previous history of admissions to an asylum, although, if other factors are taken into consideration, the estimated number of those making their first admission to any asylum is reduced to eighty-six.[1]

[1] *Vide supra*, p. 157.

Five patients, including two paupers, were stated as having been confined at Bethlem and each was admitted to Hook Norton. Fifteen patients had been admitted, previously, to the Oxford Lunatic Asylum, ten of these being admitted to Hook Norton and five to Witney. A special study of these cases was made to try to elucidate the reasons for their subsequent admission to a private licensed house. However, the only record surviving at the Warneford Hospital, Oxford, relating to this period, was a register of patients, 1826–44, in which eleven of the fifteen cases could be traced, although the information available was of very limited value. As would be expected, the two private licensed houses at Henley-in-Arden, Warwickshire, featured prominently in the list, in view of the relatively high number of admissions to Hook Norton from Warwickshire.

The private licensed houses, other than Hook Norton and Witney, the public asylums and hospitals and the county asylums which were named in the Hook Norton and Witney MSS. were as follows:

Private licensed houses
Hope House, Hammersmith; Warburton's houses at Bethnal Green and Hoxton, London; Stilwell's house, Uxbridge; the Retreat, Clapham; Peckham House, Peckham; Burman's house, and Brown's house, Henley-in-Arden, Warwickshire; Haydock Lodge, Lancashire; Duddeston Hall, near Birmingham; Belle Vue House, Devizes, Wiltshire; Brislington House, Somerset; Cleeve, near Bristol; Laverstock House, Wiltshire; and Sandfield House, Lichfield, Staffordshire.

Public asylums and hospitals
Bethlem Hospital and St Luke's Hospital, London; Oxford Lunatic Asylum; The Friend's Retreat, York; The York Asylum; Northampton General Lunatic Asylum and Morningside Asylum, Edinburgh.

County asylums
The county asylums of Surrey, Lancashire, Gloucestershire, Oxfordshire, Staffordshire and Middlesex (Hanwell).

7

◇◇◇

Aspects of the Care of the Insane in Private Madhouses and the Outcome of Treatment

◇◇◇

CRITICS of the private-madhouse system often claimed that madhouses served little or no curative function and, at best, provided only custodial care. With regard to the period in the history of madhouses under present consideration, however, there is evidence that such a generalization would be misleading. The restoration of the lunatic was the primary objective in many private madhouses during the second half of the eighteenth and early-nineteenth centuries, a period when the reputation of the madhouse system was particularly low, although it was recognized then, as at the present day, that only custodial care was possible in a number of cases. Those who treated the insane at this time, in madhouses in various parts of the country, have not received their proper acknowledgment. Amongst the examples which lend support to this view may be quoted a letter (Plate VIII), dated December 1749, from James Jeffery, owner of the madhouse at Kingsdown, Box, Wiltshire,[1] to the Trowbridge parish overseers regarding a lunatic from that parish. This letter portrays, quite clearly, Jeffery's concern for the welfare of his patient, and the following is an extract from the letter:

Gentlemen . . . concerning John Porter . . . his disorder its much worse than a raving madness and more difficult to cure he being in a sullen meross way . . . I believe need no more at present but that I shall do the best I can for his recovery.[2]

[1] Later known as Kingsdown House.
[2] Wilts. C.R.O., 206/93, Trowbridge parish records.

This letter forms part of a particularly interesting collection of parish records which includes also a letter dated 28 March 1763, in which Jeffery referred to two other patients in his madhouse, one being John Rundle, a pauper lunatic. Jeffery expressed sincere regret that he was not in a position to give a better account of his progress to the Trowbridge parish overseers, 'for altho' Rendall is not so bad as in time past yet he still persists in surprising odd Whyms & Fancys which undoubtedly might end in some bad consequence was he not under proper care'.[1] It is known that Rundle, a weaver, was admitted on 27 December 1758[2] and that he was still at Kingsdown in 1775[3] and his case is of some further interest because two letters written by him have survived in which his delusional ideas about being the King of Prussia are vividly expressed.[4] Plate IX reproduces an extract from one letter (*c.* 1765) in which he addressed his son as 'Prince Ferdinand. Prince of Brunsweke'. Such correspondence, incidentally, gives an illustration of the way in which the content of delusional ideas may reflect current events, as this was a period of turmoil in Europe during and after the Seven Years' War.

Many methods of treatment were employed in private madhouses in what, at the time, was considered to be a curative way, although some of the techniques used were condemned later as brutal and inhumane. Any attempt to provide a comprehensive review of these treatments, however, would be outside the scope of this present study. Useful sources of detailed information are provided in treatises on insanity by authors who wrote from their personal experience as owners of private madhouses, for example, Perfect and Cox. The methods described in such works can be regarded as broadly representative of the practices prevailing in the better establishments, although the accounts of these writers must have been influenced to some extent by the need to display the success of their individual houses. Few accounts are available, whose purpose was neither derogatory nor partial, concerning the methods of treatment in private madhouses in the eighteenth and early-nineteenth centuries. Amongst those that are extant, however, is an interesting description of the practice of Francis Willis senior at Greatford

[1] *Ibid.* [2] Wilts. C.R.O., 206/64, Trowbridge Overseers' Accounts.
[3] Wilts. C.R.O., 206/93, Trowbridge Overseers' maintenance agreement, 29 Sept. 1775.
[4] Wilts. C.R.O., 206/93, Trowbridge parish records.

which was published anonymously in 1796.[1] The reports of parliamentary Select Committees provide a further source of information, as do the minutes recorded, following the inspection of houses, by the Visiting Magistrates and Commissioners, although, up to the mid-nineteenth century, the information included in such minutes was very limited.

The first statutory requirements concerning medical attendants to private licensed houses were introduced by the Madhouse Act of 1828. The medical attendant had to sign the Weekly Register, which comprised a statement of the number of curable and incurable patients and of those under restraint. Under the Act of 1845, a Medical Visitation Book and a Medical Case Book had to be kept. In the latter, an entry was to be made regarding the name, age, sex, previous occupation and marital state of the patient; a description of his external appearance on admission; a descriptive account of the form of the mental disorder, together with details concerning the previous history of the cause of the patient's current illness. Entries were to be made at least weekly for the first month after admission and, thereafter, monthly in the case of recent or 'curable' cases. An accurate record of all medicines administered and remedies employed had to be kept. The fact that only two such case-books appear to be extant at the present day, those of Camberwell House, London, renders this a source of negligible value practically speaking.[2]

Mechanical restraint and 'moral management'

The use of mechanical restraint was a subject of paramount importance throughout the first half of the nineteenth century, from both the ideological and practical viewpoints. The movement to replace the traditional reliance on mechanical restraint by non-physical forms of 'management' had taken shape by the last two decades of the eighteenth century, both in this country and on the continent.[3] This was recognized by Foucault (1967), who made the point that 'what the nineteenth century formulated so ostentatiously, with all the resources of its pathos [had] already been whispered and

---

[1] Anon. (1796), 'Détails sur l'établissement du docteur Willis, pour la guérison des aliénés', *Bibliothèque britannique* (Littérature) *1*, pp. 759–73.

[2] *Vide* Appendix A, p. 300.

[3] Walk, A. (1954), 'Some Aspects of the "Moral Treatment" of the Insane up to 1854', *J. Ment. Sci. 100*, pp. 807–37.

indefatigably repeated by the eighteenth'.[1] It would be incorrect to view this process simply as the replacement of wanton cruelty by new, enlightened and humane methods. The use of restraint and 'cruelty' in the treatment of lunatics usually had been in conformity with contemporary attitudes and theoretical concepts. Thus, during the late-eighteenth century, William Cullen (1710–90), the distinguished Edinburgh medical teacher, advocated physical restraint on the basis of a body of hypotheses that were, essentially, neurophysiological,[2] although his own experience in treating insanity was limited. In his *First Lines of the Practice of Physic*, Cullen expressed the following view:

Restraining the anger and violence of madmen is always necessary for preventing their hurting themselves or others: but this restraint is also to be considered as a remedy. Angry passions are always rendered more violent by the indulgence of the impetuous motions they produce; and even in madmen, the feeling of restraint will sometimes prevent the efforts which their passion would otherwise occasion. Restraint, therefore, is useful and ought to be complete.[3]

Cullen's teaching probably had considerable influence on the practice of those of his students, such as Arnold and Hallaran, who later kept their own madhouses. In 1793, Pinel, also an admirer of Cullen's views, abolished the use of chains at the Bicêtre, Paris and substituted the 'gilet de force' as a form of moral suasion, since, in principle, he was not against the use of restraint. In England, the treatment at the York Retreat was centred on the abandonment of harsh and cruel methods, and the public subscription asylums, such as St Luke's Hospital, opened in the second half of the eighteenth century, had had similar objectives. It is likely that humane treatment was being used in many private madhouses at this time, although it is not possible to make any conclusive estimate of its extent. In 1801, Pinel observed that:

English physicians give themselves credit for a great superiority of skill in the moral treatment of insanity; and their success, frequently under the veil of secrecy, has given a sanction to pretensions to which they have no just nor exclusive claims. I have for the last fifteen years paid considerable attention to the subject ... I have discovered no secret; but, I approve of their general principles of treatment.[4]

[1] Foucault, *op. cit.*, p. 222.
[2] *Vide* Carlson, E. T. and McFadden, B. (1960), 'Dr. William Cullen on Mania', *Amer. J. Psychiat. 117*, pp. 463–5.
[3] Cullen, W. (1808). *First Lines of the Practice of Physic*, Vol. II, pp. 312–13.
[4] Pinel, P. (trans. D. D. Davis) (1806), *A Treatise on Insanity*, p. 49.

The kindly methods used by the proprietor of one licensed house, Hanham House, near Bristol,[1] were praised, in 1782, by no less a person than John Wesley. Following a visit to this house, kept by Henderson,[2] Wesley recorded in his journal: 'I particularly enquired into his whole method. There is not such another house for lunatics in the three Kingdoms—he has a peculiar art of governing his patients not by fear but by love. The consequence is that many of them recover and love him ever after.'[3] The poet, William Cowper recollected with warmth and gratitude, in many of his writings, his stay from 1763 to 1765, at Nathaniel Cotton's madhouse, the 'Collegium Insanorum', in St Albans.[4] Charles Lamb's description[5] of the care and affection which his sister, Mary, received at an Islington madhouse, also supports the view that humane treatment was practised in some eighteenth-century private madhouses. Pargeter (1792), who had no practical experience in treating the insane, was amongst the first to write about the treatment of insanity by non-physical means under the name of 'management', although he accepted the fact that 'cases of maniacal refractoriness . . . occur, which require the strongest and closest supervision'.[6] For this purpose, he considered the strait-waistcoat to be the most useful expedient, a view that had been expressed also by Cullen. Cox (1806) claimed that 'management' was 'of the highest importance in the treatment of maniacs and in almost every case is indispensable and has succeeded when the most active means have failed'.[7] He accepted

---

[1] The house was said to be at Clare Hill, but it is likely to have been that later owned by E. L. Fox, before he moved to Brislington House in 1806. This house was situated at Cleeve Hill, Downend, Bristol, but was known variously as Clover Hill (Country Register) and Clewer Hill (Report of 1807 S.C., p. 26).

[2] Henderson 'was an Irishman, who came to England in 1762, and for some years travelled . . . as one of Wesley's helpers. But he left the work, and opened at Hanham a private asylum, which won recognition and high reputation from the faculty and the public of Bristol. Wesley evidently entertained special regard for him, notwithstanding his withdrawal, and paid him frequent visits . . . the earliest of these noted in his Journal is under the date September 29, 1781.' Anon. (1902), 'Richard Henderson and his Private Asylum at Hanham', *Proc. Wesley Hist. Soc. 3*, p. 158.

[3] Methodist Archives & Research Centre, London, Journal of John Wesley, 29 July 1782.

[4] Hill, *op. cit.*

[5] Letter, Lamb to S. T. Coleridge, 3 Oct. 1796. Cited in Lucas, *op. cit.*, pp. 45–46.

[6] Pargeter, *op. cit.*, p. 131.

[7] Cox, J. M. (1806), *Practical Observations on Insanity*, p. 42.

the need for restraint in the case of the furious maniac, but disapproved of its use as a punitive measure. To Cox, the art of management depended upon the practitioner's experience and personality
and the physician's primary objective was either to gain the patient's
confidence or to excite his fear. According to Pargeter, in 'the
government of maniacs' the physician 'must employ every moment
of his time by mildness or menaces, as circumstances direct, to gain
an ascendancy over them, and to obtain their favour and pre-
possession'.[1] Similarly, Francis Willis senior is recorded as fostering
in his patients, for therapeutic purposes, a sense of fear, 'Car le
sentiment de la crainte est la première, & pendant longtems la seule
prise qu'on obtienne sur l'esprit des maniaques'.[2] Willis acquired a
reputation for gaining control over patients by catching their eye.
One writer noted that he had 'an eye like Mars, to threaten or
command ... his numerous patients stood as much in awe of this
formidable weapon, as of bars, chains or straight-waistcoats'.[3]
At the beginning of the nineteenth century, magistrates, in a few
areas, were already taking a firm line on the use of restraint. Thus,
in 1807, the Surrey Magistrates required the respective proprietors of
Great Foster House and of the house at Frimley, at both of which
chaining had taken place, 'to pledge themselves that such practice
should be discontinued and the staples and chains removed within
one week from the time of granting ... licences'.[4]

Although the establishment of the York Retreat was, undoubtedly,
an important landmark in British psychiatric history and it acquired
a pre-eminent reputation for humane treatment, it tends to be overlooked that very similar methods were employed in contemporary
private madhouses. Physical restraint was, in fact, used at the
Retreat, although no chains were employed.[5] As has been seen
already, the management of patients at Brislington House in 1815
involved little or no restraint and the régime at Laverstock House was
likened to that at the York Retreat. With regard to Brislington
House, Wakefield reported that Fox 'thinks that separate confinement is not useful; that a patient cannot easily be brought to submit
to coercion; whilst in company they only suffer the lot of others, and

[1] Pargeter, *op. cit.*, p. 49.
[2] Anon. (1796), Détails sur l'établissement du docteur Willis, pour la guérison
des aliénés, *Bibliothèque britannique* (Littérature) *1*, pp. 766–7.
[3] Reynolds, F. (1826), *The Life and Times of Frederick Reynolds*, p. 23.
[4] Surrey, R.O., QS.5/5/3, Minutes V.M., 28 Oct. 1807.
[5] Minutes of evidence 1815 S.C., p. 135.

that they coerce one another'.[1] It is interesting to note that the first matron of the Retreat, Katherine Allen (later Mrs George Jepson), had worked, previously, at Fox's first licensed house at Cleeve Hill, Bristol. In 1836, the proprietors of Brislington House stated that they had 'no hesitation in declaring their conviction that the patients derive almost as much benefit from their influence over each other, as from the combined influence of the most acute reasoning, and of the most active and skilful application of medical remedies'.[2] Ricketts, the proprietor of Droitwich Lunatic Asylum, approved of restraint for 'furious maniacs', who, if very violent, were managed in bed with the right hand and left leg secured to the bedstead. When up and about, small wrist-locks with a chain-link nine inches long were employed. He considered the strait-waistcoat to be 'one of the most inefficient and galling things which can be employed for securing a lunatic' and the overall impression of Ricketts' practice is one of a limited and selective use of restraint.[3] T. Bakewell also displayed a selective approach to the use of restraint. He utilized techniques of the 'moral' approach to promote 'lucid intervals' and advocated the use of mechanical restraint only during paroxysms of fury or violence. He quoted, as an example, the case of a woman who, on one day, might be restrained because of her raging madness, yet on the next would be nursing his infant children.[4] Bakewell used the strait-waistcoat for periods of up to forty-eight hours at a time and he employed beds with wooden canopies in which one arm and the opposite leg could be chained, thus preventing the patient from getting out of bed, but allowing a fair degree of movement. He made use also of hand-locks at night and chain hobbles that allowed short steps to be taken but which would make escape difficult.[5] Bakewell acknowledged the need for authority to be imposed on the patient and, to this end, in certain cases he recommended the whip as 'undoubtedly the best ... the most prompt, and the least disagreeable in its consequences'. He reserved its use for the punishment of violence or 'extreme rudeness', but recognized that 'it only begets opposition and obstinacy' if used 'to enforce obedience to orders, such as taking of medicine'.[6] Bakewell pointed out that the use of mechanical restraint should never be dictated by the personal

[1] *Ibid.*, p. 21. [2] Fox, F. K. and C. J., *op. cit.* In B.H.Q.N.C.N., p. 21.
[3] First Report minutes of evidence 1816 S.C., pp. 46, 52.
[4] Bakewell, T. (1815), *op. cit.*, pp. 54–60.
[5] Minutes of evidence 1815 S.C., pp. 122, 125–6.
[6] Bakewell, T. (1809), *op. cit.*, p. 39.

fears of attendants and he likened an attendant to a soldier who, if he 'shrinks from his duty from personal fear ... is a swindler that obtains money under false pretences'.[1] David Uwins (1833), physician to the Royal Free Hospital and to Peckham House, London, made a case for the use of mechanical restraint out of necessity and not convenience. It is of interest to note that he believed that 'to say that restraint and "in terrorem" measures are not frequently called for ... by madhouse inmates, were to prove ourselves either absolutely ignorant of the nature of mental aberration, or wilfully obstinate in our attachment to Utopian schemes'.[2] S. G. Bakewell (1833) stated that:

Personal restraint should seldom be resorted to, particularly with the more respectable class; their feelings are more acute than those of a humbler grade, and they do not brook with patience so humiliating an infliction. It is, however, necessary that the keeper should always be able to control them, and to assert his bodily as well as mental superiority.[3]

This observation is essentially in keeping with his father's views. Another reflection of the effect of social status on the use of restraint has been referred to already, namely, the fact that paupers could be received in greater numbers and, therefore, more cheaply, if the risks of escape, violence to others and self-injury were prevented by mechanical restraint rather than by the efforts of attendants alone. Arnold was amongst those who expressed the view that the use of chains should be restricted to poor patients, whose financial circumstances precluded the use of sufficient personal attendance to ensure their safety. In evidence before the 1815 Select Committee, Fowler stated that when the keepers at Fonthill Gifford were asked why patients were subjected to mechanical restraint, they claimed 'that it would require a larger expense than they could afford to keep servants to take care of them if they were not ironed'.[4] This rationale was referred to often throughout the first half of the nineteenth century and, although the situation was exploited, undoubtedly, in some madhouses, it is likely that financial consideration acted as a genuine brake on the introduction of milder forms of treatment, by

[1] Bakewell, T. (1815), *op. cit.*, p. 53.
[2] Uwins, D. (1833), *A Treatise on those Disorders of the Brain and Nervous System, which are usually considered and called Mental*, p. 148.
[3] Bakewell, S. G., *op. cit.*, p. 47. (In addition, *vide* Burrows (1828), *op. cit.*, pp. 690–1.)
[4] Minutes of evidence 1815 S.C., p. 46.

such persons as Arnold. The appliances used for mechanical restraint were legion, since each experienced practitioner introduced his own modifications of the standard apparatus. The basic instruments were the strait-waistcoat, strong dresses made of canvas, handcuffs, muffs and gloves, hobbles, leg-locks and various forms of the 'coercion chair'. In addition, apparatus comprising linen or leather straps, chains or a combination of both was used, generally involving attachment to the wall, bed or chair and there were many variants of this type of equipment.

Conolly defined 'non-restraint' in broad terms and, in 1860, he summarized his own views when he referred to it as 'not merely the abolition of all instruments for the mechanical coercion of the body and limbs, but all severity, all restrictions dictated by avarice, or policy, or ostentatious economy of parochial funds, including all unnecessary privations, all unfavourable domestic arrangements, and all forms of neglect'.[1] When the experiments of Conolly at Hanwell and of Hill at Lincoln had demonstrated that the total abolition of restraint was a practical proposition in asylums, the tide turned against those who advocated the combination of the moral approach with some personal restraint in certain cases. However, support for the use of restraint continued to be voiced and some of the opponents of the total non-restraint movement joined together, in 1842, to form the 'Society for Improving the Condition of the Insane'.

The itinerant Metropolitan Commissioners in Lunacy had been directed, in 1842, as part of their duties, to enquire into the use of mechanical restraint in all private licensed houses and other asylums in England and Wales. The Commissioners revealed, in their Report,[2] that manual force and seclusion, in fact, were being employed as part of the 'non-restraint' régime in establishments where it was claimed that restraint had been dispensed with completely. They noted that seclusion and solitary confinement were entering into general use and that 'great numbers of the superintendents of public, and of the proprietors of private asylums throughout the country are fitting up and bringing into use solitary cells, and padded rooms for violent and unmanageable lunatics'.[3] The Metropolitan Commissioners recommended that such treatment should be used for only short periods at a time and that details concerning its application

---

[1] Conolly, J. (1860), 'Recollections of the Varieties of Insanity', *Med. Times & Gazette 1*, p. 6.
[2] 1844 Report M.C.L., pp. 137–59.   [3] *Ibid.*, p. 146.

should be recorded for the Visitors' inspection. Restraint was stated to have been abolished entirely at two private licensed houses, Denham Park, Buckinghamshire (which received private patients only) and Fairford, Gloucestershire (which received paupers and private patients), but the Commissioners noted that, in 1843, at this latter house, they had been 'sorry to see a female ... permitted to gnaw her fingers into sores'.[1] Of the fifty-four provincial licensed houses receiving private patients only, thirty-seven were found by the Commissioners to contain none under restraint and fifteen contained only a single patient restrained. Out of the thirty-two metropolitan houses in this category, twenty-two contained none under restraint at the time of inspection. Similar figures for houses receiving paupers were not given, but the Commissioners reported the use of an excessive and censurable degree of restraint at six provincial houses, all of which received paupers, namely, the West Auckland Lunatic Asylum, Co. Durham; Lainston House, Hampshire; Plympton House, Devon; Kingsdown House, Wiltshire and Moor Cottage, East Riding of Yorkshire.

Mechanical restraint was often used, primarily, to prevent escape and its replacement by the 'vigilance and care' of attendants must have created demands that, frequently, were difficult to meet. Indeed, the problem of containing the violent patient without resort to physical or chemical restraint remains to the present day. At some private licensed houses, attendants were penalized for the escape of patients if an element of neglect was found to be present. For example, the rules for the keepers at Duddeston Hall, Warwickshire, included the following statement: 'Any keeper, nurse, or servant, from whose custody a patient escapes, through negligence, shall pay the expense of retaking the patient.'[2] Such rulings must have fostered the use of restraint. In their 1844 Report, the Metropolitan Commissioners gave examples of the difficulties which could arise from the total disuse of restraint and these examples included the death, from the effects of a bite, of the superintendent of Hilsea Asylum, Hampshire.[3] The proprietors of a number of houses provided evidence of the benefits of restraint and the Commissioners

---

[1] *Ibid.* p. 145.
[2] Warwicks. C.R.O., Q.S. lunacy records, leaflet (*c.* 1842), 'Rules and Regulations for the male and female keepers and servants at Duddeston Hall Lunatic Asylum' (Duddeston Hall was opened in 1835 and closed in 1865).
[3] 1844 Report M.C.L., p. 148.

showed sympathy for the problems encountered in the management of patients in the smaller houses and concern, particularly, for the safety of attendants. They made the important observation that,

in private asylums which receive paupers, if it be desired that the Visitors shall require an entire absence of mechanical restraint, the public must be prepared to pay an additional sum for their care and maintenance of the patients, otherwise they must either suffer long-continued solitary seclusion, which will destroy their health, or the attendants and other patients will be exposed to constant peril.[1]

There is evidence, in the Annual Reports of the Commissioners and in the minutes made following the inspection of individual houses, of the Commissioners' approval of restraint in cases of extreme violence and, also, of its acceptance, without adverse comment, under some other circumstances. For example, following a visit to Springfield House, Bedford, the Commissioners noted that Mr Harris, the proprietor, stated that he was unable to dispense with mechanical restraints as 'in some cases they are necessary for the purpose of keeping patients in their beds'.[2]

In 1847, the Commissioners observed that, at the time of their last visit, only fifty-nine of the 3,862 patients confined in provincial licensed houses were under restraint.[3] Examples of the figures for individual houses include: two patients under restraint out of fifty-seven at Hook Norton; two out of eleven at Witney; six out of eighty-seven at Duddeston Hall; five out of 185 at Belle Vue House, Devizes, and ten out of ninety-two patients at Bailbrook House, Bath.

The Commissioners published, in 1854, the findings of a survey of opinion regarding the use of restraint, amongst the medical super-intendents of county asylums or hospitals and the proprietors or medical officers of licensed houses.[4] It was stated that mechanical restraint was employed, occasionally, at ten of the fifty public institutions. No replies were received from forty-four of the 128 private licensed houses in England and Wales and fifty-three of the replies were from provincial licensed houses. The use of restraint was reported from forty-seven licensed houses, but the general trend, clearly, was for the treatment of patients without restraint wherever

---

[1] *Ibid.*, p. 150.
[2] Beds. C.R.O., LSV.3/0, Minutes C.L., 12 July 1851.
[3] Further Report (1847) C.L., Appendix B, pp. 313–17.
[4] Eighth Report (1854) C.L., Appendix G, pp. 123–209.

possible. Several proprietors stated that restraint could not be abolished entirely and its use was recommended in suicidal cases if the attendants were unreliable; for persons who were destructive, violent or threatening to others and also in cases of persistent, resistive refusal of food. It was emphasized that, in such cases, restraint was to be used as a remedial and not as a punitive measure. The proprietors of Heigham Hall, Norwich, however, regarded 'the entire and unconditional abolition of simple mechanical restraint as a piece of psychological quackery, well adapted to catch the un-reflecting sentimentality of the vulgar, but rarely . . . carried out to its fullest extent even by its warmest advocates'.[1] They believed that the occasional use of muffs or a waist-belt was less undesirable than allowing patients to jostle and struggle with attendants. The medical officer of Grove House, Acomb, near York, considered mechanical restraint to be 'a powerful remedial agent . . . a promotive of com-fort to the patient, a preventive of suicide, and injury to others, and an adjuvant to medicinal treatment in procuring quiet, and con-sequently sleep, [facts] . . . borne out by the testimony of some of the patients after recovery'.[2] Mallam's views, no doubt reflecting his practice at Hook Norton, are representative of the middle-of-the-road group. He stated that: 'I only feel called on to observe that I consider restraint in the management of the insane should not be the rule, but the exception. I feel fully persuaded that there are cases in which it is necessary for the benefit of the patient, and the safety of those who have the charge of him.'[3] In a frank review of the Com-missioners' findings, Conolly observed that the continuing use of mechanical restraint, at that time, did not necessarily indicate a leaning towards cruelty or thoughtless economy. Rather, it was evidence of ignorance and indolence and the results of a system whereby 'the habits and practice of an asylum are purchased to-gether with the patients, and the strait-waistcoats figure in the inventory with the rest of the furniture'.[4] Conolly criticized, in particular, G. Bodington, surgeon, the proprietor of Driffold House, Sutton Coldfield, who, although a kind and candid person, had condemned non-restraint as an imperfect theory, despite the fact that he had no knowledge of the practice in large public asylums and, in fact, only accommodated twelve patients in his own house. He

---

[1] *Ibid.*, p. 192. [2] *Ibid.*, p. 209.
[3] *Ibid.*, p. 194. [4] Conolly, J. (1855), *op. cit.*, p. 182.

suggested that Bodington's views were typical of those of the majority of private asylum proprietors and he added: 'On what practical subject ... in the whole range of medicine, could medical men be found on the basis of the experience of a village dispensary, utterly to condemn the practice of the whole of our large London and provincial hospitals?'[1] Conolly found fault also with Francis Willis junior, of Shillingthorpe House, for calling on the experience of his more famous predecessors in support of the use of restraint, and, in this context, he commented: 'It is painful to know that such views are still entertained by a few physicians, who are men of education, but apparently proud of adhering to ancient severities.'[2] However, Conolly pointed out that most proprietors who had been trained in public asylums had discontinued restraint and, in general, Conolly's views support the idea that an important factor in the yielding of severe treatment, in licensed houses, to a milder régime was the supervision of these establishments by more widely experienced and responsible proprietors. One of those who, naturally, was strongly in favour of non-restraint was R. Gardiner Hill, by now the proprietor of Eastgate House, Lincoln, although he fully approved of seclusion.

In 1855, the Commissioners reported on the practice, which had been introduced recently, of removing patients who were being subjected to excessive restraint to other establishments.[3] Six cases of this type, all involving females, were described. One patient was removed from each of the following houses, Castleton Lodge, Leeds; Laverstock House; Belle Vue House, Ipswich; Marfleet Lane, Hull; Terrace House, near York, and Ringmer, Sussex; and the receiving asylums were, in the first two cases, the York Lunatic Asylum, and in the remaining cases, Grove Hall, London; Gate Helmsley Retreat, York; and York Retreat and Ticehurst, respectively. All the patients transferred in this way appeared to benefit by their removal. Despite this and other similar evidence, however, opposition to total non-restraint continued, especially amongst licensed house proprietors. Thus, G. Robinson (1859), M.D., F.R.C.P., proprietor of Bensham Asylum, Gateshead, and lecturer in mental diseases at the Newcastle College of Medicine, claimed that Pinel, Prichard and the great majority of French, German and American practitioners recognized the need for mechanical restraint as a curative measure in

[1] *Ibid.*   [2] *Ibid.*, p. 183.
[3] Ninth Report (1855) C.L., pp. 26–9.

exceptional cases. Examples of such cases were the prevention of suicide attempts, the protection of post-suicidal patients from further injury, the protection of idiots and imbeciles from self-injury and serious injuries associated with maniacal excitement. Robinson was moved to state: 'I confess that it is with feelings far removed from admiration or conviction, that I observe in some modern works, an affectation of compassionate superiority towards men like Pinel and Esquirol, simply because they had too much good sense to push their own excellent and humane ideas to an extremity'.[1]

Despite the fact that the abstract principle of non-restraint was not wholly accepted, the techniques of 'moral treatment' had been adopted in the majority of licensed houses by the sixth decade of the nineteenth century. In practice, apart from the abolition of restraint, moral treatment involved the classification of patients according to clinical state (for example, the separation of dangerous lunatics from others and the restless and noisy from the more tranquil), and their separate management; the provision of indoor and outdoor amusements; the provision of facilities for exercise and for employment, primarily for the working classes; attention to religious activities and the accommodation of patients in light, well-ventilated and cheerful surroundings. In 1830, Conolly stated that, at that time, classification was found only in the larger asylums and 'a few of the more respectable lunatic houses'.[2] However, such classification rarely extended beyond the separation of the rich from the poor, of the noisy from the quiet, or, at best, of convalescent patients from the rest. Strict separation according to social class and wealth was, undoubtedly, a basic feature in the first half of the nineteenth century. In 1823, Francis Willis junior offered, in justification of the better facilities and personal attention provided for the wealthy, the reason that 'the man of fortune ... will require a greater nicety in our moral treatment of him than the poor and illiterate; for he that serves, will not feel so acutely, even under his derangement, as he that is served'.[3] Similarly, the Metropolitan Commissioners observed, in 1844, with regard to the practice in former times, that: 'If any classification existed, it was little more than a separation of persons according to their various grades in society; the poorer classes being

[1] Robinson, G. (1859), *On the Prevention and Treatment of Mental Disorders*, p. 217.
[2] Conolly, J. (1830), *op. cit.*, pp. 28–9.
[3] Willis, F. (1823), *A Treatise on Mental Derangement*, pp. 157–8.

divided from those who, by reason of larger payments, were considered to be entitled to greater personal comforts'.[1] The current practice in well-regulated asylums consisted of 'the distribution of patients with reference to their mental disorders, and in associating those persons whose intercourse is likely to be mutually beneficial, and in separating others who are in a state that renders their society a source of mutual irritation and annoyance'.[2] The Commissioners stressed the need for provisions for the segregation of dangerous and agitated lunatics and Kingsdown House and Bailbrook House, Bath, were both found deficient in this respect. In addition, arrangements for the segregation of dirty and incontinent patients were particularly deficient at four provincial houses, namely, Lainston House, Winchester; Bailbrook House; Plympton House; and Green Hill House, Derby, all of which received paupers.

The usual provisions for recreation, exercise and religious activities have been referred to in a previous section, as they formed a prominent feature in advertisements for licensed houses. Many writers supported the view expressed, in 1836, by the Fox brothers of Brislington House, that 'many of the most favourable results which have occurred in their practice ought to be mainly attributed to the constant succession of bodily exercise, and to the variety of mental recreation, which is provided for their patients'.[3] Religious observances were considered by many to have a valuable restorative function and, in this respect, reference has been made, previously, to the views and practice of Fox and Finch. S. G. Bakewell (1833) regarded religion as 'a powerful means of arresting the attention, and suspending the hallucination, and tends to tranquillize the mind', and, at Spring Vale, patients attended morning and evening prayer with the proprietor and his family.[4] Similarly, the Metropolitan Commissioners considered the effect of 'religious exercises' to be 'tranquillizing, and productive of good order and decorum, in a remarkable degree, and in some instances permanently beneficial'.[5] They advocated the appointment of local clergymen as chaplains and praised the arrangements made, in this respect, at Gateshead Fell, Co. Durham, and at Moor Cottage and Gate Helmsley, Yorkshire. At most houses, participation in religious activities was allowed

[1] 1844 Report M.C.L., p. 122.   [2] *Ibid.*
[3] Fox, F. K. and C. J., *op. cit.* In B.H.Q.H.C.N., p. 22.
[4] Bakewell, S. G., *op. cit.*, pp. 49–50.
[5] 1844 Report M.C.L., p. 159.

only for selected patients and the religious duties fell on the proprietor and his family, the attendants or, occasionally, on the patients, as at Kingsdown House, where it was recorded that 'a patient, obviously lunatic, was permitted to exhort his fellow-patients every Sunday, in reference to their religious duties, in an extemporaneous address'.[1] The beneficial effects of the regular employment of patients were always stressed by, amongst others, the Metropolitan Commissioners and many licensed houses are recorded as having gone to considerable expense in purchasing tools and in fitting up workshops where patients could carry on their accustomed trades. There is evidence that, in 1815, facilities were provided at Brislington House to employ patients in a range of occupations.[2] In the Dunston Lodge Lunatic Asylum Report for 1847, it was pointed out that lunatics could be entrusted with various agricultural implements. It was recorded in this report that:

So many as thirty-three of the patients were employed last harvest in the reaping field without any untoward accident. It would seem as if the confidence reposed in them begets a like confiding temper; cheerfulness and peace replacing discontent and clamour ... In like manner have ... joiners and shoemakers been employed, with and among their dangerous tools, and ... the restoration of reason and intellect ensued.[3]

The occupation of private patients, particularly the males, appears to have presented difficulties at many licensed houses and the accepted practice was to allow those who were not used to manual labour to amuse themselves in various less strenuous ways. Although it was easier to find employment for patients from the working classes, in general it was found more difficult, correspondingly, to engage such patients in leisure activities. In this context, it is of interest to read a contemporary account of the outdoor occupations, at the house of Francis Willis senior at Greatford, Lincolnshire:

As the unprepared traveller approached the town, he was astonished to find almost all the surrounding ploughmen, gardeners, threshers, thatchers and other labourers attired in black coats, white waistcoats, black silk breeches and stockings, and the head of each 'bien poudre, frise, et arrange'. These were the doctor's patients, and dress, neatness of person, and exercise being the principal features of his admirable system, health and

---

[1] *Ibid.*, p. 160.   [2] Minutes of evidence 1815 S.C., p. 21.
[3] Dunston Lodge Lunatic Asylum Report for 1847. Cited in (1848), 'State of Lunacy in the British Asylums', *J. Psychol. Med. & Ment. Path.* I, p. 396.

cheerfulness conjoined to aid recovery of every person attached to that most valuable asylum.[1]

A greater degree of liberty appears to have been allowed to the convalescent or well-behaved patient than has generally been considered to be the case, although the evidence relates only to individual patients in a small number of houses. An illustration, from the late-eighteenth century, is provided by the case of a former attorney, who, in 1785, was a patient at St Luke's House, Newcastle. In that year, the Visitors noted: 'He appeared to be very calm . . . He is permitted and we think very properly to visit his physician at Newcastle and to walk out at proper seasons and there is much reason to hope that he may be soon restored to his sound mind'.[2] In the second half of the nineteenth century, it came to be recognized that one particular benefit of the private asylum system was the closer proximity to normal patterns of living that it allowed. Dr J. W. Eastwood (1864), proprietor of Dinsdale Park, Darlington, stated that: 'An important object in private asylum life is to render that life as much like home as possible, and to enable those who are mentally afflicted to conduct themselves as much as they can like other members of society. The more this is done the more successful generally will be the treatment'.[3] Another aspect of the relaxation of the custodial régime in licensed houses, at this time, was the use of periods of leave of absence, granted by the Visitors, under the terms of the Act of 1845, which permitted patients to be taken, by relatives or attendants, to specified places for the benefit of their health.

The role of the attendant

The role of the private madhouse attendant or keeper and the nature of his duties changed considerably during the lifespan of the private-madhouse system. The essential change was the replacement of largely custodial duties by more directly psychotherapeutic activities. The origins of the modern profession of psychiatric nursing can be traced from the work of early private-madhouse keepers and ser-

---

[1] Extract from *Life and Times of Frederick Reynolds*. Cited by Melville, L. (1907), Farmer George, Vol. II, pp. 216–17. (*Vide* Anon. (1796), *Bibliothéque britannique* (Littérature) *1*, p. 762. Reference is made to the lodging of patients at farms within a radius of four to five miles of the madhouse.)

[2] Newcastle upon Tyne City Archives Dept., LA.1/3, Minutes V.M., 1785.

[3] Eastwood, J. W. (1864), 'On Private Asylums for the Insane', *J. Ment. Sci. 9*, p. 324.

vants, although this aspect of the history of the nursing profession has received virtually no attention. Walk (1961) has drawn attention to a number of recorded instances of praiseworthy work by madhouse attendants, such as Sam Roberts, William Cowper's attendant at Nathaniel Cotton's house, St Albans.[1] Few private-madhouse attendants either achieved prominence or made any lasting individual contribution, although many of them moved on from private madhouses to play their part in the work of county asylums and public subscription asylums. The only published work of a madhouse attendant, discovered to date, was that written, anonymously, in 1828, by W. J.,[2] which was entitled *Practical Observations on Insanity . . . addressed particularly to those who have Relatives and Friends afflicted with Mental Derangement*. The author had been a metropolitan madhouse keeper and had worked also in the provinces. In the Preface, he stated that the book had been written 'in the wards of a madhouse, during the short periods I could snatch from my duties as a keeper'. The evils of the madhouse system were stressed, but the views were not extreme. There is an interesting chapter entitled, 'On the desirableness of employing a better class of persons as immediate attendants on the insane'[3] and, also, one on the duties of keepers. One of the largest chapters was concerned with the effects of masturbation, which he considered to be the 'most pernicious and debasing vice . . . which has done more to fill our lunatic asylums, than the whole catalogue of exciting causes besides'.[4]

It was with the introduction of the techniques of non-restraint that the importance of the attendant's work became more generally acknowledged. The success of moral treatment, depended, to a large extent, on the adequacy in number and the calibre of the attendants and, in view of this, the demand for and the prestige of the attendant increased. The relationship between the status and role of the mental nurse and the methods employed for treating the insane is well described by Hunter (1956).[5] In licensed houses which catered for the wealthy, mechanical restraint could be discontinued more readily than in establishments catering for the lower classes, because it could

[1] Walk, A. (1961), 'The History of Mental Nursing', *J. Ment. Sci. 107*, p. 4.
[2] Probably W. Jones, employed by Warburton at Whitmore House in 1808 but later dismissed.
[3] Anon. (1828), *Practical Observations on Insanity*, pp. 44–53.
[4] *Ibid.*, pp. 80–1.
[5] Hunter, R. A. (1956), 'The Rise and Fall of Mental Nursing', *Lancet i*, pp. 98–9.

be replaced by increased personal attendance on the patients, despite the resultant higher charges. In pauper establishments, however, this was rarely possible, because of the pressure which existed to keep the maintenance payments for pauper lunatics as low as possible. Throughout the nineteenth century, the ratio of attendants to patients in licensed houses receiving private patients, was consistently higher than in houses receiving paupers. With the development of large establishments catering for paupers, this discrepancy in staffing became progressively more pronounced. This is illustrated by the situation in Newcastle in 1827.[1] At the Newcastle upon Tyne Lunatic Asylum, which received up to eighty patients who were largely paupers, the staff comprised the superintendent, three male keepers and five 'matrons', who were assisted by convalescent women patients. However, at Belle Grove Retreat, Newcastle, which accommodated no more than eight or nine patients of each sex, the staff comprised three experienced male keepers, a matron, four female servants and a housekeeper. In 1847, establishments receiving patients of a high class, such as Brislington House and Shillingthorpe House, could provide, on average, one attendant or servant for every two patients[2] and, in 1853, the three houses which formed the asylum at Ticehurst contained fifty-eight patients, for whom, it was claimed, there were fifty-one attendants.[3] In contrast, in that same year, at Bensham Lunatic Asylum, Gateshead, the 160 patients, largely paupers, were cared for by only eleven attendants[4] and at Fisherton House, the 214 patients were looked after by twenty-six attendants.[5] The staffing at Hook Norton and Witney has been discussed in a previous section.[6]

The qualities required of attendants were the subject of much consideration during this time of transition and emphasis was placed on the need to assist the recruitment of attendants by such measures as improving their pay, accommodation and prospects of promotion; providing relief from menial work and introducing formal training.[7] Particular difficulty was met with in recruiting and retaining the services of good male attendants because of the poor remuneration. The Commissioners in Lunacy attempted to set up a central register

[1] Mackenzie, *op. cit.*, p. 525.
[2] Further Report (1847) C.L., p. 56.   [3] P.R., 1854 (a), p. 30.
[4] *Ibid.*, p. 28.   [5] *Ibid.*, p. 31.   [6] *Vide supra*, p. 154.
[7] The first formal psychiatric instruction of nurses was given, in 1843, by Sir Alexander Morrison at the Surrey County Asylum.

of attendants, but found it a difficult task to accomplish.[1] Under 16 & 17 Vict., c. 96 & c. 97, 1853, however, the Commissioners had to be notified of all dismissals of nurses and attendants for misconduct and this information was utilized to compile a register.[2] The insufficiency in the number of attendants in many licensed houses, the frequent changes that took place, leading to the repeated introduction of new and untried persons and the general lack of experienced and trustworthy staff were important factors which contributed to the defects and abuses of the private-madhouse system, especially in the first half of the nineteenth century. This aspect will be considered in more detail in Chapter 8. However, by the mid-century, there had been a general improvement in the calibre of licensed house attendants, especially with regard to their character. Greater humanity and vigilance in their conduct came to be expected of attendants at this period and close observation of patients was one of the principal features of moral management. The vigilance which was demanded called for a new tolerance of disturbed behaviour, a quality which was developed only by experience and, not unnaturally, it was often missing during the early years of the nonrestraint era. These points are illustrated by the following contemporary descriptions of the attendant's status and role at Brislington House in 1836, which can be taken as representative of those prevailing in the best licensed houses at this time. The proprietors, Drs F. K. and C. J. Fox, stated that 'as the attendants contribute essentially to the success of every plan of treatment . . . they are selected with the greatest care, and are not permitted to have any control over the patients, until they have gained some experience in inferior departments of the institution, and have proved their good temper and forbearance'.[3] All attendants had to sign an agreement which included the following statement: 'The Drs. Fox engage to give a month's wages, or a month's warning; but any departure from the above agreement, cruelty, improper language, or other misconduct towards the patients, will warrant an immediate dismissal without reference to the above terms'.[4] In the management of a newly admitted patient, who had previously been restrained, 'the attendants, who are so arranged as to be able to entertain a constant unobserved surveillance, do not unnecessarily interfere; but permit

---

[1] Fifth Report (1850) C.L., p. 10.
[2] Ninth Report (1855) C.L., pp. 40–1.
[3] Fox, F. K. and C. J., *op. cit*. In B.H.Q.N.C.N., p. 23.　　　[4] *Ibid.*

the indulgence of many innocent vagaries, in which, because they were symptoms of insanity, he had been checked, thwarted, and thus constantly irritated at home'.[1] The Visiting Magistrates and Commissioners often praised the skill and tolerance of attendants. Thus, in 1844, following a visit to Droitwich Lunatic Asylum, the Metropolitan Commissioners noted that 'one young female, who had a propensity to eat her faeces and strip off her clothes, is prevented from doing either by the vigilant care of an attendant without the use of any restraint'.[2] The need for close observation was stressed, from time to time, in the minutes of the Visiting Magistrates and Commissioners. Thus, after noting the suicide of a patient at Springfield House, Bedford, the Visiting Magistrates observed that 'every patient should be watched for some time after his first arrival without reference to any statement in the certificate received on his admission'.[3]

The lack of experienced staff was noted by the Visiting Magistrates and Commissioners at several of the houses whose surviving records have been examined. Thus, in 1858, the Visitors to Abington Abbey, Northampton, commented on the fact that all the attendants were young men, and they recommended that at least one older and more experienced attendant should be employed.[4] Scattered information only is available concerning the previous employment and experience of licensed house attendants. In 1864, the Commissioners issued a circular letter, regarding attendants and nurses, to metropolitan licensed house proprietors, who were required to make returns in respect of the existing staff, and subsequently to keep a register.[5] Such documents in this category as have survived, therefore, furnish a useful source of information. For example, at Lea Pale House, Surrey, in 1864, the former occupations of the three male attendants were, respectively, a turnkey at Guildford Gaol, a butcher and gardener, and an attendant on an imbecile. At Great Foster House, Surrey, however, only one of the five attendants had had no previous experience as an attendant.[6] Some of the more experienced attendants, particularly in the metropolitan houses, were hired out by the proprietors for the management of single patients in private houses.

[1] *Ibid.*, p. 20.
[2] Worcs. R.O., BA.710b.125.1(i), Minutes M.C.L., 15 July 1844.
[3] Beds. C.R.O., LSV.3/O, Minutes V.M., 27 April 1846.
[4] Northants C.R.O., X.3325/J, Minutes V.M., 11 Oct. 1858.
[5] Nineteenth Report (1865) C.L., pp. 18–19.
[6] Surrey R.O., QS.5/5/7.

Many contemporary writers referred to the excessive use of restraint which was exercised under these conditions. The Commissioners observed, in 1855, that 'Attendants should combine, in their character and disposition, firmness and gentleness; and they should be able, by their education and habits, to superintend, direct, and promote the employment and recreation of patients'.[1] Conolly played an important part in formulating ideas on the choice of attendants, their qualifications and duties, but there was little uniform agreement about the role of the attendant in private licensed houses, particularly where 'superior' patients were received. The views expressed by J. G. Davey, M.D., proprietor of Northwoods, Winterbourne, near Bristol, are representative of one current attitude which regarded the attendant as a personal servant. In 1854, he observed that 'attendants themselves should not appear else than respectable domestics, nor should they be allowed to address themselves to the patients otherwise than in the accents of respect and consideration'.[2] Similarly, in 1900, the proprietors of Ticehurst Asylum stated that, if possible, they selected officers' servants or mess waiters as attendants, because, 'in addition to having acquired a sense of discipline and duty, they start with the great advantage of knowing how to speak to gentlemen . . . We adopt the view that they are body servants or valets, and this position is quite sufficient with the considerable amount of companionship with gentlefolk which we have'.[3] Upper-class patients valued the quiet and privacy which were offered generally in private licensed houses and the attendant's role was that of a personal servant or, at times, a companion. As has been shown, in many of the larger establishments accommodation was available which allowed patients to be attended by their own hired servants.

The recruitment of attendants of good character to work with pauper lunatics was, naturally, a difficult proposition and the repressive rules and regulations for attendants, known to have been applied in some licensed houses, were probably well justified. A leaflet, dated *c.* 1842, and entitled 'Rules and Regulations for the Male and Female Keepers and Servants, at Duddeston Hall Lunatic

[1] Ninth Report (1855) C.L., p. 40. (A circular issued by the C.L. re 'the duties and qualifications of attendants upon the insane', was published as an Appendix (No. 5) to the Report 1859 S.C. (Aug. 1859).)
[2] Eighth Report (1854) C.L., p. 181.
[3] Newington, *op. cit.*, pp. 68–9.

Asylum' is presented here in full. This document is of particular interest because it is the only one of its kind discovered to date relating to a private licensed house, although the content is not dissimilar from that found in corresponding documents relating to county asylums. It concerns a large establishment near Birmingham, opened in 1835 for eighteen paupers, and which contained, by 1844, twenty private patients and sixty paupers. This pamphlet is of outstanding importance for the detailed clarification it provides of the degree of responsibility which attendants were expected to assume in the daily handling of their patients:

In order that the business of this asylum may be conducted with regularity, and in an efficient manner, no person will be retained or employed therein, who does not obey the orders that may be given either personally by the proprietor, or through the medium of any other person he may authorise; and they must also conform to the following Rules and Regulations:— All engagements must be understood to be for the whole of their time; nor will any set time for going out of the premises, for any purpose be allowed; but every proper indulgence of this nature will be granted upon application to the proprietor.

First:—Every pauper patient on admission is to be stripped and washed, and it is to be carefully observed if there be any swelling in any part of the body, vermin, or spots on the skin; the hair is to be cut close and combed, and the patient is then to be clothed in the asylum dress.

Second:—Every keeper and servant is expected to rise at six o'clock; the keepers will then immediately wash and comb their patients, and observe if there be any soreness or discolouration of the skin in any part of the body. They are expected also to examine the stools and urine of the patients, so as to be able to report their state, and every other particular concerning them. On any patient appearing ill, information is immediately to be given to the proprietor or superintendent. They must also pay the strictest attention to the administering of the medicines, etc. agreeably to the directions.

Third:—At eight o'clock the patients will breakfast; as soon as breakfast is over, the keepers will clean out the rooms, and remove every kind of dirt or dirty linen, and, in fine weather, open the windows. It must be understood, that no place will be considered CLEAN which can be made CLEANER.

Fourth:—The patients will dine at one o'clock, and sup at six in winter, and seven in summer. They will go to bed as soon as supper is over, and no clothing to be allowed to remain in the room. One hour before every meal, the keepers will take down their trays and tins to the kitchen, and at the same time take from the surgery the medicines ordered for their patients; and when the bell rings (but not before) the keepers, with a patient to assist them, will go to the kitchen for the provisions. After each meal, the dishes, trenchers, etc. are to be carefully washed, and every knife, fork, and spoon is to be counted and locked up. The male keepers will shave their patients on Wednesdays and Saturdays.

Fifth:—The keepers will not be permitted to leave their wards or rooms, except at the time appointed above, unless some very urgent business demand it, when he or she will inform the superintendent of the cause of their absence; but they must not, AT ANY TIME, leave their wards without having first locked up in their rooms, any patients who are liable to be violent, or strike another, excepting such patients be properly secured. Any male keeper wanting any thing from the housekeeper or kitchen, must apply to the superintendent or housekeeper, No patient to be permitted to leave the wards in the morning, before breakfast, to assist the house-servants, without the servants personally fetching them. No patient to be allowed to fetch medicine, from the surgery.

Sixth:—The keepers are to be accountable for all bed and other linen, the patients' clothing, and the various articles belonging to the wards.

Seventh:—Any keeper striking or ill-treating a patient, will, for the first offence be admonished, and be dismissed for the second; nor are the keepers to use any harsh or intemperate language, which tends to irritate or disturb them, as their duty is uniformly to be discharged in a mild, humane manner. They are at all times to appear clean and decent in their persons, and strictly decorous in their behaviour.

Eighth:—Any keeper found making a perquisite of any kind, or selling any thing to a patient, will be admonished for the first offence, and dismissed for the second. Any keeper, nurse, or servant, from whose custody a patient escapes, through negligence, shall pay the expense of retaking the patient.

Ninth:—On Saturday, at eight o'clock in the morning, every keeper is expected to deliver a list, in writing, of the household utensils wanted in his or her ward for the following week, which will be supplied on the Monday morning. If at any time a knife, instrument, or tool, such as a brush, fire-irons, etc. shall be left unlocked up after using, or the door of the fire-guards left unlocked, each keeper shall forfeit a shilling. Any keeper leaving his or her ward or airing court, without giving notice where he or she is gone, shall forfeit one shilling; and any keeper permitting a patient to get up, and go about the ward or house, before he or she is up to take charge of or deliver the patient to the care of others, shall forfeit one shilling.

Tenth:—No person or relative, calling to see any keeper or servant, will be allowed to go into the kitchen or wards, but must remain in the hall. Each and every keeper, and servant, to attend at prayers every morning and evening, or forfeit, sixpence each, for each default.

Any keeper or nurse detected in having private communication with a patient's friends, or going to their houses without the knowledge of the proprietor, will be dismissed.

Any keeper or male servant who shall be found in any female patient's, nurse's, or female servant's room, without being directed to go there for some specific purpose, by the proprietor, superintendent, or housekeeper, will be immediately dismissed.[1]

Medical Treatment

The experience gained in the asylums opened in the second half of the eighteenth and early-nineteenth centuries, coupled with the increasing professionalism of those dealing with the insane, led to a more critical evaluation of the methods of treatment. During the eighteenth century, medical treatment continued to be influenced by primitive physiological concepts concerned with body humours, for example, bleeding, purging, vomiting, blistering and cupping and, in addition, various other forms of drugging were employed. With a buoyant certainty that is not unfamiliar at the present day, various combinations of these techniques were advocated as the cure for insanity, although few were to survive the test of experience and time and there was ample scope for quackery. Typical of the way in which hopes about a new form of treatment are raised, only to be dashed later, was the enquiry that was held, in 1813–15, to 'ascertain the extent of the process practised by Messrs. Delahoyde and Lucett, for the relief of persons afflicted with insanity'.[2] The Committee of Enquiry comprised the Dukes of Kent and Sussex, noblemen and gentlemen and one physician, J. Harness, M.D. Royal patronage for this investigation was received, in the hope that a new form of treatment could be found for George III. A considerable sum of money was subscribed for an experiment, with four confirmed lunatics from Hoxton House, London, which was carried out, initially, at Sion Vale House and, subsequently, at Ealing House, Middlesex. The secret treatment was shown later to consist of bathing the head with cold water whilst the patient lay immersed in a warm bath. In their 'Second and Final Report', the Committee observed, with regard to the patients who underwent the treatment, that 'although, at first, so essentially benefitted by the effects of the process, as to hold out the most flattering prospects of ultimate success attending the attempt, [they] did not retain the permanent benefit which had . . . been most anxiously expected'. Subsequently, the process was discredited, although it was acknowledged that there

[1] Warwicks. C.R.O., Q.S. lunacy records.
[2] Sheffield Central Lib., Wentworth Woodhouse muniments, F.64(i), Minutes of the Committee, 31 May 1813. (One of several printed reports and MSS. re this enquiry.)

were other cases in which the treatment had been successful. Lucett guarded the secret of his treatment jealously and, in 1815, published a book explaining the reasons why there had been no extension of his curative methods 'for relieving and curing Idiocy and Lunacy, and Every Species of Insanity'.[1] Further, it is of interest to note a statement of the views of Lucett in 1821, when he was the proprietor of Weston House, Chertsey and applied for a licence to open another house near the church at Ewell, Surrey. The Vestry protested vehemently, fearing disturbances during services. In reply, Lucett stated that he took no more than four patients, that there had been no complaints during his seven years at Chertsey, and that 'although I profess to relieve a person deranged in forty minutes I shall never consider my residence a madhouse or a place of confinement as never having had occasion to use those unhappy means resorted to in private and public receptacles for lunatics'.[2]

The use of a wide range of medical treatments was described in published works by private-madhouse proprietors in the late-eighteenth and early-nineteenth centuries. Preparations advocated were, generally, various emetics, laxatives and purgatives, tonics, opiates and camphor, used together with the techniques of bleeding, blistering and cupping. A good illustration of the medical treatment used in a provincial private madhouse at this time is provided in the papers relating to the insanity of a Miss Dorothy Croft, who was treated at T. Burman's licensed house at Henley-in-Arden, Warwickshire, from 1793 to 1827,[3] and examples of the details derived from this source have been given in a previous section.[4] An item of particular interest, recorded in printed sources, was the use of digitalis as an antimaniacal remedy by both Cox (1806)[5] and by Hallaran (1810).[6] Some proprietors gave medical treatment pride of place over moral management. In 1816, Ricketts strongly advocated early treatment, in the belief, which was shared by many of his

[1] Lucett, J. (1815), *An Exposition of the Reasons which have prevented the Process for relieving and curing Idiocy and Lunacy . . . from having been further extended.*

[2] Guildford Museum & Muniment Room, Ewell Vestry Minutes, 27/3/11. *Vide infra*, p. 261.

[3] Warwicks. C.R.O., Campbell, Brown & Ledbrook papers, CR.556/691.

[4] *Vide supra*, p. 125.

[5] Cox, *op. cit.*, pp. 112–16.

[6] Hallaran, W. S. (1810), *An Enquiry into the Causes producing the Extraordinary Addition to the Number of Insane, together with Extended Observations on the Cure of Insanity*, pp. 70–81.

contemporaries, that mental disorder 'in its incipient state ... [arose] ... from an undue determination of blood to the head, sometimes produced by a derangement of the digestive organs ... and almost invariably accompanied by a torpid state of the bowels, inducing inflammation of the brain and its membranes'.[1] His views led to the close cutting of hair, especially in women, to cool the head, and to reduce the 'congestion of the blood'. S. G. Bakewell (1833) claimed that the restoration of bodily health was the principal objective of medical treatment, and he believed that when this was accomplished the mind would 'very speedily regain its healthy tone'.[2]

Information regarding the number of patients in private madhouses receiving medical treatment is not available prior to the mid-nineteenth century. In 1847, returns indicated that only 167 of the 3,862 patients in provincial licensed houses were under any form of medical treatment and the emphasis placed on its use varied considerably from house to house. Thus, at Hook Norton, five out of fifty-seven patients were treated in this way; at Brislington House, eleven out of eighty-seven; at Haydock Lodge, thirty-seven out of 399, and at Northwoods, eighteen out of twenty-nine.[3] It is not clear from these returns whether the treatment was always directed at the relief of insanity rather than of bodily ailments.

By the mid-nineteenth century, a greater degree of uniformity had entered into the application of medical treatment to insanity. In 1847, the Commissioners published the findings of a survey of contemporary therapeutic methods.[4] This survey was accomplished by means of a questionnaire requesting information regarding the treatment adopted in cases of mania, epilepsy associated with insanity, paralysis associated with insanity, and melancholia. In addition, information was required concerning the use of particular remedies, such as blood-letting. Detailed replies[5] were received from forty-eight medical officers, comprising twenty-two superintendents of county asylums or registered hospitals, fifteen superintendents of private licensed houses receiving paupers and eleven proprietors of houses receiving private patients only. The list of those who replied included Mallam and the contents of his replies constitutes the only

---

[1] First Report minutes of evidence 1816 S.C., pp. 45–6.
[2] Bakewell, S. G., *op. cit.*, p. 44.
[3] Further Report (1847) C.L., Appendix B, pp. 313–17.
[4] *Ibid.*, pp. 177–231.   [5] *Ibid.*, Appendix L, pp. 389–495.

detailed account of the treatment at Hook Norton and, as such, is of considerable interest. The following observations were made by Mallam with regard to the treatment of specific disorders:

Mania: My principal remedies are sedatives, either combined with tonics or antimony and salines, according to the indications present. The form I chiefly use is the acetum opii of the Edinburgh pharmacopeia, commencing with ℩℩XX., gradually increasing to ʒi., given every six hours until the paroxysm has subsided and quiet sleep is procured, when the remedy is gradually withdrawn, or used only as circumstances require. The application of cold to the head and seclusion during the paroxysm.[1]

Melancholia: My attention is directed in the first instance to the state of the digestive organs. I frequently give one or more purgative doses of calomel. If there has been much vigilantia (and in the cases of drunkards especially) I adopt the sedative plan of treatment; in some cases the creosote, with other tonics and the cold shower bath, with occupation and amusement.[2]

Epilepsy: In young and healthy subjects, I employ drastic purgatives, especially the ol. terebinthinae. Occasionally local depletion, issues, or setons in the neck. In asthenic cases, especially in females, I employ mineral tonics during the intermissions. I deem it right to add that I have not found much success.[3]

Paralysis: I have used diuretics where there has been oedema of the feet; where the strength appeared sufficient, the elasterium; but in other cases, where there has been great apathy of the system, I have employed the creosote and other stimulants with tonics and counter-irritants; in these, as in the former class of cases, without the benefits I could wish.[4]

Mallam stated that he never employed general blood-letting as a remedy and went on to make the following observations regarding particular remedies:

Topical bleeding I have found occasionally useful. Emetics I place no confidence in. Purgatives I consider useful, especially in young plethoric subjects, many of whom are epileptic. Antimonials I occasionally combine with opiates. Sedatives, especially opium, I believe to be the most generally useful of any class of remedies in insanity in its several forms. The form I employ is the acetate of morphia. Antispasmodics I sometimes use in common with other remedies. Tonics are frequently useful. Stimulants are occasionally called for. The cold shower bath I have found very serviceable in cases of apathy of the system, where there has been no organic disease. As a general principle I consider a liberal diet necessary, and in particular cases, even more than this is required. In some epileptics I have observed considerable derangement of the digestive organs, and I am of

[1] *Ibid.*, p. 404.   [2] *Ibid.*, p. 451.
[3] *Ibid.*, p. 468.   [4] *Ibid.*, p. 484.

195

opinion that the fits have been deferred by the use of alkalies and other anti-dyspeptic remedies.[1]

Mallam's views are generally in line with those of the majority of medical officers who replied to the enquiry. Disapproval of general bleeding in mania was almost unanimous, although some approved its employment under certain conditions, such as the co-existence of mania with apoplexy. There was, however, a fairly wide acceptance of local bleeding. Mallam was included, by the Commissioners, in the group which held that 'local bleeding by leeches, and sometimes by cupping' was useful, principally in recent cases of mania associated with signs of 'cerebral congestion'. James Smith, of Hadham Palace Asylum, Hertfordshire, even recommended opening a branch of the temporal artery in certain cases.[2] Purgatives were used by the majority in the treatment of mania, but Richard Casson, of the Hull and East Riding Refuge, went further and claimed that purgatives were valuable in all cases of insanity.[3] The purgatives employed included croton oil, calomel, colocynth and senna. Emetics seem, for the most part, to have been discarded or only used where there was positive evidence of a gastro-intestinal disorder. The general view was that opium, in its various preparations, was one of the most effective remedies in many forms of mental disease, particularly in cases of extreme violence and maniacal excitement. Various forms of bathing had long been used in the treatment of lunatics, and a number of medical officers advocated the use of baths for their therapeutic as well as hygienic effects. It was held that warm baths had a sedative action, whilst the cold shower or bath was an effective means of 'subduing the paroxysm'. Casson claimed that warm bathing was beneficial in the treatment of almost all forms of insanity[4] and the Drs Fox, of Brislington House, stated: 'We attach much value to the use of hot and cold bathing. In mania we chiefly use the cold plunging and cold shower bath, and we find the warm bath and the cold shower bath, with the feet of the patient immersed in hot water, more applicable in cases of melancholia'.[5] In 1857, the Commissioners reported the findings of a survey of the use of cold and warm baths in asylums.[6] They noted that many licensed houses had no fixed shower bath and, instead, used the hand or curtain bath. Concern was expressed at the failure to distinguish between

---

[1] *Ibid.*, p. 405.   [2] *Ibid.*, p. 411.   [3] *Ibid.*, p. 398.
[4] *Ibid.*, p. 398.   [5] *Ibid.*, p. 427.
[6] Eleventh Report (1857) C.L., Appendix L, pp. 117–25.

the use of bathing as a remedial agent and as a punitive measure. A comprehensive review of the various methods of bathing in the treatment of insanity was provided by Dr Harrington Tuke in 1858 and 1859, based on his experience at his upper-class private asylum, Manor House, Chiswick.[1]

The diet received particular attention and there was general agreement that maniacal and melancholic patients required a good diet and the use of wine, beer and other 'stimulants' was often recommended. At Brislington House, it was felt that 'a generous and nutritious diet' was also necessary in cases of chronic insanity.[2] In 1816, Ricketts had advocated a reduced intake of animal food-stuffs for the 'raving maniac' and also during the summer months, when the intake of vegetables, broth and rice-milk was best increased.[3] Reference was made in the 1847 survey of therapeutic methods to difficulties in forcing resistive patients to take food and fluids. At intervals during the late-eighteenth and first half of the nineteenth centuries, concern had been expressed about the use of the technique known as 'spouting'. In this, a vessel was employed which had an attached pipe or spout that was forced between the teeth and there were claims of injury, even death, following the use of this practice in private madhouses. In cases of melancholia, all proprietors agreed on the beneficial effects of cheerful company, the distraction of patients whenever possible and the use of narcotics to promote sleep. The general impression appears to have been that epilepsy complicated with insanity was unlikely to be curable and Mallam's régime for epileptics was typical of many others. A. Iles of Fairford, Gloucestershire, used sloping 'desk-pillows' to prevent epileptics suffocating during sleep. In cases of early general paralysis, a range of treatments was employed to reduce 'vascular fullness in the head'.

Amongst other forms of treatment, the use of gyration and swinging requires particular reference. The apparatus known as the circulating swing came to be associated with the name of Cox, because of the detailed description of its use in his book in 1806,[4] although he attributed the original idea to Erasmus Darwin. Various modifications of this so-called 'Herculean remedy' were introduced.

[1] Tuke, H. (1858), 'On Warm and Cold Baths in the Treatment of Insanity', *J. Ment. Sci. 4*, pp. 532–52; and *ibid. 5*, pp. 102–14.
[2] Further Report (1847) C.L., p. 427.
[3] First Report minutes of evidence 1816 S.C., p. 52.
[4] Cox, *op. cit.*, pp. 137–76.

Hallaran (1810) strongly recommended its use[1] and, in 1815, Wakefield reported that, at Laverstock House, Finch found the rotatory chair 'most useful, as the pain it excites takes the patient's mind off to it rather than to the disease'.[2] The therapeutic effects of these methods of treatment were attributed to the vertigo, nausea and vomiting and, at times, prostration brought about by the swinging or rotation.

The curability of insanity and the outcome of treatment

The question of the curability of insanity was debated actively during the first half of the nineteenth century. Particular emphasis was placed on the duration of insanity prior to the commencement of treatment and it was generally held that the longer its duration, the less likely recovery became. The following extracts from the Visitors' Minutes, made after two inspections of G. G. Bompas's house at Fishponds, near Bristol, in 1819 and 1820, illustrate this point and display the gloomy acceptance of inevitable deterioration that was generally the case at this time. In 1819, it was recorded that:

The patients, generally speaking, appear to be as comfortable as can be expected in their unfortunate situations. In some of them there are evident appearances of amendment; and in others there are gleams of improvement; but the mental malady of the greater number continues unabated, or has sunk into irremediable fatuity.[3]

In the following year, the Visitors observed: 'The probability of cure is in a great measure to be estimated by the previous duration of the disease; and though there are occasional instances of reason having been restored after many years hallucination, the prospect of their recovery becomes every year more and more doubtful.'[4] Bethlem Hospital and St Luke's Hospital had, for some time, applied rigorous admission criteria, long-standing cases not being received and no cases being kept for longer than a year. As a result of the latter factor, it was common practice for cases regarded, after a fruitless year at Bethlem or St Luke's, as chronic and incurable, to be placed in cheap custody in a crowded private madhouse, where the chances of further improvement were poor. Indeed, the term incurable was often used to signify failure to be cured within twelve

[1] Hallaran, *op. cit.*, pp. 59–69.
[2] Minutes of evidence 1815 S.C., p. 22.
[3] Glos. R.O., Q/AL.39, Minutes V.M., 8 Jan. 1819.
[4] *Ibid.*, 29 Dec. 1820.

months. With the overcrowding of county asylums, which often occurred within a year or two of their opening, the problem of the incurable population of asylums attracted increasing attention. For example, in 1844, it was estimated that at the Lancaster County Asylum only sixty-five of the 601 patients were curable.[1] Not unnaturally, the concept of building separate establishments for the incurable began to gain support. Prior to the establishment of county asylums, workhouses constituted the principal receptacles for chronic or intractable cases which needed some form of institutional care. The more violent and unmanageable cases were often sent to a private madhouse until they became tranquil, when they were returned promptly to the workhouse, usually without any consideration being given to the possibility of cure. In 1844, it was recorded that Duddeston Hall and Hilsea Asylum, Hampshire, received pauper lunatics for this purpose.[2] As a result of such a custom, the incurable population of some private madhouses was not entirely long-stay. There is substantial evidence that the admission of paupers to private madhouses was often delayed until the disorder had become chronic[3] and this practice led, in turn, to the high estimates of the number of incurable patients amongst the pauper lunatics who required confinement in private madhouses. In Oxfordshire, for example, of the forty-three pauper lunatics in various private asylums in 1837, the high figure of thirty-five were 'believed incurable' by the parish authorities.[4]

The estimated number of curable lunatics confined in asylums in England and Wales, in January 1844, is displayed in Table 28. If Bethlem Hospital and St Luke's Hospital are excluded, because of their selective admission criteria, it is seen that provincial licensed houses contained the highest percentage of curable patients. This is particularly well marked in the case of paupers. Further, metropolitan licensed houses contained the lowest population of curable paupers in any type of asylum and, with the exception of military and naval asylums, this was also the case with regard to private patients. It is unlikely that this disparity between the estimated number of curable paupers in provincial and metropolitan licensed houses was

---

[1] 1844 Report M.C.L., p. 85.   [2] *Ibid.*, p. 42.
[3] *Vide infra*, p. 247.
[4] P.R., 1837, p. 6. (Of the total of 1,083 pauper lunatics, from 436 unions in England and Wales, confined in private licensed houses, 828 were 'believed incurable'.)

TABLE 28 *Estimated number of curable patients in asylums in England and Wales in 1844 (proportion per cent of curable to total number is given in brackets)*

Asylum	Total private patients	Number curable	Total pauper lunatics	Number curable
Provincial licensed houses	1,426	412 (28·9)	1,920	637 (33·2)
Metropolitan licensed houses	973	153 (15·7)	854	111 (13)
County asylums	245	61 (24·9)	4,244	651 (15·4)
Bethlem Hospital	265	181 (68·5)	90[a]	
St Luke's Hospital	177	93 (52·5)	31	16 (51·6)
Other public asylums/hospitals	536	127 (23·7)	343	59 (17·2)
Military and Naval asylums	168	18 (10·7)	0	0

[a] All the criminal lunatics at Bethlem Hospital were entered as paupers and no estimate was made of the number curable.
Source of data: 1844 Report M.C.L., pp. 185, 187.

related to differences in therapeutic optimism and ability, but it was attributable rather to a number of other factors. There was, undoubtedly, a greater tolerance of chronic insanity in rural communities than in the metropolitan area, so that in the provinces fewer chronic lunatics were sent for institutional care. At provincial licensed houses, the bulk of the paupers were received from a circumscribed locality, whereas many metropolitan houses received paupers from considerably further afield than the London area. Thus, in the provinces closer liaison could be maintained with parish authorities and incurable cases could be removed more readily and at lower cost, to the workhouse, or be boarded out in the neighbourhood. Moreover, provincial pauper establishments were, in general, much smaller than those in London and this facilitated more individual assessment and treatment of patients. An additional factor, referred to previously, which swelled the pool of chronic patients in metropolitan houses, was that a considerable proportion of these patients had been received as incurable lunatics from public asylums such as

Bethlem. It emerges, therefore, that the provincial private licensed house, in the fifth decade of the nineteenth century, subserved a different role from that which the county asylum was already assuming as a major part of its function, that is, as a long-term receptacle for all chronic lunatics and idiots in its catchment area. By 1860, there was a greater degree of uniformity in the proportions of patients regarded as curable, who were confined in the three principal types of asylum (Table 29). In each case, there had been a significant lowering of the percentage proportion of curable patients and, in the course of the next decade, this was particularly marked in county and borough asylums. In 1862, for example, only thirty out of 494 patients at the Oxfordshire and Berkshire County Asylum were considered to be curable.[1]

TABLE 29 *Estimated number of curable patients in asylums in England and Wales in 1860 and 1870 (proportion per cent of curable to total is given in brackets)*

Asylum	1860		1870	
	Total patients	*Number curable*	*Total patients*	*Number curable*
Provincial licensed houses	2,356	361 (15·4)	2,204	285 (12·9)
Metropolitan licensed houses	1,944	253 (13)	2,700	283 (10·5)
County and borough asylums	17,432	1,952 (11·2)	27,980	2,149 (7·7)
Registered hospitals	1,985	320 (16·1)	2,369	436 (18·4)
Military, Naval and the State Criminal Asylums	136	15 (11)	660	144 (21·8)

Source of data: Fourteenth Report (1860) C.L., p. 117 and Twenty-fourth Report (1870) C.L., p. 97.

The ability to treat insanity promptly and successfully was, naturally, the most effective advertisement for a licensed house and, during the first half of the nineteenth century, cure-rates were used

[1] P.R., 1862, p. 7.

increasingly for this purpose. There were no uniform rules concerning the degree of restoration of mental state that was required before a cure could be pronounced. Contemporary definitions of a cure, however, did fall into two groups, namely those based upon the disappearance of signs and symptoms of mental disorder and those based upon a good social remission. Evidence from a number of scattered sources allows glimpses to be obtained of the outcome of treatment in private madhouses in the eighteenth century, but there is considerably more information regarding the position in the first half of the nineteenth century. Details from a number of sources are now presented, in order to display the type of claims that were made with regard to the outcome of treatment in private madhouses.

In 1788, Addington stated that at his madhouse at Reading, in the period 1749 to 1754, two incurable patients were admitted and only two patients were not cured within a year, some recovering in three months.[1] His interpretation of a cure was, 'when the patient was able to do everything that a man in health does'.[2] In the same year, Francis Willis claimed to have cured nine out of ten lunatics, who had been placed in his care within three months of the onset of their insanity.[3] Although the validity of this claim has been questioned, the impact and repercussions of such a public declaration about the curability of insanity should not be underestimated. In his view, lunatics were cured when they were able to 'take upon themselves the conduct of their own affairs, and to do the same business they were used to doing before they fell ill'.[4] The outcome of the treatment of the 402 patients admitted to the Newcastle upon Tyne Lunatic Asylum, July 1764–July 1817, was as follows: 158 discharged cured, 49 discharged better, 69 discharged 'by their own desire', 67 dead and 59 remaining in the asylum.[5] The number of cures is surprisingly high in view of the fact that a wide range of chronic cases were accepted at this establishment. At the Droitwich Lunatic Asylum, during a period of over twenty years, probably 1792 to 1816, the admissions numbered 619. These comprised 321 'old cases', including a large number of patients removed from public hospitals as incurable, of whom only fifty-three recovered; and 298

---

[1] Report from the Committee appointed to examine the physicians who have attended His Majesty, during his illness, 1788, p. 13. (One of the incurable patients had been for many years in a private madhouse kept by 'a very skilful physician'.)
[2] *Ibid.*, p. 14.　　　[3] *Ibid.*, p. 9.　　　[4] *Ibid.*, p. 10.
[5] Newcastle upon Tyne City Lib., L.042.L.Tr.dy.51.

'recent cases' who had become insane within a few weeks or months, of whom 226 'perfectly recovered'.[1] W. Finch, the proprietor of Laverstock House, claimed, in 1815, that twenty-two of the forty-two patients admitted in a previous year were cured; seven were rendered convalescent and only a single case had relapsed.[2] In 1828, Finch stressed the need for early treatment and he provided the following figures to illustrate his point: of sixty-nine cases admitted within three months of the first attack, sixty were cured; of seventy cases admitted five months after the onset of the attack, however, only twelve were cured. The number cured fell off proportionately as the period increased and 'after two or three years the cures are very few indeed'.[3]

T. Bakewell published several sets of figures to illustrate the therapeutic success of his house, Spring Vale. He believed firmly in the segregation and wholly separate management of the curable and the incurable, even to the extent that 'those under the curative process should not breathe in the atmosphere with those given up as incurable; they should not even hear of there being any such thing as incurable lunacy'.[4] The following statement, which is based on evidence given by Bakewell before the 1815 Select Committee, indicates the outcome of treatment of the 144 patients admitted to Spring Vale during the period October 1802 to May 1815: seventy 'recent cases' (insane for up to two months): sixty-one discharged recovered, two dead, two convalescent, five remaining; forty-seven 'old cases' (two months–two years): twenty discharged recovered; and twenty-seven 'very old cases' (more than two years): two discharged recovered.[5] These figures support the prevailing opinion, at this time, that prognosis deteriorated with the increasing duration of the period of insanity. With regard to the subsequent history of those who were discharged, Bakewell stated that he had heard that, in general, they were extremely well and he claimed that: 'I could find from fifty to a hundred of my former patients in a morning's ride, who are now well and happy, and useful members of society'.[6] Bakewell held that there was little hope of cure if there had been 'no gleam of convalescence' within a year and that there was no hope of a cure after a period of four to five years had elapsed.[7] In 1844, the

[1] First Report minutes of evidence 1816 S.C., p. 51.
[2] Minutes of evidence 1815 S.C., p. 50.
[3] Minutes of evidence 1828 S.C.H.L., J.H.L., Vol. 60, p. 723.
[4] Bakewell, T. (1815), *op. cit.*, p. 22.
[5] Minutes of evidence 1815 S.C., p. 123. [6] *Ibid.* [7] *Ibid.*, p. 125.

view of the Metropolitan Commissioners was that reason was seldom regained unless recovery took place within the first year of the disorder. S. G. Bakewell (1833) stated that his father's practice was to continue treatment until at least one month after the disappearance of symptoms of mental derangement.[1] He claimed that only one relapse had occurred among twenty-five patients discharged as cured and he stated that, at Spring Vale, eight out of nine patients were cured in an average time of four months, whereas at the York Retreat eight out of twelve patients were reported to be cured in an average of eighteen months and, at Bethlem, only eight out of twenty-three patients were cured in an average time of twelve months.[2] The duration of stay of patients who were cured at other private madhouses was not infrequently claimed to be only a few months. Thus, the average periods of residence of those who recovered at Ticehurst, in 1812 and 1823, were claimed to be eight and fifteen weeks respectively.[3] In a leaflet published, in 1840, by Millard, the proprietor of Whitchurch Asylum, near Ross, Herefordshire, a case was made for the advantage of admitting pauper lunatics to private licensed houses and, not unnaturally, to his own in particular. Millard observed:

The proportion of recoveries at the different public lunatic asylums varies with the treatment—some being merely prisons or houses of safety, others hospitals or houses of recovery, but both alike yielding the palm to private establishments, as proved by the following table. The averaged portion of time taken for the cure of a patient is,

At the Stafford County Lunatic Asylum 1831–1835	$1\frac{1}{2}$ years
Gloucester County Asylum	$1\frac{3}{4}$ years
Middlesex County Lunatic Asylum	4 years and upwards
Whitchurch Private Lunatic Asylum (22 patients cured)	22 weeks and three days[4]

Millard stated that the costs for curing a patient at each of these four establishments were £35 2s., £40 19s., £153 8s. and £14 1s. 3d. respectively, claiming that this showed 'the pecuniary advantages arising to the county from the most efficient treatment of their pauper lunatics'.

An advertisement in the form of a handbill issued by the proprietors of Duddeston Hall, near Birmingham, in c. 1842,[5] included

[1] Bakewell, S. G., *op. cit.*, p. 51.   [2] *Ibid.*, p. 53.
[3] Newington, *op. cit.*, p. 64.
[4] Hereford R.O., Q/ALL/98.
[5] Warwicks. C.R.O., QS.24/a/I/5.

a statement regarding the outcome of treatment of patients admitted in the course of a period of seven years. In addition, the figures for the last three months of 1841 were compared with those for the Middlesex County Asylum at Hanwell, in order to display the high cure-rates at Duddeston Hall. The figures quoted were as follows: Number of patients admitted in the seven-year period, 353. Outcome of treatment: discharged cured, 112; discharged improved, 24; discharged, not cured, 83; died, 56 and remaining under treatment, 78. The figures for the quarter ending 31 December 1841 revealed that the average number resident at Hanwell was 992; only four patients were discharged cured and two improved. At Duddeston Hall, however, where the average number resident was eighty-eight, seven patients had been discharged cured and two improved. It is possible to cross-check the claimed statistics for Duddeston Hall by reference to the comprehensive figures presented in the Statistical Appendix to the 1844 Report of the Metropolitan Commissioners (Table XIV^A). The statistical reports relating to Abington Abbey, published by Prichard, provide a detailed analysis of the admission and discharge data, which Prichard believed was 'a sufficient answer to those who erroneously assert that in private asylums, cures are not frequently made'.[1] During the five-year period, 1854 to 1859, there were fifty-eight admissions and, at the beginning of the period, there were thirty patients in the asylum. At the time of admission, thirty-two patients were considered curable, sixteen 'doubtful' and ten incurable. By the end of the period, twenty-one of the curable patients had left cured, three were in a relieved state and eight were still in-patients. Of those considered 'doubtful' on admission, one had been cured, eleven relieved and four remained. Finally, three 'incurable' patients had left relieved, four had died and three remained.[2] With regard to the form of the disease, thirty-six of the admissions suffered from mania, fourteen from melancholia and eight from dementia.[3]

The clinical and statistical value of such published accounts of the outcome of treatment is, clearly, very limited and the principal conclusion that can be drawn is that, generally, from one-third to one-half of the admissions to private licensed houses were discharged recovered. It is difficult to establish a reliable standard of comparison and, in this context, Thurnam's compilation of the statistics of various asylums in Great Britain, in other European countries and in

---

[1] Prichard, T., *op. cit.*, p. 7.
[2] *Ibid.*, p. 6.   [3] *Ibid.*, p. 10.

America, published in his work of 1845, provides a valuable source of data.[1] The latter included a calculation of the average proportion of recoveries per cent of admissions for individual asylums and for groups of similar establishments and the following are examples of the data quoted by Thurnam: nine county asylums receiving paupers only, 36·95 per cent; six county asylums receiving private and pauper patients, 46·87 per cent; eight public subscription asylums, 40·94 per cent; metropolitan licensed houses (1839–43), 26·65 per cent (private patients 30·87 per cent and paupers 23·74 per cent); and, provincial licensed houses (1839–43), 42·24 per cent (private patients 43·5 per cent and paupers 41·5 per cent).[2]

Clinical features and the outcome of treatment at Hook Norton and Witney

No previous study of private madhouse records has been published in this country, although there has been some investigation of the records of other types of asylums in the nineteenth century. For example, Hare (1959) examined Bethlem case notes, for the period 1816 to 1818, as part of a study of dementia paralytica.[3] Klaf and Hamilton (1961) used Bethlem records, 1853–62, in a comparative study of schizophrenic features in the mid-nineteenth and mid-twentieth centuries.[4] Hassall and Warburton (1964) reviewed a brief series of records, 1852–62, relating to the Worcestershire County Asylum.[5]

The principal surviving sources of clinical data relating to patients in private madhouses, in the eighteenth and nineteenth centuries, are provided by the admission and discharge documents, although, prior to 1845, very limited information in this respect was required. Des-

---

[1] Thurnam, *op. cit.*, pp. 134–44. (In 1820, Burrows published, *A Comparative View of the Cures of Cases of Insanity in Different Institutions for Lunatics*, which included details for Laverstock House, Droitwich Asylum and Spring Vale, as presented to the 1815–16 Select Committee. Burrows (1820), *op. cit.*, p. 20.)

[2] Figures re licensed houses were stated by Thurnam to have been derived from the Statistical Appendix to the 1844 Report M.C.L.

[3] Hare, E. H. (1959), 'The Origin and Spread of Dementia Paralytica', *J. Ment. Sci. 105*, pp. 594–626.

[4] Klaf, F. S. and Hamilton, J. G. (1961), 'Schizophrenia—a Hundred Years ago and Today', *J. Ment. Sci. 107*, pp. 819–27.

[5] Hassall, C. and Warburton, J. (1964), 'The New Look in Mental Health—1852', *Medical Care 2*, pp. 253–4.

criptive and clinical data can be extracted from the medical certificates, from the statement of particulars concerning the patient which
was appended to the reception order and from the statement regarding
the mental state and bodily health of the patient at the time of
admission, made by the asylum medical officer. Much of the content
of the clinical material is equivocal in nature. Nevertheless, it has
been possible to group the terms and phrases used in the Oxfordshire medical certificates and statements in a sufficiently meaningful
way to obtain an indication of the principal presenting psychiatric
and physical features of the patients at the time of admission.
Details of the coding methods employed are given in Appendix C.
The remainder of this chapter is taken up by an account of the
clinical features and the details concerning the discharges corresponding to the admissions made to Hook Norton and Witney
during the survey-period.

Length of stay and disposal
The precise length of stay at Hook Norton and Witney is known in all
but seven of the total 745 consecutive admissions to the two madhouses and the relevant details are set out in Table 30. At Hook
Norton, nearly 62 per cent of all the admissions (including those
culminating in death in the asylum) and at Witney approximately
66 per cent, were for periods of less than twelve months. The
majority of the private patients at both houses were discharged within
a few months, for example, at Hook Norton, nearly 68 per cent of the
admission periods for private patients were of less than six months
duration. This finding is illustrated in Figure 7, which indicates also
that there was no substantial difference in the rates at which private
patients were discharged at the two houses. Although a considerable
number of paupers were discharged from Hook Norton after a short
stay, it is shown that, in general, the length of stay of this type of
patient was longer than that of private patients. Figure 8 displays a
comparison of the length of stay of admissions, for 1830 to 1839
and 1840 to 1849, at Hook Norton and Witney. It shows that the
pattern was similar at each house during the two decades, the apparent improvement at Hook Norton, during the second period,
being due, to some extent, to the withdrawal of pauper lunatics to
county asylums. Shortness of stay was also a notable feature of the
group of eighty-six first admissions, in that fifty-one of the patients
were discharged within six months, and only three patients remained

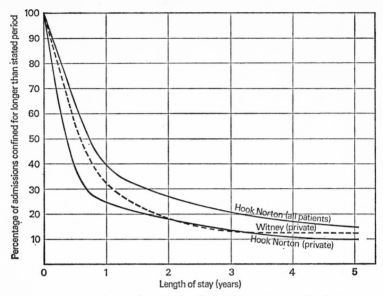

Figure 7 Length of stay of admissions for private patients at Hook Norton and Witney, and for all patients at Hook Norton.

for over five years.[1] The high proportion of short periods of stay is a finding of considerable interest and it goes some way towards refuting the general accusation that private patients were confined for prolonged periods, beyond the point of recovery, for the financial gain of the proprietor or for other corrupt motives. On the contrary, it is likely that private patients tended to be withdrawn prematurely by their relatives, so as to keep the financial outlay for their maintenance as low as possible.

The mode of disposal of patients from Hook Norton and Witney is summarized in Table 31. Very little is known of the destination of patients recorded as 'removed', particularly in the case of pauper lunatics, when the removing agency was the parish overseer or the Board of Guardians. For many chronic patients, the destination was

[1] The mean length of stay and median (months) for first admissions at Hook Norton were 9·5 and 4·5 respectively and, at Witney, 20·0 and 4·0 respectively.

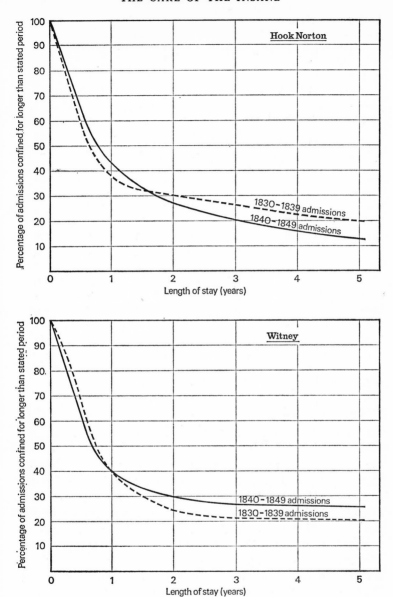

Figure 8 Length of stay of admission for decades 1830–9 and 1840–9 at Hook Norton and Witney.

TABLE 30 *Length of stay*

Length of stay	Hook Norton			Witney		
	Pauper	Private	Total admissions	Pauper	Private	Total admissions
< 1 month	35	22	57	0	12	12
1 –	71	42	113	1	20	21
3 –	88	29	117	0	23	23
6 –	55	10	65	1	12	13
9 –	39	1	40	0	4	4
1 year	76	9	85	0	19	19
2 –	26	6	32	0	1	1
3 –	25	3	28	0	2	2
4 –	9	5	14	0	2	2
5 –	45	5	50	0	6	6
10 –	21	2	23	0	4	4
15 –	3	2	5	0	0	0
20 –	0	1	1	0	1	1
25 +	0	0	0	0	0	0
Not known	4	0	4	0	3	3
Total	497	137	634	2	109[a]	111

		Mean	Median		Mean	Median
Mean stay	Pauper	26·2	9·0			
and median	Private	18·2	3·1			
(months)	Total	24·4	7·1		20·9	5·7

[a] Including two admissions in which legal status of patient was not known.

the workhouse, where maintenance costs were considerably less than at the licensed house. Recommendations made in the case of one pauper lunatic at Hook Norton, however, indicate a contemporary awareness of the benefits of returning patients to the community, with a modicum of supervision, rather than allowing prolonged confinement in the madhouse (Case (2), Appendix D). The use of periods of trial leave prior to absolute discharge, in the case of private patients, is known to have been employed at both houses and this practice is illustrated in Case (3), Appendix D. The transfer of paupers to the Littlemore Asylum took place, with one exception (Case (5), Appendix D), in 1846. Similarly, groups of patients were transferred to the county asylums of Middlesex (Colney Hatch), Buckinghamshire, Warwickshire and Worcestershire as accommodation became available in the newly opened asylums.

Clinical condition on admission and at the time of disposal
In Tables 32 and 33, the broad groupings of terms concerned with the mental state and behaviour on admission are related to the condition at the time of disposal. At Hook Norton, approximately 22 per cent of the admissions resulted in recovery or cure and a further 28 per cent in partial recovery. At Witney, 35 per cent of admissions were cured and approximately 28 per cent partially recovered. The clinical features of the group of first admissions did not differ notably from the pattern revealed by the study of the total admissions during the survey-period. Unfortunately, there is no information available regarding the criteria used when a patient at Hook Norton or Witney was considered to be cured. An examination of the terms used to describe the outcome of treatment in the case of multiple admissions of the same patient, however, revealed no obvious inconsistencies. The low overall figure for the proportion of cures at Hook Norton was related to the relatively high number of

TABLE 31 *Disposal*

Disposal	Hook Norton	Witney	Total admissions
Discharged or removed	399	96	495
Transferred to other private licensed houses	2	0	2
Transferred to public asylums	3	2	5
Transferred to Oxfordshire County Asylum	35	0	35
Transferred to other county asylums	52	0	52
Death	139	10	149
Not known	4	3	7
Total	634	111	745

pauper admissions, in that there was a significant difference in the outcome of treatment of pauper and private patients. Thus, only 103 of the 497 pauper admissions ended in recovery (20·7 per cent) whilst thirty-eight of the 137 private admissions (27·7 per cent) fell into this category. This disparity is in accordance with another finding, namely, that seventeen of the twenty-one patients who were considered as incurable at the time of disposal, were paupers. With one exception, these incurable patients were admitted once only during the survey-period. It is interesting to note that only six patients in this group stayed for a period in excess of two years and that, in seven cases, the length of stay was six months or less. The number of patients discharged as incurable is smaller than might be expected in view of the contemporary estimates of the proportion of incurable patients in asylums. In January 1844, 30 per cent of the eighty patients confined at Hook Norton were considered to be curable and this figure comprised three of the ten private patients and twenty-one of the seventy pauper lunatics.[1] This figure is in accordance with the estimate, quoted previously (Table 28), for patients in all provincial licensed houses at this time. At Witney, seven of the twelve patients were considered curable.[2]

There was a considerably higher mortality at Hook Norton, where about one-fifth (21·9 per cent) of all admissions during the survey-period resulted in death, compared with Witney, where death was the outcome of less than one-tenth (9 per cent) of the admissions (Table 31). This disparity is related, in part, to the reception, at Hook Norton, of paupers, many of whom were admitted with chronic or intractable physical and mental conditions. There were, in fact, 115 paupers amongst the 139 patients who died at Hook Norton. Twenty-nine deaths took place within four weeks of admission and the patient was a pauper in twenty-two of these cases. However, the mortality rate at Hook Norton was congruous with that at the majority of the larger provincial houses receiving paupers at this time. Burrows (1828) made the interesting observation that the mortality rates in private licensed houses did not provide a reliable index of the mortality associated with insanity, because, unlike public asylums, private licensed houses did not exclude patients with 'dangerous diseases'.[3] In 1847, the Commissioners in Lunacy published lengthy discussions regarding mortality in lunatic asylums, prompted by the

[1] Statistical Appendix to 1844 Report M.C.L., p. 10.   [2] *Ibid.*, p. 8.
[3] Burrows (1828), *op. cit.*, p. 559.

enquiries into the allegedly high occurrence of deaths at Haydock Lodge Asylum.[1,2] They emphasized the fact that mortality was likely to be higher amongst pauper lunatics because of their frequently delayed admission and poorer physical health; patients belonging to the richer classes being 'more rarely the subjects of paralysis or epilepsy'.[3]

The stated causes of death, at Hook Norton and Witney, are set out in Table 34.[4] Only two deaths from suicide were recorded and, in one of these cases, the suicide attempt had been made prior to admission. These figures are in keeping with the low recorded incidence of suicide in asylums in the mid-nineteenth century.[5] Disorders appertaining to the brain and nervous system formed the largest grouping of causes of death and examples of terms included in this category are 'softening of the brain', 'effusion on the brain', 'epilepsy', 'apoplexy' and 'paralysis'.

If the data for Hook Norton and Witney are taken in conjunction, the largest single grouping of terms used to describe the mental state and behaviour on admission, refers to an excited state associated with incoherence of speech, either with or without delusions. Of the total number of admissions for which information is available (254), over one-half (51·7 per cent), displayed excitement, incoherence or delusions, either alone or in combination. It is probable that this group included those patients who would have been considered under the broad heading of 'mania'.[6] Table III[A], which relates admissions to Hook Norton in 1843 to forms of insanity, represents the only surviving contemporary statement of this kind concerning the Oxfordshire madhouses. Of the twenty-two admissions to Hook Norton in that year, thirteen suffered from mania, in one or other of its three forms, namely, acute mania, ordinary madness, and periodical mania with comparatively lucid intervals. The majority of patients confined in asylums at this time were, in fact, diagnosed under the broad heading of mania. This fact is illustrated in Tables XII[A] and

[1] Further Report (1847) C.L., pp. 118–28.

[2] Separate report on the mortality at Haydock Lodge, made to the Board by the Commissioners who conducted the enquiry into the condition and management of that asylum. Further Report C.L. re Haydock Lodge Lunatic Asylum, March 1847, Appendix (B), pp. 44–119.

[3] *Ibid.*, p. 55.   [4] Cf. Table V[A].

[5] Cf. Table X[A]. (Five suicides occurred at Brislington House, 1830–43.)

[6] One of the ten principal forms of insanity described in a section of the 1844 Report of the M.C.L., which provides a useful introduction to the nosology of insanity at this time. 1844 Report M.C.L., pp. 102–13.

TABLE 32   *Hook Norton: mental state and behaviour on admission by the condition at the time of disposal*

Mental state and behaviour on admission	Condition at time of disposal							Total admissions
	Cured	Partially recovered	Not improved	Incurable	Dead	Other	Not specified	
Melancholic/desponding	10	7	3	0	5	0	3	28
Melancholic with incoherence and/or delusions	5	4	3	0	1	0	0	13
Excited and/or violent	13	3	2	0	6	0	2	26
Incoherent and/or deluded	13	8	11	0	6	0	5	43
Excited with incoherence and/or delusions	8	8	9	0	3	0	3	31
Idiocy	3	2	7	0	2	0	0	14
Imbecility	3	1	5	0	13	0	1	23
Other	1	2	0	0	1	0	0	4
Not known	1	1	0	0	5	0	13	20
No abnormality	0	1	0	0	2	0	0	3
Details not required on admission documents	84	142	20	20	95	12	56	429
Total	141	179	60	20	139	12	83	634

214

TABLE 33   *Witney: mental state and behaviour on admission by the condition at the time of disposal*

Mental state and behaviour on admission	Condition at time of disposal							
	Cured	Partially recovered	Not improved	Incurable	Dead	Other	Not specified	Total admissions
Melancholic/desponding	0	0	0	0	0	0	0	0
Melancholic with incoherence and/or delusions	5	2	0	0	0	0	0	7
Excited and/or violent	4	1	0	0	0	0	0	5
Incoherent and/or deluded	2	3	0	0	0	0	0	5
Excited with incoherence and/or delusions	11	6	1	0	1	0	2	21
Idiocy	0	0	0	0	0	0	0	0
Imbecility	2	1	0	0	0	0	0	3
Other	0	1	2	0	1	1	0	4
Not known	3	1	0	0	0	0	0	4
No abnormality	0	0	0	0	0	0	0	0
Details not required on admission documents	12	16	4	1	8	2	19	62
Total	39	31	7	1	10	2	21	111

215

TABLE 34 *Stated cause of death*

Cause of death	Hook Norton	Witney	Total deaths
'Decay of nature' and old age	17	1	18
Disorders of brain and nervous system	64	2	66
Disorders of respiratory system	20	1	21
Suicide	1	1	2
Other named causes	32	2	34
Not specified	5	3	8
Total	139	10	149

XVI[A], which display the admissions relative to the forms of insanity during the period 1839 to 1843, at Brislington House and Duddeston Hall. Data (not displayed) concerning the presence of an epileptic disturbance revealed that twenty-three patients admitted to Hook Norton and two to Witney, were subject to epilepsy. This figure refers, principally, to the period post-1845, but includes a small number of patients noted to have been epileptic before this information was required on the admission documents.[1]

Table 35 summarizes the data extracted from the records regarding the bodily health of patients on admission. It is significant that over 60 per cent of the admissions to Hook Norton were in a state of poor or very poor physical health and that thirty-four of the total of forty-six admissions belonging to the latter category were paupers. The relatively high number of specified disorders for the Witney patients is interesting. In many cases, the details given reflect an attempt to link together the bodily and mental state and include frequent reference to disorders of the gastro-intestinal tract and, in particular, of the liver. Febrile symptoms also feature prominently. Details relating to the incidence of suicidal and dangerous behaviour are displayed in Table 36. Information as to whether the patient was

[1] In 1844, twenty-seven of the 1,426 private patients in provincial licensed houses were epileptics, but it is significant that no less than 224 of the 1,920 pauper lunatics were epileptics. Statistical Appendix to 1844 Report M.C.L., pp. 8–10.

'suicidal or dangerous to others' was required in admission documents, for the first time, in 1845. This question led to ambiguous answers and the two items were included separately after 1853. Approximately one-half of the admissions to Hook Norton, for whom details are available, were considered to be dangerous, or dangerous and suicidal and the proportion was the same amongst the first admissions to this house. Of the sixty-three admissions stated to be dangerous alone, forty-six were paupers. It is recorded that on 1 January 1844, the seventy paupers at Hook Norton included three who were considered to be homicidal and two who were suicidal.[1] In addition, at that time, the 3,346 patients in provincial licensed houses included a total of 142 suicidal patients.[2] In only nine of the twenty-eight admissions of patients, who were stated clearly to be suicidal, was the presenting clinical picture one of melancholia.

The attack of insanity leading to admission
Information regarding the attack of insanity which precipitated admission and the interval since the first attack was not required

TABLE 35   *Bodily health*

Bodily health	Hook Norton	Witney	Total admissions
Satisfactory/good	61	9	70
Poor	83	3	86
Very poor	46	1	47
Specific disorders	15	32	47
Not known	0	4	4
Not applicable	429	62	491
Total	634	111	745

before 1845. It is likely that the details recorded were unreliable and only a few points from this part of the study are presented. The disorder leading to 113 of the 254 admissions for which information was required (ninety-six to Hook Norton and seventeen to Witney),

[1] Statistical Appendix to 1844 Report M.C.L., pp. 10–11.
[2] 1844 Report M.C.L., p. 185.

TABLE 36   *Suicidal and/or dangerous behaviour*

Condition	Hook Norton	Witney	Total admissions
Suicidal	14	14	28
Dangerous	63	5	68
Suicidal and dangerous	44	4	48
Not suicidal or dangerous	56	20	76
Not known	28	6	34
Not applicable	429	62	491
Total	634	111	745

was noted as the first attack; in eighty-nine cases, it was not the first attack and the information was not known in the case of fifty-two admissions. Table 37 summarizes the details given regarding the length of the existing attack at the time of admission. The total number of admissions for which positive information is available is reduced by the high number of Hook Norton admissions in which the details were specified as not known. The available data, however, does suggest that private patients were admitted more promptly than paupers, and this was particularly the case at Witney, where over three-quarters of the admissions had a history of preceding derangement of less than six months. The number of paupers admitted to Hook Norton with long-standing disorders is perhaps lower than would be expected, in view of the observations made during the first half of the nineteenth century regarding the state of paupers admitted to asylums. This can be accounted for, probably, by the fact that after the opening of the Oxfordshire and Berkshire County Asylum in 1846, Hook Norton received an unrepresentative sample of pauper lunatics from outside the immediate neighbourhood. The details concerning paupers admitted to the Littlemore Asylum present a different picture. For example, in 1848, thirty-nine of the 106 admissions had a history of over two years duration and William Ley, the superintendent, noted that it was evident that 'lunatics who have been harmless in their demeanour and not in bad health, have been retained in union workhouses until emergency or illness has suggested the necessity for their removal hither'.[1] By 1850, the duration of insanity prior to admission of one-half of the patients admitted to the Littlemore Asylum was of two years or more.[2]

TABLE 37   *Duration of existing attack*

Duration of attack	Hook Norton			Witney			Total admissions
	Pauper	*Private*	*Total*	*Pauper*	*Private*	*Total*	*sions*
< 1 month	26	14	40	0	25	25	65
1 −	48	13	61	0	13	13	74
6 −	11	5	16	0	1	1	17
1 year	5	3	8	0	2	2	10
2 −	14	3	17	0	3	3	20
10 +	4	1	5	0	0	0	5
From infancy	8	0	8	0	0	0	8
Not known	44	6	50	0	5	5	55
Not applicable	337	92	429	2	60[a]	62	491
Total	497	137	634	2	109	111	745

[a] Including two admissions in which legal status of patient was not known.

This volume can only attempt to indicate the range of clinical conditions which were treated at Hook Norton and Witney, but it is considered, nevertheless, that the data presented demonstrate what a valuable and wholly unexplored source of research material is embodied in madhouse records. For example, despite its limitations and the difficulties in the interpretation of the terminology used, such material provides an additional means for examining the historical and semantic development of certain psychiatric terms. The use of the term 'imbecility' and the study of cases described in this way provides one example of the potential interest and value of such records. There were twenty-six cases admitted to Hook Norton and Witney, in which imbecility was the principal presenting feature and each was admitted once only during the period of study. The number included twenty-two paupers, all of whom were Hook Norton patients; the sexes were equally represented. The age on admission ranged from twenty-two to seventy-six years, the greater

[1] Littlemore Asylum, Superintendent's Report, 1849, pp. 3–4.
[2] *Ibid.*, 1851, p. 7.

majority of patients being aged between fifty and seventy and the mean age was fifty-four. Illness prior to admission was often short. In only two cases was the disorder lifelong, and, in fourteen cases, the duration of illness was less than six months. Thirteen of the patients died, some dying shortly after admission and six of those who died had a history of six months or less. Five patients were discharged cured and two relieved. The length of stay of patients in this group ranged from three days to over eight years but nineteen patients were discharged within twelve months and in eight cases the stay was for eight weeks or less. Many of the cases were admitted in a poor physical condition and the imbecile state of the patient was attributed, in some of the records, to such factors as 'fever . . . with derangement of the digestive organs', 'advanced age' and a 'debilitated state'. In only one instance was the term 'idiocy' used in addition. At this time, clearly, imbecility was being used to describe a disturbance of mental state which was secondary to a physical disorder, often of recent onset. This is of particular interest in view of the fact that by the end of the nineteenth century the term was being used quite precisely and consistently to refer to mental defectiveness of a lesser degree than idiocy.

8

◇◇

The Principal Abuses and Defects of the Private-Madhouse System: A Review of the Evidence

◇◇

THROUGHOUT its history, and especially during the period under present consideration, the private-madhouse system was subjected to persistent disparagement and censure. By the mid-nineteenth century, the standing of the private madhouse in the community had been enhanced considerably compared with its position at the beginning of that century, but the system as a whole never escaped from the shadow of its past. The basic flaw, around which all the known and alleged defects were centred, was the 'principle of profit' upon which the system was founded.

One of the aims of this research has been to review, as comprehensively as possible, the source material, both printed and manuscript, relating to the defects and abuses of the private-madhouse system and to evaluate its contents. The source material which was considered for this purpose can be grouped as follows: (a) observations regarding private madhouses and their supervision in contemporary works on insanity; (b) writings by alleged lunatics and former inmates of private madhouses; (c) newspapers and periodicals; (d) novels and biographies; (e) minutes of the Visiting Magistrates and the Commissioners in Lunacy; (f) reports of special enquiries into the affairs of individual houses; (g) reports and proceedings of parliamentary Select Committees; (h) minute books, papers, and annual and other reports of the Commissioners in Lunacy; (i) reports of parliamentary proceedings; (j) law reports; (k) miscellaneous items.

In the search for material, particular attention was given to provincial private madhouses, although evidence concerning metropolitan houses was not excluded since it played an essential part in the evaluation of the system as a whole. In fact, the main body of the available evidence for the late-eighteenth and early-nineteenth centuries relates to metropolitan madhouses.

Improper confinement and prolonged detention for corrupt motives

Pargeter (1792) summed up the late-eighteenth-century public attitude towards the private madhouse in the following way:

The idea of a mad-house is apt to excite ... the strongest emotions of horror and alarm; upon a supposition not altogether ill-founded, that when once a patient is doomed to take up his abode in those places, he will not only be exposed to very great cruelty; but it is a great chance, whether he recovers or not, if he ever sees the outside of the walls.[1]

Pargeter quoted three newspaper articles which had appeared in 1791 and 1792.[2] The first, entitled 'Mad-Houses', contained the following passage:

The masters of these receptacles of misery, on the days that they expect their visitors, get their sane patients out of the way; or, if that cannot be done, give them large doses of stupifying liquor, or narcotic draughts that drown their faculties, and render them incapable of giving a coherent answer. A very strict eye should be kept on these gaolers of the mind; for if they do not find a patient mad, their oppressive tyranny soon makes him so.

The second article stated that justice was being flaunted so overtly 'that any man may have his wife, his father or his brother confined for life, at a certain stipulated price'. The third article was directed, similarly, against those places 'which were originally a refuge for the insane only', but had become 'pension houses for those whose relatives wish to be the guardians of their fortunes, overseers of their estates, and receivers of their rents'. The wrongful confinement of alleged lunatics and their maltreatment had constituted the principal public grievances against private madhouses throughout the eighteenth century and fears of this nature continued to haunt the system for the greater part of the next. It is not unnatural that the possibility of the violation of an individual's liberty, by incarceration in a madhouse, should have aroused public concern, but surviving evidence in support of the view that sane persons were detained in this way is not, in fact, substantial. The 1815 Select Committee, for

---

[1] Pargeter, *op. cit.*, p. 123.   [2] *Ibid.*, pp. 126–8.

example, considered that, in that year, the grounds for complaint were based upon 'very slender means of information'.[1]

In 1739[2] and 1754,[3] Alexander Cruden, the compiler of a Biblical concordance, described his confinement in private madhouses, which, he claimed, was wholly unjust and brought about by malevolent trickery. His accounts relate to a stay of ten weeks at Matthew Wright's madhouse at Bethnal Green[4] in 1738 and to a period of seventeen days, in 1753, in a Chelsea madhouse kept by Peter Inskip. Cruden had had a period of derangement as a young man. When these writings are seen in the context of his other works, the whole picture suggests an eccentric, grandiose, paranoid personality.[5] Earlier, Defoe, one of the first serious campaigners for the official supervision of madhouses, had drawn attention to cases of wrongful detention.[6] In 1728, he called for the suppression of 'pretended madhouses, where many of the fair sex are unjustly confin'd, while their husbands keep mistresses, etc, and many widows are lock'd up for the sake of their jointure'.[7] Defoe made proposals to protect sane persons from confinement under the pretence of madness and also concerning the licensing and official inspection of madhouses. Although these reforms were reasonable, the more sensational aspects of his illustrative stories cannot be taken too seriously and lack corroboration. Other writers also referred to the use of madhouses for the confinement of women so as to allow their husbands to live adulterously with their mistresses. For example, J. A. Gaitskell (1835), a Bath physician, described the case of one of his patients, a mother of eight children, who had been confined by her husband in a metropolitan licensed house for five years, until she was discharged by the Commissioners of the College of Physicians. This woman was 'rather weak in her intellects', but not insane. It was claimed that 'on the contrary, she conducted her domestic affairs and brought up

---

[1] Report 1815 S.C., p. 4.

[2] Cruden, A. (1739), *The London-Citizen exceedingly injured.*

[3] Cruden, A. (1754), *The Adventures of Alexander the Corrector.*

[4] The notorious White House of the early-nineteenth century. Not closed until 1921.

[5] *Vide* Olivier, E. (1934), *The Eccentric Life of Alexander Cruden.*

[6] *Vide supra*, p. 9. (Cf. an advertisement regarding 'Applications . . . for licences to dispose of husbands, wives, sisters, and such near relations into madhouses, when it may serve on occasion to say they are lunatick', in Defoe, D. (1710), *A Review of the State of the English Nation 6*, p. 572.)

[7] Defoe, D. (1728), *Augusta Triumphans: or, the Way to make London the most Flourishing City in the Universe*, p. 30.

her family with credit, till her husband became fascinated with a lady of superior attractions'.[1]

Prior to the Act of 1774, the only legal way by which persons detained in madhouses without sufficient cause could obtain their release was by a writ of habeas corpus and even then, the Court of King's Bench would order an examination of the patient by proper persons, before making an order of discharge. The cases of Rex v. Turlington (1761)[2] and Rex v. Clarke (1762)[3] illustrate this point, as they were concerned with the suspected illegal detention of alleged lunatics in madhouses. At this time, in the absence of laws relating to madhouses, a keeper might justify his actions by a plea of necessity, claiming that he had acted in good faith, for the patient's best interest.[4] Under the Act of 1774, keepers of madhouses were not given any special protection and in all proceedings under a writ of habeas corpus, the parties complained of were obliged to justify their actions according to the course of common law.

In 1763, publicity was given, in *The Gentleman's Magazine*, to the state of private madhouses and to the 'many unlawful, arbitrary, cruel, and oppressive acts', which had been committed in such places.[5] A plea was made for their proper regulation, as it was felt that the system might 'endanger the liberty of every person, whose confinement may become the interest and convenience of such as are wicked enough to contrive, and bold enough to attempt, the seizing and shutting them up in those dreadful places of confinement, from which neither rank nor sex have been found to be any protection'.[6] The parliamentary Select Committee of 1763 confirmed that the wrongful confinement of sane persons in madhouses, for various corrupt reasons, had occurred. The scope of the enquiry conducted by the Committee, however, was very limited and the evidence presented was almost entirely concerned with two London madhouses,

---

[1] Gaitskell, J. A. (1835), *On Mental Derangement*, p. 98.

[2] English Reports, Vol. 97, p. 741. (Mrs Deborah D'Vebre, who had been confined by her husband, at Robert Turlington's house, Chelsea, was found to be 'absolutely free from the least appearance of insanity', and, consequently, she was discharged.)

[3] *Ibid.*, pp. 875–6. (An affidavit by Dr Monro, confirming the insanity of Mrs Anne Hunt, confined in Clarke's madhouse at Clapton, was accepted. As a result, the writ was withdrawn and a commission of lunacy was issued.)

[4] *Vide* Rex v. Coate (1772). *Ibid.*, Vol. 98, pp. 539–40; Brookshaw v. Hopkins (1773). *Ibid.*, pp. 627–8, 630–2.

[5] Anon. (1763), 'A Case humbly offered to the Consideration of Parliament', *Gentleman's Magazine 33*, pp. 25–6.

[6] *Ibid.*, p. 25.

Turlington's at Chelsea and Miles's house at Hoxton, only one case from each being reported in detail. Perhaps the most striking revelations were those made by King, Turlington's 'agent' at the Chelsea house, where the rule was to admit everyone who was taken there. King stated that he had

admitted several for drunkenness, and for other reasons of the same sort, alleged by their friends or relatives bringing them, which he had always thought a sufficient authority . . . he frankly confessed that out of the whole number of persons whom he had confined he had never admitted one as a lunatic during the six years he had been entrusted with the superintendency of the house.[1]

Battie and John Monro, the two most eminent psychiatric physicians of the day, supported the view that wrongful confinement in madhouses did take place. The former quoted, as an example, a case in which a man had tried to confine his wife in Battie's madhouse and had justified his conduct by the belief that the house was 'a sort of Bridewell, or place of correction'.[2] Reference to the findings of this Committee and to the prevailing abuses was made in 1866, by a writer who signed himself L.T.F.[3] A description was given of a narrative, in MS., dated 1746, in which a lady of distinction was confined in a madhouse, by her husband's authority, because of her extravagance and indifference towards him. Other inmates of this particular madhouse, near Harrow, had been placed there for such reasons as drunkenness, violent tempers and, in the case of two young girls, to break off love-affairs which did not meet with their parents' approval. Also amongst those reputed to have been improperly confined in madhouses in the eighteenth century were individuals from the ranks of the early Methodists, the revivalist field-preachers and their followers, who were so often exposed, at this period, to persecution and derision. As an example, the following lines are quoted from a poem, entitled 'The mechanic inspir'd: or, the Methodist's welcome to Frome. A ballad', published by Samuel Bowden, M.D., in 1754, but probably written some years before:

> Struck with puritan looks, and bare fac'd assertion,
> They stake all below, for the skys in reversion,

[1] Report 1763 S.C., J.H.C., Vol. 29, p. 488.
[2] *Ibid.*
[3] Anon. (1866), 'Private Madhouses a Century ago', *Notes and Queries 9*, pp. 367–8.

'Till politic Satan cuts off the entail,
And sends them to Bedlam, to Box or to Jail.[1]

In 1774, Samuel Bruckshaw published an account of what he claimed to be his wrongful confinement in a madhouse.[2] Bruckshaw, a Lincolnshire woolstapler, was detained for 284 days, in 1770 to 1771, at Wilson's madhouse, Stamford, Lincolnshire. The account, addressed to the Lord Mayor of London, was lengthy and circumstantial, but indicated the use of much brutality in his treatment. W. Belcher (1796) published a pamphlet,[3] which, like those of Cruden and Bruckshaw, was typical of many others written by ex-inmates of madhouses at this time. The pamphlet included one section entitled 'The trade of lunacy' (Plate XI) and another part called 'A sketch of a Helleborean Savage, or Smiling Hyena famous in a province over which the devil is said to do his business, by which the author was severely bitten, and Sir John Scott was induced to declare it was a D – d ODD THING'. Belcher was confined in a Hackney madhouse from 1778 to 1795 and was released following the declaration of his sanity by Dr Thomas Monro, physician to Bethlem Hospital and the intervention of Sir John Scott, the Lord Chancellor. As 'a victim to the trade of lunacy', Belcher pledged himself to expose its brutal and horrible abuses and his pamphlet contains a spirited tirade against the madhouse proprietor, the brutal treatments practised by him, the corruption of the official visitors and the legal malpractice of the day. His revealing sketch of the madhouse proprietor, symbolized as the 'Smiling Hyena', which illustrates his sardonic humour, is reproduced in full:

This animal is a non-descript of a mixed species. Form obtuse—body black
—head grey—teeth and prowess on the decline—visage smiling, especially
at the sight of shining metal of which its paws are extremely retentive—
heart supposed to be of a kind of tough white leather.
N.B. He doth ravish the rich when he getteth him into his den.

A letter received in 1814 by Samuel Whitbread, M.P. for Bedford, referring to the state of private madhouses in Scotland, is probably representative of the kind of correspondence addressed to lunacy

[1] Bowden, S. (1754), *Poems on Various Subjects; with Some Essays in Prose, Letters to Correspondents, &c. and a Treatise on Health*, p. 216. (Box was the location of a private madhouse, later referred to as Kingsdown House.)

[2] Bruckshaw, S. (1774), *One more Proof of the Iniquitous Abuse of Private Madhouses*.

[3] Belcher, W. (1796), *Address to Humanity*. (Belcher wrote a number of essays and, in 1787, he published *The Galaxy*, a collection of poems.)

reformers of this time. The writer expressed well-defined ideas of persecution and denounced the laws of Scotland which could condemn 'anyone who shall displease a Noble Scots Earl, to ever-lasting misery in a dungeon of a madhouse; without trial . . . without mercy'.[1] In another letter, which Whitbread endorsed 'Mad', the writer H. Wynnitt, referred to the persecution to which he had been submitted by his father because of his religious opinions, and he described the way in which he was removed from his lodgings at Bromsgrove, 'in the middle of the day before the whole town and conveyed to Droitwich Asylum for lunatics'.[2] At this licensed house, 'they soon found I was not a fit subject for the place' and he was liberated in about three months.

John Mitford published (1825?) two pamphlets describing 'the crimes and horrors' of Warburton's private madhouses at Hoxton and Bethnal Green, London.[3] Two years previously, Mitford had petitioned Parliament, unsuccessfully, to enquire into the situation at these houses. The abuses which Mitford described, often luridly, included the confinement of sane persons by their relatives out of malice and self-interest; the certification of patients by medical men who had never seen or examined the patient and the capturing of alleged lunatics by keepers armed with pre-signed certificates. Mitford suggested also that madhouses were often used to harbour criminals and to protect them from rightful punishment. More bio-graphical information is available for Mitford (1782–1831) than is usually the case for other writers of this type. After a short career in the Royal Navy, Mitford was working as a poet and journalist in London in 1811, when he was certified and confined in a madhouse for about two years. Subsequently, he lapsed into alcoholism, leaving his family in the care of his cousin, Lord Redesdale. One account of his last years included the following description:

The only way his publisher could compel him to write . . . was to limit him to a shilling a day—twopence for bread, cheese, and an onion, the rest for gin. His later work was written anonymously, for the most part in a

---

[1] Beds. C.R.O., Whitbread MSS. 5082, letter, Alexander Fraser to Samuel Whitbread, 1 Dec. 1814.

[2] Beds. C.R.O., Whitbread MSS. 3073, letter, H. Wynnitt to Samuel Whitbread, 11 Sept. 1813.

[3] Mitford, J. (1825?), *A Description of the Crimes and Horrors in the Interior of Warburton's Private Mad-house at Hoxton* [i.e. Part 1]. *Part Second of the Crimes and Horrors of the Interior of Warburton's Private Mad-houses at Hoxton and Bethnal Green* [i.e. Part 2]. (The first part was published anonymously but is undoubtedly attributable to Mitford.)

cellar ... Finally he went to the workhouse and died there ... Mitford was utterly untruthful, dissipated, and half-crazy, but his earlier poems at least are racy tales in verse written with flowing ease.[1]

Mitford's recollections would, therefore, appear to be of limited value, although there is evidence from other sources which confirms the fact that conditions in Warburton's houses were bad during the early decades of the nineteenth century. The White House, Bethnal Green, which received paupers from three of London's wealthiest parishes, featured prominently in the report of the 1827 Select Committee and it was shown, conclusively, that patients in this establishment had been subjected to much cruelty and neglect.[2] Lengthy references were made to Warburton's madhouses in the parliamentary debate at the time of the introduction of the 1828 Madhouse Bill.[3]

Similar accounts to those of Mitford were given by John Tempest (1830)[4] and Richard Paternoster (1841).[5] Paternoster's pamphlet was essentially a compilation of a number of articles published previously in the *Satirist* and was centred on his stay of forty-one days at Finch's madhouse, Kensington. He exposed the circumstances of his wrongful seizure, which had been arranged by his father following a disagreement on money matters. He was released after the attention of the police and the press had attracted much publicity to his case. He described several other metropolitan houses but, apart from a reference to an enquiry at Hereford Lunatic Asylum, no mention was made of conditions outside London. Paternoster, who had worked in the Madras Civil Service, dealt fairly objectively with the defects of the madhouse system, many of which he rightly attributed to 'the absurdities of the Lunacy Act' and this pamphlet is probably the most valuable of the published self-accounts of former inmates in madhouses. The illegal detention, in 1838, of Lewis Phillips, a London businessman, at one of Warburton's houses seems indisputable and detailed reference to this case was

---

[1] Kunitz, S. J. (ed.) (1936), *British Authors of the Nineteenth Century*, p. 440.

[2] *Vide* Gordon, S. and Cocks, T. G. B. (1952), *A People's Conscience*, Chapter V: 'The case of the White House at Bethnal Green, pp. 101–51. (Gives a graphic account of conditions at this house and its early history.)

[3] H.P.D., Vol. XVIII, 19 Feb. 1828, H.C., cols. 575–85.

[4] Tempest, J. (1830), *Narrative of the Treatment experienced by John Tempest Esq., of Lincoln's Inn, Barrister at Law, during Fourteen Months Solitary Confinement under a False Imputation of Lunacy.*

[5] Paternoster, *op. cit.*

made in Parliament in 1845[1] by Thomas Duncombe, M.P. for Finsbury, who presented a petition concerning Phillips. He referred, also, to petitions regarding other alleged lunatics, whom, he claimed, had been imprisoned under a false plea of lunacy, namely, William White,[2] William Bailey[3] and Captain Digby,[4] and he outlined the case of Mrs Ellen Finn.[5] These cases were presented to display the deficiencies of the Metropolitan Commissioners and the defects of the existing legislation and Duncombe pressed for a full enquiry into the latter before any further legislation on the subject was passed. The novelist, H. Cockton (1840) in his work, *The Life and Adventures of Valentine Vox, the Ventriloquist*, vehemently denounced 'the system of private lunatic asylums' under which sane men could,

at any time be seized, gagged, manacled, and placed beyond the pale of the constitution, within the walls of an asylum; there to be incarcerated for life, with no society save that of poor idiots and raving maniacs, shut out for ever from the world as completely as if they were not in existence, without the power of communicating with a single friend, or of receiving from a single friend the slightest communication.[6]

Charles Reade (1863), similarly, gave a vivid description, in his somewhat sensational novel *Hard Cash*, of the way in which the trickery and self-interest of relatives could lead to an individual's unjust confinement in a madhouse[7] and the content is closely reminiscent of Paternoster's experiences. As in *Valentine Vox*, emphasis was placed on the ways in which the victim's pleas to the Visitors were muffled and upon the ineptitude of the Lunacy Commissioners. Plate X reproduces an engraving from one edition of *Valentine Vox*. In this illustration, Goodman, who had been seized forcibly and detained illegally in 'Dr Holdem's Den', is 'goaded to madness' by being chained to his bed and having his feet tickled with a feather shortly before the Commissioners visited, so that he would present in a state of raving madness and be unable to complain rationally to them. Reade boasted of the factual basis of his story, but his use of facts in a work of fiction led one contemporary reviewer to observe, 'the

[1] H.P.D., Vol. LXXXII, 11 July 1845, H.C., cols. 409–13.
[2] *Ibid.*, cols. 395–6.   [3] *Ibid.*, col. 413.   [4] *Ibid.*, cols. 413–14.
[5] *Ibid.*, cols. 414–16.
[6] Cockton, H. (1840), *The Life and Adventures of Valentine Vox, the Ventriloquist*, p. vi.
[7] Reade, C. (1863), *Hard Cash. A Matter of Fact Romance*. (This novel was first published in a serial form as *Very Hard Cash* in Charles Dickens's weekly journal, *All the Year Round*. It appeared at a time when public opinion was particularly hostile towards private asylums.)

incautious reader is apt to imagine mad doctors to be scientific scoundrels, lunatic asylums to be a refined sort of Tophet, and the commissioners in lunacy and visiting justices to be a flock of sheep. This is the untruthful exaggeration of fact jumbled with fiction.'[1] It is relevant to note that several of the characters in the novel are readily identifiable as well-known, contemporary figures, such as Dr Conolly who is portrayed as Dr Wycherley.[2]

J. T. Perceval published an account of his experiences in two mad-houses, which appeared in two volumes in 1838 and 1840. These works are probably the best known, at the present day, of any nineteenth-century self-accounts by lunatics, and they were re-printed and edited by Bateson in 1962.[3] Perceval, who was the fifth son of Spencer Perceval, the Prime Minister who was assassinated in 1812, was confined at Brislington House in 1831 to 1832 and was moved later by his family to Ticehurst Asylum, which he left in 1834. In his books, he claimed that at Brislington House he was exposed to barbarous cruelties, callous neglect and degradation at the hands of attendants and submitted to much ill-treatment by such methods as excessive mechanical restraint, the use of cold baths and blood-letting. In particular, he objected to what he termed 'public confinement without any privacy'.[4] He made the thought-provoking comment, on one occasion, that 'the humanity of the asylum consisted in the conduct of the patients, not in that of the system and of its agents' and claimed that had the patients given expression to their rightful indignation they might well have been murdered.[5] For about two weeks at Brislington House, he was accommodated on straw in an 'out-house', because of incontinence. He reviled his family for abandoning him to such treatment and for allowing his confinement to be continued despite the restoration of his sanity. Perceval was, undoubtedly, acutely psychotic at the time of his admission to Brislington House. He remained deluded and hallucinated for some time and it would appear that, at times, his behaviour was negativistic and resistive. By the time he was transferred to Ticehurst, the psychotic process had subsided, although some paranoid preoccupation continued. At Ticehurst, he was treated

---

[1] *The Times*, 2 Jan. 1864.

[2] Hunter, R. A. and Macalpine, I. (1961), 'Dickens and Conolly. An Embarrassed Editor's Disclaimer', *Times Lit. Suppl.*, 11 Aug. 1961.

[3] Bateson, G. (1962), *Perceval's Narrative: a Patient's Account of his Psychosis*.

[4] Perceval (1840), *op. cit.*, p. 17.

[5] Perceval (1838), *op. cit.*, p. 256.

without harshness and allowed considerably greater personal privacy and liberty. Despite the paranoid vehemence of his writings, however, Perceval's contribution was an important one, in that, like Paternoster, his aims were more far-reaching than those of other alleged lunatics who published accounts of their cases. His objectives were the reform of lunacy law, particularly with regard to the protection of insane patients in asylums, and the reform of the management of lunatic asylums. In addition, he hoped to be able to educate the relatives of mentally deranged persons, so that they might avoid the errors which, he claimed, had been committed by his own family. He sought to 'stir up an intelligent and active sympathy, in behalf of the most wretched, the most oppressed, the only helpless of mankind, by proving with how much needless tyranny they are treated—and this in mockery—by men who pretend indeed their cure, but who are, in reality, their tormentors and destroyers'.[1] His subsequent career in the movement for the reform of lunacy legislation and the treatment of the insane confirms the sincerity of his purpose.[2] Paternoster was one of the alleged lunatics on whose behalf Perceval intervened. In 1845, Perceval helped to form the Alleged Lunatics' Friend Society[3] and, in the following year, he became the honorary Secretary.[4]

Later in the nineteenth century, the cases of Louisa Lowe and Georgiana Weldon fanned the renewed sentiments of concern that were being expressed during the seventies that the lunacy laws did not provide adequate protection for the alleged lunatic. In 1872, Louisa Lowe, a spiritualist, published an account of her case, in which she had charged the Commissioners with concurring in her improper detention at Brislington House and, later, at The Lawn, Hanwell, Middlesex.[5] Her case was not proved, but, subsequently, she became the Secretary of the newly formed Lunacy Law Reform Association and published a series of pamphlets and books.[6]

---

[1] Perceval (1838), *op. cit.*, p. 2. (*Vide* Perceval (1840), *op. cit.*, pp. iii–xxviii, for a re-statement of his objectives and views.)

[2] *Vide* Hunter, R. A. and Macalpine, I. (1962), 'John Thomas Perceval (1803–1876) Patient and Reformer', *Med. Hist. 6*, pp. 391–5.

[3] This society did not gain substantial support or publicity but its influence was not unimportant. Reports were published in 1851 and 1858.

[4] *Vide* advertisement in *The Times*, 21 March 1846.

[5] Lowe, L. (1872), *Report of a Case heard in Queen's Bench, November 22nd 1872.*

[6] *Vide* Lowe, L. (1883), *The Bastilles of England; or the Lunacy Laws at Work.* Also a number of undated pamphlets in a series entitled, *Quis custodiet ipsos*

Louisa Lowe's allegations were given further detailed consideration by the Select Committee of 1877.[1] She was involved in the case of Georgiana Weldon, who was also an eccentric spiritualist and whose multiple legal actions, stemming from an attempt to certify her as insane, attracted much publicity to the case for the amendment of the lunacy laws.[2]

In 1809, the younger Duncan observed disparagingly that 'from the very nature of a mad-house it is a place of constraint and conceal-ment',[3] but it is important not to lose sight of the fact that secrecy and concealment in the treatment of insanity were factors much sought after by the relatives and sincere friends of lunatics, especially amongst the upper classes. A number of examples in support of this view have been discovered in private-madhouse MSS. For example, there was admitted to St Luke's House, Newcastle, in 1784, a young woman 'who would not speak tho' its probable she cou'd', whose name was unknown. According to the keeper, she had been brought to the house by persons presumed to be her mother and brother and, 'it appeared to him that they did not wish to have her name known'.[4] The opportunities for concealment offered at such establishments, clearly, could be abused very readily. Fears centred on such abuses must have been amplified by the fact that protestations of illegal confinement could be dismissed so easily as a symptom of insanity. In this setting, the role of the official visitor and the link that he provided with disinterested parties outside the madhouse was of cardinal importance. In an attempt to discourage the tendency to abandon patients in madhouses, it was enacted, in 1828, that patients should be visited at least once in six months by the person who had ordered their admission or by persons acting on behalf of the latter-named. However, this plan was not well received by madhouse proprietors, chiefly because it was believed that such visits might provoke disturbance. For example, in 1829, Thomas Burman, proprietor of a well-established house at Henley-in-Arden, Warwick-shire, reported that many patients were visited by authorized persons

custodes? including: *Gagging in Madhouses as practised by Government Servants; My Outlawry, a Tale of Madhouse Life; The Lunacy Laws and Trade in Lunacy in a Correspondence with the Earl of Shaftesbury; A Nineteenth Century Adaptation of Old Inventions to the Repression of New Thoughts and Personal Liberty.*

[1] Report and minutes of evidence 1877 S.C., pp. 236–49.

[2] *Vide* Weldon, G. (1878), *The History of my Orphanage or the Outpourings of an Alleged Lunatic.* [3] Duncan, *op. cit.*, p. 18.

[4] Newcastle upon Tyne City Archives Dept., LA.I/3, Minutes V.M., 13 Dec. 1784.

but he considered that 'the visit of such persons often causes a degree of excitement which is injurious to the patient'.[1] Such reasons could be misconstrued and be seen as an attempt to sever, for corrupt motives, the patient's contact with his family and friends. However, throughout the period under consideration, an important feature of the treatment of insanity was, in fact, the strong belief in the therapeutic value of severing the patient's association with his home and the prevention of early or indiscriminate visiting by relatives and acquaintances. Many contemporary authors supported this view. In *c.* 1806, E. L. Fox stressed the importance of removing

the insane from their own houses and friends, not only on account of the distress and confusion they there produce, but because there, the circumstances that excite a maniacal paroxysm more frequently exist. Their recovery is promoted by associating with persons under similar circumstances, and they submit more patiently to discipline from strangers . . . than from relations and dependants, who are timid, unskilled and frequently the objects of irritation.[2]

According to Prichard (1835), Willis asserted that 'insane persons from the Continent, who came to seek his advice, recovered more frequently than his countrymen'.[3] S. G. Bakewell (1833) stated that his father was convinced that a patient had not got a fair chance of recovery without removal from home and gave as a reason for the very rapid recovery of those patients who came from the greatest distance, their removal 'from all associations connected with their hallucination, and all causes of excitement from collision with their friends'.[4] Similarly, it was believed that too early a return home generally resulted in relapse. Bakewell acknowledged the fact that the views of his father might be regarded with suspicion, simply because he was a madhouse proprietor. By way of contrast, it is interesting to note that by the late-nineteenth century the Commissioners in Lunacy actually recommended that relatives and friends of patients should stay in licensed houses, in accordance with legislative provisions, both for the benefit of the patient and as a means of reducing the likelihood of malpractice.[5]

[1] Warwicks. C.R.O., QS.24/a/I/7, Minutes V.M., 1829.

[2] Reprint of notice re Brislington House, B.H.Q.N.C.N., p. 1.

[3] Prichard, J. C., *op. cit.*, p. 281. (*Vide* Anon. (1796), 'Détails sur l'établissement du docteur Willis, pour la guérison des aliénés', *Bibliothèque Britannique* (Littérature) *1*, p. 771.)

[4] Bakewell, S. G., *op. cit.*, p. 48.

[5] Thirty-third Report (1879) C.L., pp. 113–14.

The Oxfordshire madhouse records contain very little evidence concerning the visiting of patients by relatives, friends, or, in the case of paupers, by parish officials. As far as can be ascertained, no cases of illegal confinement took place at the Oxfordshire madhouses. The propriety of the detention of one patient (Edward Bishop) at Witney, in 1847, was questioned and this patient's interesting case history is summarized in Case (1), Appendix D. Three patients were admitted to Hook Norton, who, at the time of admission, did not display any evidence of mental disorder. Two of them, however, were in a dying state and both died within a short time of admission.[1] In the third case,[2] 'indications of insanity' were 'dependent on the use of stimulants', there was a record of previous admissions elsewhere and the patient was discharged relieved over two years after admission. The only indication that some improper procedure may have occurred was the fact that, from 1832 onwards, sixteen admissions to Witney took place on the strength of a single medical certificate, the second being completed shortly after admission. Only two such cases occurred at Hook Norton. The 'special circumstances' quoted were generally related to the urgency for admission,[3] the acuteness of the disorder or ignorance of the statutory requirements and, in one case, it was stated that if the patient had been examined by two medical men the reason would have been suspected and the patient would have fled. The medical certificate illustrated in Plate VII was used, in fact, to admit the patient, a second being provided later to regularize the admission. The reasons quoted for the irregularity were, 'The patient being removed in haste and the Trustee not knowing that it required two certificates'.[4] Cockton (1840), with his characteristically bitter mistrust of lunacy legislation, drew attention to the fact that the 'special circumstances' clause was abused deliberately to procure the improper and hasty admission of alleged lunatics.[5]

There is evidence that, in the first half of the nineteenth century, the Visitors were more alert to the possibilities of improper detention than they were to other abuses of the madhouse system. They were empowered, for the first time, by the Act of 1828 (9 Geo. IV, c. 41) to

---

[1] O.C.R.O., QSL.II/3 and QSL.II/7. Michael Kenney, pauper, admitted 18 Aug. 1847 and died three days later; and Sophia Marks, pauper, admitted and died on 5 July 1851.

[2] O.C.R.O., QSL.II/2. William Archer, pauper, admitted 9 Nov. 1846 and discharged 15 Feb. 1849.   [3] *Vide* Case (3) Appendix D.

[4] O.C.R.O., QSL.I/15. Sarah S. Jackson, admitted 11 Jan. 1832, discharged 3 June 1832.   [5] Cockton, *op. cit.*, p. ix.

set at liberty persons whom they considered to be improperly confined, if, after three visits, at least twenty-one days apart, the patient continued to appear to be detained without sufficient cause. Although this provision was a useful safeguard, there still remained the possibility that sane persons, who were allegedly lunatic, could spend a lengthy period in a madhouse. However, in 1828, E. L. Fox claimed that he had never had a sane person referred for admission to his madhouse, with the exception of two patients who had been referred in error by inexperienced medical men[1] and W. H. Ricketts of Droitwich Lunatic Asylum supported him in this claim.[2] Subsequent legislation gave the Visitors power to discharge lunatics, other than those who were criminals or those found lunatic by inquisition. Under the Act of 1845, the Visitors were empowered to discharge a patient if he appeared, on two distinct and separate visits, to be detained without sufficient cause. In 1844, the Metropolitan Commissioners offered the following general rule regarding the suitability of persons for confinement: 'wherever a man of ordinary intellect is able so to conduct himself, that he is not likely to do injury, in person or property, to himself or others, he is unfit to continue as the inmate of a lunatic asylum.'[3] Special enquiries were held if any doubt was raised about the correctness of a patient's confinement. For example, in 1833, the Warwickshire Visitors enquired into the case of a female patient at Burman's house, following the receipt of a letter from John Conolly suggesting that she was illegally confined. No evidence in support of this suspicion, however, came to light.[4] The Metropolitan Commissioners stated in 1836 that, during the previous year, no case had been revealed in licensed houses within their jurisdiction, in which they had seen 'just ground for supposing that the patient was originally confined without due cause, or from improper motives'.[5] In their Report of 1844, the Metropolitan Commissioners observed that rarely had they found any evidence of a sane person being confined.[6] They stated, however, that: 'Occasionally, the reasons for confining a patient at a great

[1] Minutes of evidence 1828 S.C.H.L., J.H.L., Vol. 60, pp. 711–12.

[2] *Ibid.*, p. 721.

[3] 1844 Report M.C.L., p. 170.

[4] Warwicks. C.R.O., QS.24/a/I/7, Report of a Special Meeting of V.M., 23 April 1833.

[5] Annual Report (1836) M.C.L. In Copies of Annual Reports M.C.L., 1835–41, p. 1.

[6] 1844 Report M.C.L., p. 176.

distance from his home, or for affording him an allowance apparently incompatible with his means',[1] were not always explained satisfactorily, although there had been very few instances where the patient's mental state did not justify confinement. However, the Commissioners observed that there had been many cases in which confinement had been prolonged unduly and that this situation was, not infrequently, due to reluctance on the part of the patient's relatives or the parochial officers to remove the patient when convalescent. Sometimes this reluctance was attributable to the relatives' timidity or their desire to conceal the patient's disorder and, in the case of parish officials, to their unwillingness to re-accept potentially troublesome patients. With reference to patients from the middle and upper classes, however, T. Prichard (1859) observed:

As regards the detention of patients after their apparent recovery, the commonly-received notion that their friends are careless of their position or anxious to prolong their detention, is totally at variance with fact, in so far as my experience goes. The contrary is the fact—they are too ready to remove them; and they frequently do this with imprudent haste; consequently, a relapse is the result.[2]

In 1849, the case of a Miss Nottidge, who was confined at Moorcroft House, Hillingdon, London, from 1846 to 1848, provoked considerable medico-legal attention. The evidence suggests that this woman was properly confined, despite the claims to the contrary and the publicity stemmed chiefly from statements made by the Lord Chief Baron, Sir Frederick Pollock, who presided at the trial of Nottidge v. Ripley.[3] He expressed the view that no person ought to be confined in a lunatic establishment unless he was suicidal or dangerous to others and that any persons not thus dangerous ought to be set at liberty. These dicta were clearly erroneous and they were regarded by the Commissioners in Lunacy as 'likely seriously to mislead the medical profession and the public'.[4] John Conolly condemned these statements in 'A remonstrance with the Lord Chief Baron',[5] with which he included the history of the case written by the proprietor of the house, Dr A. Stilwell.

[1] *Ibid.*   [2] Prichard, T., *op. cit.*, p. 11.

[3] Sittings at Nisi Prius, in Middlesex, before the Chief Baron and a Special Jury, 23–6 June 1849. *Vide* (1849), 'Judicial Insanity. Trial of Nottidge v. Ripley', *J. Psychol. Med. & Ment. Path. II*, pp. 630–5.

[4] Copy of a letter to the Lord Chancellor from the Commissioners in Lunacy, with reference to their duties and practice, under the Act 8 & 9 Vict., c. 100, p. 4.

[5] Conolly, J. (1849), *op. cit.*

Two commissions of lunacy held in 1858 attracted considerable publicity and gave rise to a popular outcry against private asylums. The first related to a Mrs Turner, who was a patient at Acomb House, near York. The jury declared her to be of sound mind and commented adversely upon the conduct of Mr Metcalf, the proprietor, who was accused of using grossly offensive language and of improper behaviour towards Mrs Turner. His licence was revoked and he received a good deal of public censure.[1] The second commission concerned a Mr Ruck, who had been confined at Dr Stilwell's asylum, Moorcroft House, and again the jury declared the patient sane.[2] The newspaper publicity given to these cases, which was associated with an attack by several influential journals, on private asylums in general, was condemned in an editorial comment in the *Journal of Mental Science*,[3] from which the following extracts have been taken:

A greater act of injustice has never been perpetrated by the press, than the attack which it has made upon private lunatic asylums under the calumnious imputation that the gentlemen by whom they are conducted, are capable of the unworthy conduct to which in one solitary instance the anonymous scribes are able to point.[4]

Doubt was cast upon the validity of the evidence establishing the sanity of the two persons concerned and it was suggested that the inquisitions had not proved that sane persons were actually placed in confinement under the pretext of insanity. Instead, these commissions had the effect of drawing attention to the defects of the operative lunacy legislation:

All this outcry . . . has been raised upon grounds no more relative than this, that if two ignorant or corrupt medical men choose to certify to the insanity of a sane person, and the proprietor of a private asylum chooses to receive and detain him, there is no official machinery to frustrate or prevent such iniquity . . . the defects of the lunacy law have been most unjustly attributed as faults to those acting under it. The possibility of unrighteous detention may certainly now be regarded as a defect in the law, notwithstanding that it may never have been made use of. If no one . . . has been injured by it, except the maligned proprietors of private asylums, for their honour and interest . . . it should no longer be left possible to attribute to them the crime of false imprisonment.[5]

[1] (1859), 'Commission of lunacy on Mrs. Turner', *J. Ment. Sci. 5*, pp. 114–22.
[2] 'Commission of lunacy on Mr. Ruck', *Ibid.*, pp. 122–46.
[3] 'The newspaper attack on private lunatic asylums', *Ibid.*, pp. 146–54.
[4] *Ibid.*, p. 148.   [5] *Ibid.*, p. 151.

In fact, it was claimed that, at that time, the majority of private asylums were licensed to 'high-minded and philanthropic medical men'.

In evidence given before the Select Committee of 1859, Perceval, the Honorary Secretary of the Alleged Lunatics' Friend Society, claimed that he could provide a list of twenty-six persons or more who had been unjustly confined during the period 1837 to 1858, and he pressed for the total abolition of private asylums, as the only solution to the problem of improper confinement.[1] Despite his strong views against private asylums, Lord Shaftesbury stated his belief, before this Select Committee, that 'very few have been really shut up without cause, but I have no doubt that very many indeed have been detained beyond the time when they might have been at liberty'.[2] Similarly, Conolly declared that, in his long experience, he did 'not recollect the case of a patient being put into an asylum, or scarcely ever, who was not a proper person to be placed under superintendence at all events of some kind',[3] and he thought that detention beyond the time of perfect recovery very seldom, if ever, took place. The Committee reviewed the safeguards against illegal confinement and consideration was given to the proposal that the alleged lunatic should have the right to have his case tried by a magistrate before admission. The Committee, however, concluded that, as the cases in which admission had been shown to be unwarranted were rare, 'the evil of acting on the present law without enquiry before a magistrate is more imaginary than real'.[4]

During the eighteenth and the first half of the nineteenth centuries, the ignorance and corruption of the certifying medical men probably contributed substantially to the apparent defects of the private-madhouse system. Professional standards were varied and were generally low and, during the earlier period, a person might set himself up as an apothecary after a brief apprenticeship to a surgeon or a druggist. Following the Act of 1774, the justification for the confinement of private patients depended solely upon a single medical certificate, which could be signed by a physician, surgeon or apothecary of unspecified qualification. However, it was not until an Act of 1853 (16 & 17 Vict., c. 96) that a person certifying lunatics had to state the qualification entitling him to practice as a physician, surgeon or

---

[1] Report 1859 S.C. (Aug. 1859), pp. 15–16.
[2] Report 1859 S.C. (April 1859), p. 22.   [3] *Ibid.*, p. 179.
[4] Report 1859 S.C. (July 1860), p. viii.

apothecary. Cox clearly recognized the abuses that could result from the ignorance of medical men and he believed that the law assigned too much power to the inferior grades of the profession. In 1806, he observed that he had 'witnessed shameful abuses of this power' and he recalled 'an instance where a son of Esculapius signed a certificate Sarjeant instead of Surgeon'.[1] Cox held enlightened views and in his *Practical Observations on Insanity*, he provided guiding rules regarding the certification of lunatics for the use of 'the younger and inexperienced classes of medical men'.[2] Views similar to those of Cox were expressed by others who were concerned with private madhouses. In 1815, Finch gave an excellent illustration of the ignorance and near illiteracy of some apothecaries at that time: a medical certificate was received by him in March 1809:

He[y] Broadway A Potcarey of Gillingham Certefy that Mr. James Burt Misfortin hapened by a Plow in the Hed which is the Ocaisim of his Ellness & By the Rising and Falling of the Blood And I think A Blister and Bleeding and meddeson Will be A Very Great thing But Mr. Jame Burt wold not A Gree to be Don at Home, H[ay] Broadway.[3]

Finch stated that Broadway kept a village druggist's shop and occasionally attended poor people. The principal accusation against medical practitioners was that they falsely certified sane persons as lunatics, often without conducting a personal examination, in return for payments made by parties interested in the disposal of the alleged lunatic or by the proprietor of a madhouse as an inducement to increase his trade. There are a number of examples of the prosecution of medical men for signing false certificates, but, in general, the paucity of corroborative material makes it extremely difficult to evaluate the validity of the accusations that were made.

In 1811, James Parkinson, a London medical practitioner, published a short book,[4] principally to vindicate his conduct in the case of an alleged lunatic named Mary Daintree. In 1807, this woman had been admitted to Holly House, Hoxton, London, by direction of her nephew, but without a medical certificate. Later, Parkinson provided a certificate on what appeared, subsequently, to have been largely hearsay evidence. Mrs Daintree was released three months later and

[1] Cox, *op. cit.*, p. 183.   [2] *Ibid.*, pp. 181–97.
[3] Minutes of evidence 1815 S.C., p. 51.
[4] Parkinson, J. (1811), *Mad-houses. Observations on the Act for regulating Mad-houses. (Vide* McMenemey, W. H. (1955), 'A Note on James Parkinson as a Reformer of the Lunacy Acts', *Proc. R. Soc. Med. 48*, pp. 593–4.)

in 1810, she won her case against her nephew for having committed her to a madhouse although she was sane. Parkinson's conduct led to much personal criticism, which the Commissioners of the College of Physicians encouraged him to refute publicly. In his book, Parkinson discussed the defects of the lunacy laws that had been involved in the Daintree case and he recommended modifications, many of which were incorporated in later legislation. His principal concern was for the medical practitioner who had to sign the certificate and he stressed the considerable judgment required in making a decision as to whether a patient, although insane, would be properly confined in an asylum. He referred to the difficulties which arose from the need to distinguish true madness from other states of mental disturbance, especially when the patient was not overtly insane at the time of examination and the principal evidence of insanity was second-hand. This particular difficulty received legal recognition in 1853 (16 & 17 Vict., c. 97), when it was enacted that evidence of insanity observed by the medical practitioner had to be stated separately from that communicated to him by other persons. Parkinson felt that a medical man placed in these circumstances needed greater legal protection and he made a suggestion which was supported by many of his contemporaries, that it would be advantageous if the admitting authority for all patients was always a magistrate. He also proposed the appointment of an arbitrator who could be called in by any of the parties concerned, but this suggestion was not fulfilled until the Mental Health Act of 1959 made provision for Mental Health Review Tribunals. Parkinson's views undoubtedly gave impetus to the movement for the repeal of the Act of 1774. In a complimentary review of Parkinson's pamphlet, which appeared in *The Gentleman's Magazine* in 1811, the following observations were made regarding the Act:

The Act, as it stands, affords a very incompetent protection either to the publick from the mischievous disposition of cunning lunaticks, or to the physician that may be called to give his opinion, the relations who may think confinement necessary, or lastly to the keepers of mad-houses, to whose care they must ultimately be committed.[1]

Many of the critics of the madhouse system asserted that proprietors bribed medical men to patronize their houses. Rogers (1816) claimed that masters of public asylums often received 'a douceur of five hundred a year' for transferring patients to certain private mad-

[1] (1811), 'Review of New Publications, 27', *Gentleman's Magazine 81*, pp. 254–5.

houses[1] and, according to one J. Blackman, in *c.* 1814, the apothecary at St Luke's received half a guinea or more for sending patients to Warburton's houses at Bethnal Green.[2]

Fears about the unnecessary prolongation of the stay of patients were related closely to the fact that private madhouses were essentially trading speculations, often owned, during the early-nineteenth century, by persons of low integrity and having no special experience. S. W. Nicoll (1828), the Recorder of Doncaster and York, who had a deep interest in asylum supervision, stated clearly the view that the proprietor and keepers 'must have a strong tendency to consider the interest of the patients and their own at direct variance'.[3] He felt this was more likely to be the case when the proprietor was non-resident and the hired superintendent's salary and job depended upon his ability to keep the outlay as small and the income as large as possible.[4] In 1831, fifteen of the thirty-eight metropolitan houses were superintended by persons other than the named proprietors,[5] but, although details are not available concerning all provincial houses, it is likely that the proportion of resident proprietors was greater outside London. Earlier, T. Bakewell (1815) had stated that, at some madhouses, the pecuniary interest of the proprietor and the secret wishes of the lunatics' relatives, led not only to the neglect of all means of cure, but also to the deliberate prevention and delay of recovery, conduct which he considered 'a crime that may be perpetrated with perfect impunity as to human laws'.[6] This statement is in keeping with what Mitford (1825?) claimed to be the rule at Warburton's house, namely: 'If a man comes in here mad, we'll keep him so; if he is in his senses, we'll soon drive him out of them.'[7] Similarly, 100 years previously, Defoe had stated that if persons were not mad on entering a madhouse, they were soon made so 'by the barbarous usage they there suffer ... Is it not enough to make one mad to be suddenly clap'd up, stripp'd, whipp'd, ill fed, and worse us'd?'[8] C. Crowther (1838) observed that in private-madhouses the rich did not recover in the same proportion as the poor, although he

---

[1] Rogers, *op. cit.*, pp. 16–17.

[2] Beds. C.R.O., Whitbread MSS. 5079, letter, J. Blackman to Samuel Whitbread, *c.* 1814.

[3] Nicoll, S. W. (1828), *An Enquiry into the Present State of Visitation in Asylums*, pp. 2–3.

[4] *Ibid.*, p. 33.   [5] P.R., 1831, pp. 2–3.

[6] Bakewell, T. (1815), *op. cit.*, p. 10.   [7] Mitford, *op. cit.*, (Part 1), p. 1.

[8] Defoe (1728), *op. cit.*, p. 31.

recognized that, in addition to purely mercenary reasons, other factors could operate, such as the difficulty in confining such persons at an early and curable stage and also the problem of procuring suitable therapeutic occupation for them.[1] In contrast to some of the claims of certain madhouse proprietors, Millingen (1840) stated that cures were more frequent in public than in private asylums.[2]

The case of the pauper lunatic must not be overlooked in any discussion of improper confinement. During the period of operation of the Act of 1774, 'The mere Fiat of a parish officer [could] send any individual of the whole class of parochial paupers into a madhouse, there to remain unnamed and unseen'.[3] The reasons underlying the improper detention of paupers were, in general, neglect and disinterest rather than the corrupt motives which might apply in the case of wealthier patients. Several contemporaries drew attention to the fact that it was possible to admit private patients at the same low rates as paupers. By being classed with the paupers, these patients were exempt from inspection and from inclusion in returns. Prolonging the stay of pauper patients was a less likely abuse because of the smaller profit margin, but large numbers of paupers, confined with the utmost economy, could prove, nevertheless, financially rewarding. Their confinement was not complicated by the troublesome enquiries of relatives or friends and the parish officers were often indifferent towards the welfare and progress of paupers previously in their charge. The case of the proprietor of Haydock Lodge Asylum, Charles Mott,[4] illustrates a form of abuse that may well have occurred more widely than is known. Mott, who had been an Assistant Poor Law Commissioner, acted as superintendent of the asylum whilst holding the position of auditor to the neighbouring Poor Law Union. His position, clearly, allowed him to influence the parishes to send their paupers to his asylum and, in this way, some paupers may have been confined unjustifiably. Even in 1900, the Commissioners felt it proper to comment severely on the practice, indulged in by the proprietors of certain licensed houses receiving paupers, of bribing relieving officers to favour them with their patients.[5]

[1] Crowther, C. (1838), *Observations on the Management of Madhouses*, pp. 92–3.
[2] Millingen, *op. cit.*, p. 181.
[3] (1817), 'Lunatic Asylums', *Edinburgh Review 28*, p. 466.
[4] *Vide infra*, p. 277.
[5] Fifty-fourth Report (1900) C.L., p. 50.

The maltreatment of lunatics in private madhouses

The content of the rules and stated objectives of many of the public asylums founded in the eighteenth century affords some indirect indication of the conditions prevailing in private madhouses at that time. Thus, the Manchester Lunatic Hospital, opened in 1766, was intended to benefit the poor, to relieve the parishes of their difficult cases and to provide accommodation for a better class of patients, who, thereby, would be saved the heavy charges and the brutalities of private madhouses.[1] The brutal handling of patients was described in many of the accounts of conditions in private madhouses during the eighteenth and early-nineteenth centuries. A description was given, in 1763, of the typical events associated with the forcible seizure and detention in a madhouse of a sane person. Any protestation of sanity by the alleged lunatic would be regarded as evidence of insanity; he would be severely 'reduced by physic' and deprived of all contact with the outside world. The anonymous author speculated: 'What . . . must a rational mind suffer, that is treated in this irrational manner? Weakened by physic; emaciated by torture; diseased by confinement; and terrified by the sight of every instrument of cruelty, and the dreadful menaces of an attending ruffian.'[2] Some writers went as far as saying that the treatment in private-madhouses both induced and perpetuated insanity. Reid (1808), physician to the Finsbury Dispensary, London, proclaimed this view in a bold way, calling madhouses 'depots for the premature captivity of intellectual invalids . . . nurseries for, and manufactories of, madness . . . arsenals for the destruction of human reason . . . slaughter houses for the dislocation and murder of the human mind'.[3] Evidence of the maltreatment of lunatics in madhouses during the late-eighteenth and the first half of the nineteenth centuries relates, almost entirely, to a small number of metropolitan houses and one is left to speculate about the conditions elsewhere. Perceval's account of his treatment at Brislington House, in fact, provides the most detailed description of alleged abuses practised in a provincial madhouse.

[1] *Vide* Brockbank, E. M. (1933), 'Manchester's Lead in the Humane Treatment of the Insane', *Brit. Med. J. 2*, p. 540.

[2] Anon. (1763), 'A Case humbly offered to the Consideration of Parliament', *Gentleman's Magazine 33*, p. 26.

[3] Reid, J. (1808), 'Report of Diseases', *Monthly Magazine, 25*, pp. 166–7. (In 1816, such statements were reiterated in his *Essays on Hypochondriacal and other Nervous Affections*, pp. 205–6.)

Rogers (1816), a former apothecary and accoucheur at Warburton's madhouses in London, described, in a pamphlet,[1] the atrocities perpetrated at these houses and also gave evidence before the 1816 Select Committee, together with his sister, Mary Humières, who had worked as a housekeeper at the White House. The cruelties and abuses which he described included prolonged restraint, theft and misuse of the patient's personal belongings and clothing, beating, whipping, raping of married and single women, inhumane procedures, such as the 'mopping-down' of incontinent patients under an outside pump and the brutal use of instruments such as the 'spout', which, he alleged, had led to the death of patients. Many others amongst the critics of the madhouse system commented on the misuse of patients' personal possessions and the failure to fulfil obligations to patients and relatives in accordance with the agreed terms. It is difficult, however, to evaluate the validity of the statements made by Rogers and his sister. Matthew Talbot, superintendent of the White House, accused them both of deliberate falsification of the facts and even of theft[2] and the Select Committee reached no adverse conclusions regarding the conduct of Warburton himself. Rogers also gave evidence before the 1827 Select Committee, in the course of which he admitted that he had been ruined by the keepers of madhouses, as a result of his earlier disclosures.[3] Mitford, similarly, painted lurid pictures of the atrocities at Warburton's madhouses and, he declared, in the alarmist style that invariably characterized the work of this type of writer, that 'the advocates for the extinction of foreign slavery will do well to look at home—to the slavery of the whites, in private mad-houses, there they are worse treated than negroes—the maniacs are there abused as an inferior cast of beings, as a degraded, and malignant race, and they are made so by cruel treatment'.[4] To the contrary, Nicoll (1828) stressed that such evils as did exist were not wilful but secondary upon factors such as the overcrowding, the inadequate accommodation and the provocative, often directly violent behaviour, which the keepers had to withstand, which could lead readily to 'an alternation of reciprocal violence between the prisoner and the gaoler'.[5] According to Conolly (1856), patients from the lower and middle classes, in particular, were subjected to fearful maltreatment earlier in the century.

---

[1] Rogers, *op. cit.*   [2] First Report minutes of evidence 1816 S.C., p. 23.
[3] Report 1827 S.C., pp. 144–6.   [4] Mitford, *op. cit.*, (Part 1), p. 31.
[5] Nicoll, *op. cit.*, p. 32.

Concerning the handling of this class of patient, he commented:

Fetters and chains, moppings at the morning toilet, irregular meals, want of exercise, the infliction of abusive words, contemptuous names, blows with the fist, or with straps, or with keys, formed almost a daily part of the unprotected daily life of many wretched beings, previously accustomed to comfort, and decency, and kindness and reasonable enough to feel the bitterness of being debarred from all.[1]

The attendant's occupation was, undeniably, a hazardous one; the working conditions were generally poor and, until the second half of the nineteenth century, there was no professional training or recognition. Many writers commented on the moral defects and general unsuitability of a large number of attendants and quoted instances of the display of frank malevolence and deliberate brutality. Pinel drew attention to the dangers of delegating too much power to attendants and cited, as an example, the practice of Francis Willis senior:

In the establishment under his direction in the vicinity of London, it would appear that every lunatic is under the control of a keeper, whose authority over him is unlimited, and whose treatment of him must be supposed, in many instances, to amount to unbridled and dangerous barbarity: a delegated latitude of power totally inconsistent with the principles of a pure and rigid philanthropy.[2]

In 1850, an anonymous writer, possibly Conolly, made reference to 'ignorant, idle and ferocious keepers, acting without conscience or control'.[3] Conolly observed, in 1855, that many attendants belonged to 'the dangerous classes of society; their appearance announces it; their effect on the terrified or disgusted patients, declares it; and their manners, habits and conduct... frequently prove it'.[4] A Parliamentary Return, published in 1854, recorded the dismissal, for misconduct, of seven attendants in provincial licensed houses and of fifteen in metropolitan houses; the provincial houses thus named being, Dunston Lodge, Gateshead; Grove Place, Hampshire; Norwich Infirmary, Norfolk; Brislington House; Longwood House, Somerset; and Gate Helmsley Retreat, York.[5] From 1853 on, there was a statutory obligation to make such returns to the Commissioners and this applied to both public and private asylums. In evidence before the 1859 Select Committee, Perceval claimed that he had extensive

---

[1] Conolly, J. (1856), *op. cit.*, p. 143.   [2] Pinel, *op. cit.*, p. 66.
[3] Anon. (1850), *Familiar Views of Lunacy*, p. 122.
[4] Conolly, J. (1855), *op. cit.*, p. 182.   [5] P.R., 1854, pp. 26–31.

evidence of the cruelty practised by attendants, particularly in public asylums[1] and W. G. Campbell, one of the Commissioners in Lunacy, reported that, from 1847 to 1858, forty-eight male attendants and twenty female 'nurses' had been dismissed for cruelty, from various private licensed houses.[2]

The misuse of mechanical restraint featured prominently in allegations of maltreatment of lunatics at this time and the principal reasons for its excessive use in private madhouses were the structural deficiencies of the houses; the conduct of unenlightened or mercenary proprietors and the inadequacy of the number of attendants, who were often of low calibre. The successful implementation of the non-restraint system, depended, to a large extent, on the attendants and, as has been noted in a previous section, by the mid-nineteenth century, the importance of recruiting a better class of attendant had been recognized. Lack of proper supervision of the attendant's conduct, due to the negligence and ignorance of proprietors or their hired superintendents, must be held responsible for a large part of the maltreatment of lunatics that took place. A medical attendant's ability to modify adverse conditions was limited by the fact that he was an employee of the proprietor and, in the early-nineteenth century, his role was generally confined to the treatment of bodily illness and he had little responsibility in the management of the patient's mental disturbance.[3]

Evidence of maltreatment of patients was produced in a number of special enquiries into the management of individual licensed houses and several of such enquiries are described later in this chapter. The enquiry, relating to Hunningham House, Warwickshire, conducted by the Visiting Magistrates in 1849, was concerned particularly with charges of maltreatment.[4] The enquiry was the result of complaints, made by a former medical officer at the house, Alfred Carr, M.D., M.R.C.S., who claimed that there had been wilful neglect and abuse of patients. The Visitors' enquiry lasted three days and the evidence of twenty witnesses was taken. The charges against the proprietor, Mr Harcourt, included disregard for sick and dying patients, the punitive use of solitary confinement without clothing or bedding and tolerance of violence on the part of attendants, when

---

[1] Report 1859 S.C. (Aug. 1859), pp. 34–6.   [2] *Ibid.*, p. 56.
[3] *Vide* Report of 1815 S.C., p. 4.
[4] Warwicks. C.R.O., QS.24/a/I/1, draft of Special Report by the Committee of Enquiry, 5 March 1849.

directed, for example, towards patients who refused food. It was re-vealed, however, that all the charges were exaggerated, that some had occurred before Harcourt became proprietor and, indeed, that some of them could be dismissed as frivolous. Carr's case was weakened by the fact that, in the previous year, he had written an article in the local newspaper describing Hunningham House as a model establishment. Later, however, he had quarrelled with Harcourt, when rebuked by him for neglect of his duties. He even assaulted Harcourt and was both convicted and fined for his be-haviour. Carr's motives for raising the charges were questioned by the Visitors and the whole case was clearly related to the feud between the two medical men. The Visitors concluded that they were sure that Harcourt had always encouraged his attendants to use kind-ness and that the alleged maltreatment had arisen more from errors of judgment in the management of patients by the attendants, than from intentional harshness or neglect. Nevertheless, it seems unlikely that Carr would have gone to the extent that he did, unless the char-ges had some basis of truth. This example illustrates the considerable difficulties presented in the evaluation of the case against private madhouses. There were instances, however, where the abuses were glaring and the Visitors were able to take decisive action. Thus, in 1853, the Hampshire Visiting Magistrates recommended the dis-continuation of the licence granted to the proprietor of Grove Place, Nursling, largely because of the substantiated evidence of the cruel and severe treatment of a patient confined there.[1] One special en-quiry, initiated by the Visiting Magistrates of Cumberland and Westmorland and taken up by the Commissioners in Lunacy, con-cerned the remarkably cruel treatment of a male pauper at Dunston Lodge, Co. Durham.[2] In 1851, after biting the arm of the proprietor, J. E. Wilkinson, this patient was placed in a strait-jacket, then flogged and secluded. Later, his two upper incisor teeth were removed by the medical attendant. There was some conflicting evidence about the management of the patient, but Wilkinson was found guilty 'of the most flagrant cruelty' and the renewal of his licence was prohibited by the Commissioners in Lunacy.[3]

Despite the widely held belief in the value of early treatment, the admission of both private and pauper patients was often delayed until the condition of the lunatic became acutely disturbed or hope-

[1] Eighth Report (1854) C.L., pp. 19–20.   [2] *Ibid.*, pp. 25–7.
[3] In 1853, the licence was transferred to Mr Cornelius Garbutt.

lessly chronic. This was, undoubtedly, an important factor in the perpetuation of treatment, which, at a later date, could be regarded as neglectful and harsh, as patients in such a condition generally presented the greatest management problems. Writers, such as T. Bakewell, attributed this delay preceding admission, in the case of paupers, to the parsimony of parish officials and, in the case of private patients, to the ignorance, wickedness or desire for secrecy of relatives. Bakewell gave examples of cases in which admission to a madhouse had been preceded by long periods of confinement as a single lunatic in a private dwelling house[1] and many other references to this practice have been found. For example, in 1846, a male pauper was admitted to Dunston Lodge heavily fettered and chained. His history indicated that

his two sisters, with the view of retaining the command of some property belonging to him, had kept him in an outhouse chained hand and foot, and fastened to a staple in the floor. In this horrible situation, naked, save a few canvas rags, with no other bed other than a little straw and a few leaves, and compelled by the shortness of his chain to remain constantly in a crouching attitude, had he for twelve years continued[2]

until his case came to the attention of the local magistrates. Ricketts confirmed the fact that it was common practice for pauper lunatics to be confined, often chained, in a workhouse 'till the disease becomes highly alarming or incurable'.[3] In 1836, W. J. Gilbert, an Assistant Poor Law Commissioner, summarized the position then prevailing in Devonshire with regard to pauper lunatics, as follows:

At the moment we do not know what to do with a pauper lunatic ... I believe that many lunatic paupers might have been cured if the disorder had been properly treated in an early stage, but the expense of sending them to an asylum, there being no county asylum, is so great, that they have been kept in the workhouses until they become so troublesome, that it is desirable to remove them even at considerable expense; but in the meantime the disease has become inveterate and recovery is hopeless.[4]

There can be little doubt that such observations were relevant for other areas of the country at this period. The Metropolitan Commissioners reported, in 1844, with regard to Hook Norton: 'The majority of the paupers sent into the asylum are old cases which have previously

[1] Minutes of evidence 1815 S.C., pp. 123–4.
[2] Dunston Lodge Lunatic Asylum Report, 1847. Cited in (1848), 'State of Lunacy in British Asylums', *J. Psychol. Med. & Ment. Path. I*, p. 396.
[3] First Report minutes of evidence 1816 S.C., p. 46.
[4] Second Annual Report (1836) Poor Law Commissioners, p. 326.

been kept for some time in the workhouse, a circumstance which is considered to operate unfavourably to their recovery.'[1] Following a comment on the large number of 'dirty patients' at Droitwich Lunatic Asylum, the Metropolitan Commissioners observed that it was 'the custom of the neighbouring Unions to send patients in a very bad state, after they have been kept in workhouses until their condition has become truly deplorable'.[2] In 1847, the Commissioners criticized the conduct of officers of unions and parishes, whose duty it was to provide promptly and efficiently for the welfare of lunatics, but, 'whose want of prudence and humanity has, without doubt, tended in numberless cases to render the disease permanent; and has thereby increased the burthens of their parishes more than all the accidental causes to which insanity is referable'.[3] Many other similar reports about the condition of paupers on admission to licensed houses confirm the fact that often they had been detained over-long in workhouses and that, frequently, they were dirty, ill-clothed, violent and physically dilapidated.

Unsuitable premises and bad physical conditions

There is considerable evidence that, in the early part of the nineteenth century, private madhouses were, in general, structurally ill-suited for the reception of lunatics and very few indeed were purpose-built. Overcrowding was a common feature in pauper establishments and in houses catering for the poorer class of paying patients. Under such conditions, the maintenance of adequate security and classification was rendered difficult. The provisions of the Act of 1774 did little to discourage overcrowding, since the licensing fees were not related to the number of lunatics which a house could receive but were charged according to whether the number resident was greater or less than ten. This arrangement was changed in 1828. As far as can be ascertained, the available evidence regarding these defects concerns only a small number of licensed houses and, prior to the 1844 Report of the Metropolitan Commissioners, there is little information relating to provincial establishments.

Only six provincial licensed houses were named in evidence before the 1815–16 Select Committee and these were, Brislington House; Laverstock House; Droitwich Lunatic Asylum; Langworthy's

[1] 1844 Report M.C.L., p. 229.
[2] Worcs. R.O., BA.710.b.125. 1(i), Minutes M.C.L., 15 July 1844.
[3] Further Report (1847) C.L., p. 128.

house (Kingsdown House), Box, Wiltshire;[1] Spencer's house, Fonthill Gifford, Wiltshire; and Gillett's house at Taunton, Somerset. With the exception of Droitwich, these madhouses were all concentrated in a circumscribed area of South-West England and had been visited by Edward Wakefield, who combined his business travels as a land-agent with philanthropic tours of inspection of asylums in England. The houses of Fox, Finch and Ricketts, referred to in a previous section, appear to have been establishments of some merit. At Langworthy's house, Box, where there were forty patients and nine servants, Wakefield was not permitted to see the men, ostensibly because it was not a day when they were allowed up. He did see two women, however, nearly naked on straw in a cellar and four others entirely naked in a completely dark room, about whom Wakefield commented, 'in the course of my visiting these places I never recollect to have seen four living persons in so wretched a place'.[2] At Gillett's house, formerly a large, old farmhouse, he was refused permission to see the paupers, although he could hear the noise they made. Wakefield saw little there that was either praiseworthy or blameworthy, but he commented on the 'ignorant and brutal manners' of the proprietor, in comparison with those of men such as Fox and Finch.[3] The house at Fonthill Gifford was kept by Arthur Spencer, who had been its proprietor for twenty or thirty years. The local Medical Visitor, Dr Richard Fowler,[4] was called as a witness before the Committee and he described the conditions at the house in 1812, referring to the Minutes made by himself and the Visiting Magistrates in November of that year.[5] The Visitors' Minutes were reproduced in full, together with a groundplan of the house (Figure 9). Prior to this time, the house had never been officially visited and inspected. Fowler found that some lunatics were confined in cells without light or ventilation and were in a pallid, offensive and filthy state. One man had been chained in an oblong wooden trough and was allowed out only once in every one or two weeks. A further visit to the house, in 1815, revealed that considerable improvements had been carried out by the new proprietor, Spencer's nephew, who

---

[1] Probably Charles C. Langworthy, M.D., proprietor in 1819. P.R., 1819(a).
[2] Minutes of evidence 1815 S.C., p. 21.
[3] *Ibid.*, p. 22.
[4] (1765–1863), M.D., F.R.S., physician to Salisbury Infirmary. A respected practitioner of integrity, the author of a number of scientific and medical publications.
[5] Minutes of evidence 1815 S.C., pp. 43–8.

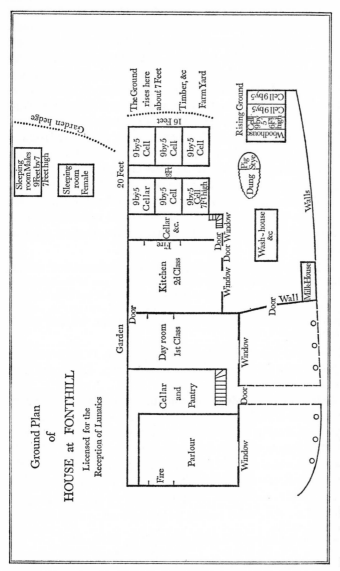

Ground Plan
of
HOUSE at FONTHILL

Licensed for the
Reception of Lunatics

Garden hedge

Sleeping room Males
9Feet by 7
7feet high

Sleeping room Female

20 Feet

The Ground rises here about 7 Feet

Timber, &c

Farm Yard

16 Feet

9 by 5 Cell

9 by 5 Cell

9 by 5 Cell

3Ft

9 by 5 Cellar

9 by 5 Cell

9 by 5 Cell 7Ft high

Cellar &c.

Fire

Pig Stye

Dung

Cell 9 by 5

Cell 9 by 5

Woodhouse Cell 9 by 5 6Ft high

Rising Ground

Door

Door Window

Window

Kitchen 2d Class

Garden

Door

Day room 1st Class

Cellar and Pantry

Parlour

Fire

Window

Door

Window

Window

Door

Wall

Wash-house &c

Walls

Milk House

Figure 9   Ground plan of the house at Fonthill Gifford, Wiltshire, 1812, as reproduced in the Minutes of evidence of the 1815 Select Committee, p. 45.

planned to rebuild the asylum on a new site. Physical restraint with handcuffs and fetters was still being used, nevertheless, because of the lack of security afforded by the premises and the insufficiency of keepers. In 1829, however, the Visitors were able to make favourable comments on this establishment and approved of the use of restraint on two of the twenty-two patients.[1] The principal metropolitan houses referred to in the minutes of evidence of the 1815–16 Select Committee were, Miles's house, Hoxton; Whitmore House, Hoxton; Talbot's house and Rhodes's house at Bethnal Green (i.e. Warburton's White and Red Houses). Some of the evidence, particularly that of Rogers, suggested appalling conditions at the White House, a state of affairs that was confirmed by the 1827 Select Committee, which was fearful that similar abuses prevailed elsewhere. As far as can be ascertained, in the intervening period the London Commissioners had done little to remedy conditions at this house. Richard Holt's house at Blackheath[2] was named also in the report of the 1827 Select Committee. Dr John Bright read part of the Visitors' Minutes made in 1820:

In a close room in the yard two men were shut by an external bolt, and the room was remarkably close and offensive. In an outhouse at the bottom of the yard, ventilated only by cracks in the wall, were enclosed three females, the door was padlocked; upon an open rail-bottomed crib herein, without straw, was chained a female by the wrists, arms and legs, and fixed also by chains to the crib.[3]

There appears to have been very little improvement in the conditions at this house over the course of the next few years, despite the visits of the Commissioners.

The following descriptions of conditions at Ringmer Asylum, Sussex, embodied in the Visitors' Annual Report for 1830, demonstrate its unsuitability as the sole institution for paupers in that county.[4] The defects were not outrageous but were typical of those in many establishments at this time. The building which housed the asylum was formerly an artillery barrack and was first licensed in 1829.[5] The Visitors stated that 'to allow proper classification the day-

---

[1] Wilts. C.R.O., Q.S. lunacy records (private asylums), Annual Report of Clerk of Peace, 1829.

[2] In 1819, this house contained seven patients. P.R., 1819(a), p. 2.

[3] Report 1827 S.C., pp. 157–8.   [4] E. Sussex C.R.O., QAL/1/8/E.2.

[5] In that year, the proprietors transferred their patients from another house at Balsdean, Rottingdean, first licensed in 1825. In 1830, Ringmer housed over twenty patients, but by 1832, the number had been reduced to four private patients and remained at about this level till the asylum was closed in 1855.

rooms should be more numerous and a separate bedroom or cell be allowed to each patient, were this obtained a less degree of bodily restraint would be necessary both in the day and at night'. Facilities for employment and exercise were poor. 'The day room and dormitory of the men are too far removed (about 100 yards) from the residence of the superintending surgeon to make the appeal to him by the keepers sufficiently easy and prompt.' In addition, they noted that, 'the residence of the licensed proprietors, who are the principal medical attendants, is too remote (being 12 miles distant) to allow of the necessary visiting and reference to them'. Up to twenty paupers were received and the Visitors observed that the maintenance charge of 15s. per week seemed unduly high. They commented that the situation could only be remedied, 'where a considerably greater number of pauper patients can be placed under the same roof and where the building has been fitted up expressly for these purposes'.

In their 1844 Report, the Metropolitan Commissioners named nine provincial licensed houses which deserved 'almost unqualified censure'.[1] These were the houses at West Auckland and Wrekenton, Co. Durham; Green Hill House, Derby; Lainston House, Winchester and Grove Place, Nursling, Hampshire; Kingsdown House, Wiltshire; Plympton House, Devon; Moor Cottage, Yorkshire and West Malling Place, Kent. All of these were houses which received paupers. Two others, Bailbrook House, Bath, and Duddeston Hall, were considered unsuitable for the reception of paupers. The chief defects comprised wretched, filthy and overcrowded accommodation, with the paupers often confined in outhouses; excessive and cruel restraint; lack of proper classification and deficient facilities for the employment, exercise and amusement of the patients. The following account of the Commissioners' findings at West Auckland is characteristic of the conditions prevailing in these houses at this period. This house was first visited in 1842, when there were thirteen male and sixteen female patients:

Each sex had only one sitting-room, with windows that did not admit of any prospect from them, and the violent and quiet, and the dirty and clean were shut up together. There was only one small walled yard, and when the one sex was in it, the other was locked up ... There were two small grass closes belonging to the House, but they appeared to be little used for the employment of the males. In the small, cheerless day-room of the males, with only one unglazed window, five men were restrained, by leg-locks ... and two were wearing, in addition, iron hand-cuffs and fetters

[1] 1844 Report M.C.L., p. 46.

from the wrist to the ankle: they were all tranquil. The reason assigned for this coercion was, that without it they would escape ... Chains were fastened to the floors in many places, and to many of the bedsteads. The males throughout the house slept two in one bed.[1]

At the Wrekenton Asylum, heavy chaining was practised and the bedding and the sleeping rooms were filthy and offensive.[2] At Green Hill House, Derby,

the straw in the paupers' beds was found filthy, and some of the bedding was in a disgusting condition from running sores, and was of the worst materials, and insufficient. Two cells, in which three sick epileptic paupers slept, were damp, unhealthy, and unfit for habitation. The beds of some of the private patients were in an equally bad state.[3]

Conditions at Plympton House were exceptionally repressive and foul and, at West Malling, the use of six wholly unsuitable sleeping places for males, not indicated on any plans, was discovered. Paupers were accommodated in converted stables and out-houses at Lainston House, at Grove Place and at West Malling. By 1847, both the West Auckland Asylum and Lainston House had closed and several others, including Plympton House, had been improved substantially. The number of new instances of abuse and severely defective conditions that were being revealed, by this time, was small and the Commissioners were able to comment that, with a few exceptions, the condition in licensed houses 'may be represented as being on the whole satisfactory. The condition of some of them indeed appears to be excellent.'[4] This observation is given support in some of the reports made by members of the Manchester Lunatic Hospital Committee, in 1845–6, following visits paid by them to certain private licensed houses in Yorkshire, having vacancies for private patients at that time. The visiting deputation was set up when arrangements had to be made for the accommodation of patients from the Lunatic Hospital during the interval between its removal from Manchester to a new site at Cheadle.[5] Acomb House, near York, under the proprietorship of Mr H. B. Hodgson, was reported as being in 'a most highly satisfactory state'.[6] The deputation was impressed favourably with Mr I. Taylor's house, Grove House, Acomb[7] and with Terrace House, Osbaldwick, the latter being run by Mrs E. Tose, in whom they expressed considerable confidence.[8] The visitors were unable to

---

[1] *Ibid.*, pp. 53–4.   [2] *Ibid.*, pp. 55–6.   [3] *Ibid.*, p. 56.
[4] Further Report (1847) C.L., p. 105.
[5] The present Cheadle Royal Hospital, Cheshire.
[6] Manchester Royal Lunatic Hospital Committee Book, Minutes, 8 Dec. 1845.
[7] *Ibid.*, 26 March 1846.   [8] *Ibid.*

refer 'in unqualified terms of commendation' regarding Mr B. Hornby's house at Dunnington, near York, although they stated that the rooms offered to the patients from Manchester were satisfactory.[1] After visiting other establishments, these four houses were selected for twenty-two patients from the Manchester Lunatic Hospital. There is evidence, nevertheless, that some serious deficiencies did exist in certain provincial establishments and, in the course of the next few years, the licences of several houses had to be withdrawn. For example, the licence to Joseph Beale, proprietor of Moor Cottage, Nunkeeling, Yorkshire, was discontinued, in October 1851,[2] after he had been warned, in 1850,[3] that his licence would not be renewed unless the premises were improved.

Only three provincial licensed houses were named as being especially defective in the 1850 Report of the Commissioners: Fisherton House, Belle Vue House, Devizes,[4] and Kingsland Asylum, Shrewsbury. In the case of the latter, the whole establishment was considered unsuitable for the reception of lunatics. The gutters, privies and airing-courts were dirty and offensive, the drainage deficient, the walls damp and the clothing and bedding filthy and inadequate. All three houses received paupers and the adverse conditions were tolerated by the Commissioners only because of the anticipated transfer of paupers to the new county asylums.

Although the Act of 1808 had been implemented very slowly during the first half of the nineteenth century, its provisions, nevertheless, had created a threat to the proprietors of houses which received paupers. When the erection of county asylums for paupers became compulsory in 1845, there was little incentive for proprietors to invest capital in improving their pauper departments in accordance with contemporary requirements. In view of this, it is of interest to read the praise afforded by the Commissioners to the proprietors and medical officers of licensed houses, in 1847, for assisting the process of improving conditions within their houses, despite the financial burden involved and with little hope of substantial monetary return.[5] In some private licensed houses, the Commissioners observed that the paupers were exceedingly well taken care of, under conditions

[1] *Ibid.*   [2] E.R. Yorks. C.R.O., QAL.3/15, Sessions Order, 14 Oct. 1851.
[3] E.R. Yorks. C.R.O., QAL.3/14, memorandum, Oct. 1850.
[4] In 1853 the Commissioners recommended closure of the pauper department, but the justices re-licensed it.
[5] Further Report (1847) C.L., pp. 63–4.

which were superior to those in some county asylums. But the improvement of such establishments, in general, was not rapid enough and, in 1848, the Commissioners 'would have felt themselves justified in insisting upon considerable outlays of money in some licensed houses, had it not been for the progress now making towards the erection of county asylums, the completion of which must ere long necessarily drain all private establishments of their pauper patients'.[1] One of the houses which was reported to be defective in 1852, was Amroth Castle, Pembrokeshire.[2] This house, formerly a large mansion, was licensed in 1851, to Dr J. H. Norton, for fifty-six patients. The accommodation for paupers was created by converting the stables into wards, using boarding and whitewash. The male dormitory was in the loft over the stables and there was no means of heating this chamber. Former horse-stalls were used to make single rooms. This establishment was objected to, strongly, by the Commissioners in Lunacy, but it was regarded as satisfactory by the Visiting Magistrates. Finally, however, in October 1856, the licence was not renewed and the thirty-eight paupers were transferred to Vernon House, Briton Ferry, on the Commissioners' instructions.[3] The conditions at Vernon House had been little better, as pauper wards were, similarly, the converted stables and offices of the mansion.[4] In 1854, however, the Commissioners observed that such defects were unlikely to be removed as 'the remedy would involve an amount of alteration and an outlay of capital, for which, as the law now stands, the proprietors could not reasonably expect to receive an adequate compensation.[5] A more important factor was that, in many areas, private licensed houses provided the major part, if not all, of the accommodation for pauper lunatics and the Commissioners were not in a position to be too harsh with the proprietors. Not unnaturally, few licensed houses could compete favourably with county asylums, in regard to their pauper accommodation. In 1855, the Commissioners noted: 'Many of them are content to remain at a certain point of advancement; and require, indeed, the constant stimulus of official supervision to prevent their relapsing into the unsatisfactory condition from which by great care and vigilance they have been raised.'[6] During the remainder of the nineteenth century, a

---

[1] Third Report (1848) C.L., p. 7.   [2] Seventh Report (1852) C.L., p. 27.
[3] Glam. C.R.O., Vernon House MSS., Q/S. L/VH.12.
[4] Seventh Report (1852) C.L., p. 26.   [5] Eighth Report (1854) C.L., p. 15.
[6] Ninth Report (1855) C.L., p. 19.

small number of houses were animadverted upon in annual reports, chiefly for their defective and dilapidated premises, overcrowding, and the lack of cleanliness, comfort or adequate furnishing for the patients. For the most part, however, reports relating to provincial licensed houses were not unfavourable.

Many of the critics of the madhouse system produced evidence of the failure, on the part of proprietors, to fulfil obligations to patients and relatives, with regard to accommodation and treatment. In 1850, the Commissioners expressed concern that private patients in licensed houses did not always receive their due in return for the payments made, whilst acknowledging that some proprietors provided a standard of comfort and accommodation that exceeded the level required by the maintenance payments.[1] In 1852, the Commissioners reported that at Duddeston Hall, Warwickshire, the second class of private patients were 'mixed with the paupers, and occupy the pauper wards. Although the payments made for this class of patients are generally small, the accommodation appears to . . . be inferior to that usually provided for patients of similar rank in other establishments'.[2] Similar observations were made with regard to High Beech Asylum, Essex.

If a valid interpretation is to be made, the adverse conditions in private madhouses have to be contrasted with those in other asylums and, for this purpose, some selected examples are now quoted. The Select Committee of 1815 revealed horrible abuses and very bad physical conditions at the York Asylum and at Bethlem Hospital. At the York Asylum, established in 1777, conditions had been deteriorating since at least 1790, when the death of a female patient occurred under suspicious circumstances and was wrapped in secrecy. This incident, in fact, led William Tuke to establish the York Retreat. It was in 1815 that the renowned case of James Norris came to light at Bethlem. Norris was found to have been restrained in irons, under the most horrifying conditions, for nine years, with the full knowledge of Haslam, the apothecary. The effect of such revelations on the general public was considerable and must have heightened fears and misgivings about all places for the confinement of lunatics. According to Wakefield's evidence before the 1815 Select Committee, at St Luke's Hospital many cells were unglazed, the privies were offensively dirty and many patients were chained to their

---

[1] Fifth Report (1850) C.L., pp. 15–16.
[2] Eighth Report (1854) C.L., p. 23.

beds, nearly naked and covered only with rags. At the ward for incurable lunatics at Guy's Hospital, Wakefield found two patients naked in straw and conditions in this lunatic ward remained unsatisfactory until it was finally closed in 1861. The only county asylum considered by the Select Committee was that at Nottingham, where conditions appear to have been good and the treatment humane. In 1829, Halliday described Bethlem as 'long little better than a miserable dungeon for lunatics . . . like the Bastile of Paris—a prison from which few were ever liberated'[1] and there is considerable evidence regarding the deficiencies of 'Bedlam' during the eighteenth century.

The Metropolitan Commissioners made the following observations in 1844, with regard to county asylums:

It is apparent . . . that although a few . . . are well adapted to their purpose, and a very large proportion of them are extremely well conducted; yet some are quite unfit for the reception of the insane, some are placed in ineligible sites, some are deficient in the necessary means of providing outdoor employment for their paupers, some are ill contrived and defective in their internal construction and accommodations, some are cheerless and confined in their yards and airing-grounds, and some are larger than seems consistent with the good management of their establishments and the proper care and health of their patients.[2]

Amongst the public asylums and hospitals, the Commissioners commented adversely on St Luke's Hospital, Bethel Hospital, Norwich and the Manchester Lunatic Asylum. By far the worst abuses and defects, however, were found at the asylum at Haverfordwest, Pembrokeshire,[3] which was formerly the town gaol, but which had been taken over, in 1822, for the accommodation of lunatics and declared a county asylum by a special Act of Parliament. When they first visited the asylum, in 1842, the Metropolitan Commissioners found that little modification of the gaol had been carried out. The rooms were dark, dirty and ill-ventilated and contained little furniture. There were holes in the walls and ceilings, the airing courts were, 'very small and cheerless . . . and . . . were both strewn with large stones, which had fallen or been forced from the building'.[4] The patients' dress was dirty and ragged, linen and bedding was deficient, provisions were scarce and there were no facilities for the employ-

---

[1] Halliday (1829), *op. cit.*, p. 25.
[2] 1844 Report M.C.L., p. 29.
[3] *Ibid.*, pp. 46–52.   [4] *Ibid.*, p. 47.

ment or amusement of patients. By 1847, limited improvement had been effected but the asylum remained entirely unsuitable for the treatment and cure of the insane.

During the course of the second half of the nineteenth century, the county asylums were planned and built with great care. Instances of neglect and ill-treatment of patients did occur from time to time, but kindly, custodial care of patients was the general rule. Many observers, however, came to be disturbed, in turn, by the way in which patients were managed in these asylums. For example, following a visit to a recently opened county asylum, W. Napier Reeve, Clerk of the Peace and Clerk of the Visitors of the Leicestershire and Rutland County Asylum, observed:

It was simply a larger prison and the inmates sitting listlessly and depressed in the lengthened corridors served only to be mocked by the polished floor and costly furniture to which they had been unaccustomed and of which they took no heed.[1]

Already the situation had changed insidiously since 1866, when Sir George Paget described, proudly, the many fine attributes of the English pauper lunatic asylums, the sight of which he claimed to be 'the most blessed manifestation of true civilization that the world can present'.[2]

Administrative irregularities and illegal practices by madhouse proprietors

There is considerable evidence relating to the failure by proprietors to fulfil all the statutory requirements concerned with the management of their houses and the treatment of patients. The relatively frequent changes in lunacy legislation from 1828 onwards must itself have been the cause of many minor administrative irregularities. The Clerk of the Peace was required to send an abstract of relevant new legislation to madhouse proprietors and a copy of the current Acts had to be at hand in every house, a point upon which the Visitors were required to check. Shortly after the Act of 1845 came into operation, Mallam observed, 'the change is so sudden the public are not aware of it', and he commented on the unavoidable delay which was likely to take place before all new admission orders and notices were made on the

---

[1] Reeve, W. N. (*c.* 1880), *Report to the Visitors of the Leicestershire and Rutland Lunatic Asylum as to the Proposed New Asylum at Newton Unthank.*
[2] Paget, G. E. (1866), *The Harveian Oration*, pp. 34–5.

amended forms.[1] Consideration will now be given to examples of the principal types of irregularities which occurred.

The confinement of patients in unlicensed premises or unlicensed parts of an asylum was a practice to which the Visiting Magistrates and Commissioners were particularly alert. In 1813, the case of Budd v. Foulks[2] made it clear that any person detaining two or more lunatics in an unlicensed house, was guilty of a misdemeanour, even if, thereby, they were not receiving any profit. In this case, Mary Foulks, a servant, was found guilty of keeping, in London, an unlicensed house, which was owned by a Mr Dunston.[3] The Metropolitan Commissioners, in 1837, sentenced one William Moseley to twelve months imprisonment for having kept a house, for a considerable period, without a licence.[4] They discovered, also, that 'he had publicly assumed and advertised for patients in the name of Willis, that being a name very attractive and familiar to persons conversant with lunacy'.[5] Moseley appealed against the sentence and, because of inconsistencies in the evidence, he was released after three months. He resumed his illegal practices, but the Commissioners were reluctant to proceed against him again because of the difficulties in obtaining the necessary evidence and the great expenses involved. In 1844, the Metropolitan Commissioners referred to the occurrence of this practice at High Beech, Essex, and at Laverstock House, Salisbury.[6] Finch had a second house in Salisbury, which was unlicensed but often was used, illegally, to house more than a single lunatic. It has been pointed out, in a previous section, that the inclusion of the two parts of Hook Norton under a single licence was probably illegal, but it was corrected in 1842 before the Metropolitan Commissioners started their provincial tours.[7] Early in 1852, Eli Lawrence, formerly superintendent of Haydock Lodge Asylum, opened a house at Abbot's Grange, near Chester, for the reception, as boarders, of lunatics who had been under his care previously at Haydock Lodge. The law was clearly violated, as the house had no licence and

[1] O.C.R.O., QSL.X/1/C, letter, Mallam to Oxfordshire Clerk of Peace, 8 Sept. 1845.
[2] *English Reports*, Vol. 170, p. 1,426. (The prosecution was instituted by direction of Dr Budd, Treasurer of the College of Physicians. A similar case was heard in Somerset in 1819. Report 1827 S.C., p. 46.)
[3] Possibly Thomas Dunston (d. 1830), master of St Luke's Hospital, London.
[4] Annual Report (1837) M.C.L. In Copies of Annual Reports M.C.L. 1835–41, pp. 4–5.
[5] *Ibid.*, p. 4.　　　[6] 1844 Report M.C.L., pp. 37, 39.
[7] *Vide supra*, p. 139.

the patients were not certified, but by the time this irregularity had been brought to the notice of the Commissioners, the house had been closed and Lawrence could receive only severe censure and an admonition.[1]

The reception and accommodation of patients without properly completed orders and certificates or the failure to provide proper notification of an admission, were punishable from 1774 on and, from 1828, these regulations applied to both pauper and private patients. In 1807, Cox was fined £50 for detaining a male patient at Fishponds licensed house without a certificate.[2] Many patients were found to have been received without regular certificates at Spencer's house, Fonthill Gifford, in 1812. A fine of £1,800 was imposed but only £200 was exacted, the rest being remitted on account of Spencer's poverty.[3] In August 1823, James Lucett, who kept a house at Chertsey, Surrey, was prosecuted for keeping a patient at his house without a certificate. The patient in question was a surgeon and Lucett claimed that he had not admitted him formally, 'out of delicacy to his character'.[4] Lucett was found guilty, but little further is known of the outcome of the affair, other than that he was later committed to the county gaol as an insolvent debtor.[5] The surviving records relating to this incident contain a reference made by Powell, Secretary to the Commissioners of the College of Physicians, to a similar prosecution that had been instituted by the Somerset Clerk of the Peace. There are examples, however, of the acceptance by the Visiting Magistrates, without adverse comment, of resident boarders, despite the fact that they were fully alert to the possibility of illegal detention. Thus, in 1791, the Surrey Visitors observed that two patients at Great Foster House, Egham, were 'remaining there as boarders and lodgers having been cur'd some years past and now continuing there at their own will and pleasure'.[6] Amongst similar examples from the Surrey records is a note made in 1821 by the Visitors that a patient named Stackhouse 'appeared to us to be free from any symptoms of insanity and under no restraint and stated

---

[1] Seventh Report (1852) C.L., pp. 29–30.   [2] Glos. R.O., Q/AL.41, accounts of Clerk of Peace, Feb. 1807.   [3] Minutes of evidence 1815 S.C., p. 47.

[4] Surrey R.O., QS.5/5/4, Minutes V.M., 4 Jan. 1823; and accounts of Clerk of Peace, 15 July 1823 to 24 May 1824.

[5] It is amusing to note, in minutes made by the Visiting Magistrates to The Recovery, Mitcham, Surrey, a reference to a patient certified by Mr James Lucett of Mitcham, 'who is stated in the certificate to be a Professor in the cure of insanity'. *Ibid.*, Minutes V.M., 14 Oct. 1825.

[6] Surrey R.O., QS.5/5/3, Minutes V.M., 2 Aug. 1791.

himself to be residing at Great Foster House by his own desire'.[1]

In 1838, evidence was placed before a Select Committee of enquiry at Hereford, that pauper lunatics had been received at the Hereford Lunatic Asylum with improperly signed certificates, a fact that had been noted first by the magistrates two years previously.[2] Three houses were named, in the 1844 Report of the Metropolitan Commissioners in Lunacy, for receiving patients without proper admission documents.[3] At the Reverend Dr J. Chevallier's house, Aspall Hall, Suffolk, there were, in 1842, three certified patients and eight others reported as not insane, who were living at the house as boarders. The magistrates found that several of these boarders were, in fact, insane. The Commissioners' findings were similar at G. S. Ogilvie's house at Calne, Wiltshire, and Ogilvie was reported as advertising that he received 'nervous' as well as insane persons in his establishment. The Visiting Magistrates decided to refer this matter to the Court of Quarter Sessions when Ogilvie applied for the renewal of his licence, but within a few months the boarders had left.[4] The third house named was High Beech whose proprietor, Allen, was a strong advocate of the voluntary admission of patients in order to facilitate early treatment, rather than allowing the disorder to reach a point where certification was clearly justifiable, although the chances of recovery were correspondingly diminished. It was stated that Allen had admitted to receiving 'low-spirited' or 'desponding' persons as boarders. The Commissioners concluded that 'nervous, imbecile, and dejected persons' should not be received in houses licensed for the insane. The admission of such persons, without orders or certificates, was illegal and was liable to great abuse as 'The practice is, or may be, made a subterfuge for receiving, as nervous, those who are manifestly of unsound mind'.[5] The Commissioners felt strongly that it was 'questionable, whether a proprietor . . . who receives boarders of this class, or who permits deeds to be executed by persons who are under confinement as patients, [as Allen claimed to have done] ought to be entrusted with a license'.[6] This mistrust was probably ill-founded and an Act of 1862 granted authority to licensed-house proprietors to receive private patients as voluntary

[1] *Ibid.*, 5 July 1821.   [2] *Vide infra*, p. 274.
[3] 1844 Report M.C.L., pp. 35–8.
[4] Wilts. C.R.O., Q.S. lunacy records (private asylums), Minutes V.M., 9 Aug. 1844 and May 1845.
[5] 1844 Report M.C.L., p. 38.   [6] *Ibid.*

boarders. A few instances of forged medical certificates have been discovered[1] and also examples of certificates being signed by one of the proprietors of the establishment to which the patient was admitted.[2]

Failure to maintain properly the various books and registers, according to statutory requirements, was a relatively common misdemeanour. This deficiency was noted, amongst other irregularities, in the evidence given in enquiries into the affairs of Hereford Lunatic Asylum in 1838 and Fishponds in 1848. In 1842, the Dorset Justices refused to renew the licence of the proprietor of Boardhay's House, Stockland, partly because no returns had been made to the Clerk of the Peace since the Act of 1832 came into operation.[3] The Third Report of the Commissioners in Lunacy contained references to several instances of neglect, at unnamed houses, in keeping Case Books and Medical Visitation Books. In the case of one provincial house, the neglect was so gross that the Commissioners planned to prosecute the offending party.[4] At the Oxfordshire madhouses, only a small number of irregularities were noted by the Visitors and Commissioners. In 1848, for example, E. A. Batt erroneously recorded his own observations about patients in the Patients' Book.[5] Three years later, Batt was reprimanded by the Commissioners for failing to record, in the Medical Journal, the use of mechanical restraint in the case of one patient. In addition, it was noted that the Case Book was, 'not kept so carefully or fully' as the statutes required. The entries regarding the last two admissions were meagre and there was no record of the treatment adopted.[6] However, criticisms were not made again.

Mention has to be made, in addition, of more trivial faults and misdemeanours which were committed. Examples which may be quoted include omitting to display a plan of the house in a conspicuous place, or failing to comply with the letter of the Act in applying for renewal of a licence. Particular importance was attached, by the licensing authorities, to the submission of detailed plans

---

[1] e.g. in 1837, at Samuel Brown's house, Henley-in-Arden, a certificate was proved to have been a forgery. Warwicks. C.R.O., QS.24/a/I/7, Minutes V.M., 12 July 1837.

[2] e.g. at Great Foster House and Lea Pale House, Surrey, in 1815. Surrey R.O., QS.5/5/3, Minutes V.M., 21 March 1815.

[3] P.R., 1842, p. 8.   [4] Third Report (1848) C.L., p. 5.

[5] O.C.R.O., QSL.VII/4, Minutes C.L., 16 June 1848.

[6] *Ibid.*, 6 Feb. 1851.

because there were instances where patients had been hidden in concealed and unknown parts of asylums.

Deficiencies in the supervisory role of the magistrates

It is known that in the early-nineteenth century unlicensed private madhouses existed in many parts of the country and this fact was due both to the ignorant or illegal practice of the proprietors and to the neglect of their duties by the magistrates. The following extract from a letter received, in 1813, by Powell, Secretary to the London Commissioners, was sent by the Worcestershire Clerk of the Peace in reply to his request for information regarding madhouses in that county. The contents of the letter reflect the degree of indifference towards the care of the insane and suggest the resistance to change that was probably prevalent in many other counties at this time:

No step whatever has been taken in this county respecting lunatic asylums, nor has any account of Mr. Ricketts's house at Droitwich been made to the Sessions, or the Clerk of the Peace, or any license been taken out by him; I have laid accounts of postages, etc. for these kinds of business before the magistrates, who are so very particular in their allowances in this county, that they have told me they cannot allow them, and have advised me, when I receive such applications, not to attend to them.[1]

In 1838, the Metropolitan Commissioners observed, with regard to the facts stated in the returns of that year, regarding all licensed houses in provincial England and Wales, that

the salutary provisions of the Act by which it is required that all houses . . . shall be annually licensed and periodically visited and reported upon by the Visiting Magistrates, have been in a great degree neglected or violated, and that even now considerable ignorance with respect to their duties in this respect prevails, as well on the part of the proprietors of such establishments as of the Clerks of the Peace and the Visiting Magistrates.[2]

They noted that there were no recorded asylums in some of the largest English counties, or in the whole of Wales and stated that these circumstances could not be reconciled with other information in their possession. It was concluded that:

It would seem to be a not unfair inference that, besides the houses for which licences have been taken out, in conformity with the Act of Parliament, there must exist in different parts of the country other and unlicensed establishments in which persons are confined as insane patients (perhaps

[1] Minutes of evidence 1815 S.C., p. 169.
[2] Annual Report (1838) M.C.L. In Copies of Annual Reports M.C.L., 1835–41, p. 6.

even without medical certificates) in contempt and defiance of the law . . . this practice . . . is one which may obviously lead to the most glaring and dangerous abuses, and which therefore strongly calls for a searching investigation and an effectual remedy.[1]

Although the provisions made in the Act of 1774, for the visitation and inspection of licensed houses, constituted a great advance, they contained obvious weaknesses, such as the prohibition on visiting by night and their value was diminished by the fact that licences could not be revoked or refused, however adverse the Visitors' reports were. This situation was modified, however, by the Madhouse Act of 1828 and by later legislation. It has been indicated, in a previous section, that, despite the great importance of the Visitors' inspections, their reports, prior to c. 1842, suggest only a cursory inspection, often made less frequently than was required by law. Such visits constituted virtually the only opportunity for the patient to make known his wishes and grievances to unbiased persons, and there is evidence that the magistrates often failed to fulfil their obligations in this respect.[2]

John Conolly gained first-hand experience of the role of the Visiting Magistrate in the provinces, whilst acting as a Medical Visitor to the Warwickshire private licensed houses from 1824 to 1828. Although the minutes he signed at that time were stereotyped and lacking in detail and gave no hint of the work he was to undertake later, his experiences clearly made an impression upon him. In 1860, he recollected that:

When official visits were made, all presented their best appearance, but the general spectacle was distressing. The patients who could be exhibited at large were usually turned into two or three airing-courts . . . of small dimensions, where no grass grew, no flower relieved the eye, and no tree afforded shade. Noise and confusion combined to disturb and affright the Visitors, who were glad to retreat from a scene they deplored and considered unavoidable. Patients too mischievous or too furious to be congregated with others were cautiously locked up in their rooms, into which few Visitors ventured even to look. In those days, the superintendents affected an imposing manner, even an imposing dress, and they believed to govern their patients by their looks. It was concluded that they knew everything, and did everything that could be done; and they maintained their authority by despising or resenting any suggestions.[3]

In a previous work, Conolly had stressed the difficulties confronting the Visiting Magistrates, particularly when the proprietor was 'a

---

[1] *Ibid.*   [2] *Vide* Perceval (1838), *op. cit.*, pp. 266–7.
[3] Conolly, J. (1860), *op. cit.*, p. 9.

most respectable man, a neighbour, a friend perhaps, and the asylum is his fortune; to depreciate it, or to cast doubt upon a case where he has none, may be to ruin him; and the sense of duty in an honorary Visitor could hardly lead him to run such a risk'.[1] In 1849, he referred, similarly, to the 'unwillingness of country gentlemen, in general, to perform a task which is unpleasant, and troublesome, and difficult, and exposes them to unmeasured censure and annoyance'.[2] The deficiencies of the magistrates' visits had been stressed in the Report of the 1815 Select Committee and the hope was expressed that the Visiting Magistrates would improve their vigilance and would regard it as their duty to watch closely over the conduct of the keepers and the treatment of the patients.[3] In evidence before this Committee, Fowler described the particular difficulties experienced by himself and the Visiting Magistrates in ascertaining whether any parts of the asylum had been concealed from them and, also, in distinguishing between lucid intervals and the permanent return of the sanity of madhouse inmates. Nicoll (1828) reviewed, quite objectively, the different kinds of official visitation then in operation and their influence in the modification of the adverse conditions in asylums. His conclusion was that the overall effect of visitation, in this respect, was trivial. He summarized what transpired during the Visiting Magistrates' inspection of private madhouses as follows:

A tolerable exterior of things in the house, a little adroit civility in its owner, a willingness on the part of the justice to finish his job as soon as he can, and an equal willingness in the manner that it should be speedily concluded, will get over the business with great ease to all parties; and then, for nearly half a year, there is reasonable certainty of no further obtrusion.[4]

Certainly, there appears to have been a strong aversion amongst magistrates to undertake the inspection of madhouses. Some contemporary writers claimed that inspection was rendered more difficult by the atmosphere of mystery which the private-madhouse proprietor fostered deliberately. Thus, in 1827, Halliday observed, that 'the mystery which was made to hover round the precincts of a madhouse, was sufficient to baffle common enquiry; and the utter seclusion, so insidiously inculcated, made it next to impossible to discover the scenes of horror that took place within its walls'[5]. It

[1] Conolly, J. (1830), *op. cit.*, p. 6.   [2] Conolly, J. (1849), *op. cit.*, p. 33.
[3] Report 1815 S.C., p. 5.   [4] Nicoll, *op. cit.*, pp. 68–9.
[5] Halliday (1827), *op. cit.*, p. 7.

emerges also that during the inspection of houses which accommodated large numbers of paupers, it was the usual practice to attempt
to see all the private patients but to make only general comments
concerning the paupers.

Crowther, one-time physician to the West Riding of Yorkshire
County Asylum, expressed the view, upon a number of occasions,
that magistrates were, in general, ignorant, biased and irresponsible
and, in 1849, he devoted one chapter in his book to 'the unfitness of
magistrates to govern madhouses'.[1] However, J. S. Bolton (1928),
who made a careful study of Crowther's writings, concluded that he
became 'a monomaniac on asylum abuses in consequence of his
fancied wrongs while a visiting physician to Wakefield Asylum'.[2]
Certainly, Crowther's views were exaggerated and motivated, generally, by personal bitterness. There is considerable contemporary
evidence, nevertheless, that medical men did resent the inspection
and supervision of the magistrates, particularly when it involved
clinical decisions, such as whether or not a patient was sufficiently
recovered to be discharged. This resentment is displayed clearly in
the statements made in evidence before the 1828 Select Committee
of the House of Lords by E. L. Fox, W. Finch and E. T. Monro,
three reputable private-madhouse proprietors. Finch claimed that,
some two years previously, the Visiting Magistrates had threatened
to refuse the renewal of his licence because he would not agree to
certain proposals made by them, regarding the notification of the
whereabouts of patients after recovery, and the freedom of his
patients to consult an attorney or another medical practitioner without prior consultation with him.[3]

Appointment to the Bench was dependent, largely, upon social
position, and usually the justices were chosen from amongst the
ranks of the nobility, the local gentry and the clergy. It is likely that
the range of their ever-increasing duties alone must have resulted in
many magistrates having little more than a cursory knowledge of the
intricacies of lunacy law and only a limited understanding of their
own role as Visitors. The Oxfordshire MSS., for example, reveal
many attempts by the Clerk of the Peace to guide the magistrates in

---

[1] Crowther, C. (1849), *Observations on the Management of Madhouses*, Part III,
p. 6. (The term 'madhouse' was used by Crowther to refer to both public and
private asylums.)
[2] Bolton, J. S. (1928), 'The Evolution of a Mental Hospital, Wakefield, 1818–
1928', *J. Ment. Sci. 74*, p. 596.
[3] Minutes of evidence 1828 S.C.H.L., J.H.L., Vol. 60, p. 723.

such matters as the framing of their reports. On one occasion, following the entry of the Visitors' Minutes in the incorrect book, the Clerk of the Visitors commented, with an air of resignation, that he had done all he could to keep the magistrates on the right course. The Commissioners in Lunacy issued circulars, from time to time, to clarify specific legal points and to advise the magistrates, generally, with regard to their duties. For example, in June 1847, a circular was issued which reminded the Visiting Magistrates of their right to visit licensed houses at night, a practice that seemed insufficiently used.[1]

In the provinces, the Medical Visitors were physicians, surgeons or apothecaries, but in the London area they were, almost invariably, physicians. The main condition to the appointment of the Medical Visitor was that he should not have any financial interest in an asylum. He was precluded from signing any certificates for the admission of a patient and from attending professionally any patient in a licensed house, unless directed to do so by the person upon whose order the patient was admitted, or by the order of the Secretary of State or the Lord Chancellor. There was no requirement that he should have any special knowledge of insanity. It is likely that the Visiting Magistrates often left all but the formal part of the enquiry to the Medical Visitor, who was the only Visitor to be paid. Payment was made for the time during which he was actually employed in his duties and the amount of the fee rested with the magistrates. The following are examples of payments made in Oxfordshire. In 1834, G. Coles, surgeon, of Woodstock, was considered to be entitled to two guineas for each visit to Witney.[2] Some twenty years later, the same fee was being paid to John Farwell, surgeon, of Chipping Norton, for each visit to Hook Norton.[3] Acting as a Medical Visitor in a rural area is unlikely to have been a much sought-after appointment. In particular, inspecting the premises of another medical man, perhaps a close colleague in the neighbourhood, could be unpleasant and travelling was still a considerable undertaking until the road improvements of the latter half of the nineteenth century facilitated movement. In the light of these facts, it is not surprising that difficulties in obtaining a Medical Visitor to undertake the statutory

[1] O.C.R.O., QSL.X/1/C.
[2] O.C.R.O., QSL.X/1/A, letter, Clerk of Visitors to Clerk of Peace, 7 Nov. 1834.
[3] O.C.R.O., QSL.X/1/C, receipt, 18 Oct. 1856.

visits to Hook Norton and Witney are revealed in the accounts of the Oxfordshire Clerk of the Peace. During the years 1828 and 1829, the Clerk recorded[1] that he had had to write many times to Doctors Bourne,[2] Williams,[3] Kidd[4] and Ogle[5] before the necessary arrangements could be made. It is noteworthy that such eminent Oxford physicians were included in the list of Medical Visitors at this time.

The nation-wide inspection of licensed houses by the Metropolitan Commissioners, which began in 1842, led to the introduction of a greater uniformity in the standard of management of patients and into the general conditions in the houses. This additional system of visitation and inspection had its defects, but the Commissioners took their obligations seriously and carried out their duties with the meticulous attention to detail that was characteristic of the times. From the outset, the Metropolitan Commissioners' inspections demonstrated the advantages of the visitation of licensed houses by official persons, who were unlikely to have undue local sympathy for, or prejudice against, individual proprietors. The Commissioners considered that their role was a key one and, in 1847, indicated clearly that the improved state of private madhouses was attributable, principally, to their visitation, the withdrawal of which would lead to a prompt revival of all the former abuses.[6] The Metropolitan Commissioners had made similar observations regarding their role with respect to metropolitan licensed houses. In 1836, the Commissioners felt that they had 'great reason to be satisfied with the improvements which have taken place in all the asylums within their jurisdiction'.[7] In their 1844 Report, they drew attention to the deficiencies of the inspection carried out by the Visiting Magistrates. It was claimed that the reports of the Visitors were couched, usually, in ill-defined, general terms and they were often limited to a description of the number, cleanliness and bodily condition of the patients and the

[1] O.C.R.O., QSL.IX/1 and QSL.X/1/B.
[2] Robert Bourne (1761–1829), M.D., F.R.C.P., Physician to Radcliffe Infirmary and Prof. Clinical Medicine, 1824.
[3] George Williams (1763–1834), M.D., F.R.C.P., Physician to Radcliffe Infirmary.
[4] John Kidd (1775–1851), M.D., F.R.C.P., Physician to Radcliffe Infirmary and Regius Prof. of Physic, 1822–51.
[5] James Adey Ogle (1792–1857), M.D., F.R.C.P., Physician to Radcliffe Infirmary and to Warneford Lunatic Asylum; Regius Prof. of Physic, succeeding Kidd.
[6] Further Report (1847) C.L., p. 93.
[7] Annual Report (1836) M.C.L. In Copies of Annual Reports M.C.L., 1835–41, p. 3.

general state of the premises, whilst the mental state of the patients, and their treatment, was neglected. Failure to fulfil statutory requirements with regard to the frequency of visitation was a common failing. The Metropolitan Commissioners reported that, in October 1843, the Oulton Retreat had not been visited for two and a half years and Shillingthorpe House and Great Wigston Asylum, only once in twelve months. At one house, Heigham Hall, Norfolk, the visitations had been regular, but their value had been rendered 'comparatively useless', because the Visitors had always sent for the Visitors' Book beforehand, in so doing, warning the proprietor of their intended visit.[1] In 1847, the Commissioners reported that a number of houses had been visited less frequently than seven times, as should have been the case, during the previous one year and nine months; for example, Hook Norton was included in a group of seven houses which had only been visited three times.[2]

Frequent difficulties arose in Oxfordshire concerning visitation by the magistrates. In 1829, the Clerk of the Peace had to point out to the Visitors that the number of visits to Hook Norton and Witney in the previous year had been insufficient.[3] Table 16 displays the number of visits made to the Oxfordshire houses annually, from 1829 to 1857.[4] Again, in April 1833, the Clerk observed that no visits, which fulfilled the statutory provisions, had been made to either house in that year.[5] Subsequent correspondence reveals that the Visitors attempted to interpret the law in a way that allowed inspection by a single magistrate to be legally proper and that they objected to repeating visits which did not fulfil statutory requirements because they had made them singly. One magistrate, A. J. Rawlinson, wrote:

I have not an open day before the end of the month to visit . . . Hook Norton . . . and indeed if I had I should consider it a perfect piece of mockery to repeat my visit so soon again . . . if the Act of Parliament, however, require it to be done it is only right that some of the other Visitors should make themselves acquainted with the state of the house in question.[6]

The Clerk of the Peace then requested the advice of the Metropolitan Commissioners, whose Clerk, E. Du Bois, replied abruptly that it was not the Commissioners' 'province or duty to construe Acts of Parliament for the government of the Oxfordshire Commissioners.

[1] 1844 Report M.C.L., p. 68. [2] Further Report (1847) C.L., pp. 131–2.
[3] O.C.R.O., QSL.X/1/B, letter, 10 June 1829. [4] *Vide supra*, p. 143.
[5] O.C.R.O., QSL.X/1/A, letter, Clerk of Peace to V.M., 22 April 1833.
[6] *Ibid.*, letter, Rawlinson to Clerk of Peace, 23 June 1833.

the role of the Visitors when, in 1859, he summed up the part played by them in the following way:

When . . . first appointed they did their work laxly, they did not seem to understand it, but of late years really many of them have done their work very well; they are very regular in their visits, and they make good reports, not so full as we do, but . . . they are very much disposed to act in conformity with us, and we have of late had no collisions with them at all, and I think that we can speak with very great approbation of their labours.[1]

In general, the Commissioners felt that the Visiting Magistrates exercised their power to discharge patients with discretion, although, in 1844, their judgment in two cases was questioned. One of these cases involved a patient at the licensed house at Nunkeeling, Yorkshire and the other was a patient at Witney. The following is an extract of the Metropolitan Commissioners' account of the latter case:

The Visiting Justices (with their medical attendant), examined a patient, who was confined there, and had been guilty of violence, twice in one day, and thereupon expressed their desire that the proprietor of the asylum (a respectable medical man), would open his doors and let the patient out at once. He refused to do this without an order. The justices urged this liberation, on the advice of their medical attendant, who had never seen the patient until that day; and they soon afterwards brought the matter before our consideration, and two members of our body accordingly investigated the case; but they, after repeatedly examining the lunatic, and hearing the evidence of various persons respecting his conduct and general habits, whilst out of the asylum did not feel themselves justified in liberating him.[2]

It is unfortunate that the reports of the Visiting Commissioners to Witney prior to 1845 have not survived, but the patient in question can be identified, with reasonable certainty from other sources, as Edward Bishop. On a subsequent admission to Hook Norton, this patient attracted further attention and the surviving details of his case history are given in Case (1), Appendix D.

Special enquiries into the management and conditions in individual licensed houses

In the course of this volume, reference has been made to the findings of a number of special enquiries held by the Visitors or Commissioners in Lunacy. Such enquiries provide a useful source of information about the houses concerned, their staff, the role of the Visitors

[1] Report 1859 S.C. (April 1859), p. 17.
[2] 1844 Report M.C.L., pp. 171–2.

and the prevailing attitudes towards the management of the insane. In most cases, the alleged abuses and defects were multiple and, in order to prevent the disruption of the total picture which results from the separate consideration of the defects, a short account is now given of the enquiries made into the management of three provincial houses, namely, Hereford Lunatic Asylum; Fishponds, Bristol and Haydock Lodge.

Hereford Lunatic Asylum

In 1839, the Herefordshire Visiting Magistrates petitioned Parliament to set up a Select Committee to enquire into the affairs of the Hereford Lunatic Asylum, which had been licensed to a surgeon, John Gilliland.[1] A Committee, empowered to report to the House of Commons, was convened and its members included Lord Ashley. The enquiry was held in April 1839 and the report and the minutes of evidence were published, together with the magistrates' petition and some explanatory remarks by the medical superintendent, W. L. Gilliland, M.D.[2] The specific purpose of this Committee was to investigate the alleged mismanagement of the house and its re-licensing by the Hereford City Magistrates, after the county justices had refused renewal of the licence at the Michaelmas Sessions in 1838. The events leading up to the enquiry have to be traced back to 1835, when J. Gilliland, accompanied by his brother, W. L. Gilliland, took over the establishment. In that year, the Visitors

ascertained to their great satisfaction, and to the great credit of Dr. Gilliland, the resident physician, and Mr. Gilliland, the resident surgeon, that under their judicious treatment a system of unusual mildness has been adopted towards the unfortunate inmates . . . and no personal punishment, coercion or restraint . . . has been practised.[3]

A year later, however, numerous faults were reported, including irregularities concerning the admission documents and the statutory books, failure to hold religious services and the overcrowding of patients.[4] Although the proprietor complied with suggestions regarding the legal regulations, over the next two years several adverse

[1] *Vide supra*, p. 63, for details regarding the earlier history of this establishment.

[2] Report S.C. re house kept by John Gilliland at Hereford, Minutes of evidence and Appendix, June 1839. (Also Hereford R.O., Q/ALL/95, Minutes of evidence (printed), 23 April 1839.)

[3] Hereford R.O., Q/ALL/64, Minutes V.M., 13 Sept. 1835.

[4] Hereford R.O., Q/ALL/77, Minutes V.M., 29 Oct. 1836.

reports were made by the Visitors. For example, in May 1838, they condemned the practice of forcibly plunging patients into cold baths as a punishment for tearing their clothes or quarrelling. It was revealed that some patients had been treated in this manner at least fifty times.[1] Later, the Visitors investigated complaints of ill-treatment and neglect made by the wife of a patient who had died shortly after being discharged, his body showing numerous bruises and sores.[2] This incident was attributed by the Visitors to a serious deficiency in the number of attendants, a factor which had also allowed fighting to occur amongst the patients. The structure of this asylum was condemned frequently, chiefly because it precluded adequate classification of the patients. At the Michaelmas Quarter Sessions, 1838, the Visitors submitted a Special Report, in which the establishment and its management was criticized strongly. They came to the unanimous conclusion that: 'The Hereford Lunatic Asylum was not in that state, either as relates to ventilation, to classification, to employment, to moral treatment, to recreation and religious consolation of convalescents, which they would wish to prevail.'[3] Subsequently, the assembled justices in Quarter Sessions refused to renew the licence to J. Gilliland. However, a licence was granted shortly afterwards, to W. Gilliland, by the Hereford City Magistrates, since the house was situated in a parish which was within the liberties of the city. The final report of the Select Committee was inconclusive. The insufficiency in the number of attendants was acknowledged, but the Committee was guarded about the propriety of the magistrates' decision not to renew the licence, despite the fact that the evidence presented required serious consideration by the licensing authority. Considerable attention was given to the remarkable circumstances of the licensing of the house by the city magistrates, and the Recorder of the city was acquitted of improper motives in allowing this to occur.

Fishponds licensed house

In 1848, an extensive enquiry was held by the Gloucestershire Magistrates into the conditions at the licensed house at Fishponds, near Bristol[4] and the evidence taken was printed in a voluminous publica-

---

[1] Hereford R.O., Q/ALL/108, Minutes V.M., 24 May 1838.
[2] *Ibid.*, 30 June 1838.
[3] *Ibid.*, Special Report V.M. to Q.S., Michaelmas 1838.
[4] This enquiry took place on 22–5 and 29 Nov.–2 Dec. 1848.

tion.[1] The proprietor of this house, which accommodated forty to fifty patients, was Dr J. C. Bompas and he was accused of numerous misdemeanours. These included the reception of patients without proper certificates (one patient had no order or certificates and four had only a single medical certificate); failure to maintain the books and registers in accordance with the statutory requirements, for example, omitting to record the use of restraint in the Medical Journal; and several less important errors, such as failing to display a plan of the house, in a conspicuous place. In addition, evidence was presented of the harsh and neglectful treatment of patients and of the unsuitability of the premises as a whole for use as an asylum. Specific defects included gloomy courtyards; cheerless accommodation for the 'second-class' men; lack of furniture; inadequate facilities for recreation; the existence of only two baths and one water-closet; and an inadequately padded strong-room, whose door was of such great thickness that sounds of disturbance within could not be heard by attendants outside. The Visitors' Minutes during the preceding year[2] had indicated a growing dissatisfaction with the management of the asylum and, finally, it appears that a determined attempt was made to fault Bompas on every possible score. The Visitors decided to grant Bompas a licence for six months only, during which time he was to dispose of the asylum. Bompas refuted the Visitors' accusations in a printed statement[3] and endeavoured 'to remove the false impressions under which all alike are suffering by a plain statement of facts'. He requested a full judicial enquiry into the whole affair.

The content of the evidence taken during this enquiry is of particular interest because the expert witnesses called upon included John Conolly; Dr W. Wood, resident apothecary at Bethlem and Dr F. R. Philp, one of the visiting physicians to St Luke's Hospital and proprietor of Kensington House, London. Both Wood and Philp supported the selective use of mechanical restraint. The committee of enquiry upheld the magistrates' decision not to renew Bompas's licence and the asylum was managed, subsequently, by other members of the family,[4] until 1852, when it was taken over by Dr J. D. F.

---

[1] Glos. R.O. Lib. The evidence taken in the enquiry into the management of the Fishponds private lunatic asylum, December 1848. (A large collection of MSS. re this enquiry has survived. Glos R.O., Q/AL.43.)

[2] *Ibid.*, Appendix included copies of Minutes V.M. and C.L., 21 April 1847–14 Nov. 1848.

[3] Glos. R.O., Q/AL.43.

[4] Including Dr J. C. Cox, 'late of Naples', who claimed in an advertisement

Parsons, previously proprietor of White Hall House, near Bristol. The establishment was closed, finally, in 1859 and the Bristol Borough Asylum was opened, in the Fishponds district of Bristol, in 1861.

Haydock Lodge Asylum

One of the most notable series of enquiries, during the first half of the nineteenth century, was that relating to Haydock Lodge Asylum, Lancashire,[1] at the time when its resident superintendent was Charles Mott.[2] The instigator of these enquiries was Dr O. O. Roberts, a medical practitioner and an ardent social reformer, from Caernarvonshire, North Wales. In 1844, Roberts accompanied one of his patients, a local clergyman, to Haydock Lodge. Following this visit, he expressed concern that, although the establishment catered for a large number of paupers from the North Wales counties, there was only one Welsh-speaking attendant. Later, at Mott's request, Roberts hired two 'respectable' Welsh women as nurses.[3] In 1846, when it was learned that patients were being treated with cruelty at the asylum, the clergyman was brought home. He was found, in fact, to be in a filthy, neglected state and bore bruises and scars suggestive of harsh physical treatment. The explanations offered by Mott regarding the patient's condition did not satisfy Roberts, who complained to the Commissioners in Lunacy. The Commissioners, in accordance with their usual practice, referred the matter to the local Visiting Magistrates of the Kirkdale Sessions, who held a short enquiry, in March 1846, and acquitted the keepers of any ill-conduct or malpractice. However, when Roberts and a colleague, Dr Williams, indicated that they were still dissatisfied, the Commissioners themselves held an enquiry, in May 1846. They found some grounds for complaint, but concluded that they saw little purpose in holding a further enquiry and that the situation could be resolved by the dismissal of the offending parties and by a general reform of the establishment. Nevertheless, in June 1846, Roberts petitioned Parliament to enquire into the whole affair.[4] In his petition, he outlined the

that the house had been remodelled and that the treatment was 'based on the improved views of modern psychological science', *The London and Provincial Medical Directory* (1851), p. 668.

[1] Opened Jan. 1844, licensed to Miss Louisa Coode.

[2] *Vide* Further Report C.L. re Haydock Lodge Lunatic Asylum, March 1847. Gives details concerning the whole investigation.

[3] U.C.N.W. Lib., *Caernarvon and Denbigh Herald*, 18 May 1844, advertisement by Roberts.   [4] Petition, 12 June 1846, LH. 77, U.C.N.W. Lib.

evidence concerning the alleged cruelty and neglect practised at Haydock Lodge; he revealed that there had been a remarkably high death rate at the asylum and stressed the need for a county asylum in North Wales. He disclosed the fact that Charles Mott had been an Assistant Poor Law Commissioner and Roberts's principal charge was that the 'asylum was established as a joint speculation by parties directly and officially connected with the Poor Law Commission'. He petitioned that measures should be taken to prevent persons connected with the Poor Law Commission from becoming proprietors of asylums which received paupers, or from having any financial interest in such establishments.[1] Returns made by Mott, in 1846[2] indicated that, in January of that year, the house was licensed for 450 patients, including paupers who were drawn from nineteen counties, including thirty-seven from North Wales and even three from Oxfordshire. There was one resident surgeon, 'capable of partially conversing with Welsh patients', an assistant dispenser, two visiting physicians and forty-three attendants.

In the enquiries that followed Roberts's petition, it was revealed that Mott had, in fact, ceased to be an Assistant Poor Law Commissioner in December 1842, before the house was opened. However, from October 1845, Mott had been the Poor Law Auditor of the large district in which the asylum was situated, although the Poor Law Commissioners had not acknowledged this fact. In addition, it emerged that the landlord of the establishment, George Coode, was employed as one of the Assistant Secretaries to the Poor Law Commissioners and was a relative of Mott. Coode promptly resigned this appointment,[3] at the request of the Poor Law Commissioners. Mott gave up his position at Haydock Lodge in August 1846 and was succeeded as superintendent by Mr Whelan. However, the whole affair had a number of repercussions in Parliament. The Hon. W. O. Stanley, M.P. for Anglesey, claimed that Mott had been under the patronage of the Home Secretary, Sir James Graham and, on his behalf, he had run an unsuccessful journal, *The Poor Law Guide*.[4] In a stirring speech in Parliament,[5] Edward Wakley, M.P., reviewed the whole case. He drew attention to the mortality at the

---

[1] *Vide* leading articles and correspondence in *The Times* 17, 18 and 19 June 1846.

[2] Returns re Haydock Lodge Lunatic Asylum, 1846.

[3] Coode remained the owner of Haydock Lodge.

[4] Published 11 March–30 Dec. 1843.

[5] H.P.D., Vol. LXXXVIII, 26 Aug. 1846, H.C., cols. 1023–56.

asylum,[1] which he considered to be abnormally high,[2] although it had not been commented upon adversely by the Commissioners or the Visitors and he described the wholesale transfer of paupers to Haydock Lodge as 'one of the greatest violations of law which has ever fallen under my notice'. He stated clearly that the conduct of both the Poor Law Commissioners and the Commissioners in Lunacy had been evasive and reflected an attempt to suppress enquiries. He pressed for the appointment of a commission to enquire into the whole affair, but later withdrew this request. It was felt widely that the Commissioners in Lunacy had failed in their duties and the editorial columns of a North Wales newspaper included the following observations:

The public mind cannot but be deeply impressed with the total unfitness of the Commissioners in Lunacy to occupy the office they hold. They are in fact undeserving of all public trust . . . traitors to the cause which it was their duty to protect, they deserve as severe a reproach as the very wretches into whose alleged misdeeds it was their duty fairly and fully to enquire.[3]

It is significant that by October 1846, when the Commissioners carried out a further detailed enquiry[4] and entered a lengthy report in the Visitors' Book,[5] it was recorded that considerable alterations were in progress and that they were well satisfied with the management of the establishment. Earlier, John Conolly had been appointed a visiting physician to Haydock Lodge. His first report listed numerous deficiencies and suggestions for improvement, but he was able to comment, to Coode, that with his 'kind and judicious intentions, and the able assistance of Mr Whelan in the details, and the concurrence of Dr Fortune [the resident medical officer], I see no difficulty, with the unrivalled advantages you possess at Haydock Lodge, in making it a most comfortable and healthy asylum for the insane'.[6]

[1] *Vide* Separate report on the mortality at Haydock Lodge, made to the Board by the Commissioners who conducted the inquiry into the condition and management of that asylum, March 1847, Appendix (B), pp. 44–119. (*Vide supra*, p. 212.)

[2] e.g. during the period 1 Jan. 1844–20 Oct. 1846, of the 977 admissions, 208 died. *Ibid.*, p. 54.

[3] U.C.N.W. Lib., *Caernarvon and Denbigh Herald*, 29 Aug. 1846.

[4] Report made to the Board by the Commissioners who conducted the inquiry into the state and management of the lunatic asylum at Haydock Lodge (in explanation of the mode in which the inquiry was carried on), Dec. 1846. Further Report C.L. re Haydock Lodge Lunatic Asylum, March 1847, Appendix (A), pp. 37–43.

[5] Entry made by the Visiting Commissioners, in the Visitors' Book at the asylum, 23 Oct. 1846. *Ibid.*, Appendix II, pp. 19–21.

[6] Report made by Dr John Conolly to Mr Coode, as to the condition of Haydock Lodge, 10 Sept. 1846. *Ibid.*, Appendix IV, p. 25.

By 1847, the Visitors and Commissioners were able to report favourably on the condition of the asylum,[1] which was then licensed to C. F. J. Jenkins, surgeon. Haydock Lodge was closed in 1851, but was re-opened a year later by John Sutton, formerly master of the Manchester workhouse, who conducted the establishment in an admirable way.[2]

Finally, in the consideration of the abuses and defects of the private-madhouse system, reference must be made to the numerous proposals for the reform of private-madhouse management that were made in the course of the eighteenth and nineteenth centuries and which, in general, reflected the essential flaws of the madhouse system. Typical examples of the recommendations that were made were those by Ellis (1815),[3] Burrows (1820),[4] Millingen (1840)[5] and E. T. Conolly (1858).[6] The chief objective of such proposals was, in general, to safeguard the treatment of lunatics in private madhouses from being influenced by the interests of personal profit on the part of the proprietor. Ellis, for example, suggested that the best licensed houses should be purchased by the county authorities and then supervised, directly, by the magistrates. Competent, medically trained proprietors could be kept on as directors of these establishments, on a salaried basis, whilst those of an inferior rank might be trained as principal keepers. It was suggested that compensation should be paid to proprietors of houses which were unsuitable for purchase. Despite his criticisms of the madhouse system, however, Ellis admitted that it was necessary not to be unjust to private-madhouse proprietors, 'to whom . . . the country is indebted for providing for the insane, who would otherwise have been totally neglected'.[7]

---

[1] Further Report (1847) C.L., pp. 166–7.
[2] Sixteenth Report (1862) C.L., pp. 25–7.   [3] Ellis, *op. cit.*, pp. 35–6.
[4] Burrows (1820), *op. cit.*, p. 279.   [5] Millingen, *op. cit.*, pp. 179–90.
[6] Conolly, E. T., *op. cit.*   [7] Ellis, *op. cit.*, p. 35.

9

◇◇

Summary and Conclusions

◇◇

INTERPRETATION and discussion has been employed freely throughout the text and, at this stage, little more needs to be done than to bring together the main conclusions and to make a tentative evaluation of the themes and events that have been described. At the outset, it needs to be recorded that the preparatory research for this book had not progressed far, before it became clear that a study of this nature would not be restricted by any lack of material. On the contrary, one of the most important findings of this research was that such an extensive body of information could be accumulated from a wide range of printed and MS. material. Quarter Sessions lunacy records constitute the largest single category of source material and the documents relating to private licensed houses, filed with the Oxfordshire Quarter Sessions records, have been shown to be representative of the most comprehensive series which have survived in England and Wales. The investigative survey of lunacy MSS. in 142 record repositories in England and Wales revealed the remarkable fact that some manuscript material has survived for a very large number of madhouses, despite the ravages of war and time. The bulk of this MS. material remains untouched, often only partly sorted and, undoubtedly, when taken as a whole, it provides considerable potential for further research by the medical historian. This finding is of particular relevance in the case of provincial madhouses, which tended to receive less publicity and attention than those in the metropolitan area. Only a very small quantity of

281

madhouse records preserved in non-official custody has been located to date.

From a historical viewpoint, the madhouse system may be seen to comprise three relatively distinct phases. Firstly, a period extending from the first emergence of private madhouses, as named places of confinement, in the mid-seventeenth century, up to the latter end of the eighteenth century, a phase which represents the rise of the private-madhouse system but which is the least well documented. Secondly, a period which covers the last quarter of the eighteenth and the first half of the nineteenth century and which can be called the heyday of the system. Thirdly, a period of decline, covering the remainder of the lifespan of the private-madhouse system. It was during the second period that private licensed houses attained their greatest prominence and fulfilled their most important role. Considerable expansion in the number of houses took place; the number of provincial houses rising from approximately twenty at the start of the century to 100 in 1844, after which the peak was maintained for some five years. This process of expansion was related, closely, to the rapid increase in the number of pauper lunatics in England and Wales. The highest number of paupers was accommodated in provincial licensed houses during the closing years of the fifth decade, although the contribution of the madhouse, relative to other types of asylum, had, in fact, been considerable in the previous decade. This expansive phase was brought to an end by the widespread establishment of county and borough asylums, following the Act of 1845, which led to the withdrawal of pauper lunatics and idiots from licensed houses and, consequently, to a sharp decrease in the number of pauper establishments. The decrease was offset, however, by a consolidation in the position of licensed houses receiving private patients, a state of affairs which was maintained until the close of the century. During the third period, these houses catered for the bulk of the insane of the middle and upper classes and, to a lesser extent, for the poorer class of paying patients, who were not otherwise provided for adequately.

The major public service which private madhouses rendered in the late-eighteenth century and in the nineteenth century has not received the recognition it merits due, in part, to a too ready acceptance of the more sensational disclosures and also to longstanding prejudice. It must be emphasized that madhouses were the principal form of institution catering for the insane in anything approaching a specialized way until the mid-nineteenth century and, by 1848, one-half of the total number of lunatics confined in asylums in England and Wales were in private licensed houses. During the first half of the century, they had made available accommodation for pauper lunatics, at a time when public provisions, in the form of county asylums, were extremely slow in developing and, in the second half of the century, they met a legitimate, if diminishing, demand from the upper and middle classes for facilities that were not widely available elsewhere. There is evidence that the value of licensed houses, with regard to paupers, continued well into the second half of the nineteenth century, in that they were used, in some areas, to compensate for the lack of county asylums or for the overcrowding of those which did exist. In a few provincial areas, licensed houses receiving paupers, which had been closed with the advent of county asylums, were even re-opened for this purpose. Further, their contribution in relation to both criminal lunatics and idiots must not be overlooked. In these ways, private licensed houses remained indispensable throughout the nineteenth century, despite the resentment that their continued existence and their prosperity aroused amongst the antagonists of the system.

In reviewing the geographical distribution of provincial licensed houses, a notable finding was that, as their number increased, the geographical distribution of licensed houses widened to produce a veritable network of madhouses. In fact, the number of counties containing houses doubled during the period 1807 to 1844. The location of these licensed houses appears to have been related both to the density of population and to the existence of other provisions for lunatics within the area. A significant increase in the number of new houses took place in the fourth decade of the nineteenth century. The lifespan of private madhouses showed considerable variation, ranging from establishments of an ephemeral nature to those which ran throughout the nineteenth century, some of which, indeed, had had their roots in the eighteenth and extended forward into the present century. With regard to the relative capacities of provincial licensed houses, it was shown that the greater number contained, or were licensed to receive, up to twenty-five patients. The largest houses were those which catered chiefly for paupers and the number of these establishments increased up to the mid-nineteenth century and then declined. Throughout the greater part of the century, London contained several houses which consistently accommodated several hundred patients, although there were only two houses of a similarly large capacity in the provinces, namely Haydock Lodge and Fisherton House, both of which accommodated an unusually large number of patients.

The late-eighteenth and the early-nineteenth century witnessed the gradual substitution of the medical for the non-medical proprietor. The principal contribution of the private-madhouse system, in terms of the theoretical and practical aspects of the growth of psychiatry, was made at this time, when medically qualified madhouse pro-prietors were gaining prestige and the 'trade in lunacy' was acquiring some degree of professional respectability. Notable contributions, in this respect, were made by several provincial madhouse proprietors, including Arnold, Perfect and Cox, whose combined achievement was, for a time, influential. During the first half of the century and for the greater part of the second half also, not more than two-thirds of the provincial licensed houses had medical proprietors. It is significant that the ranks of the latter included a number of well-known physicians and superintendents and medical officers of public hospitals and county asylums. The lay proprietors often included women, who, generally, were the widows or daughters of former proprietors. The rapid expansion of the private-madhouse system, in the early nineteenth century, attracted into the 'trade', an in-creased number of unsuitable persons, who exploited the situation to obtain a good living. Their conduct and speculative commercialism affected, adversely, public opinion about medical and non-medical proprietors alike and was responsible, in part, for bringing the private-madhouse system into prolonged, but not altogether justi-fiable, disrepute. Lay proprietors, some of whom appear, beyond doubt, to have been ignorant and illiterate persons of low integrity, were considered to be more likely to be corrupt, negligent and avaricious than their medical colleagues, although there were notable exceptions to this generalization. Many proprietors displayed a responsible attitude towards their duties and recognized that the continued success of licensed houses depended, to a large extent, on the personal reputation of the proprietor and the public con-fidence which he held. The available evidence certainly suggests that keeping a madhouse could be very lucrative, but there has been little acknowledgment of the fact that a large capital outlay could be involved in opening such an establishment and in keeping it running properly. Not infrequently, individual proprietors displayed humane and charitable attitudes towards their patients and expended large sums of money on pauper departments, when the incentive of financial reward was diminished by the anticipated establishment of county asylums.

Naturally, it is difficult to describe a typical private madhouse, chiefly because of the wide variation in the type of premises and accommodation available. It is possible, however, to combine information from a range of sources to construct a composite picture of what was, or what was intended to be, the pattern of activities in such an establishment. The accounts given of four fairly well-documented provincial houses, namely, Brislington House, Laverstock House, Ticehurst Asylum and Droitwich Lunatic Asylum afford glimpses, not only into their individual history and functioning, but also, when set against the fuller accounts of the Oxfordshire houses, provide a frame of reference for the comparison and evaluation, of other provincial madhouses.

Neither of the Oxfordshire madhouses had any particular claim to fame, but each is broadly representative of many other provincial licensed houses. The house at Witney was a small establishment, opened in the third decade of the nineteenth century and it catered chiefly for middle-class patients, predominantly women, drawn from the immediate neighbourhood. Hook Norton exemplifies an establishment founded in the early-eighteenth century, which operated on a small, local scale until it was expanded in the fourth decade of the nineteenth century to accommodate a greatly increased number of pauper lunatics. The latter were received from Oxfordshire and from all the adjoining counties. The proprietors of both houses were members of well-known, professional families in the locality, who ran their respective houses with integrity. Both licensed houses were so sited as to form an integral part of the village community. The physical conditions at Hook Norton and Witney appear to have been consistently satisfactory and there is no evidence of any outstanding abuses or deficiencies. The only recorded instances of the use of excessive mechanical restraint occurred at Witney, in 1853 to 1855, when the house was superintended by the widow of the former proprietor. The surviving records in Oxfordshire and elsewhere, indicate clearly that the Visiting Magistrates and the Lunacy Commissioners generally did not disapprove of the use of instrumental restraint in cases of extreme violence, when the safety of attendants or of other patients was endangered.

The unbroken series of admission and discharge documents for the two Oxfordshire private licensed houses, 1828–57, affords a rewarding subject for statistical investigation. The findings of this local study have wider implications, in that they serve to illuminate many aspects of the functioning and role of the provincial madhouse. They demonstrate, in addition, both the potential value and the limitation of this wholly unexplored source of research material for the study of insanity in the nineteenth century. The study involved a total of 745 consecutive admissions to the two houses, relating to 604 individual patients, during a defined period. A noteworthy finding was the high proportion of short periods of stay, particularly amongst the private patients, the length of stay of the paupers being consistently longer. Such a finding confirms the statements made by other contemporary proprietors concerning the outcome of treatment in their establishments and goes some way towards refuting the general accusation that private patients were confined for prolonged periods, beyond the point of recovery, for a variety of corrupt motives. At Hook Norton, nearly one-quarter of the admissions resulted in recovery and just over one-quarter in partial recovery; at Witney, the proportion partially recovered was the same, but the proportion cured was over one-third. These figures are broadly in keeping with those available for other contemporary private licensed houses. The proportion of cures amongst the paupers, who constituted over three-quarters of the total admissions to Hook Norton during the survey-period, was lower than amongst the private patients and the small group of incurable cases was almost entirely composed of paupers. The reception of paupers resulted in a higher overall mortality at Hook Norton than at Witney, as many of the paupers were admitted in a poor physical state. All these latter features correspond with those described in relation to other madhouses and were due, principally, to the parsimony of parish officials, which led to delayed admission until the pauper's physical or mental condition was acute or intractably chronic. Such factors contributed to the perpetuation within licensed houses of conditions and forms of treatment which, by later standards, could be regarded as neglectful and harsh. With regard to the range of presenting psychiatric disturbances, over one-half of the total number of admissions, for which such information is available, displayed excitement, violence, incoherence of speech or delusions, either alone or in combination and the next most common type of disturbance was melancholia.

The late-eighteenth and the early decades of the nineteenth century witnessed a great increase in concern about the outcome of institutional care of the insane. The early years of the county asylum movement were characterized by an upsurge of therapeutic optimism, but it is important not to overlook the activities and prevailing attitudes in private madhouses at this time. In 1844, provincial licensed houses contained the highest percentage of curable patients, both pauper and private, in any type of asylum, if Bethlem Hospital and St Luke's Hospital are both excluded because of their selective admission criteria. A marked disparity existed, with regard to estimates of the curability of paupers, between provincial and metropolitan licensed houses. This difference in outcome was influenced by the smaller size of provincial houses, the admission of patients from a more local area, allowing closer liaison with parish officials and, finally, by the greater tolerance of chronic insanity which prevailed in rural communities. There is evidence which suggests that a number of provincial pauper establishments did not function as long-term receptacles for chronic lunatics, in that patients were returned to their parishes as soon as their acutely disturbed condition had subsided. It goes without saying that in any discussion of the curability of insanity, recurrent problems arise from the poverty of information concerning the criteria employed in the assessment of curability and recovery.

The modes of treatment practised at Hook Norton and Witney are probably representative of those in many contemporary provincial licensed houses. There has been insufficient awareness, generally, of the curative aims and achievements of private madhouses, at many of which the emphasis was clearly upon the rapid restoration and rehabilitation of the patients. It is known that at many provincial licensed houses, in the early-nineteenth century, only minimal restraint was employed and establishments such as Brislington House and Laverstock House adopted methods of treatment that were probably as advanced as those of the York Retreat, although they never enjoyed the publicity gained by the latter establishment. The principles of moral management were widely accepted in licensed houses by the middle of the century, although mechanical restraint was still used selectively. However, the advances of the non-restraint school of lunacy reformers within the county asylum movement overshadowed the achievements of the private madhouses. Important factors in the perpetuation of the use of restraint were the over-crowding, lack of classification and the inadequate security which occurred in cheaply and ill-adapted premises, together with the conduct of a number of reactionary proprietors, who were ignorant and disinterested in new methods of management. Further, with regard to pauper establishments, the various factors which operated to keep the charges for paupers as low as possible, such as the competition for contracts between rival houses, served to delay the introduction of the non-restraint system and to foster the continuance of the merely custodial confinement of lunatics. Only a very small number of houses were purpose-built and many of the unsatisfactory premises utilized converted outbuildings for the accommodation of paupers.

During the period under consideration, the general lack of experienced and trustworthy attendants of reputable character was an important contributory factor to the defects and abuses of the madhouse system. The introduction of moral management made demands, with regard to the adequacy of the numbers and the calibre of attendants, which could not easily be met, particularly in houses receiving paupers. Greater recognition should be given to the private-madhouse attendant, whose work made an important contribution in the founding of the modern profession of mental nursing.

A considerable part of this study had to be devoted to the investigation of the alleged abuses and defects, firstly, because it was upon these facts that contemporaries and posterity have formed their broad judgments and, secondly, because these adverse aspects, in the case of many establishments, received the fullest documentation. The changing pattern of the madhouse system's deficiencies may be seen, broadly, in terms of three phases, related essentially to legislation. Prior to the Act of 1774, no legislation existed for the licensing and inspection of private madhouses or for the protection of persons confined in them. The Act itself had major short-comings, particularly regarding the inspection of madhouses, and it was followed by a protracted delay in legislative progress, until it was repealed, finally, in 1828. During this period, the deficient provisions of the Act allowed private madhouses to flourish without uniform or effective control and the situation was amplified by the disproportionate expansion of the pauper section of the community and by the delay, on the part of the counties, in implementing the County Asylum Act of 1808. By the mid-nineteenth century, however, the lunacy laws had multiplied and an elaborate framework of legislation had been established for the supervision of private licensed houses and for the safe-guarding of patients. There is considerable evidence that, by this time and thereafter, the private-madhouse system was free from major deficiencies and abuses. A good deal is known about the types of abuses which, it is claimed, prevailed in madhouses in the late-eighteenth and early-nineteenth centuries, but, despite the view that such abuses were widespread, surviving evidence for this is limited and often is based upon sensational accounts by persons of doubtful reliability. The bulk of the published evidence for this period relates to a small number of metropolitan houses. Later in the century, however, more reliable evidence is available, as a result of the official inspection of houses and of the publication of the findings of committees of enquiry.

Writers dealing with the history of lunacy in general have exaggerated, almost without exception, the adverse aspects of the conditions prevailing in madhouses in the late-eighteenth and the nineteenth centuries and have overstated the significance of forms of treatment of lunatics which, by later standards, seemed inhumane. One of the reasons for this appears to be that retrospective condemnation has been embarked upon without attempting to assess either contemporary attitudes towards insanity or social conditions in general. When seen out of context and judged by later standards, in particular those of the era of moral treatment, the prevailing conditions appeared disproportionately harsh and brutal. Despite the fact that a rational approach towards the study of insanity was developing during the second half of the eighteenth century, earlier beliefs continued to exert their influence, in particular, the view that insanity had to be overcome by forceful means using coercion, restraint and physical treatments. Harshness and squalor, in fact, pervaded many aspects of daily life until well into the nineteenth century. John Howard's tours of inspection of prisons and hospitals, in the late-eighteenth century, revealed putrid, infested and overcrowded conditions, with a disregard for hygiene and human suffering.[1] The punitive measures then adopted appear, at the present day, to have been excessively severe. Until the criminal-law reforms of the second quarter of the nineteenth century, for example, crimes such as theft, forging, shoplifting and sheep-stealing were punishable by death and punishments such as public whipping took

[1] Howard, J. (1777–80), *The State of the Prisons in England and Wales*; and (1789), *An Account of the Principal Lazarettos in Europe*.

289

place. The progressive modification and humanizing of the conditions and of the treatment of the insane has to be seen, therefore, not as an isolated sequel to the previous handling of the insane, but as part of the general awakening of social conscience in defence of the wronged and the afflicted members of society.

The principal public grievance which led to the notorious reputation of the late-eighteenth-century madhouse was the possibility of improper confinement of sane persons as alleged lunatics and their prolonged detention therein for corrupt motives. Fears of this kind flared up, at intervals, throughout the nineteenth century. It is likely that outrages did occur, due to the deficiencies of the legislation; the machinations of self-interested and malicious relatives or associates of the alleged lunatic; the conduct of unscrupulous, mercenary proprietors and the complicity of ignorant and corrupt medical men, who signed the necessary certificates. However, there is little well-documented evidence of such practices, particularly in provincial houses. Much of the hue and cry stemmed from the published recollections and accounts of alleged lunatics and ex-inmates of private madhouses. With regard to the maltreatment of lunatics in madhouses, confined under bad, often appalling, physical conditions, the evidence is considerably more substantial and refers, especially, to pauper departments during the first half of the nineteenth century. In the course of the period of expansion of the madhouse system to accommodate paupers, premises ill-suited for use as asylums were often licensed by the magistrates and allowed to continue in use because of the acuteness of the demand for accommodation.

The deficiencies of the system of visitation by local magistrates must have contributed to the perpetuation of many abuses, although, in general, their role in the improvement of the provincial-madhouse system cannot be disregarded. It is probably true to say that the Visiting Magistrates and the Medical Visitors were often ignorant of the provisions and purposes of the lunacy laws and their inexperience rendered them ill-suited to give opinions about the care of lunatics or the management of asylums. The surviving records in Oxfordshire, as in many other counties, reveal the fact that the Visitors often failed to fulfil their statutory duties, particularly in terms of the frequency of visitation by properly constituted groups and also in the adequacy of their actual inspection. The Commissioners in Lunacy, however, introduced some degree of uniformity into the management of patients and into the conditions in provincial licensed houses. They demonstrated, in the execution of their duties, the advantages of regular visitation and inspection by a body of experienced men who were beyond suspicion of local partiality.

The private madhouse could not aspire to competition with the newly built county and borough asylums in terms of properly planned accommodation or financial resources. The county asylums achieved some degree of consistency in treatment, albeit custodial and lacking in facilities for the individual management of patients, particularly towards the end of the nineteenth century. This could not be said of private madhouses, however, which, over the centuries, comprised a wide range of types of establishment and showed marked disparity in conditions. This was chiefly a reflection of the fact that madhouse proprietors formed a heterogeneous group and, for the major part of the nineteenth century, private madhouses featured characteristics of merit or demerit in close association with the character and ability of the proprietors. It was, perhaps, during the second half of the nineteenth century that private asylums subserved their most fitting role by making good provision for the middle and upper classes in relatively small, well-staffed houses, where privacy and a considerable amount of personal liberty could be enjoyed. In this respect, private asylums had considerably more to offer than the registered hospitals or the private departments of the county asylums. One of the limitations of the private-madhouse system was that it never achieved the corporate identity of a 'movement', and this fact also is related to the wide variations in the calibre and qualifications of the proprietors. During the second half of the nineteenth century, this undermined attempts both to raise the professional and public status of private asylums and to achieve closer identification with other types of asylum.

Throughout its history, the private-madhouse system was subjected to persistent disparagement and censure, due, principally, to the fact that patients were received for profit and, thereby, became the objects of financial speculation. The great lunacy reformers found this 'trade in lunacy' intolerable and indefensible. By the mid-century, the standing of the private madhouse had been enhanced considerably compared with its position at the beginning of the century. Nevertheless, all the achievements of private madhouses and the contributions which resulted from the enterprise of private individuals could not outweigh the real and fancied defects of a system based on the principle of profit. The periodic outcries against the madhouses have to be seen in the setting of the ever-changing public attitudes towards insanity and, in this context, the telling observations of Bucknill are particularly apt:

The tide of public opinion has set strongly against asylums; soon, however, it will be slack water, and then a few outrages will probably turn the prejudices of the fickle public against the liberty of mad folk. A few striking examples either way are sufficient to turn the direction of public opinion.[1]

The private-madhouse system, in fact, suffered from all the misgivings and suspicions that are still often felt for any system of private care and treatment, but more acutely, because of the particular fears that insanity has always aroused. Even at the present day, despite extensive education of the general public, misconceptions and mistrust about what goes on in mental hospitals are only too common.

Basic to this entire study has been a conviction that the application of historical data and principles is crucial to the understanding of psychiatry at its present stage of development. Although the application of scientific methodology rightly must play the foremost part in extending psychiatric knowledge, the full evaluation of current issues and theories cannot be achieved without historical perspective. One outcome of this study, for example, has been the possibility of effecting a better evaluation of the county-asylum movement by extending what is known about the setting in which it evolved. The relevance of this lies in the fact that the county asylum system continues to exert a substantial effect on the structure, problems and prevailing attitudes in British psychiatry. The nomenclature and nosology of psychiatry still lack standardization, concepts of aetiology are tentative, often contradictory, and treatment is largely empirical. In practical terms, therefore, it follows that we cannot yet afford to overlook any information which can be derived from historical sources about the management in the past of those problems that still perplex us at the present day.

[1] Bucknill (1860), *op. cit.*, p. 511.

Appendix A

Manuscript Sources

THE principal sources of record material relating to private madhouses and to lunacy, in the eighteenth and nineteenth centuries, fall into the following general categories: (a) *Public records of central origin*: preserved in P.R.O., London. (b) *Parish records*: to be found either in the parish chest of the parish of origin or deposited in the diocesan or local record office. (c) *Poor Law records*: usually contained in local record offices. (d) *Private papers*, e.g. family muniments and solicitors' papers: privately held or deposited in a public repository. (e) *Quarter Sessions records*: generally preserved, in England and Wales, in the county, city or borough record office. (f) *Miscellaneous documents*. Each of these categories of documents is now considered in greater detail and their importance as source material for the study of the private madhouse is evaluated.

(a) *Public records of central origin*
These comprise records of the Commissioners in Lunacy, 1845–1913, and, later, of the Board of Control. The detailed, indexed Minute Books and special enquiry reports complement the printed Annual Reports and clarify the Commissioner's supervisory role relating to private licensed houses.

(b) *Parish records*
The account books of the overseers of the poor contain weekly disbursement figures, some of which make reference to lunatics. Scattered items of information can be gleaned from such material and they contribute, in some measure, to an understanding of the management of lunatics in the seventeenth, eighteenth and nineteenth centuries. In a few areas direct references to madhouses have been discovered in parish records, but, in general, information from this source is limited or fragmentary.

(c) *Poor Law records*
Poor Law records relating to lunacy usually comprise such items as report books, asylum maintenance accounts, registers from various parishes and

293

unions of lunatics in asylums and returns of pauper lunatics. A considerable body of Poor Law material has been lost, but, in the case of certain documents, for example, returns of pauper lunatics, duplicate copies may be found filed with the Quarter Sessions records. Such records provide useful background information relevant to the history of lunacy in general, they supply little information dealing with private licensed houses.

(d) *Private papers*

The National Register of Archives constitutes the principal index to those privately owned records which are still held in private custody or placed on deposit in record repositories. Of the seventy-three references listed in the 'lunacy' index in 1967, only a few included a direct reference to a private madhouse, and an extensive search of original MSS. scattered all over the country would be required to evaluate the individual importance of these references.

(e) *Quarter Sessions records*

Lunacy records filed with the records of the Court of Quarter Session fall into two main categories:

(1) *Records of the Court in Sessions* The Sessions Rolls and Order Books contain scattered and fragmentary information regarding the management of lunatics by the justices of the peace. Such references are to be found chiefly during the seventeenth and first half of the eighteenth centuries, as later there was less call for intervention by the magistrates once parishes had started to place those in need of relief directly in workhouses. References of this type in the Oxfordshire Quarter Sessions records are typical of those to be found in many other areas, and deal chiefly with the problems and threats to law and order which the behaviour of individual lunatics caused within the community. Information derived from this source contributes to the background of one of the roots of origin of the private madhouse system, namely the method adopted by the parishes for the disposal of lunatics placed in their charge by the magistrates.

(2) *Administrative records* These records may be grouped as follows:

   (i) *Returns of pauper lunatics in parishes and unions.* An Act of 1815, 55 Geo. III, c. 46, required parish overseers to submit returns of all pauper lunatics and idiots in their areas to the Clerk of the Peace, but few returns from this period have survived. Most surviving records are post-1828, and in Oxfordshire, records for the period 1828 to 1841 are extant, although numerous parishes defaulted from making proper returns.[1] In 1842 the duties of the overseer, with regard to the preparation of annual returns of lunatics, were transferred to the Clerk of the Guardians, by the Act of 5 & 6 Vict., c. 57.

[1] O.C.R.O., QSL.IV.

(ii) *Records relating to county and borough lunatic asylums.* In some areas, these records date from as early as 1808, although more generally, from the mid-nineteenth century, since the majority of county asylums were established following the Act of 1845.

(iii) *Records relating to private licensed houses.* This group of documents occurs following the Act of 1774. The survival of such material, in considerable quantity, is attributable directly to the supervisory work of the local justices, which led to the enrolment of licensing data upon the Quarter Sessions Rolls and to the depositing of certain documents, regularly, with the papers of the Clerk of the Peace.

(f) *Miscellaneous documents*

Into this category are allocated certain documents of considerable interest which do not fall readily into any of the preceding groups of MSS. Amongst these documents, the Country Register for 1798–1812 may be singled out as an item of outstanding value in this research. The legal and administrative distinctions drawn, by the Act of 1774, between provincial England and Wales and the metropolitan area, led to the creation of two distinct series of registers recording the names of the proprietors of madhouses and a list of the patients admitted. These became known as the Country and Town Registers. In 1912, the Royal Commission on Public Records indicated that the Registers for the period 1774–1828 were all available. In 1932, two Town Registers were extant but an extensive search, reported by Hunter, Macalpine and Payne (1956),[1] resulted only in the tracing of a single volume, the Country Register for the period 1798–1812.[2] Recent investigations by the writer have confirmed that no other volumes of the Town or Country Register are known to have survived to the present day. The surviving Country Register consists of a list of the proprietors of private licensed houses arranged alphabetically according to the proprietor's name, the names of patients admitted to these houses, with the dates of admission and notification of the College of Physicians. In addition, the name and address is given of the person by whose direction the patient was admitted and the name of the physician, surgeon or apothecary who recommended his confinement. A name index of patients is provided at the beginning and of the proprietors at the end of the volume.

The only surviving manuscript material dealing with the supervision of licensing and inspection of metropolitan madhouses by the College of Physicians is the Treasurer's Account Book, 1774–1828.[3] This consists of a ledger in which are recorded receipts and payments by the Treasurer of the College. It includes details of the licences issued annually and the number of visits made by the Commissioners appointed by the College.

[1] Hunter, Macalpine, and Payne, op. cit.
[2] Preserved in the custody of the Legal Department, Ministry of Health, London.
[3] R.C.P.L. Lib., MSS. C.362.2.

A survey of private madhouse MSS. extant in record repositories in England and Wales

In order to evaluate the Oxfordshire collection and to base an assessment of the private-madhouse system, as far as possible, on primary sources, a survey was conducted by the author of the lunacy records in the principal repositories in England and Wales. This enabled the main catalogued collections of manuscript material relating to private madhouses to be located. A summary of the findings of this survey is given in Appendix B.

In the first place, a circular letter, requesting information about lunacy records in general and private madhouses in particular, during the eighteenth and nineteenth centuries, was sent to all record repositories in which such material was at all likely to be held. The repositories circulated were selected from the list prepared by a joint committee of the Historical Manuscripts Commission and the British Records Association.[1] This list includes repositories of public records; county, city and borough record offices; public libraries and museums; libraries and archive departments of universities and colleges; repositories maintained by various religious denominations; and finally, those maintained by certain societies, institutions, banks, etc.

In addition to this survey, an attempt was made to locate private-madhouse records and other relevant material, held in non-official custody, for example, in hospitals and in private hands. A circular letter of enquiry was sent to the persons in charge of all the registered mental nursing homes which were known to have functioned as private licensed houses during the nineteenth century. To date, the amount of material discovered has been very limited e.g. registers of admissions for Grove House, Shropshire, *c.* 1853,[2] and Visitors' Books for Court Hall, Kenton, Devon, *c.* 1870.[3]

Quarter Sessions records re private licensed houses

Quarter Sessions records constitute the bulk of the surviving MS. material relating to private licensed houses. The volume and format of these records changed considerably during the period under review, in accordance with developments in lunacy legislation.

(a) *Documents re the licensing of private madhouses*

Under the provisions of the Act of 1774, every house for the reception of more than a single lunatic had to be licensed. In the provinces, a licence could be granted by the justices of the peace in Quarter Sessions to any person who applied for one, but recognizances of £100 had to be taken for their good behaviour. These duties were laid on the College of Physicians in the metropolitan area. The fee for a licence, when up to ten lunatics were

[1] *Record Repositories in Great Britain*, 1966.
[2] Preserved at The Grove House, Church Stretton, Shropshire.
[3] Preserved at Cliffden, Teignmouth, Devon (Cliffden was opened in 1927, as a branch of Court Hall which was closed in 1946).

received, was £10 and, if more than ten were confined, it was £15. The licence was renewable annually, but had to be forfeited if the proprietor refused to admit the official visitors and there was a penalty of £500 for keeping an unlicensed house. The power to revoke licences or to refuse their renewal was not, however, given to the licensing bodies, even in the presence of severely adverse reports about a particular house or proprietor. The licensing duties of the magistrates remained substantially unchanged by subsequent legislation. Even under the National Health Service Act of 1946, the licensing magistrates retained their duties.

The Madhouse Act of 1828 introduced more rigorous criteria for licensing. Notices of application for licences which had to be submitted fourteen days prior to the Quarter Sessions, now had to include some details concerning the proposed proprietor, for example, his previous occupation and whether or not he intended to reside at the madhouse. A declaration had to be made of the greatest number of patients proposed to be received. It became necessary to submit an accompanying plan, displaying the proposed madhouse, drawn to the scale of one-eighth of an inch to a foot, together with a description of the premises and of every apartment in the house. Any subsequent alteration to this plan had to be approved by the Visiting Magistrates and notice given to the Clerk of the Peace. The licensing fee was now 2s. 6d. for every proposed parish patient and 10s. for each private patient and the minimum payment for a licence was raised to £15. Under this Act, power was given to the Secretary of State to revoke licences on the recommendations of any five Metropolitan Commissioners or any three Visiting Magistrates and this power was transferred to the Lord Chancellor under the Act of 1845. Finally, private licensed houses for upwards of 100 patients were required to have a resident medical attendant, whilst smaller houses were to be visited by a medical man not less than twice a week. Modifications in detail only were made to the licensing regulations under the Act of 1845. Under the terms of the Lunatics Law Amendment Act of 1862, no new licence could be granted by the magistrates until the plans and the proposed premises had been approved by the Commissioners and this provision applied also to alterations and additions.

Documents concerned with licensing in the Oxfordshire Quarter Sessions lunacy records cover the period Epiphany 1775 to Michaelmas 1857 and are representative of those found in many other counties. Only a few examples of early licences have survived, such as those granted to Joseph Mason in 1774 and 1776 for his house at Fishponds, Stapleton, near Bristol.[1]

(b) *Documents re the visitation and inspection of licensed houses*

In addition to their licensing duties, the justices of the peace were directed by the Act of 1774 to visit and inspect any licensed houses within their respective counties or boroughs. Outside the London area, two magistrates and a medical practitioner were to be appointed for this purpose

---

[1] Gloucester City Lib., OF.9.2, 3.

by the Court of Quarter Sessions. These Visitors, as the Visiting Magistrates were called, were required to take an oath to perform their duties faithfully and were ordered not to give prior notice to the proprietor of any house of the time of their proposed visit. Visitation was to be carried out not less than once annually, between the hours of eight in the morning and five in the afternoon. A report of the visit could be made and submitted to the Clerk of the Peace to be entered in a book kept for the purpose and, from time to time, copies of these reports were to be sent to the College of Physicians. Visits could, however, be made without minutes being recorded. Adverse reports had to be displayed in the Censor's room at the College of Physicians, but there is evidence that, although this was done for a number of years, the practice was nugatory, since no one had access to the reports. Later on, adverse reports were recorded in a book which anyone authorized to make an enquiry was allowed to see.[1] Special additional visitations could be authorized by the Lord Chancellor and the Chief Justices of the Courts of King's Bench and Common Pleas.

The Madhouse Act of 1828 directed that three or more magistrates and one or more medical men were to be chosen as Visitors at each Michaelmas Sessions, but a number considerably in excess of this was usually appointed. In addition, a Clerk to the Visitors was chosen. Prior to the Act of 1845, the usual practice was to appoint Visitors for named houses, whereas, subsequently, the magistrates at the Michaelmas Quarter Sessions were required to appoint a body of Visitors, whether or not any licensed houses existed in that area, since licences could be granted now at other Sessions or by Visiting Magistrates between Sessions. Under the Act of 1828, houses were to be visited not less than four times a year by at least two of the Visitors, who were authorized now to make visits by night as well as by day, with or without prior notice. Minutes, in the form of a report, were to be entered by the Visitors in a book kept in every licensed house and these were to be transcribed by the Clerk of the Visitors into a book kept by the Clerk of the Peace. The substance of these reports was to be included in an Annual Report relating to licensed houses and their occupants, which was prepared by the Clerk of the Peace. The Annual Report had to include details concerning all the patients admitted during the preceding twelve months, the dates of visits by the Visiting Magistrates and a summary of the observations made by them. A copy of this report was to be sent to the Secretary of State and to the Clerk to the Metropolitan Commissioners. The Visitors were given little in the way of guidance as to the form of their inspection by the Madhouse Act of 1828, apart from the recommendations that particular enquiry should be directed into the religious activities of the house. Their findings in this respect, were to be reported in the Visitors' Book, with the proprietor's reasons for not holding Divine Service, if this was the case. The statutory requirements concerning visitation were changed by the Act of 1832. Three Visiting Magistrates, together with a Medical Visitor, were required to visit provincial licensed houses three times a year, whilst the Metropolitan

---

[1] Minutes of evidence 1828 S.C.H.L., J.H.L., Vol. 60, p. 718.

Commissioners had to make four visits per annum in the metropolitan district. The Visitors' Minutes were to be considered by the Court of Quarter Sessions before a licence could be renewed.

The Act of 1842 authorized the Metropolitan Commissioners to visit and report on private licensed houses in the provinces. Later, the Act of 1845, provided for visits to provincial houses by the Commissioners in Lunacy at least twice a year, together with at least four visits per annum by a minimum of two Visitors, one being the Medical Visitor. The Visitors and Commissioners were now required to enter Minutes concerning the condition of the house and its inmates in the Visitors' Book kept at the house and any observations regarding individual named patients were to be entered in the Patients' Book. The Medical Visitation Book, which included the medical attendant's observations, had to be examined and a statement made therein to confirm that it had been inspected. The proprietor or superintendent of the house was required to send a copy of these entries, within three days, to the Clerk of the Visitors and to the Commissioners. Throughout the period considered in this study, therefore, copies of the Visitors' Minutes were required to be deposited in the custody of the Clerk of the Peace.

The contents of the Visitors' Minutes altered a good deal during the period 1774 to 1850. The surviving Minutes for the period 1774 to 1828 suggest that the Visitors did not use their potentially wide powers of inspection very fully. In general, the reports have a stereotyped pattern and little detailed information is provided, beyond a statement of the number of patients admitted and discharged and of those confined in the house. A general statement was usually made about the condition of the house and the management of the patients, together with a note as to whether or not the admission documents were in order.

The tours of inspection of the Metropolitan Commissioners from 1842, and of the Commissioners in Lunacy after 1845, made considerable impact upon the character of the minutes and produced a more detailed and uniform standard of recording. The Visiting Magistrates now had the benefit of referring to the Minutes of the Commissioners and, in general, must have been concerned to display a responsible attitude for the benefit of the Commissioners. In some counties, the Visitors demonstrated their independence by not always agreeing with the recommendations of the Commissioners, a factor which often had the effect of fostering the persistence of abuses. In these cases in particular, the Visitors' Book became the medium for dialogue between the Visitors and the Commissioners. Under the terms of the Act of 1845, the official visitors of private licensed houses were directed to enquire when Divine Service was performed at the house, how many patients attended the services and what was its effect upon them. They were also to enquire about the occupations and amusements provided and the benefits derived from them; to discover whether any system of non-restraint was employed and, if so, to comment on its efficacy. The classification of patients, the condition of pauper patients when first received and their dietary were also to receive scrutiny. A list of the patients, distinguishing paupers from private, and specifying which

299

were deemed curable, had to be produced by the proprietor or super-intendent, together with the books required to be kept by the Act, namely Registers of admissions, discharges and deaths, the Medical Journal and the Medical Case Book.[1] The current licence and the orders and certificates of patients admitted since the last visit had to be inspected and any irregularities noted, and the visitors were to be shown every part of the establishment and grounds and were to inspect every patient. When visiting provincial licensed houses, the Visiting Commissioners were directed to give special attention to the state of mind of any patient whose detention seemed in any way improper and the attention of the Visitors was to be drawn to such cases. Models for the type of minutes to be made by the Visiting Commissioners following the inspection of metropolitan and provincial licensed houses were included in the Appendix of the Report from the 1859 Select Committee.[2]

In some counties, papers have survived which relate to the appointment of the Visitors, the Medical Visitor and the Clerk of the Visitors, who was usually the Clerk of the Peace, but could, in some cases, be some other person appointed by the Court of Quarter Sessions. There is often a good deal of surviving correspondence between the Visitors and their Clerk, regarding such matters as the time and place of meetings and enquiries and directions concerning the implementation of the statutory require-ments.

(c) *Documents re the admission, discharge, removal and death of patients*

Although the foundation for all future legislation was laid by the Act of 1774, its inadequacies were soon patent and its lack of provision for paupers was a major deficiency. The admission order and accompanying medical certificate introduced by this Act applied solely to non-pauper patients and the only other information required at the time of admission concerned the persons by whose direction the lunatic was to be received. Notice of the reception of a lunatic by the proprietor of a provincial licensed house had to be sent to the Clerk of the Peace and to the Secretary of the London Commissioners within fourteen days. The Act of 1819 required parish overseers to present any insane person or 'mischievous idiots', who were chargeable to their parish, before two or more justices of the peace. The justices were authorized to call a medical person to their assistance and, if necessary, to direct the overseers to convey the lunatic to an asylum or licensed house. The form of the certificate was prescribed and this Act made the first provisions for the formal medical certification of pauper lunatics.

Extensive changes in detail were introduced by the Madhouse Act of 1828. The confinement of non-pauper, or 'superior' patients now required certification by two medical men, who had examined the patient separ-ately. Some details concerning the patient had to be furnished, including

[1] The only Case Books known to have survived are those for Camberwell House, London (two vols) 1847–53, now in the private collection of Dr R. A. Hunter.
[2] Report 1859 S.C. (April 1859), Appendix 2, pp. 287–9.

his former occupation, the name of any other licensed house or asylum in which he had been confined previously, and whether or not he had been found lunatic under a commission issued by the Lord Chancellor. Any special circumstances which prevented the provision of two medical certificates had to be stated, so as to allow the correction of the deficiency within one week. The admission of pauper patients required an order signed by two magistrates, or by one of the parish overseers and the officiating clergyman of the patient's parish of legal settlement. In addition, a single medical certificate was required, stating, as in the case of 'superior' patients, that the person was of unsound mind and, therefore, a proper person to be confined. No clinical details had to be given and no further particulars concerning pauper lunatics were required in the admission documents until 1845. Notices of the reception of pauper and private patients and a copy of the order and certificates had to be sent to the Clerk of the Visitors within seven days and notices of removal or death within three days. Hence for the first time, information became available regarding the total number of lunatics and idiots admitted. The Act of 1832 reproduced the 1828 legislation without any major alteration and the admission and discharge documents remained substantially unchanged. Details of the marital state of the patient were now required, together with a note about any special circumstances which precluded the insertion of any particulars. The state of mind of the patient at the time of removal had to be recorded on the notice of discharge or removal and, in the case of pauper patients, a statement regarding the cause of death had to be made.

The admission documents were modified considerably by the Act of 1845. The admission notice for pauper and private patients by the proprietor or superintendent of a licensed house had to be accompanied by a statement concerning the mental and bodily condition of the patient at the time of reception. The superintendent was now required to send a copy of the order and certificates and the notice and statement to the Commissioners, within seven days, and further copies had to be sent to the Clerk of the Visitors. The format of the reception order for pauper patients was essentially unchanged, but the parish overseer or relieving officer now had to provide a statement concerning certain of the patient's particulars, which were the same as those required for private patients. The range of particulars had been extended to include religion; length of time insane; whether or not the current illness was the first attack; age, if known, at the time of the first attack and whether suicidal, dangerous or subject to epilepsy. In the case of private patients, the medical certificates required a statement, by the certifying physician, surgeon or apothecary, of the [facts upon which he had formed his opinion. This represented a theoretical advance of considerable importance, although the data supplied by the attesting practitioner, in support of his opinion, was often very limited and in some cases non-existent.

Further modification of the statement of the patient's particulars and of the medical certificates was introduced in 1853 by the Act of 16 & 17 Vict., c. 96, and the statement now required a note on the supposed cause of the insanity. Particulars as to whether the patient was suicidal or dangerous to others were now included in two separate questions, thereby avoiding the ambiguity which had existed in answers to this question under the Act of 1845. The standardization of particulars in the documents for paupers and private patients was completed with the removal of minor, but nevertheless significant, differences in terminology. The medical certificates required the examining medical person to distinguish between those facts indicative of insanity, which he had observed personally, from those which had been communicated to him by others. No lunatic was to be received into a licensed house with a certificate founded entirely on facts communicated by others. This provision was a sound one, as it was possible for the certifying medical person's opinion to be founded largely upon the testimony of others, with only cursory corroborative observations of his own. In view of the new provisions for the safeguarding of patients introduced by the Act of 1853, it is interesting to note that a fourteen-day period was still allowed for defective orders and certificates to be corrected. In addition, a number of other provisions were introduced by this Act. The person certifying had to state the qualifications which entitled him to practice as a physician, surgeon or apothecary. Notices of recovery for every patient had to be sent to their friends and relatives and, in the case of paupers, to the parish officers. If not discharged within fourteen days of the proposed date for removal, the Visitors or Commissioners were to be informed. Finally, in the case of deaths, a statement had to be made to the coroner.

(d) *Accounts of the Clerk of the Peace re licensed houses*

The accounts of the Clerk of the Peace relating to private licensed houses, as presented annually to the Court of Quarter Sessions, provide a record of the expenses incurred in the execution of the lunacy laws at a county level. In some areas, such records, particularly those concerned with licensing, provide the only useful information about the number and location of private licensed houses and the names of their proprietors. It was intended that the income derived from the licensing fees should be applied towards the payment of the administrative expenses incurred. Any excess that accrued was to go into the county stock, but the Sessions could order any deficiency to be paid out of the county rates. In addition to licensing fees, other items detailed included payments made to the Medical Visitors; the Visitors' travelling expenses; fees for considering applications for licences, and afterwards granting and making out a licence; the cost of advertisements for Visitors; and the costs incurred by the Clerk of the Visitors in the course of his statutory duties, such as the maintenance of the appropriate books and corresponding with the Visitors.

(e) *Miscellaneous items*

The final category of Quarter Sessions records relating to private licensed houses comprises miscellaneous items such as correspondence, circulars and orders for Parliamentary Returns. Search of such miscellaneous material has proved rewarding on a number of occasions, since this type of source has the advantage of containing documents of a less formal character, for example, letters. These are of considerable interest for revealing the more human and personal aspects of lunacy law administration.

Appendix B

A Summary of the Results of the Survey of Private-Madhouse Records extant in Record Repositories in England and Wales

A TOTAL of 142 repositories were circularized to locate any catalogued MS. material relating to private licensed houses and, of this number, nine record offices failed to reply to the circular. Section I indicates the names of repositories holding records relevant to this enquiry. The names which follow in brackets refer to those private licensed houses for which there is documentation at that specific record office, although the quantity may vary from a single item to a considerable number of documents. Section II lists repositories which held no catalogued material relating to private licensed houses when the circular was dispatched in 1967. Within these two sections, the order adopted for listing follows that set out in the hand-list *Record Repositories in Great Britain* (Historical Manuscripts Commission, 1966), dealing separately and successively with repositories situated in England, Wales and London. References to private licensed houses located in the index of the National Register of Archives, under the heading of 'lunacy', are dealt with under the appropriate repositories in which the records are currently preserved. Reference needs to be made also to certain relevant items known to be preserved outside either record repositories or public libraries. For example, at St Nicholas's Hospital, Gosforth, are kept MSS. relating to Newcastle upon Tyne Lunatic Asylum, and to St Luke's House, Newcastle; at Cheadle Royal Hospital, Cheshire, a Committee Book refers to twenty-six private licensed houses in Lancashire and Yorkshire 1845–6; Registers of admissions for Grove House, Church Stretton, remain in custody at The Grove House, Church Stretton, Shropshire.

Section 1   Repositories containing catalogued MS. material relating to private licensed houses

A   England

Bedfordshire: County Record Office (Springfield House, Kempston; Hinwick House; The Pines, Aspley Heath).

Buckinghamshire: Buckinghamshire Record Office (Denham Park, nr. Uxbridge; Mr MacKay's house, Stony Stratford).

Cheshire: Chester City Record Office (Haydock Lodge).

Derbyshire: Derbyshire Record Office (Wye House, Buxton).

Devon: Plymouth City Library (74 Lisson Grove, Mutley, Plymouth; Plympton House, Plympton St Maurice).

Dorset: Dorset Record Office (Portland House, Halstock; Cranbourne; Boardhayes, Stockland).

Durham: Durham County Record Office (Gateshead Fell; Gateshead; Bensham nr. Gateshead; Wrekenton, Gateshead Fell; West Auckland; Dunston Lodge, Gateshead; Dinsdale Park, nr. Darlington).

Essex: Essex Record Office (Fair Mead House, High Beech/Beach, nr. Epping; Leopard's Hill Lodge, High Beech, nr. Epping; house in Maldon Lane, Witham).

Gloucestershire: 1 Gloucestershire Records Office (Castleton House, Charlton Kings, Cheltenham; Moorend House, Charlton Kings; Sandywell Park, Dowdeswell, Cheltenham; The Retreat, Fairford; Croft House, Fairford; Northwoods, Frampton Cotterill; Tusculum House, Mitcheldean; Ridgeway House, Stapleton, nr. Bristol; Whitehall House, St Georges, Bristol; Fishponds, Stapleton, nr. Bristol).

Gloucestershire: 2 Gloucester City Library (Fishponds, Stapleton, nr. Bristol).

Hampshire: Hampshire Record Office (Westbrooke House, Alton; Bury/Berry House, Alverstoke; Carisbrooke House of Industry, Isle of Wight; Hilsea Asylum, Portsea Island, Portsmouth; Lainston House, Winchester; Grove Place, Nursling; Moorton House, Ringwood; Stubbington House, Titchfield).

Herefordshire: County Record Office (Hereford Lunatic Asylum; Whitchurch Asylum, nr. Ross, otherwise known as Portland House; Peterchurch House).

Hertfordshire: County Record Office (Hadham Palace, Much Hadham; Harpenden Hall; house of Mary Thornton, Cheshunt; house of Dr Nathaniel Cotton, St Albans; house of John Rumball, St Albans).

Kent: Kent Archives Office (West Malling Place, West Malling; house of Rebecca Law, Windmill Terrace, Gravesend; Northgrove House, Hawkhurst; Goudhurst; Spring Croft House, Beckenham; Cavendish House, Ramsgate; Northwood House, St Lawrence, Thanet).

Lancashire: Lancashire Record Office (Billington, nr. Blackburn; Prescot; Blakeley, nr. Manchester; Bury; West Derby, Liverpool; Newton, nr. Manchester; Walton-on-the-Hill, Liverpool; Haydock Lodge; Clifton; Marsden Hall; Shaftesbury House (Raven Meols Lane Asylum),

Formby; Overdale, Outwood, Prestwich; Scout Mill, Ashton-under-Lyne; Cronton; Stanerick Hill, Ashton-under-Lyne; Hollingrove, Habergham Eaves).

Leicestershire: Leicestershire Record Office (Wigston House, Great Wigston).

Lincolnshire: Lincolnshire Archives Office (Greatford/Gretford; Shillingthorpe House, Stamford).

Norfolk: Norfolk and Norwich Record Office (Loddon).

Northamptonshire: Northamptonshire Record Office (Abington Abbey, Northampton).

Northumberland: Newcastle upon Tyne City Archives Office (Newcastle upon Tyne Lunatic Asylum, Bath Lane; St Luke's House, Newcastle, post-1795 known as Bellegrove Retreat/House/Lunatic Asylum; Dr Pemberton's house; house of Dr William Luck, Newcastle).

Nottinghamshire: County Record Office (Mansfield; Burton Joyce).

Oxfordshire: 1 County Record Office ((i) Hook Norton; (ii) Witney). Duplicate copies of orders, medical certificates and notices of reception of lunatics into (i) and (ii) and notices of death, discharge and removal 1832–45, QSL.I/1–15; for 1845–56, QSL.II/1–12; eleven plans for (i) and eight plans for (ii) 1828–54, QSL.III/1–2; draft licences for (i) and (ii) 1835–56, QSL.V/1; licences for (i) (pauper and private departments) 1842, QSL.V/2i–ii; licence for (ii) 1845, QSL.V/2/iii; book of copy licences for (i) and (ii) 1842–56, QSL.V/3; licence renewal applications and lists of patients in (i) and (ii) 1842–56, QSL.V/4; Register of admissions to (i) and (ii) 1832–45, 1845–56, 1828–32, QSL.VI/1, 2, 3; copy Minutes of Visiting Magistrates to (i) and (ii) 1833–57, QSL.VII/1; copy Minutes of Visiting Magistrates to (ii) 1833–57, QSL.VII/2, and to (i) 1833–54, QSL.VII/3; copy Minutes of Commissioners in Lunacy to (ii) 1845–57, QSL.VII/4, and to (i) 1843–54, QSL.VII/5; book of proceedings (including notes re appointment of Visitors, Medical Visitors and Clerks; Minutes of Visitors' meetings; transcripts of Visitors' reports) 1828–39, QSL.VII/6; notices of appointment of Visiting Magistrates to (i) and (ii) and of the Clerk of the Visitors, 1845–57, QSL.VIII/1; licensing details for (i) 1775–1834 and for (ii) 1823–34 QSM.I and II; annual accounts of the Clerk of the Peace 1828–57, QSL.IX/1; miscellaneous correspondence, papers, returns, etc., 1829–56 QSL.X/1A–E. (Outside dates of the total collection 1775–1857.)

Oxfordshire: 2 Bodleian Library, Oxford (Greatford, Lincolnshire; Dr Thomas Arnold's house, Leicester).

Shropshire: Salop Record Office (House of Industry, Kingsland, Shrewsbury; Grove House, Church Stretton; Boreatton Park).

Somerset: Somerset Record Office (Amberd House, nr. Taunton; Bailbrook House, Batheaston; Beaufort Villa, Keynsham; Belle Vue; Bindon House, Langford Budville; Bowyes House, Kingston; Brislington House, nr. Bristol; Cleeve House, Yatton, Clevedon; Colford Asylum, nr. Bishops Lydeard; Downside Lodge, Midsomer Norton; Fairwater House, Staplegrove, nr. Taunton; Fivehead House; Longwood House, Ashton, nr. Bristol; Monument Asylum, Wellington;

Portishead Asylum; Temple Combe House; Upper House, Bath; West Fullands House, Wilton).

Staffordshire: Staffordshire Record Office (Spring Vale, Stone; Moat House, Tamworth; Oulton House/Retreat, Stone; Bilston).

Suffolk: Ipswich and East Suffolk Record Office (Aspall Asylum, nr. Debenham).

Surrey: 1 Surrey Record Office (Lea Pale House, Stoke-next-Guildford; Great Foster House, Egham; Church Street House, Epsom; Timberham House, Charlwood, nr. Crawley; Frimley House, Frimley; Weston House, Chertsey; Canbury House, Kingston; Croshams, Sutton; Sutherland House, Surbiton; Chalk Pit House, Sutton; Woodcote End, Epsom; house of William Finch M.D., Mitcham; The Recovery, Mitcham; Abele Grove, Epsom).

Surrey: 2 Guildford Museum and Muniment Room (Weston House, Chertsey; house in the parish of Ewell).

Sussex: 1 West Sussex County Record Office (Langcroft House, New Shoreham; Craywell, Aldwick).

Sussex: 2 East Sussex County Record Office (Ticehurst Asylum and House, the latter otherwise known as Highlands; Balsdean Asylum, transferred to Ringmer; Knole House, Frant; Stillwood House, Brighton; St George's Retreat, Ditchling; Myskyns, Etchingham; Periteau House, Winchelsea; Ashbrooke Hall, Rollington).

Warwickshire: Warwickshire County Record Office (Watchbury House, Barfold; house of Dr Griffin, Gravelly Hall, Erdington; house of Mr Harcourt, Hunningham House, Harbury; house of Mr Dartnell, Henley-in-Arden; Hurst House, Henley-in-Arden; house of Mr S. Brown, Henley-in-Arden; house of Mr T. Burman, Henley-in-Arden; Glendosil, Henley-in-Arden; Midland Counties Idiot Asylum; Clare House, Leamington Priors; house of Dr Seaton, Stoke; house of Edward Price, Southam; house of William and Mary Roadknight, Henley-in-Arden; house of John Blunt, Warwick, later removed to Great Wigston, Leicestershire; house of Miss Mary Gibbs, Hough/Haugh House, Packwood, Wootton Wawen; house of Miss Mary Gibbs, Aylesbury House, Packwood; Duddeston Hall, Birmingham; house of Benjamin Gibbs, Buckley Green, Beaudesert, Henley-in-Arden).

Wiltshire: Wiltshire Record Office (Fonthill Gifford; Calne; Fisherton House; Kingsdown House, Box; Laverstock House; Fiddington House, Market Lavington; Belle Vue Asylum, Devizes).

Worcestershire: Worcestershire Record Office (Droitwich Lunatic Asylum).

Yorkshire: 1 East Riding County Record Office (Field House; Moor Cottage, Nunkeeling, nr. Brandsburton; Cottingham Retreat; Dunnington House, nr. York; Hessle House, nr. Hull; Kilham Retreat; Rillington House/Retreat, nr. New Malton; Sculcoates Refuge, Hull; Southcoates Retreat, Hull; Weaverthorpe Asylum, nr. Sledmere).

Yorkshire: 2 North Riding County Record Office (Gate Helmsley, nr. York; Osbaldwick, nr. York; Heworth, nr. York; Terrace House, Osbaldwick; Clifton House, York; Claxton Grange).

Yorkshire: 3 North Riding: City Library, York (Gillygate; Acomb

House, Acomb, nr. York; Grove Hall, Acomb; St Maurice House, York).

Yorkshire: 4 West Riding: The Clerk's Department, County Hall, Wakefield (Greta Bank Private Asylum, Burton-in-Lonsdale; The Grange Private Asylum, Rotherham; Grove House Asylum, Acomb; Lune Tree House Private Asylum, Acomb).

Yorkshire: 5 West Riding; Sheffield City Library (Sion Vale House, London).

B. Wales

Glamorgan: County Record Office (Vernon House, Briton Ferry).

C. London

1 Public Record Office (Forty-two metropolitan houses in Annual Reports of M.C.L., 1829–31; numerous provincial and metropolitan houses in Minute Books and papers of C.L., 1845 on).

2 Methodist Archives and Research Centre (Hanham House, Clare Hill, nr. Bristol).

3 Royal College of Physicians (Metropolitan licensees, 1774–1827, listed in Treasurer's Account Book, maximum nos forty-eight in 1826 and 1827).

4 Glyn Mills and Company (Mr Stroud's house, Bilstone, Staffordshire; Mr Chadwick's house, Lichfield, Staffordshire).

5 Corporation of London Records Office, Guildhall (Hoxton House, Shoreditch; Warburton's Asylum, Bethnal Green; Peckham House; Camberwell House).

6 Greater London Record Office; London Records (Hoxton House).

Section 2   Repositories containing no catalogued MS. material relating to private licensed houses

A   England

Berkshire Record Office; Reading University Library; Buckinghamshire Archaeological Society; Cambridge County Record Office; Cambridge University Library; Cambridge University Archives; Cheshire Record Office; Cornwall County Record Office; Cumberland, Westmorland and Carlisle Record Office; Devon Record Office; Exeter City Library; Bristol Archives Office; Portsmouth City Record Office; Southampton Civic Record Office; Southampton University Library; Winchester City Record Office; Isle of Wight County Record Office; Huntingdonshire County Record Office; Liverpool Record Office; Canterbury Cathedral Library and City Record Office; Liverpool University Library; Manchester Central Library; Manchester, Chetham's Library; Manchester, John Rylands Library; Warrington Public Library; Wigan Local History and Archives Department; Leicester Museums, Department of Archives; Grimsby Borough Archives Office; Lincoln Public Library; Great Yarmouth Borough Records; Northumberland Record Office; Newcastle upon Tyne City Library; Newcastle upon Tyne University Library; Nottingham City Libraries and Guildhall Muniment Room; Nottingham University, Department of MSS; Oxford City Record Office; Shrewsbury Borough Archives; Bath, Victoria Art Gallery and Municipal Libraries; Keele University Library; Bury St Edmunds and West Suffolk Record Office; Birmingham City Library; Birmingham University Library; Coventry City Record Office; York, Borthwick Institute of Historical Research; Leeds Public Libraries; Leeds, Brotherton Library; Leeds University School of Medicine; Sheffield University Library.

B Wales

The National Library of Wales, Aberystwyth; Anglesey County Record Office; Caernarvonshire Record Office; Bangor, University College of North Wales Library; Carmarthenshire County Record Office; Flintshire Record Office; Cardiff Central Library; Swansea University College Library; Merioneth County Record Office; Monmouthshire County Record Office; Pembrokeshire Record Office.

C London

Church Commissioners; Duchy of Cornwall Office; House of Lords Record Office; British Museum; National Monuments Record; Science Museum and Library; Baptist Union Library; Congregational Library; Dr William's Library; Presbyterian Church of England Library; Inner Temple Library; Lincoln's Inn Library; Middle Temple Library; Royal College of Surgeons; St Bartholomew's Hospital; St Thomas' Hospital; Society of Genealogists; Wellcome Historical Medical Library; University of London Library; Kings' College London Library; Bank of England; Barclays Bank Ltd; Coutts and Co; C. Hoare & Co; Midland Bank Ltd; Guildhall Library; Greater London Record Office (Middlesex Records); Lambeth Minet Library.

Appendix C

Explanatory Notes on the Coding Methods Employed in the Statistical Analysis of Data extracted from the Admission and Discharge Documents

SELECTED data, extracted from the admission and discharge documents, 1828–57, relating to Hook Norton and Witney private licensed houses were coded and transferred to eighty-column punch cards. Specific items, transcribed in every case from the admission documents, but not selected for coding were as follows:

(a) Information as to whether the patient was found lunatic by inquisition and the date of such an enquiry. This information was required for private patients by the Act of 1832 and subsequent Acts, but only a single case occurred in the Oxfordshire records.

(b) Special circumstances preventing the patient being examined separately by two medical practitioners. This information was required for private patients by the Act of 1828 and subsequent Acts. Circumstances of this kind were recorded on eighteen occasions in the series and they are discussed separately in the text.

(c) Special circumstances preventing the inclusion of any particulars relating to the patient. This information was required by the Act of 1832 and subsequently, but no circumstances of this kind were recorded in the series.

(d) 'Age on first attack'. This information was not required prior to the Act of 1845. See notes re Col. 25 below.

(e) 'Supposed cause' of insanity. This information was not required prior to the Act of 1853 (16 & 17 Vict., c. 96). Ten variants were recorded in the series.

Coding methods

Cols. 1–3   *Overall admission number*
Numbering 001–999.

The documents were found sorted roughly into annual bundles, with

310

admission and discharge papers generally filed together. Three separate series, relating to the Acts of 1828, 1832 and 1845, had been numbered but the method of numbering was unreliable and often related to the chronological order of the admission.

All relevant data relating to individual admissions were transcribed on to index cards and missing information was supplied from other sources whenever possible. The cards were then arranged in chronological order of admission and numbered 1–754. Fourteen cases, where the precise date of admission was unknown, were included at the end of the series (numbers 755–68), the numbers being allocated in chronological order of death, discharge or removal. The admissions numbered 1–754 fall into two distinct groups, firstly, a consecutive series of admissions during the period 24 August 1828 to 11 May 1856 (numbers 10–754 inclusive) which, as far as can be ascertained, is quite complete and constituted the basis of this statistical study; and, secondly, nine admissions which took place prior to the commencement of the consecutive series, during the period 14 January 1814 to 31 May 1828 (numbers 1–9 inclusive). These admissions were excluded from the statistical analysis.

Cols. 4–5   *Year of admission*
            Code: Last two digits of year of admission as written 01–98
            Not known 99

Col. 6   *Quarter of admission*
            Code: 1 Jan.–March
                  2 April–June
                  3 July–Sept.
                  4 Oct.–Dec.
                  5 Not known

Col. 7   *Individual case admission number*
            Code: As written 1–9

In order to allow examination of the case-histories of individual patients, a detailed name index of patients was compiled and cross-referenced with the overall admission numbers. The first and subsequent admissions of individual patients, within the survey-period, were numbered 1, 2, 3, etc.

Col. 8   *Admitting authority*
            Code: 1 Justices of the peace
                  2 Parish or Poor Law officials
                  3 Relatives (including persons with the same surname as patient and those persons of specified familial relationship)
                  4 Others (friends, guardians, trustees and persons of unspecified connection)
                  5 Not known

Col. 9   *Name of licensed house*
           Code: 1 Hook Norton
                 2 Witney

Col. 10   *Legal status*
           Code: 1 Pauper lunatic
                 2 Private patient
                 3 Not known

Cols. 11–12 *Age*
           Code: As written
                 Not known 98
                 Not applicable 99

A statement of age in the case of pauper lunatics was not required on admission documents before 1845; in the case of private patients it was required from 1828.

Col. 13   *Sex*
           Code: 1 Male
                 2 Female

A statement of the patient's sex was not required before 1845. However, throughout the whole series, the information was available or could be ascertained from other sources.

Col. 14   *Previous place of abode*
           Code: 1 Oxfordshire
                 2 Gloucestershire
                 3 Berkshire
                 4 Warwickshire
                 5 Northamptonshire
                 6 Buckinghamshire
                 7 Worcestershire
                 8 London, including Middlesex
                 9 Other English counties
                 0 Elsewhere
                 X Not known

The counties coded were those in which the usual, or last known, place of abode was situated, or, in the case of paupers, those containing the parish to which the patient was legally chargeable. Difficulties in the correct identification of counties were presented in a small number of cases, in which the name of a parish only was given and also in areas where boundary changes are known to have occurred.

Col. 15   *Marital status*

> Code: 1 Single
>   2 Married
>   3 Widowed
>   4 Not known
>   5 Not applicable

A statement of the patient's marital status was not required for private patients before 1832 and for paupers before 1845. The term 'widowed' was included in the admission documents for the first time in 1845.

Col. 16   *Religion*

> Code: 1 Church of England (including the terms Churchman and Established Church)
>   2 Nonconformist (including Methodist, Independent, Baptist, Wesleyan, Dissenter, Quaker)
>   3 Protestant (frequent use of this ambiguous term made necessary its inclusion as a separate item)
>   4 Roman Catholic
>   5 Specified as 'None'
>   6 Other
>   7 Not known
>   8 Not applicable

Details of the patient's religion were not required on the admission documents before 1845.

Col. 17   *Occupation*

> Code: 1 Professional and other educated persons
>   2 Farmers
>   3 Employed in retail trade
>   4 Employed in handicraft or manufacture as masters or workmen
>   5 Agricultural labourers
>   6 Labourers (work unspecified) and domestic workers
>   7 Gentlefolk and persons specified as having no occupation
>   8 Not known
>   9 Not applicable

In the case of women and dependants without specified occupation, the occupation of husband or father, if available, was used for coding purposes. A statement of the patient's occupation was not required for private patients prior to 1828 and, in the case of paupers, before 1845. The method of coding employed was, essentially a modification of the occupational categories used in the 1831 census.

Col. 18   *Mental state and behaviour on admission*

    Code: 1 Melancholic/desponding
          2 Excited and/or violent
          3 Incoherent and/or deluded (the term incoherence
            being used generally to refer to speech)
          4 Melancholic with incoherence and/or delusions
          5 Excited with incoherence and/or delusions
          6 Idiocy
          7 Imbecility
          8 Other
          9 Not known
          0 No abnormality
          X Not applicable

Information regarding the mental state of patients was not required in admission documents, for pauper or private patients, before 1845. Data coded in this way comprised the most prominent psychiatric features noted in the medical certificates, and in the statements made by the medical officer of the licensed house in the notices of admission.

Col. 19   *Bodily health on admission*

    Code: 1 Satisfactory (e.g. good, healthy, tolerable)
          2 Poor (e.g. debilitated, delicate, feeble, weak, infirm)
          3 Very poor (e.g. in a very bad state, very weak)
          4 Specific disorders (e.g. in pre-coma, part-paralysed,
            febrile, ascites, ulceration of bowels)
          5 Not known
          6 Not applicable

Information regarding the bodily health of patients on admission was not required before 1845. Data coded in this way was derived from the statements on the bodily health and condition of patients which formed part of the notices of admission.

Col. 20   *Epilepsy*

    Code: 1 Subject to epilepsy
          2 Not subject to epilepsy
          3 Not known
          4 Not applicable

This information was not required before 1845. However, occasional references to epileptic disturbances were made before this time and such information was coded.

Col. 21   *Suicidal or dangerous*

    Code: 1 Suicidal
          2 Dangerous
          3 Suicidal and dangerous
          4 Not suicidal or dangerous

314

5 Not known
6 Not applicable

This information was not required before 1845. The phrase 'whether suicidal or dangerous to others', which was included as part of the statement on the admission order, led, inevitably, to a number of ambiguous answers and some interpretation was required in order to group all the terms employed in the above categories. Under the Act of 1853 (16 & 17 Vict., c. 96), the information was requested under two headings, 'whether suicidal' and 'whether dangerous to others'.

Col. 22   *Previous place of confinement*
Code: 1 Hook Norton
2 Witney
3 Other licensed house(s)
4 Public asylum(s) or hospital(s)
5 County asylum(s)
6 More than one type of establishment
7 Not known
8 As stated previously
9 Not applicable
0 Not previously confined

This information was not required for private patients before 1828 and, in the case of paupers, before 1845. The details coded in this way were those which appertained to periods of confinement prior to the first admission during the period delineated by the consecutive series of admissions. In the case of multiple admissions within this period, a restatement of information given previously, i.e. at the time of first admission, was coded 8 and readmissions to Hook Norton or Witney, within the survey-period, were dealt with similarly.

Col. 23   *Whether first attack*
Code: 1 First attack
2 Not first attack
3 Not known
4 Not applicable

This information was not required before 1845.

Col. 24   *Duration of existing attack*
Code: 1 < 1 month
2 1 −
3 6 −
4 1 year
5 2 −
6 10+
7 From infancy
8 Not known
9 Not applicable

This information was not required before 1845.

315

Col. 25   *Interval since first attack*

        Code: 1 < 5 years
             2 5 −
             3 10 −
             4 20 +
             5 As given for 'duration of existing attack'
             6 Not known
             7 Not applicable

This information was calculated using the 'age on first attack' (an item first included in the admission documents in 1845) and the age on admission. When the 'interval since first attack' was equal, as far as could be ascertained, to the 'duration of existing attack', i.e. in cases stated to be first admissions or of life-long disorders, where no separate attacks are specified, the interval was coded 5.

Cols. 26–27 *Year of discharge*

        Code: Last two digits of year of discharge as written 01–98
              Not known 99

Col. 28   *Quarter of discharge*

        Code: 1 Jan.–March
             2 April–June
             3 July–Sept.
             4 Oct.–Dec.
             5 Not known

Cols. 29–31 *Duration of stay*

        Code: Less than 1 month 000
              Completed months as written 001–998
              Not known 999

Col. 32   *Disposal*

        Code: 1 Discharged or removed
             2 To other licensed house
             3 To public asylum or hospital
             4 To Oxfordshire County Asylum
             5 To other county asylums
             6 Died
             7 Not known

Col. 33   *Condition at time of disposal*

        Code: 1 Recovered/cured
             2 Partially recovered
             3 Not improved

4 Incurable
5 Dead
6 Other terms not classifiable under 1–5
7 Not specified

This information, generally, was available throughout the series. The terms to be used were not specified before 1845. Subsequently, three terms were suggested, namely, recovered, relieved and not improved.

Col. 34   *Stated cause of death*

Code: 1 Terms denoting decay of nature, old age, etc.
2 Terms denoting disorders of brain and nervous system (e.g. softening of the brain, effusion of the brain, epilepsy, and apoplexy)
3 Terms denoting disorders of the respiratory system (e.g. pulmonary consumption, bronchitis, and inflammation of the chest)
4 Other conditions not classifiable under 1–3 (e.g. peritonitis, erysipelas and ill-defined terms such as fever, debility and exhaustion)
5 Suicide
6 Not specified
7 Not applicable

Cols. 35–37 '*Overall admission number*' *allocated on first admission*

Code: As written 001–998
First admission 999

The 'overall admission number' allocated to the first recorded admission, during the survey-period, of an individual patient was coded, as written, on the second and on any subsequent admissions of that patient. This procedure was employed to enable the location and linkage of data to be carried out in the case of multiple admissions of the same patient.

Appendix D

Case Histories referred to in the Text, derived from the Oxfordshire MSS.

(1) *The case of Edward Bishop*[1]

Details are available regarding admissions, as a private patient, to Witney on 7 November 1842, and to Hook Norton, on 20 November 1847. There had been an earlier admission to Witney, for which there are no records.

Little clinical material is available for the first of these admissions, when he was aged thirty-seven, which ended in his being discharged 'not improved' and he was admitted, that same day, to Hook Norton. There is indirect evidence that, in 1843, his case was the subject of a special examination by the Metropolitan Commissioners, who upheld the proprietor's decision to refuse to comply with the Visitors' request to discharge him. In August 1846, the Visitors reported that Bishop appeared 'somewhat excited, but assigns as the reason the injustice of his detention'. Subsequently, his name featured frequently in the Patients' Book and, on 24 June 1847, the Visitors noted that 'Mr. Bishop appears to complain very much of his long continued confinement . . . we cannot ourselves perceive any ground for his detention'. The Commissioners in Lunacy observed on 13 August 1847, that Bishop

did not in his manner or demeanour exhibit any indications of insanity. He is, however, of an obviously excitable temper and is in a rather moody and depressed state of mind. Having regard to his previous history and proceedings we feel much hesitation in urging his discharge. At the same time, the report of Mr. Batt is so favourable, that we feel very anxious that some arrangements should be made with his relations for giving him a trial, the rather as the prolongation of his confinement seems likely to produce permanent despondency of mind. In the meantime, we recommend Mr. Batt to give him, during the day, as much liberty in going about as he thinks may be safely and properly allowed to him.

Initially, the Visitors agreed with this view and greater freedom was permitted. However, by November 1847, the recurrence of excited be-

[1] O.C.R.O., QSL.I/11.371 and QSL.II/3.83.

haviour was attributed to the change in his management and Batt, the proprietor, observed 'his manner appears to me greatly altered since he has had his liberty. He has a wild look with his eyes—speaks unnaturally quick, and if in the least contradicted his countenance is full of anger. He is perfectly rational, in conversation appears under no illusion'.

The reason for his 'transfer' to Hook Norton is not recorded. One of the medical certificates at the time read 'he is labouring under mental delusion of an absurd character, easily excited under ordinary circumstances, especially under the influence of stimulating liquor'. He was considered 'unsafe . . . to be at large' and possibly 'dangerous to others unless under proper and judicious restraint'. On admission, however, he was 'correct in conversation . . . peaceable' and in good physical health. He was admitted to the Upper House, in accommodation for the poorest class of paying patients. Whilst at Hook Norton, concern about his management continued to be expressed. It appears that he remained deluded, but the Commissioners observed, on 1 January 1850, that

if he could be removed from the pauper wards, prevailed on to occupy himself, attend church, and have the advantage of an occasional interview with a clergyman, he would be placed in a situation . . . better calculated to promote complete restoration, or at all events, a better means could be afforded of judging how far he is capable of resisting the temptation to take intoxicating liquors, the effect of which it appears have caused him to commit serious acts of violence on former occasions.

Bishop took advantage of these recommendations, but in April 1850, it was noted that he was 'shortly to be pauperized or removed, as his brother refuses to pay any longer for him'. Mallam requested the Commissioners' advice. They recommended Bishop's transfer to the county asylum,[1] but he was removed by his brother in October 1850.

(2) *The case of Sarah Westbury*[2]

This unmarried field-worker from Gloucestershire was admitted as a pauper lunatic to Hook Norton on 23 November 1846, by order of the parish overseer and the officiating clergyman. She was aged 28, this was her first attack and she was reported to have been insane about three years. On admission, she was 'suicidal' and suffering from 'melancholy'. She was in a very feeble state physically. On 10 June 1849, the Commissioners noted in the Patients' Book that she was 'of weak mind and not fit to be entirely her own mistress . . . at the same time if there was some trustworthy relative or employer who would keep a surveillance over her or she were kept under the eye of the Matron of the Workhouse, she might perhaps be trusted with a greater degree of liberty than she can enjoy in her present situation'. A week later, she was discharged, 'relieved' and removed by the Board of Guardians.

[1] P.R.O., M.H. 50, Minute Book C.L., Vol. 4, 11 April 1850.
[2] O.C.R.O., QSL.II/2.50.

(3) *The case of Anne Hopwood*[1]

This middle-aged, widowed gentlewoman, initially from Gloucester and later a resident of the town of Witney, was admitted to Witney nine times between 1849 and 1856. In 1850, her age was given as forty-nine years. She was a chronic alcoholic and her admissions followed bouts of acute intoxication, lasting days or weeks, when she became greatly excited and, at times, suicidal. On her first admission to Witney during the survey-period, she was known to have had five previous attacks and two admissions, to the Gloucester County Asylum, and to the Warneford Asylum, Oxford, respectively.

On the occasion of her third admission to Witney, on 7 July 1851, she was received with only a single medical certificate and the following 'special circumstances' were stated: 'This patient was found in a state of insensibility two miles from home and brought in a cart to the Asylum and seen by the Surgeons the same evening'. One of the medical certificates described the incident: 'She left her home this morning, entered a cottage at Ducklington and sent for a large quantity of ardent spirits which she drank until she became insensible—so much so, that I consider her unfit to be at large—she is habitually addicted to drinking and is at times dangerous to herself'. By 1854, it was reported that she was behaving improperly in the public streets and was 'a nuisance to her friends and the neighbourhood'. On admission, in May 1854, her physical condition was deteriorating and she was 'in a low, weak state with great gastric derangement and tremulous action of the muscles generally of the body'. At the time of admission in October 1854, her sixth admission to Witney, one certificate stated that 'the functions of the brain very much impaired by the constant intemperate use of spirituous liquors . . . Her conversation is very incoherent'. Her mental and physical deterioration continued and, in March 1856, it was recorded that 'she has lost all control over her actions, talks incoherently, is at times very violent . . . she walks about the whole of the night and is lost to all senses of decency by improperly exposing herself when almost naked'.

The duration of her periods of confinement was, on five occasions, less than four months and only once more than a year. On each occasion, she was discharged 'recovered', by the authority of a cousin, who acted as her guardian. In two instances, her final discharge took place after a period of trial leave, of up to six months duration. This practice was permitted under the provisions of the Act of 1845. Thus, on 30 January 1852, the Commissioners observed in the Patients' Book:

Miss Hopwood seems now so much recovered that notwithstanding her former history and her unfortunate propensities we think she is well enough to have a trial at large. Perhaps this might be most prudently and conveniently effected in the first instance by a leave under the 86th Section of 8 & 9 Vict. c. 100 and if she went on well during her probationary liberation for a short period, she is then to receive an absolute discharge.

[1] O.C.R.O., QSL.II/5.131; QSL.II/6.178; QSL.II/7.198; QSL.II/9.228; QSL.II/10.240, 245; QSL.II/11.248 and QSL.II/12.250.

On this occasion, she left Witney on 4 February 1852 and was finally discharged, 'cured', on 6 May 1852. No further details are available following her discharge from Witney in October 1856.

(4) *The case of William Marriott Clinch*[1]

This thirty-year-old, unmarried Witney man, of no occupation, was admitted to Witney on 12 May 1853, by the authority of his mother. This was stated to be his first admission and his first attack of insanity, the duration of which was two to three months. He was not epileptic nor considered to be suicidal or dangerous. One medical certificate stated that he was 'affected with idiocy and imbecility of mind and . . . his conduct lately, when in female society has been such as to render it necessary he should be placed under proper restraint'. The other certificate gave a similar description of his disorder, and, on admission, his condition was summarized as 'imbecile and unable to take care of himself. He is immodest and consequently exposes his person'. On 24 June 1853, the Commissioners in Lunacy made the following note: 'He is described in the certificates as being addicted to disgusting habits, especially in the presence of females and yet, we find that he is attended solely by a female attendant, who sleeps in his room at night, a practice the propriety of which appears to us to be extremely questionable'. The patient was, in fact, discharged, 'relieved', four weeks later.

(5) *The case of William John Wakelam*[2]

This pauper lunatic was admitted to Hook Norton on 15 December 1853, by order of two justices, after he had been found wandering at large and had been taken to the police station at Bourton-on-the-Water. He was reputed to be chargeable to the parish of Stow-on-the-Wold, Gloucestershire, although Long Island, America, was given as his previous place of abode. He was admitted to Hook Norton, because there was no room for male paupers, at that time, in the Gloucestershire County Asylum. According to the statement attached to the admission order, he was married, aged fifty-eight, a Quaker by religion and his occupation was a 'music-maker' (the supposed cause of his disorder, in fact, was considered to be the 'study of music'). He was reputed to have had his first attack at the age of forty-two and to have had two admissions to the Radcliffe Asylum, Oxford. This latter fact has been confirmed in the records of the Warneford Hospital; the two admissions were 30 May–23 June 1835, and 4 July–11 August 1835. On these occasions, he was described as a maltster from Burford and was twice discharged 'cured'.

At the time of his admission to Hook Norton, the medical certificates referred to his 'general maniacal irritability of manner and incoherent discourse'. His admission was precipitated by the fact that he had created 'a disturbance during the performance of service in the Baptist Chapel,

[1] O.C.R.O., QSL.II/9.231   [2] O.C.R.O., QSL.II/9.235.

Bourton-on-the-Water, claiming it as his own property'. Mallam described him as 'rambling and incoherent in his conversation and irritable and threatening in his conduct'. He remained insane and, when Hook Norton closed, he was transferred to the Oxfordshire County Asylum, at Littlemore, where his condition was described in the Case Book as 'Mania'. He died at Littlemore on 4 January 1862.

Appendix E

Abstracts of Published Statistics relating to Hook Norton, Brislington House and Duddeston Hall

THE source of the data presented in this Appendix was as follows:

(i) For the period up to 1843, the Statistical Appendix to the 1844 Report of the Metropolitan Commissioners in Lunacy, pp. 130–2 (Brislington House), pp. 181–2 (Hook Norton) and pp. 191–2 (Duddeston Hall).

(ii) For the period 1849 to 1853, the Eighth Report (1854) of the Commissioners in Lunacy, Appendix H, p. 305 (Hook Norton only).

The original format of the tables has been retained, although the content has not been reproduced in full in each case. The original captions and column headings have been preserved.

TABLE I *Hook Norton: Table of admissions (1839–43)*

| | Total number in the asylum 31 December 1838 | | | 1839 | 1840 | 1841 | 1842 | 1843 | Total | | |
	M.	F.	Total						M.	F.	Total
Private	} 43	26	69 {	9	9	6	3	3			
Pauper				33	31	35	31	19			
Total of cases (including re-admissions)	43	26	69	42	40	41	34	22	125	123	248
Deduct re-admissions	0	0	0	5	10	6	5	7	14	19	33
Total of patients	43	26	69	37	30	35	29	15	111	104	215

TABLE II *Hook Norton: Discharges, deaths, etc. (1839–43)*

		1839	1840	1841	1842	1843	Total M.	Total F.	Total
Cured	Private	2	2	4	4	1	3	10	13
	Pauper	16	15	19	20	13	36	47	83
Not cured (including removals and escapes)	Private	2	0	0	1	2	3	2	5
	Pauper	4	4	3	10	1	6	16	22
Died	Private	3	3	3	3	1	9	4	13
	Pauper	5	10	4	8	3	14	16	30

TABLE III *Hook Norton: Admissions during 1843, relative to forms of insanity*

Forms of Insanity	1843 M.	F.	Total
Mania:			
Acute mania (raving madness)	1	1	2
Ordinary madness (conversation, or conduct, absurd and irrational)	3	2	5
With intervals comparatively lucid	3	3	6
Dementia	0	2	2
Melancholia	1	0	1
Monomania	2	0	2
Moral insanity	1	0	1
General paralysis (paralysis des aliénés)	0	1	1
Epilepsy	1	1	2

TABLE IV *Hook Norton: Admissions during 1843, relative to hereditary predisposition to, and exciting causes of, insanity*

Predisposition to, and exciting Causes of, Insanity	1843		
	M.	F.	Total
Hereditary predisposition ascertained	5	2	7
Exciting Causes:			
Intemperance	2	1	3
Vice; sensuality	0	3	3
Poverty and distress; sudden changes of fortune	1	0	1
Grief; disappointment	1	1	2
Bodily disorder	2	0	2
Various physical causes	6	5	11

TABLE V *Hook Norton: Causes of death during five years (1839–43)*

Assigned Causes of Death	In the year 1839	In the year 1840	In the year 1841	In the year 1842	In the year 1843
Decay of constitution	3	3	2	1	0
Erysipelas	1	0	0	0	0
Inflammation of brain	2	1	2	1	0
Paralysis	1	2	1	0	0
Apoplexy	1	1	0	3	1
Dropsy	0	2	0	1	0
Consumption	0	1	0	1	0
Diabetes	0	1	0	0	0
Inflammation of the bowels	0	1	0	0	0
Diseased liver	0	1	0	0	0
Effusion on the brain	0	0	1	1	2
Diseased lungs	0	0	1	0	0
From the effects of a burn	0	0	0	1	0
Atrophy	0	0	0	1	0
Diseased brain	0	0	0	1	0
Diseased prostate gland	0	0	0	0	1

TABLE VI *Hook Norton: Admissions, including re-admissions (1849–53)*

Years	Males	Females	Total
1849	15	8	23
1850	14	16	30
1851	13	11	24
1852	7	8	15
1853	3	0	3
Totals	52	43	95

TABLE VII *Hook Norton: Discharges, removals and deaths (1849–53)*

| Years | Discharged or removed | | | | | | Died | | |
| | Recovered | | | Not recovered | | | | | |
	M.	F.	Total	M.	F.	Total	M.	F.	Total
1849	5	6	11	8	13	21	4	4	8
1850	4	5	9	2	2	4	7	6	13
1851	6	5	11	6	4	10	2	5	7
1852	6	3	9	12	20	32	2	3	5
1853	1	1	2	7	8	15	0	0	0
Totals	22	20	42	35	47	82	15	18	33

TABLE VIII *Hook Norton: Numbers of patients on the 1st January, and average numbers in each year (1849–53)*

| Years | 1 January | | | Average numbers | | |
	M.	F.	Total	M.	F.	Total
1849	32	41	73	31	32	63
1850	28	27	55	29	34	63
1851	30	32	62	30	31	61
1852	29	30	59	24	21	45
1853	16	13	29	11	5	16

TABLE IX *Brislington House: General table of admissions, including all cases of re-admission (1830–43)*

	Total number from opening of asylum[a] to 31 Dec. 1838			1839	1840	1841	1842	1843	Total		
	M.	F.	Total						M.	F.	Total
Private	178	101	279	26	19	24	24	20	241	151	392
Pauper	31	15	46	0	0	0	0	0	31	15	46
Total of cases (including re-admissions)	209	116	325	26	19	24	24	20	272	166	438
Deduct re-admissions	27	5	32	5	4	2	1	7	35	16	51
Total of patients	182	111	293	21	15	22	23	13	237	150	387

[a] Although the asylum was opened in 1806, the statistics presented dated from 31 Dec. 1829, when the asylum contained 89 patients, of whom 71 were incurable.

TABLE X *Brislington House: Discharges, deaths, etc. (1830–43)*

		Total from opening to 31 Dec. 1838			1839	1840	1841	1842	1843	Total		
		M.	F.	Total						M.	F.	Total
Cured	Private	72	28	100	9	14	12	8	8	100	51	151
	Pauper	10	7	17	0	0	0	0	0	10	7	17
Not cured[a] (including removals & escapes)	Private	34	19	53	10	4	7	0	12	49	37	86
	Pauper	12	6	18	0	0	0	0	0	12	6	18
Died (including suicides)	Private	22	16	38	4	1	7	5	5	37	23	60
	Pauper	9	2	11	0	0	0	0	0	9	2	11
Suicides		3	0	3	0	0	1	1	0	3	2	5

[a] Including those discharged in a temporarily convalescent or improved state.

TABLE XI *Brislington House: Average number, and percentages of deaths and cures, in each year (1834–43)*

	1834	1835	1836	1837	1838	1839	1840	1841	1842	1843
Average number of patients	87	88	87	85	84	82	86	87	84	90
Percentage of deaths	+9	−6	+9	−6	+7	−5	+1	8	6	−6
Percentage of cures	+18	−15	+10	−12	+20	+10	+16	−14	−10	−9

TABLE XII *Brislington House: Admissions during five years, ending 31 December 1843, relative to forms of insanity*

Forms of insanity	1839	1840	1841	1842	1843	Total		
						M.	F.	Total
Mania:								
Acute mania (raving madness)	5	2	4	3	7	9	12	21
Ordinary madness (conversation, or conduct, absurd and irrational)	2	6	2	3	4	12	5	17
With intervals comparatively lucid	3	2	5	7	3	14	6	20
Dementia:								
Consequent upon protracted mania	1	0	0	0	0	0	1	1
Arising from other causes	2	1	6	4	4	9	8	17
Melancholia	10	5	4	4	1	9	15	24
Monomania	1	2	0	2	0	3	2	5
Moral insanity	0	0	0	1	0	0	1	1
General paralysis (paralysie des aliénés)	1	0	1	0	0	2	0	2
Epilepsy	1	1	2	0	0	4	0	4

TABLE XIII *Duddeston Hall: General table of admissions, including all cases of re-admission (1831–43)*

	Total number from opening[a] to 31 Dec. 1838			1839	1840	1841	1842	1843	Total		
	M.	F.	Total						M.	F.	Total
Private	39	43	82	30	13	20	22	24	101	90	191
Pauper	48	49	97	26	39	39	25	31	117	140	257
Total of cases (including re-admissions)	87	92	179	56	52	59	47	55	218	230	448
Deduct re-admissions	6	2	8	8	4	8	14	9	28	23	51
Total of patients	81	90	171	48	48	51	33	46	190	207	397

[a] 24 April 1831.

TABLE XIV *Duddeston Hall: Discharges, deaths, etc. (1831–43)*

		Total from opening to 31 Dec. 1838			1839	1840	1841	1842	1843	Total		
		M.	F.	Total						M.	F.	Total
Cured	Private	17	14	31	10	2	3	12	8	41	25	66
	Pauper	10	7	17	14	16	16	8	6	41	36	77
Not cured (including removals and escapes)	Private	6	16	22	17	12	8	12	9	33	47	80
	Pauper	2	6	8	6	11	17	20	7	31	38	69
Died	Private	4	3	7	5	2	2	4	4	16	8	24
	Pauper	9	11	20	6	6	6	6	5	26	23	49

TABLE XV *Duddeston Hall: Average number, and percentages of deaths and cures, in each year (1839–43)*

	1839	1840	1841	1842	1843
Average number of patients	72	74	86	69	71
Percentage of deaths	11	10	9	14	12
Percentage of cures	33	24	22	29	20

TABLE XVI *Duddeston Hall: Admissions during five years, ending 31 December 1843, relative to forms of insanity*

Forms of insanity	1839	1840	1841	1842	1843	Total		
						M.	F.	Total
Mania:								
Acute mania (raving madness)								
Ordinary madness (conversation or conduct, absurd and irrational)	37	36	41	36	40	95	95	190
With intervals comparatively lucid								
Dementia:								
Consequent upon protracted mania	2	1	4	1	0	6	2	8
Melancholia	3	4	2	4	0	0	13	13
Monomania	1	2	1	2	0	2	4	6
Congenital idiotcy	0	0	1	0	0	1	0	1
General paralysis (paralysie des aliénés)	1	1	5	3	6	13	3	16
Epilepsy	4	3	4	1	4	12	4	16

Bibliography

Public general statutes

17 Ed. II, c. 9 & 10	Praerogativa Regis, 1324.
43 Eliz., c. 2	Poor Law Act, 1601.
12 Anne, c. 23	An Act for reducing the Laws relating to Rogues, Vagabonds, Sturdy Beggars and Vagrants, into one Act of Parliament; and for the more effectual punishing such Rogues, Vagabonds, Sturdy Beggars and Vagrants, and sending them whither they ought to be sent, 1714.
17 Geo. II, c. 5	Vagrant Act, 1744.
14 Geo. III, c. 49	Regulation of Madhouses Act, 1774.
19 Geo. III, c. 15	An Act to continue the Regulation of Madhouses Act, 1779.
26 Geo. III, c. 91	An Act for making perpetual the Regulation of Madhouses Act, 1786.
39 & 40 Geo. III, c. 94	Criminal Lunatics Act, 1800.
48 Geo. III, c. 96	Lunatics (Paupers or Criminals) Act, 1808 (County Asylum Act).
51 Geo. III, c. 79	Act to amend the Lunatics (Paupers or Criminals) Act, 1811.
55 Geo. III, c. 46	Act to amend the Lunatics (Paupers or Criminals) Act, 1815.
59 Geo. III, c. 127	An Act for making provision for the better care of Pauper Lunatics in England, 1819.
9 Geo. IV, c. 40	Lunatic Asylums & Pauper or Criminals Maintenance Act, 1828 (County Lunatic Asylums Act).
9 Geo. IV, c. 41	Treatment of Insane Persons Act, 1828 (Madhouse Act).
10 Geo. IV, c. 18	An Act to explain, amend, and alter the Treatment of Insane Persons Act, 1829.

2 & 3 Will. IV, c. 107	Care and Treatment of Insane Persons Act, 1832.
3 & 4 Will. IV, c. 36	An Act to diminish the Inconvenience and Expence of Commissions in the Nature of Writs De lunatico inquirendo; and to provide for the better Care and Treatment of Idiots, Lunatics, and Persons of unsound mind, found such by Inquisition, 1833.
4 & 5 Will. IV, c. 76	Poor Law Amendment Act, 1834.
5 & 6 Vict., c. 57	An Act to continue the Poor Law Commission; and for the further Amendment of the Laws relating to the Poor in England, 1842.
5 & 6 Vict., c. 84	Lunatics Property Act, 1842.
5 & 6 Vict., c. 87	Lunatic Asylums Act, 1842.
8 & 9 Vict., c. 100	Lunatics Act, 1845.
16 & 17 Vict., c. 70	Lunacy Regulation Act, 1853.
16 & 17 Vict., c. 96	Lunatics Care and Treatment Amendment Act, 1853.
16 & 17 Vict., c. 97	Lunatic Asylums Amendment Act, 1853.
23 & 24 Vict., c. 75	Criminal Lunatics Asylums Act, 1860.
24 & 25 Vict., c. 55	Irremovable Poor Act, 1861.
25 & 26 Vict., c. 111	Lunatics Law Amendment Act, 1862.
49 & 50 Vict., c. 25	Idiots Act, 1886.
51 & 52 Vict., c. 41	Local Government Act, 1888.
53 Vict., c. 5	Lunacy Act, 1890.
20 & 21 Geo. V, c. 23	Mental Treatment Act, 1930.
9 & 10 Geo. VI, c. 81	National Health Service Act, 1946.
7 & 8 Eliz. II, c. 72	Mental Health Act, 1959.

Parliamentary and official publications

Hansard's Parliamentary Debates, London.
Journals of the House of Commons.
Journals of the House of Lords.

Reports

Annual Reports of the Poor Law Commissioners, 1835 on.
Reports from the Select Committee on the Poor Law Amendment Act of 1834, 1838.
Report of the Select Committee appointed to inquire into the state of private madhouses in this Kingdom, 1763 (*Journals of the House of Commons*).
Reports from the Committee appointed to examine the physicians who have attended His Majesty, during his illness, 1788 and 1789.
Report from the Select Committee on the state of criminal and pauper lunatics and the laws relating thereto, 1807.
Report from the Select Committee on the better regulation of madhouses in England, July 1815. Reports (4) of minutes of evidence taken before the Committee, May–June 1815.

Reports (3) from the Select Committee on the better regulation of madhouses in England, April–June 1816.

Report from the Select Committee on the state of pauper lunatics in the county of Middlesex, and on lunatic asylums, 1827.

Minutes of evidence taken before the Select Committee of the House of Lords on the Bills relating to lunatics and lunatic asylums, 1828 (*Journals of the House of Lords*).

Report of the Metropolitan Commissioners in Lunacy made to the Home Office, 1829.

Report from the Select Committee appointed to inquire into the manner in which the house kept by John Gilliland ... at Hereford, has been conducted, and to whom several petitions were referred; with Minutes of evidence and Appendix, 1839.

Copies of Annual Reports made by the Metropolitan Commissioners in Lunacy to the Lord Chancellor, from 1835 to 1841, both inclusive, 1841.

Report of the Metropolitan Commissioners in Lunacy to the Lord Chancellor and Statistical Appendix to the Report, 1844.

Supplemental Report of the Metropolitan Commissioners in Lunacy relative to the general condition of the insane in Wales, 1844.

First Annual Report of the Commissioners in Lunacy to the Lord Chancellor, June 1846. Second and Third Annual Reports of the Commissioners, 1848–49. Ditto for 1850–1914, Fourth to Sixty-Eighth Annual Reports.

Further Report of the Commissioners in Lunacy to Her Majesty's Principal Secretary of State for the Home Department, relative to the Haydock Lodge Lunatic Asylum, with plans, March 1847.

Further Report of the Commissioners in Lunacy to the Lord Chancellor, June 1847.

Reports (3) of the Select Committee on the operation of the Acts and Regulations for the care and treatment of lunatics and their property, April & August 1859 and July 1860.

Reports of the Select Committee on the operation of the lunacy law, so far as regards security afforded by it against violations of personal liberty, 1877 and 1878.

Annual Reports of the Board of Control to the Lord Chancellor, 1916–1959.

Report of the Royal Commission on lunacy and mental disorder, 1926.

Report of Royal Commission on the law relating to mental illness and mental deficiency, 1957.

Returns and papers

Papers relating to the management of insane officers, seamen, and marines, belonging to His Majesty's Naval Service, 1814.

Return of houses licensed for the reception of lunatics, 1819(a).

Return of the number of lunatics confined in the different gaols, hospitals, and lunatic asylums; specifying the number in each, and distinguishing the males from the females, 1819(b).

Return of counties in which there are lunatic asylums; and of lunatics confined in gaols and houses of correction, 1824.

Return of the number of licensed houses within the Bills of Mortality and also within the county of Middlesex and of the number of lunatics contained therein, 1813–1821 inclusive, and 1822, 1823 and 1824, printed 1825.

Returns respecting licensed houses for the reception of lunatics, and lunatics in asylums and gaols in Great Britain, from 1815 to 1824, printed 1826.

Summary abstract of returns made to Clerks of the Peace in England and Wales, specifying the numbers of lunatics and idiots, of the dangerous and the harmless, and of those confined in regular asylums and of those not confined, 1830.

Returns of the number of public and private lunatic asylums in England and Wales; number of patients; number discharged or deceased; names of proprietors, and whether of the medical profession, 1831.

Returns of the number of pauper lunatics and idiots in each county in England and Wales; and of criminal lunatics, with their places of confinement, 1837.

Return from the Clerks of the Peace of the several counties of England and Wales (except Middlesex), of all houses to which licences have been granted, during each of the last three years, for the reception of insane persons, 1838.

Returns, for each of the last five years, of houses licensed for the reception of insane persons; of the sums paid to the credit of the County stock in regard to licences of asylums; of the number of visitations made by the Visitors to each licensed house; and, of all houses in regard to which licences have been refused to be renewed, suspended or revoked, 1842.

Return of the number of patients for which Haydock Lodge Asylum is licensed; number confined, 1st January 1846; greatest number admitted at one time since 1844; number of deaths since 1st January 1845; also copies of correspondence, and further reports of the Commissioners, relative to the treatment of lunatics in Haydock Lodge, 1846.

Copy of letter to the Lord Chancellor from the Commissioners in Lunacy, with reference to their duties and practice under the Act 8 & 9 Vict., c. 100 (case of 'Nottidge *v.* Ripley'), 1849.

Return of the visits made to each provincial licensed house by the Visitors, and to metropolitan and provincial licensed houses by the Commissioners in Lunacy, during the year ending Michaelmas 1853; and of licensed houses, the numbers for which licensed, the number of patients therein; the number of attendants, and the number dismissed for misconduct in each house, 1854(a).

Returns of the number of persons found to be lunatic under inquisition by the Court of Chancery, who are residents in private asylums, and the amount of their respective incomes and allowances for maintenance; etc., 1854(b).

Return of the number of lunatics in lunatic asylums of England and Wales, classified as curables, incurables, and idiots, 1862.

Journals and newspapers

Asylum Journal, 1853–5 (Vol. 1 bound as the *Asylum Journal of Mental Science*); continued as the *Asylum Journal of Mental Science*, 1856–7, and later, the *Journal of Mental Science*. Now the *British Journal of Psychiatry*.

British Medical Journal.

Caernarvon and Denbigh Herald.

Edinburgh Review.

Gentleman's Magazine, The.

Gloucester Journal, The.

Hull Advertiser.

Jackson's Oxford Journal.

Journal of Psychological Medicine and Mental Pathology, 1848–60. (Continued as *The Medical Critic and Psychological Journal*, 1861–3.) New series, 1875–83.

Lancet.

Medical History.

Proceedings of the Royal Society of Medicine.

Salisbury and Winchester Journal.

Times, The.

Books, pamphlets and articles

ABEL-SMITH, B. (1964). *The Hospitals 1800–1948*. London: Heinemann.

ALLEN, M. (1831). *Cases of Insanity, with Medical, Moral and Philosophical Observations upon them*. London: Swire.

—— (1833). *Allen versus Dutten*. London: Swire.

—— (1837). *Essay on the Classification of the Insane*. London: Taylor.

ANON. (1662). *Mirabilis annus secundus; or, the Second Year of Prodigies*. London.

—— (1763). 'A Case humbly offered to the Consideration of Parliament.' *Gentleman's Magazine, 33*, pp. 25–6.

—— (1796). 'Détails sur l'établissement du docteur Willis, pour la guérison des aliénés,' *Bibliothèque Britannique* (Littérature) *1*, pp. 759–73.

—— (1807). *The Moorland Bard; or, Poetical Recollections of a Weaver in the Moorlands of Staffordshire; with notes*, 2 vols. Hanley: Allbut.

—— (1828). *Practical Observations on Insanity and the Treatment of the Insane; addressed particularly to those who have Relatives or Friends afflicted with Mental Derangement: also Hints on the Propriety of making the Study of Mental Disorders a Necessary Adjunct to Medical Education*. London: for the author.

—— (1848). *The Asylum for Idiots*. London: for the author.

—— (1850). *Familiar views of Lunacy and Lunatic Life*. London: Parker.

—— (1853). *Cretins and Idiots. A Short Account of the Progress of the Institutions for their Relief and Cure*. London.

—— (1860). *Our Holiday at Laverstock House Asylum; how we visited Stonehenge and what we learned there*. London: Churchill.

BIBLIOGRAPHY

(1866). 'Private Madhouses a Century ago', *Notes and Queries 9*, pp. 367–8.

(1902). 'Richard Henderson and his Private Asylum at Hanham', *Proc. Wesley Hist. Soc. 3*, pp. 158–61.

ARCHER, J. (1673). *Every Man his own Doctor, compleated with an Herbal ... The Second Edition, with Additions, viz. A Treatise of Melancholly and Distraction, with Government in Cure.* London: for the author.

ARLIDGE, J. T. (1859). *On the State of Lunacy and the Legal Provision for the Insane with Observations on the Construction and Organization of Asylums.* London: Churchill.

(1860). 'Thirteenth Report of the Commissioners in Lunacy to the Lord Chancellor', *J. Ment. Sci. 6*, pp. 141–55.

ARNOLD, T. (1806). *Observations on the Nature, Kinds, Causes, and Prevention of Insanity*, 2nd ed., 2 vols. London: Phillips.

BAKEWELL, S. G. (1833). *An Essay on Insanity, translated from the Author's Latin Inaugural Dissertation composed on that Subject.* Edinburgh: Neill & Co.

BAKEWELL, T. (1809). *The Domestic Guide in Cases of Insanity. Pointing out the Causes, Means of Preventing, and Proper Treatment, of that Disorder.* Newcastle: for the author.

(1815). *A Letter addressed to the Chairman of the Select Committee of the House of Commons, appointed to enquire into the State of Madhouses: to which is subjoined Remarks on the Nature, Causes, and Cure of Mental Derangement.* Stafford: for the author.

BARNET, M. C. (1965). 'Matthew Allen, M.D. (Aberdeen) 1783–1845', *Med. Hist. 9*, pp. 16–28.

BATEMAN, F. and RYE, W. (1906). *The History of Bethel Hospital at Norwich.* Norwich: Gibbs & Waller.

BATESON, G. (1962). *Perceval's Narrative: a Patient's Account of his Psychosis.* London: Hogarth Press.

BATTIE, W. (1758). *A Treatise on Madness.* London: Whiston & White.

BELCHER, W. (1796). *Address to Humanity, containing a Letter to Dr. Thomas Monro; a Receipt to make a Lunatic, and seize his Estate and a Sketch of a True Smiling Hyena.* London: for the author.

BOLTON, J. S. (1928). 'The Evolution of a Mental Hospital, Wakefield, 1818–1928', *J. Ment. Sci. 74*, pp. 587–633.

BOWDEN, S. (1754). *Poems on Various Subjects; with Some Essays in Prose, Letters to Correspondents, &c. and a Treatise on Health. Dedicated to Charles Boyle, Lord Viscount Dungarvan.* Bath: for the author.

BOWERS, W. H. and CLOUGH, J. W. (1929). *Researches into the History of the Parish Church and Parish of Stone, Staffordshire.* Birmingham: Midland Educational Co. Ltd.

BRAND, J. (1789). *The History and Antiquities of the Town and County of the Town of Newcastle upon Tyne*, Vol. 1. London: White & Son: Egerton.

Brief History of the Warneford Hospital, compiled for the Committee of Management, 1926.

336

BROCKBANK, E. M. (1933). 'Manchester's Lead in the Humane Treatment of the Insane', *Brit. Med. J.* 2, p. 540.

BROWNE, W. A. F. (1837). *What Asylums were, are, and ought to be: being the substance of Five Lectures delivered before the Managers of the Montrose Royal Lunatic Asylum.* Edinburgh: Black.

BRUCKSHAW, S. (1774). *One more Proof of the Iniquitous Abuse of Private Madhouses.* London: for the author.

BUCKNILL, J. C. (1857). 'Tenth Report of the Commissioners in Lunacy to the Lord Chancellor', *Asylum J. Ment. Sci.* 3, pp. 19–30.

(1860). 'Annual Reports of Lunatic Asylums', *J. Ment. Sci.* 6, pp. 495-513.

(1861). 'Presidential Address', *J. Ment. Sci.* 7, pp. 1–23.

BURDETT, H. C. (1891–3). *Hospitals and Asylums of the World; their Origin, History, Construction, Administration, Management, and Legislation.* 4 vols. London: Churchill.

BURROWS, G. M. (1820). *An Inquiry into Certain Errors relative to Insanity; and their Consequences; Physical, Moral and Civil.* London: Underwood.

(1828). *Commentaries on the Causes, Forms, Symptoms, and Treatment, Moral and Medical, of Insanity.* London: Underwood.

CARLSON, E. T. and MCFADDEN, B. (1960). 'Dr. William Cullen on Mania', *Amer. J. Psychiat.* 117, pp. 463–5.

CLAY, R. M. (1909). *The Medieval Hospitals of England.* London: Methuen.

COCKTON, H. (1840). *The Life and Adventures of Valentine Vox, the Ventriloquist.* London: Tyas.

CONOLLY, E. T. (1858). *Suggestions for the Amendment of the Laws relating to Private Lunatic Asylums.* London: Shaw & Sons.

CONOLLY, J. (1830). *An Inquiry concerning the Indications of Insanity, with Suggestions for the Better Protection and Care of the Insane.* London: Taylor.

(1849). *A Remonstrance with the Lord Chief Baron touching the Case Nottidge versus Ripley*, 3rd ed. London: Churchill.

(1855). 'Fourth Notice of the Eighth Report of the Commissioners in Lunacy', *Asylum J. Ment. Sci.* 1, pp. 180–5.

(1856). *The Treatment of the Insane without Mechanical Restraints.* London: Smith, Elder & Co.

(1860). 'Recollections of the Varieties of Insanity', *Med. Times & Gazette 1*, pp. 6–9.

(1861). 'Licences and Certificates', *J. Ment. Sci.* 7 (No. 37), pp. 127–36.

COX, J. M. (1806). *Practical Observations on Insanity; in which some Suggestions are offered towards an Improved Mode of treating Diseases of the Mind . . . to which are subjoined, Remarks on Medical Jurisprudence as connected with Diseased Intellect*, 2nd ed. London: Baldwin & Murray.

CROWTHER, C. (1838). *Observations on the Management of Madhouses, illustrated by Occurrences in the West Riding and Middlesex Asylums.* London: Simpkin, Marshall & Co.

337

(1849). *Observations on the Management of Madhouses, Part III.* London: Simpkin, Marshall & Co.

CRUDEN, A. (1739). *The London-Citizen exceedingly injured . . . an Account of the Unparallel'd Case of a Citizen of London . . . who was . . . sent . . . by . . . a Mere Stranger, to a Private Madhouse. Containing an Account of the Said Citizen's Barbarous Treatment . . . and of his Rational and Patient Behaviour, whilst chained, handcuffed, strait-wastecoated and imprisoned in the Said Madhouse: where he probably would have been continued, or died under his Confinement, if he had not most providentially made his Escape. . . . The Whole humbly addressed to the Legislature, as plainly shewing the Absolute Necessity of regulating Private Madhouses in a More Effectual Manner than at present.* London: Cooper & Dodd.

(1754). *The Adventures of Alexander the Corrector, wherein is given an Account of his being unjustly sent to Chelsea, and of his Bad Usage during the time of his Chelsea-Campaign . . . with, an Account of the Chelsea-Academies, or the Private Places for the Confinement of such as are supposed to be deprived of the Exercise of their Reason.* London: for the author.

CULLEN, W. (1808). *First Lines of the Practice of Physic*, 2 vols. Edinburgh: Bell & Bradfute *et al.*

DAINTON, C. (1961). *The Story of England's Hospitals.* London: Museum Press.

DEFOE, D. (1706). *A Review of the State of the English Nation 3*, pp. 327, 353–6; and ibid *6*, p. 572.

(1728). *Augusta Triumphans: or, the Way to make London the most Flourishing City in the Universe.* London: Roberts.

DEWHURST, K. (1962). 'A seventeenth century symposium on manic-depressive psychosis', *Brit. J. med. Psychol. 35*, pp. 113–25.

DICKINS, M. (1928). *A History of Hook Norton.* Banbury: The Banbury Guardian.

DICKSON, T. (1852). *Observations upon the Importance of establishing Public Hospitals for the Insane of the Middle and Higher Classes.* London: Churchill.

Dictionary of National Biography. London.

Directory, Durham County. Hagar & Co., 1851.

The Local Government Manual and, 1938. London: Knight & Co.

The London Medical, 1845–7.

The London and Provincial Medical, 1847 onwards.

The London and Provincial New Commercial, 1830. Pigot & Co.

The Medical, of Great Britain and Ireland, 1845.

DUNCAN, A.. sen., (ed.) (1809). *Observations on the Structure of Hospitals for the Treatment of Lunatics.* Edinburgh: Ballantyne.

EASTWOOD, J. W. (1864). 'On Private Asylums for the Insane', *J. Ment. Sci. 9*, pp. 319–27.

ELLIS, W. C. (1815). *A Letter to Thomas Thompson, Esq., M.P., containing Considerations on the Necessity of Proper Places being provided by the Legislature for the Reception of all Insane Persons and on Some of the*

Abuses which have been found to exist in Madhouses, with a Plan to remedy them. Hull: for the author.

English (Law) Reports. Edinburgh.

FALLOWES, T. (1705). *The Best Method for the Cure of Lunaticks. With some Account of the Incomparable Oleum Cephalicum used in the same, prepared and administered by Tho. Fallowes, M.D. at his House in Lambeth-Marsh.* London: for the author.

FAULKNER, B. (1789). *Observations on the General and Improper Treatment of Insanity: with a Plan for the more Speedy and Effectual Recovery of Insane Persons.* London: for the author.

FESSLER, A. (1956). 'The Management of Lunacy in Seventeenth Century England. An Investigation of Quarter Sessions Records', *Proc. R. Soc. Med. 49*, pp. 901–7.

FOUCAULT, M. (1967). *Madness and Civilization. A History of Insanity in the Age of Reason.* London: Tavistock.

FOX, *Genealogical Memoranda relating to the Family of Fox of Brislington, etc., 1872.* London: for the authors.

FOX, A. (1906). 'A Short Account of Brislington House, 1804–1906', *The Brislington House Quarterly News Centenary Number*, pp. 4–14.

FOX, F. K. and C. J. (1836). 'History and Present State of Brislington House, near Bristol', Reprinted in *Brislington House Quarterly News Centenary Number* (1906), pp. 16–23.

GAITSKELL, J. A. (1835). *On Mental Derangement; its Causes, Symptoms and Treatment, with some Observations relative to Lunatic Asylums.* Bath: Binns.

GASKELL, S. (1860). 'On the Want of Better Provision for the Labouring and Middle Classes when attacked or threatened with Insanity', *J. Ment. Sci. 6*, pp. 321–7.

GILES, J. A. (1852). *History of Witney, with Notices of the Neighbouring Parishes and Hamlets.* London: for the author.

GORDON, S. and COCKS, T. G. B. (1952). *A People's Conscience.* London: Constable & Co.

GRANVILLE, J. M. (1877). *The Care and Cure of the Insane, being the Reports of the Lancet Commission on Lunatic Asylums, 1875–1877, for Middlesex, the City of London and Surrey*, 2 vols. London: Hardwicke & Bogne.

GREIG, J. W. and GATTIE, W. H. (1915). *Archbold's Lunacy and Mental Deficiency*, 5th ed. London: Butterworth & Co.

HALÉVY, E. (1961). *A History of the English People in the Nineteenth Century*, Vols. 1 and 2. London: Benn.

HALL, J. (1767). *A Narrative of the Proceedings relative to the Establishment, etc. of St. Luke's House.* Newcastle upon Tyne: for the author.

HALLARAN, W. S. (1810). *An Enquiry into the Causes producing the Extraordinary Addition to the Number of Insane, together with Extended Observations on the Cure of Insanity; with Hints as to the Better Management of Public Asylums for Insane Persons.* Cork: Edwards & Savage.

HALLIDAY, A. (1827). *A General View of the Present State of Lunatics, and Lunatic Asylums, in Great Britain and Ireland, and in some other Kingdoms.* London: Underwood.

(1829). *A Letter to Lord Robert Seymour: with a Report of the Number of Lunatics and Idiots in England and Wales.* London: Underwood.

HARE, E. H. (1959). 'The Origin and Spread of Dementia Paralytica', *J. Ment. Sci. 105*, pp. 594–626.

HARE, S. (1838). *Practical Observations on the Causes and Treatment of Curvatures of the Spine.* London: Simpkin & Marshall.

HASSALL, C. and WARBURTON, J. (1964). 'The New Look in Mental Health—1852', *Medical Care 2*, pp. 253–4.

HASTINGS, C. (1860). 'Presidential Address', *J. Ment. Sci. 6*, pp. 3–13.

HILL, B. (1967). ' "My little physician at St. Albans". Nathaniel Cotton 1705–1788', *Practitioner 199*, pp. 363–7.

HISTORICAL MANUSCRIPTS COMMISSION, *Record Repositories in Great Britain*, 2nd ed., 1966. London: H.M.S.O.

HODGKINSON, R. G. (1966). 'Provision for Pauper Lunatics 1834–1871', *Med. Hist. 10*, pp. 138–54.

HOELDTKE, R. (1967). 'The History of Associationism and British Medical Psychology', *Med. Hist. 11*, pp. 46–65.

HOLLINGSHEAD, J. (1895). *My Lifetime*, 2 vols. London: Sampson Low, Marston & Co.

HOOD, W. C. (1855). *Statistics of Insanity; being a Decennial Report of Bethlem Hospital, from 1846 to 1855 inclusive.* London: Batten.

HOWARD, J. (1777–80). *The State of the Prisons in England and Wales, with Preliminary Observations and an Account of some Foreign Prisons.* Warrington.

(1789). *An Account of the Principal Lazarettos in Europe.* Warrington.

HUNTER, R. A. (1956). 'The Rise and Fall of Mental Nursing', *Lancet i*, pp. 98–9.

(1959). 'Some notes on the importance of manuscript records for psychiatric history', *Archives IV*, pp. 9–11.

and MACALPINE, I. (1961). 'Dickens and Conolly. An Embarrassed Editor's Disclaimer', *Times Lit. Suppl.*, 11 Aug. 1961.

and —— (1962). 'John Thomas Perceval (1803–1876) Patient and Reformer'. *Med. Hist. 6*, pp. 391–5.

and —— (1963). *Three Hundred Years of Psychiatry 1535–1860.* London: Oxford University Press.

and —— (1964). Introduction to '*An Inquiry concerning the Indications of Insanity with Suggestions for the Better Protection and Care of the Insane' by J. Conolly.* London: Dawsons.

—— and PAYNE, L. M. (1956). 'The Country Register of Houses for the Reception of "Lunatics", 1798–1812'. *J. Ment. Sci. 102*, pp. 856–63.

and WOOD, J. B. (1957). 'Nathaniel Cotton, M.D., Poet, Physician and Psychiatrist', *King's Coll. Hosp. Gazette 36*, p. 120.

IRISH, D. (1700). *Levamen infirmi: or, Cordial Counsel to the Sick and Diseased.* London: for the author.

JONES, K. (1955). *Lunacy, Law and Conscience, 1744–1845*. London: Routledge & Kegan Paul.

—— (1960). *Mental Health and Social Policy, 1845–1959*. London: Routledge & Kegan Paul.

KLAF, F. S. and HAMILTON, J. G. (1961). 'Schizophrenia—a Hundred Years ago and Today', *J. Ment. Sci. 107*, pp. 819–27.

KUNITZ, S. J. (ed.) (1936). *British Authors of the Nineteenth Century*. New York: Wilson Co.

LEIGH, D. (1961). *The Historical Development of British Psychiatry*, Vol. 1. Oxford: Pergamon Press.

LEWIS, A. (1955). 'Philippe Pinel and The English', *Proc. R. Soc. Med. 48*, pp. 581–6.

LOWE, L. (1872). *Report of a Case heard in Queen's Bench, November 22nd 1872, charging the Commissioners in Lunacy with concurring in the Improper Detention of a Falsely-alleged Lunatic and Wrongful Tampering with her Correspondence*. London: Burns.

—— (1872?). Pamphlets in a series entitled *Quis custodiet ipsos custodes?*

(1) *A Nineteenth Century Adaptation of Old Inventions to the Repression of New Thoughts and Personal Liberty.*

(2) *Gagging in Madhouses as practised by Government Servants, in a Letter to the People, by One of the Gagged*. London: Burns.

(3) *How an Old Woman obtained Passive Writing and the Outcome thereof*. London: Burns.

(4) *My Outlawry, a Tale of Madhouse Life.*

(5) *The Lunacy Laws and Trade in Lunacy in a Correspondence with the Earl of Shaftesbury.*

—— (1883). *The Bastilles of England; or the Lunacy Laws at Work*. London: Crookenden & Co.

LUCAS, E. V. (ed.) (1905). *The Works of Charles and Mary Lamb*, Vol. 6. London: Methuen.

LUCETT, J. (1815). *An Exposition of the Reasons which have prevented the Process for relieving and curing Idiocy and Lunacy, and Every Species of Insanity, from having been further extended*. London: Martin.

MACALPINE, I. and HUNTER, R. (1969). *George III and the Mad-business*. London: Penguin Press.

MACKENZIE, E. (1827). *A Descriptive and Historical Account of the Town and County of Newcastle upon Tyne, including the Borough of Gateshead*. Newcastle upon Tyne: Mackenzie & Dent.

MCMENEMEY, W. H. (1955). 'A Note on James Parkinson as a Reformer of the Lunacy Acts', *Proc. R. Soc. Med. 48*, pp. 593–4.

MELVILLE, L. (1907). *Farmer George*, 2 vols. London: Pitman.

MILLINGEN, J. G. (1840). *Aphorisms on the Treatment and Management of the Insane, with Considerations on Public and Private Lunatic Asylums, pointing out the Errors in the Present System*. London: Churchill.

MITFORD, J. (1825?). *A Description of the Crimes and Horrors in the Interior of Warburton's Private Mad-house at Hoxton, commonly called Whitmore House*. London: Benbow. (This work was published anonymously but is undoubtedly attributable to Mitford.)

(1825?). *Part Second of the Crimes and Horrors of the Interior of War- burton's Private Mad-houses at Hoxton and Bethnal Green; and of these Establishments in general with Reasons for their Total Abolition.* London: Benbow.

MONK, W. J. (1894). *History of Witney.* Witney: Knight.

MONRO, H. (1850). *Remarks on Insanity: its Nature and Treatment.* London: Churchill.

(1852). *Articles on Reform in Private Asylums.* London: Churchill.

MORRIS, A. D. (1958). *The Hoxton Madhouses.* March: for the author.

Munk's Roll, Vols. I–III (1878) and IV (1955). London: Royal College of Physicians.

NEWINGTON, H. H. and A. (1901). 'Some Incidents in the History and Practice of Ticehurst Asylum'. *J. Ment. Sci. 47,* pp. 62–72.

NICOLL, S. W. (1828). *An Enquiry into the Present State of Visitation in Asylums for the Reception of the Insane; and into the Modes by which such Visitation may be improved.* London: Harvey & Darton.

NOBLE, D. (1853). *Elements of Psychological Medicine: an Introduction to the Practical Study of Insanity. Adapted for Students and Junior Practitioners.* London: Churchill.

OLIVIER, E. (1934). *The Eccentric Life of Alexander Cruden.* London: Faber & Faber.

PAGET, G. E. (1866). *The Harveian Oration.* Cambridge: Deighton, Bell & Co.

PARGETER, W. (1792). *Observations on Maniacal Disorders.* Reading: for the author.

PARKINSON, J. (1811). *Mad-houses. Observations on the Act for regulating Mad-houses, and a Correction of the Statements of the Case of Ben- jamin Elliott, convicted of illegally confining Mary Daintree; with Remarks addressed to the Friends of Insane Persons.* London: Sher- wood *et al.*

PARRY-JONES, B. (1965). 'A Calendar of the Eldon-Richards Corres- pondence c. 1809–1822', *J. Merioneth Historical and Record Soc.* 5 (1), pp. 39–50.

PATERNOSTER, R. (1841). *The Madhouse System.* London: for the author.

PAUL, G. O. (1812). *Observations on the Subject of Lunatic Asylums, ad- dressed to a General Meeting of Subscribers to a Fund for building and establishing a General Lunatic Asylum near Gloucester.* Gloucester: for the author.

PERCEVAL, J. T. (1838 and 1840). *A Narrative of the Treatment experienced by a Gentleman, during a State of Mental Derangement; designed to explain the Causes and the Nature of Insanity, and to expose the Injudicious Conduct pursued towards many unfortunate Sufferers under that Calamity.* London: Effingham Wilson.

PERFECT, W. (1787). *Select Cases in the Different Species of Insanity, Lunacy or Madness, with the Modes of Practice as adopted in the Treatment of Each.* Rochester: Gillman.

(1791). *A Remarkable Case of Madness, with the Diet and Medicines used in the Cure.* Rochester: for the author.

PHILLIPS, H. T. (1970). 'The Old Private Lunatic Asylum at Fishponds', *Bristol Medico-Chirurgical J. 85*, pp. 41–4.

PINEL, P. (trans. DAVIES, D. D.) (1806). *A Treatise on Insanity, in which are contained the Principles of a New and more Practical Nosology of Maniacal Disorders than has yet been offered to the Public.* Sheffield: Cadell & Davies. (A translation of the 1801 edition of Pinel's *Traité médico-philosophique sur l'aliénation mentale, ou la manie.* Reproduced in facsimile, 1962, New York: Hafner).

PLOMER, W. (ed.) (1964). *Kilvert's Diary.* London: Jonathan Cape.

POWELL, R. (1813). 'Observations upon the Comparative Prevalence of Insanity at Different Periods', *Medical Transactions 4*, pp. 131–59.

POYNTER, F. N. L. (ed.) (1962). *The Evolution of Hospitals in Britain.* London: Pitman.

PRICHARD, J. C. (1835). *A Treatise on Insanity and other Disorders affecting the Mind.* London: Sherwood, Gilbert & Piper.

PRICHARD, T. (1859). *Statistical Report of Cases of Insanity treated in Abington Abbey, Northampton, from January 1st, 1854, to December 31st, 1858.* Northampton: for the author.

READE, C. (1863). *Hard Cash. A Matter of Fact Romance*, 3 vols. London: Sampson Low *et al.*

REEVE, W. N. (*c.* 1880). *Report to the Visitors of the Leicestershire and Rutland Lunatic Asylum as to the Proposed New Asylum at Newton Unthank.* Leicester.

REID, J. (1808). 'Report of Diseases', *The Monthly Magazine 25*, pp. 166–7, 374–5.

—— (1816). *Essays on Hypochondriacal and other Nervous Affections.* London: Longman *et al.*

Reports, Littlemore Asylum, Oxford, 1847–1861.

REYNOLDS, F. (1826). *The Life and Times of Frederick Reynolds, by himself,* Vol. II. London: Colburn.

ROBERTSON, C. L. (1856). 'The Military Lunatic Hospital', *Asylum J. Ment. Sci. 2*, pp. 31–40.

—— (1857). 'The Military Lunatic Hospital; a Summary of the Minutes of Evidence taken before the Select Committee on the Medical Department (Army) so far as they relate to the Re-establishment of that Hospital', *Asylum J. Ment. Sci. 3*, pp. 271–6.

—— (1881). 'Lunacy in England', *J. Psychol. Med. & Ment. Path.* (New Series) *VII*, pp. 174–92.

ROBINSON, B. and HUDLESTON, C. R. (1938). 'Two Vanished Fishponds Houses', *Trans. Bristol & Gloucester Archeol. Soc. 60*, pp. 238–59.

ROBINSON, G. (1859). *On the Prevention and Treatment of Mental Disorders.* London: Longman *et al.*

ROGERS, J. W. (1816). *A Statement of the Cruelties, and Frauds which are practised in Mad-houses.* London: for the author.

ROSEN, G. (1968). *Madness in Society. Chapters in the Historical Sociology of Mental Illness.* London: Routledge & Kegan Paul.

SEYMOUR, E. J. (1859). *A Letter . . . on the Laws which regulate Private*

Lunatic Asylums; *with a comparative View of the Process 'De lunatico inquirendo', in England, and the Law of 'Interdiction', in France.* London.

SHARPE, J. B. (1815). *Report, together with the Minutes of Evidence, and an Appendix of Papers, from the Committee appointed to consider of Provision being made for the Better Regulation of Madhouses in England.* London: Baldwin Cradock & Joy.

SIMMONS, S. F. (ed.) (1783). *The Medical Register.* London: Johnson.

STEWARD, J. B. (1845). *Practical Notes on Insanity.* London: Churchill.

TEMPEST, J. (1830). *Narrative of the Treatment experienced by John Tempest, Esq., of Lincoln's Inn, Barrister at Law, during Fourteen Months Solitary Confinement under a False Imputation of Lunacy.* London: for the author.

THEOBALD, H. S. (1924). *The Law relating to Lunacy.* London: Stevens & Sons.

THOMAS, V. (1827). *An Account of the Origin, Nature and Objects of the Asylum on Headington Hill, near Oxford, considered as a Benevolent Institution for the Reception, Relief and Cure of the Insane.* Oxford: for the author.

THURNAM, J. (1845). *Observations and Essays on the Statistics of Insanity.* London: Simpkin, Marshall & Co.

TRENCH, C. C. (1964). *The Royal Malady.* London: Longmans.

TREVELYAN, G. M. (1941). *History of England,* 2nd ed. London: Longmans, Green & Co.

TROSSE, G. (1714). *The life of the Reverend Mr. Geo. Trosse, late Minister of the Gospel in the city of Exon, who died January 11th, 1712/3. In the eighty second year of his age, written by himself, and publish'd according to his order.* By J. H. Exeter: White.

TUKE, D. H. (1882). *Chapters in the History of the Insane in the British Isles.* London: Kegan Paul, Trench & Co.

—— (1889). *The Past and Present Provision for the Insane Poor in Yorkshire, with Suggestions for the Future Provision for this Class.* London: Churchill.

TUKE, H. (1858). 'On Warm and Cold Baths in the Treatment of Insanity'. *J. Ment. Sci. 4,* pp, 532–52; and *ibid. 5,* pp. 102–14.

UWINS, D. (1833). *A Treatise on those Disorders of the Brain and Nervous System, which are usually considered and called Mental.* London: Renshaw & Rush.

WALK, A. (1954). 'Some Aspects of the "Moral Treatment" of the Insane up to 1854'. *J. Ment. Sci. 100,* pp. 807–37.

—— (1961). 'The History of Mental Nursing'. *J. Ment. Sci. 107,* pp. 1–17.

WEBB, S. and B. (1910). *English Poor Law Policy.* London: Longmans Green.

WELDON, G. (1878). *The History of my Orphanage or the Outpourings of an Alleged Lunatic.* London: for the author.

WILLIS, F. (1823). *A Treatise on Mental Derangement, containing the Substance of the Gulstonian Lectures for May, MDCCCXXII.* London: Longman *et al.*

WILLIS, T. (trans. PORDAGE, S.) (1683). *Two Discourses concerning the Soul of Brutes, which is that of the Vital and Sensitive of Man.* London: Dring.

WINSLOW, F. B. (1858). 'Presidential Address'. *J. Ment. Sci.* 4, pp. 4–16.

—— (1860). *On Obscure Diseases of the Brain, and Disorders of the Mind.* London: Churchill.

Index of Private Madhouses

This index lists houses referred to in the text and does not include all those named in Appendix B.

347

General Index